AMISH SOCIETY

THE JOHNS HOPKINS UNIVERSITY PRESS

BALTIMORE AND LONDON

Amish Society

THIRD EDITION

John A. Hostetler

To the memory of

MOSES LAPP,

an inspiring man of the Amish faith,

and

ABDUL HAMID M. el-ZEIN,

a Temple University colleague who, in the search for
social reality, combined the love of knowledge
with humility

Contents

vii

PART II. STABILITY AND FULFILLMENT

PART III. PATTERNS OF CHANGE

PART IV. SURVIVAL

Preface

卫

THIS, THE THIRD edition of *Amish Society*, is a completely rewritten volume. While the best has been retained from the previous editions, not a single chapter or page remains the same. This new book was made necessary by changes in Amish society, by new discoveries from research, and by changes in my own point of view. At mid-century, sociologists predicted that the Amish would be absorbed into the larger society within twenty-five years. It was thought that once the vitality of the European tradition was exhausted the Amish would be assimilated by the larger social forces of the dominant society. The predictions were wrong. The Amish population has since doubled and the assimilation rate has not changed significantly. The cultural energy of the Amish is healthy.

Popular misconceptions still abound as they did twenty-five years ago, all in spite of more research and widely available publications. Two extreme views still prevail. One is the traditional view of pity for persons who will not modernize and ease the burdens of life through the convenience of twentieth-century ways and who will not be enlightened by the creativity of individual self-determination. The other extreme is embodied in the comment of the industrialist who insisted that "the Amish are the only honest Christians left in the modern world." Because of the qualities of sainthood ascribed to them, the Amish are viewed by some as a rare species, a people who raise their crops "naturally," who live by extraordinary standards of honesty and uprightness.

Any society that is perceived as "standing still" will soon become a tourist attraction. The Amish are viewed as a slow-changing people, but they are not an "archaeological discovery." The paradigm they have worked from is different from that of the larger culture; therefore they have reached different conclusions about how to live in the modern world. The present revitalization of ethnic and religious groups calls for a reevaluation of traditional social theories. Amish communities are not relics of a bygone era. Rather, they are demonstrations of a different form of modernity.

The first edition of *Amish Society* was preceded by ten years of preparation and appeared in 1963. It was slightly enlarged in 1968. These earlier editions embody the perspectives of the times in which they were written. It is time for a new interpretation. The Amish have changed, world society has changed, and Americans generally have shifted their thinking about culturally diverse peoples within their borders. Modern scholarship has refocused its method of inquiry, resulting in new perspectives.

The clash of "civilized ways" with "Amish ways" is still as apparent in Amish settlements as it was several decades ago. The notion that the Amish suffer from more human stress by denying themselves or their children the uses of modern technology and convenience or by living a more austere life than others is today in serious doubt. Civilization has indeed taught us how to survive in large numbers, how to prolong life, how to transform tribal societies into urban ones, and how to ease the burdens of labor. American rural communities generally have been transformed into landscapes for development, investment, and commercial gain. Without preachment the Amish have taught us something of the human cost when old values are cast away, when parents are alienated from children, when neighbors are treated as strangers, and when man is separated from his spiritual tradition.

This book provides a context for evaluating technical change, human values, and the alternatives confronting human communities in many parts of the world. The purpose is to communicate a knowledge of Amish life to the inquiring reader. The scope of the material is comprehensive rather than regional, integrative rather than specialized or esoteric. Although the special terms of the social sciences are in evidence, it is hoped that such terms will serve as a structure for the description of the people. A discussion of the origins, values, maintenance, and social relationships of the Amish community will be followed by a consideration of the problems, conflicts, and costs of being Amish. The book attempts to widen our knowledge of the diversity of human cultures—their customs and conflicts—and to convey the depth of human experience.

How did the Amish formulate their beliefs and develop their community life? How have the Amish managed to circumvent the forces of mainstream civilization? What is the character and scope of personal, family, and community life? What are the consequences of living in a slow-changing culture? What is the logic of introducing more efficient technology if in the process the human qualities of *Gemeinschaft* (the "natural groupings") are cut into shreds? These and other questions have relevance for human communities anywhere, from university and municipal communities to the small villages in Africa and Asia that are faced with radical change in their age-old customs.

The ethnographic material in this volume is based on the three largest Amish settlements, which are located respectively in Pennsylvania, Ohio, and Indiana. Many smaller settlements also were visited. I have conducted research on socialization, schooling, family patterns, population trends, and occupational patterns since the first edition of *Amish Society* was published. Mifflin County, Pennsylvania, where I lived as a member of an Amish family, and Washington and Johnson counties, Iowa, where I spent my youth until the age of twenty-two, taught me much about the depth and diversity of Amish culture. I have experienced the ties of kinship and faith, but I have also seen the tragedies of division, exclusion, and fragmentation.

The natural history of the Amish people has been enriched by the discovery of new sources. Some have come to light through the efforts of the Amish people themselves, who have taken a vital interest in their own heritage. Other sources have emerged through the research and publications of European scholars who have subsequently "discovered" the Amish. My understanding of Amish origins was greatly aided by a stay in Alsace, France, Switzerland, and Germany, where I visited villages, families, and congregations of descendants from the first followers of Jacob Ammann.

The specialized studies of others, both colleagues and students, have helped to round out the description of agriculture, demography, education, geography, medical studies, and tourism. These contributions are acknowledged and appreciated, for they add significant knowledge to the total perspective. All the chapters have been rewritten. Where enlightening, new material has been added, while some of the more dated technical terminology has been removed. The organization of the material, as in previous editions, is grounded in a holistic understanding of the small society.

Any society that falls under the scrutiny of scientific investigation is liable to have its internal strengths and weaknesses exposed. The risks of discovery become the responsibility of the investigator. To any reader who may feel that the strengths and weaknesses of Amish society have been disproportionately emphasized here, and especially to Amish readers, I extend the assurance that there has been no ill intent.

Acknowledgments

For the financial support that made possible my archival and European field studies, as well as the basic research essential to this volume, I thank the National Endowment for the Humanities.' For assistance in the collection of data I thank many of the Amish people.

I also wish to thank Jean Jacques Hirschy, Rene Hege, Willy Hege, Claude Jerome, Willy Nafziger, André Nussbaumer, Prof. F. Raphael, and Prof. Jean Séguy of France; Paul Ammann and Dr. Theo. Gantner of Switzerland; and Edwin Hochstättler, Paul Schowalter, Gary Waltner, and Dr. Karl Scherer of Germany.

For critical readings of one or more sections of the manuscript, often involving engaging discourses, I thank in addition to many unnamed Amish informants, Allen Alexander, Richard Beam, John W. Bennett, Roy Buck, Eugene Ericksen, Julia Ericksen, Joshua Fishman, Ivan Glick, Thomas Gallagher, Hugh Gingerich, Leonard Gross, Paul Herr, Gertrude Enders Huntington, James Hurd, Victor A. McKusick, Mervin Smucker, Don Yoder, John H. Yoder, and the late Abdul Hamid M. el-Zein. Elizabeth Horsch Bender translated many German sources, Nancy Gaines provided bibliographic help, and Doris Weiland drew the maps and charts.

I am greatly indebted to Beulah Stauffer Hostetler, my wife, for thinking out with me many of the ideas of the book. Ann Hostetler, my daughter, performed commendable editorial work on the entire manuscript.

Part I

Foundations

CHAPTER 1

Models for Understanding
Amish Society

SMALL COMMUNITIES, with their distinctive character—where life is stable and intensely human—are disappearing. Some have vanished from the face of the earth, others are dying slowly, but all have undergone change as they have come into contact with an expanding machine civilization. The merging of diverse peoples into a common mass has produced tension among members of the minorities and the majority alike.

The Old Order Amish, who arrived on American shores in colonial times, have survived in the modern world in distinctive, viable, small communities. They have resisted the homogenization process more successfully than others. In planting and harvest time one can see their bearded men working the fields with horses and their women hanging out the laundry in neat rows to dry. Many American people have seen Amish families, with the men wearing broad-brimmed black hats and the women in bonnets and long dresses, in railway depots or bus terminals. Although the Amish have lived with industrialized America for over two and a half centuries, they have moderated its influence on their personal lives, their families, communities, and their values.

The Amish are often perceived by other Americans to be relics of

3

the past who live an austere, inflexible life dedicated to inconvenient and archaic customs. They are seen as renouncing both modern conveniences and the American dream of success and progress. But most people have no quarrel with the Amish for doing things the old-fashioned way. Their conscientious objection was tolerated in wartime, for after all, they are meticulous farmers who practice the virtues of work and thrift.

In recent years the status of the Amish in the minds of most Americans has shifted toward a more favorable position.[1] This change can scarcely be attributed to anything the Amish have done; rather, it is the result of changes in the way Americans perceive their minority groups. A century ago, hardly anyone knew the Amish existed. A half-century ago they were viewed as an obscure sect living by ridiculous customs, as stubborn people who resisted education and exploited the labor of their children. Today the Amish are the unwilling objects of a thriving tourist industry on the eastern seaboard. They are revered as hard-working, thrifty people with enormous agrarian stamina, and by some, as islands of sanity in a culture gripped by commercialism and technology run wild.

In the academic community several models have been advanced for understanding Amish society. Social scientists, like other Americans, have been influenced by the upward push of an advancing civilization and changes in the social discourse between the dominant society and its minorities. University teachers have traditionally taught their students to think of the Amish people as one of many old-world cultural islands left over in the modern world. The Amish have been considered "a sacred society," a "familistic society," as maintaining "organic solidarity," an "integrative social system," "primary" (face-to-face) rather than "secondary" relationships, and "Apollonian" instead of "Dionysian" orientations to life. They may be viewed from any one of these perspectives, but such objective models and abstractions leave out things that are important for understanding the whole perspective of Amish society.

The Amish are a church, a community, a spiritual union, a conservative branch of Christianity, a religion, a community whose members practice simple and austere living, a familistic entrepreneuring system, and an adaptive human community. In this chapter

---

1. In selecting a theme for the bicentennial of the founding of the United States of America, the *Michigan Farmer* chose to feature the Amish when only a few years previously the state had prosecuted them for maintaining uncertified schools. The narrative was written by an Amish girl, Mary Miller, and appears in the July 1976 issue.

several models will be discussed in terms of their usefulness and limitations as avenues for understanding Amish society as a whole. By models I mean structured concepts currently used by anthropologists to characterize whole societies. The serious reader will want to transcend the scientific orientation and ask, What is the meaning of the Amish system? What, if anything, is it trying to say to us?

A COMMONWEALTH

The Amish are in some ways a little commonwealth, for their members claim to be ruled by the law of love and redemption. The bonds that unite them are many. Their beliefs, however, do not permit them solely to occupy and defend a particular territory. They are highly sensitive in caring for their own. They will move to other lands when circumstances force them to do so.

Commonwealth implies a place, a province, which means any part of a national domain that geographically and socially is sufficiently unified to have a true consciousness of its unity.[2] Its inhabitants feel comfortable with their own ideas and customs, and the "place" possesses a sense of distinction from other parts of the country. Members of a commonwealth are not foot-loose. They have a sense of productivity and accountability in a province where "the general welfare" is accepted as a day-to-day reality. Commonwealth has come to have an archaic meaning in today's world, because when groups and institutions become too large, the sense of commonwealth or the common good is lost. Thus it is little wonder that the most recent dictionaries of the American English language render the meaning of commonwealth as "obsolescent." In reality, the Amish are in part a commonwealth. There is, however, no provision for outcasts.

It may be argued that the Amish have retained elements of wholesome provincialism, a saving power to which the world in the future will need more and more to appeal. Provincialism need not turn to ancient narrowness and ignorance, confines from which many have sought to escape. A sense of province or commonwealth, with its cherished love of people and self-conscious dignity, is a necessary basis for relating to the wider world community. Respect for locality, place, custom, and local idealism can go a long way toward checking the monstrous growth of consolidation in the nation and thus help to save human freedom and individual dignity.

2. For a discussion of wholesome provincialism and community self-consciousness, see Josiah Royce, *Race Questions, Provincialism, and Other American Problems* (n.p., 1908), p. 62.

The Amish world view is reflected in the orderliness,
careful maintenance, and simplicity of the home.

A SECTARIAN SOCIETY

Sociologists tend to classify the Amish as a sectarian society. Several
European scholars have compared the social structure of "sect" and
"church" types of religious institutions.[3] The established church was
viewed as hierarchic and conservative. It appealed to the ruling
classes, administered grace to all people in a territorial domain, and
served as an agency of social control. The sect was egalitarian. Essentially a voluntary religious protest movement, its members separated
themselves from others on the basis of beliefs, practices, and institutions. The sects rejected the authority of the established religious
organizations and their leaders. The strains between sect and church
were viewed as a dialectic principle at work within Christianity.
The use of an ideal type helped to clarify particular characteristics of
the sectarian groups. The Anabaptists, for example, were described
as small, voluntary groupings attempting to model their lives after
the spirit of the Sermon on the Mount (Matt. 5,6,7) while also

3. Ernst Troeltsch, *The Social Teachings of the Christian Churches*, 2 vols.
(New York: Macmillan, 1931). Troeltsch, the pioneer in this field, drew his observations from the sects arising out of medieval and modern Christianity before 1800.

exercising the power to exclude and discipline members. Absolute separation from all other religious loyalties was required. All members were considered equal, and none were to take oaths, participate in war, or take part in worldly government.[4]

Sects have employed various techniques of isolation for maintaining separateness. Today the extreme mobility of modern life brings people together in multiple contexts. The spatial metaphors of separation (i.e., valley, region, sector, etc.) are fast becoming obsolete. Nevertheless, modern sectarians turn to psychic insularity and contexts that protect them from mainstream values and competing systems.[5] Members of the sect remain segregated in various degrees, chiefly by finding a group whose philosophy of history contradicts the existing values so drastically that the group sustains itself for a generation or more. To the onlooker, sectarianism, like monasticism, may appear to serve as a shelter from the complications of an overly complex society. For its participants, it provides authentic ways of realizing new forms of service and humility as well as protection from mainstream culture.

Sectarians, it is claimed, put their faith first by ordering their lives in keeping with it. The established churches compromise their faith with other interests and with the demands of the surrounding environment. Sectarians are pervasively religious in that they practice their beliefs in everyday life. Sects are often considered marginal or odd groups of alienated people with fanatic ideas. Yet the sects have had an immense influence in shaping the course of history. The British sociologist Bryan Wilson has observed that sects are "self-conscious attempts by men to construct their own societies, not merely as political entities with constitutions, but as groups with a firm set of values and mores, of which they are conscious."[6] The growth of religious toleration in America has resulted in the development of religious pluralism in a manner that has not been realized in Europe. Wilson, who has characterized modern Christian sects into several types, classes the Amish as *introversionist* rather than *conversionist* or *reformist*. "Salvation is to be found in the community of those who withdraw from involvement in the affairs of mankind."[7] The Amish recognize the evil circumstance of man, attempt to moderate its influence upon them, and retreat into a community to

4. Ibid., 2:705.
5. Martin Marty, "Sects and Cults," *Annals of the American Academy of Political and Social Science* 332 (1960): 125–34.
6. Bryan Wilson, *Religious Sects* (New York: McGraw-Hill, 1970), p. 22.
7. Ibid., p. 39.

experience, cultivate, and preserve the attributes of God in ethical relationships.

The sectarian model lends itself to a historical, religious context. As a model, it offers some insight into the proliferation of groups with a negative orientation during a specific time period. Today there are many types of movements that did not exist in the early stages of industrialization. Sects may lose their spontaneity in a variety of ways. While the model may teach us something of how sects originate and grow from a protest movement to a separate religious entity, it does not provide us with a knowledge of the dynamics of the group. The Amish, for example, are not sectarians in the sense that they demand that others conform to their practices. Nor do they claim to base all actions on holy writ. They are not in conflict with the dominant culture in the same way, or with the same intensity, as are a number of sects such as the "apocalyptic" or "manipulationist" types.[8]

Many sectarian societies, including the Amish, make little or no attempt to communicate their message. They recognize instinctively that authentic communication would mean greater literacy, education, and sophistication, and this would mean the beginning of the end. "The contribution of the sect to the larger society is," according to Martin Marty, "made best through the sympathetic observer who carries with him a picture of the advantages or particularity and assertiveness back to the word of dialogical complexity."[9] In the Amish case, the message of the sectarian society is exemplary. A way of living is more important than communicating it in words. The ultimate message is the life. An Amish person will have no doubt about his basic convictions, his view of the meaning and purpose of life, but he cannot explain it except through the conduct of his life.

A FOLK SOCIETY

Anthropologists, who have compared societies all over the world, have tended to call semiisolated peoples "folk societies," "primitives," or merely "simple societies." These societies constitute an altogether different type in contrast to the industrialized, or so-called civilized, societies. The "folk society," as conceptualized by Robert Redfield,[10] is a small, isolated, traditional, simple, homogeneous society in which

8. Ibid.
9. Marty, "Sects and Cults." p. 134.
10. Robert Redfield, "The Folk Society," *American Journal of Sociology* 52 (January 1947): 293–308. See also his book *The Little Community* (Chicago: University of Chicago Press, 1955).

oral communication and conventionalized ways are important factors in integrating the whole of life. In such an ideal-type society, shared practical knowledge is more important than science, custom is valued more than critical knowledge, and associations are personal and emotional rather than abstract and categoric.

Folk societies are uncomfortable with the idea of change. Young people do what the old people did when they were young. Members communicate intimately with one another, not only by word of mouth but also through custom and symbols that reflect a strong sense of belonging to one another. A folk society is *Gemeinschaft*-like; there is a strong sense of "we-ness." Leadership is personal rather than institutionalized. There are no gross economic inequalities. Mutual aid is characteristic of the society's members. The goals of life are never stated as matters of doctrine, but neither are they questioned. They are implied by the acts that constitute living in a small society. Custom tends to become sacred. Behavior is strongly patterned, and acts as well as cultural objects are given symbolic meaning that is often pervasively religious. Religion is diffuse and all-pervasive. In the typical folk society, planting and harvesting are as sacred in their own ways as singing and praying.

The significance of the Amish as an intimate, face-to-face primary group has long been recognized. Charles P. Loomis was the first to conceptualize the character of the Amish. In his construction of a scale he contrasted the Amish as a familistic *Gemeinschaft*-type system with highly rational social systems of the *Gesellschaft*-type in contemporary civilization.[11]

The folk model lends itself well to understanding the tradition-directed character of Amish society. The heavy weight of tradition can scarcely be explained in any other way. The Amish, for example, have retained many of the customs and small-scale technologies that were common in rural society in the nineteenth century. Through a process of syncretism, Amish religious values have been fused with an earlier period of simple country living when everyone farmed

11. Charles P. Loomis and J. Allan Beegle, *Rural Social Systems* (Englewood Cliffs, N.J.: Prentice-Hall, 1951), pp. 11–30. Further refinements on the Amish as a social system appeared in subsequent publications. See also Ferdinand Toennies, *Community and Society*, ed. and trans. Charles P. Loomis (East Lansing: Michigan State University Press, 1957).

The self-imposed isolation of Amish society suggests that they are neither folk nor peasant but "a voluntary contrived folk society," says Gertrude Enders Huntington in what is the most discerning dissertation ever written on an Amish community ("Dove at the Window: A Study of an Old Order Amish Community in Ohio" [Ph.D. diss., Yale University, 1956], p. 107).

with horses and on a scale where family members could work together. The Amish exist as a folk or "little" community in a rural subculture within the modern state, as distinguished from the primitive or peasant types described in anthropological literature. Several aspects of Redfield's folk-society model and features of the Toennies-Loomis *Gemeinschaft* aid us in understanding the parameters of Amish society. They are *distinctiveness, smallness of scale, homogeneous culture patterns,* and the *strain toward self-sufficiency.*

Distinctiveness. The Amish people are highly visible. The outsider who drives through an Amish settlement cannot help but recognize them by their clothing, farm homes, furnishings, fields, and other material traits of culture. Although they speak perfect English with outsiders, they speak a dialect of German among themselves.

Amish life is distinctive in that religion and custom blend into a way of life. The two are inseparable. The core values of the community are religious beliefs. Not only do the members worship a deity they understand through the revelation of Jesus Christ and the Bible, but their patterned behavior has a religious dimension. A distinctive way of life permeates daily life, agriculture, and the application of energy to economic ends. Their beliefs determine their conceptions of the self, the universe, and man's place in it. The Amish world view recognizes a certain spiritual worth and dignity in the universe in its natural form. Religious considerations determine hours of work and the daily, weekly, seasonal, and yearly rituals associated with life experience. Occupation, the means and destinations of travel, and choice of friends and mate are determined by religious considerations. Religious and work attitudes are not far distant from each other. The universe includes the divine, and Amish society itself is considered divine insofar as the Amish recognize themselves as "a chosen people of God." The Amish do not seek to master nature or to work against the elements, but try to work with them. The affinity between Amish society and nature in the form of land, terrain, and vegetation is expressed in various degrees of intensity.

Religion is highly patterned, so one may properly speak of the Amish as a tradition-directed group. Though allusions to the Bible play an important role in determining their outlook on the world, and on life after death, these beliefs have been fused with several centuries of struggling to survive in community. Out of intense religious experience, societal conflict, and intimate agrarian experience, a mentality has developed that prefers the old rather than the new. While the principle seems to apply especially to religion, it has also become a charter for social behavior. "The old is the best, and the

A white-top carriage along a back mountain road
in Pennsylvania.

new is of the devil," has become a prevalent mode of thought. By
living in closed communities where custom and a strong sense of
togetherness prevail, the Amish have formed an integrated way of
life and a folklike culture. Continuity of conformity and custom is
assured and the needs of the individual from birth to death are
met within an integrated and shared system of meanings. Oral tradition, custom, and conventionality play an important part in maintaining the group as a functioning whole. To the participant, religion

and custom are inseparable. Commitment and culture are combined to produce a stable human existence.

These are some of the qualities of the little Amish community that make it distinctive. "Where the community begins and where it ends is apparent. The distinctiveness is apparent to the outside observer and is expressed in the group consciousness of the people of the community."[12] The Amish community is in some aspects a functional part of modern society but is a distinctive subculture within it.

Smallness of Scale. The basic social unit of the Amish community is small. Wherever the Amish live, this primary, self-governing unit is the "church district." The rules of life are determined by this face-to-face group, which is kept small by the ceremonial functions of assembling in a single household and by the limitation imposed by horse-and-carriage travel. In most places the Amish live adjacent to non-Amish farm neighbors, but all Amish households in a geographic proximity form a unit. This small unit, from thirty to forty households, is the congregation. Households take turns hosting the biweekly religious services in their homes as there is no central building or place set aside for ceremonial functions. Families may migrate from one settlement to another, or from one state to another, but in so doing they affiliate with a local district. A settlement may be large, but the basic social unit remains small and indigenous.

The rules that are formulated by each district cover the range of individual experience. In this little community, which survives by keeping the world out, there are many taboos, and material traits of culture become symbolic. Conformity to styles of dress is important.

Smallness of scale is assured in Amish life by the multiple functions of the family. When asked about the size of his congregation an Amish bishop thinks in terms of families, not individuals. Persons who make up the society are associated with genealogical position. Most people in this society have orderly kinship and coherent social connections with one another so that virtually the whole society forms a body of relatives. Outsiders who join the Amish community —although in fact very few do—identify with the ethnic and kinship values of Amish life. Persons who defect from the little community break not only with Amish beliefs but also with normal ties with their relatives.

The Amish people maintain a human rather than an organizational scale in their daily lives. They resisted the large, consolidated school and the proposition that big schools (or farms) were better than small

12. Redfield, *The Little Community,* p. 4.

The Amish farm: a blending of human labor, stewardship,
and diligence with nature

ones. A bureaucracy that places pupils together within narrow age
limits and emphasizes science and technology to the exclusion of
sharing values and personal responsibility is not tolerated. The
Amish appreciate thinking that makes the world, and their own lives,
intelligible to them. When human groups and units of work become
too large for them, a sense of estrangement sets in. When this happens
the world becomes unintelligible to them and they cease participating
in what is meaningless.

Each Amish community exhibits a local culture, though in its
basic orientation it is like other Amish communities. Organization,
roles, authority, sanction, facility, and controls governing relations
with the outside world are much alike in all Amish communities.
Smallness in the Amish community is maintained by a functional
unit no larger than a group of people who can know one another
by name, by shared ceremonial activity, and by convention. Like the
Redfield model, the Amish community "is small, so small that either
it itself is the unit of personal observation or else, being somewhat
larger and yet homogeneous, it provides in some part of it a unit of
personal observation fully representative of the whole."[13]

13. Ibid.

Homogeneous Culture Patterns. The Amish community is homogeneous in the totality of its culture and psychology. Ways of thinking and behaving are much alike for all persons in corresponding positions of age and sex. "States of mind" are much alike from one generation to the next. Egalitarian patterns are manifest in socially approved means of subsistence, production, and consumption. Physiological homogeneity among the Amish has been recognized by persons who associate inbreeding with facial types. The first American Mennonite historian, C. Henry Smith (1875–1948), who earned a Ph.D. from the University of Chicago in 1907, was born of Amish parents. He says: "My ancestors were of Mennonite faith and race. I say race deliberately, for like the Jews they had developed in the course of time not only spiritual homogeneity, but a physical solidarity as well, which, through a process of inbreeding, had accumulated many of the characteristics of a distinct human type."[14]

Psychological homogeneity finds expression through preference for traditional and shared knowledge. All have the same amount of education, and the aspirations of one generation repeat those of the preceding one. Critical thought for its own sake has no function in the little community. Agricultural lore and tradition still provide potent sources of knowledge. Science is "worldly" wisdom, although in his farming operations the Amishman cannot help being influenced by outside knowledge.

Amish communities constitute some of the most productive and stable agricultural societies in the United States. The Amish have no great desire for wealth other than owning family-size farms that serve the purposes of the community. Their rejection of trends that characterize other rural communities, such as migration to the cities, consolidation of schools, and urban recreation and associations, is a function of cohesive homogeneity. Placing a high value on farming and farm-related occupations has tended to preserve a total way of life in a little community.

Homogeneous patterns in the Amish community can be observed in the parts that people play, their activities, and the roles that govern life. Such functions correspond with those of the preceding generations. The infant born into an Amish home is received with joy; his given name will be similar to that of his grandparents, cousins, uncles, and aunts. His last name will, of course, be the same as his father's, which will be one of several common family names. He will grow up conforming to patterns of life like his older brothers and sisters,

14. C. Henry Smith, *Mennonite Country Boy* (Newton, Kans.: Faith and Life Press, 1962), p. 12.

playing and experimenting with things within the Amish farm environment.

Wisdom accumulates with age, and with age comes respect. Old people retain the respect of children and grandchildren. Obedience to parents is one of the most common themes in Amish preaching—in family relations in particular, and in extended kinship relations generally—so that it becomes a life principle. Those who honor father and mother have the biblical promise of long life. Since the wisdom of the aged carries more weight than the advice of younger men, the conservation of the entire community is assured and the religious ideals are protected from too much change. The aged father and mother are content if their children are all married in the Amish faith, if they are all located on farms, and if they abide by the rules of the church. They may confidently face a sober death knowing that their children and a large group of relatives will continue to live a stable, believing life according to the Amish pattern. In the Amish community, the career of one generation repeats that of the preceding.

Strain toward Self-sufficiency. Although Amish communities are highly integrated, they are not economically self-sufficient. In the everyday operations of the farm, total separation is neither sought nor desired. The communities are dependent on local markets, merchants, hospitals, and medical services. The Amish community is self-sufficient in its religious life, socialization patterns, and educational functions. The basic needs of the individual are met within the community.

The attempt to retain self-sufficiency is associated with agrarianism and occupations close to nature. Closeness to the soil, to animals, to plants, and to weather is consistent with the Amish outlook on life and with limited outside contact. Hard work, thrift, mutual aid, and repulsion of city ways such as leisure and nonproductive spending find support in the Bible and are emphasized in day-to-day experience. With practical knowledge and hard work, a good living can be made from the soil; and this, the Amish contend, is the only fit place for a family.

The Amish woman's sphere and work are at home, not in the factory or in a paid profession. Cooking, sewing, gardening, cleaning, whitewashing fences, tending to chickens, and helping with the milking keep her occupied. Caring for the children is, of course, her principal work. Her place in the religious life of the community is a subordinate one, though she has voting rights in congregational meetings and in the nomination of persons for the ministry. An

Amish woman's work, like the work of any American woman, is never done. But she is always with her children, and to break the monotony, there are weddings, quiltings, frolics, auction sales, and Sunday services. For her satisfaction in life she turns to brightly colored flowers in the garden, or in the winter, to rug-making, embroidery work on quilts, pillowcases, and towels, and to shelves of colored dishes in her corner cupboard. Some the work of her hands, these are her prized possessions, made for the enjoyment of the household and her host of relatives. Within her role as homemaker she has a greater possibility of achieving status recognition than the suburban housewife; her skill, or lack of it, has direct bearing on her family's standard of living. She sews all their clothes; plants, preserves, and prepares the food her family eats; and adds beauty to life with quilts, rugs, and flowers. Canning her own food, making her chow-chow, and spreading the dinner table with home-prepared food are achievements that are recognized and rewarded by her society.

The Amish have no schools of higher learning, but they have built elementary schools to avoid the external influence that comes with the centralized school system. As soon as the law will allow, Amish children are taken out of school for work at home. The Amish viewpoint is that "if a boy does little hard work before he is twenty-one, he probably never gets to like it afterward. In other words, he will not amount to much as a farmer."[15]

The need for leisure and social enjoyment is met by informal institutions within the community. Kinship duties require extensive visiting. Recreation consists primarily of meaningful social experiences, group solidarity, and rites of passage within the community. Work bees, such as barn-raisings, woodcuttings, husking bees, quiltings, preparations for church services, weddings, and funerals (including casket-making), all combine work and recreation. The social life of the young people is centered in the Sunday evening singing. One of the most important life ceremonies is the wedding, which calls for a large amount of festivity, food, kinship duties, and ritual. What matters most about the prospective bride and bridegroom is not whether they come from a wealthy family, but whether they show promise of being a good housekeeper and a good farmer, respectively, within the bounds of the community.

The little Amish community is not a communal society with an exclusive economic system, and property ownership is not unlike that in the dominant society. However, the Amish have been able to maintain patterns of mutual aid and ways of sharing economic re-

15. Anonymous Amish comment.

wards and misfortunes. Their vital linkages with outside institutions are conditioned by their distinctive core values and by the special rules that govern such relationships. By making agriculture a sacred occupation, the Amish avoid the drift toward the complex world of labor relations and the professions. Farm produce may not be delivered or picked up on the Lord's Day. Religion prevents members from taking an active part in activities that are beyond "necessity" on Sunday. Amish farmers are not integrated with farm organizations, local political groups, or consolidated schools.

Self-sufficiency is the community's answer to government aid programs such as farm subsidy and social security benefits. The Amish are opposed to receiving direct government aid of any kind, whether old-age pension, farm subsidy, or compensation payments, and to having their children and grandchildren fall heir to such handouts. To admit that the government has a responsibility for Amish members is to deny the faith. This, they say, would undermine their own stable community and their form of mutual aid. Amish security requires a high degree of personal relations and responsibility in times of stress, fire, sickness, old age, or death. Strictly commercial or federal means of providing for these needs are regarded as secular, if not sinful. Amish life is not segmented into cliques, clubs, or special-interest groups, but approximates a cradle-to-the-grave arrangement as an integral whole; the little community "provides for all or most of the activities and needs of the people in it."[16]

Amish society, developed along the lines of the folk model of Robert Redfield, is a type of human community that is realized in many parts of the world. These "little" communities that remain at the edges of expanding civilizations share certain characteristics. The Amish, however, are neither primitive nor peasant in the manner of the older and more geographically isolated groups.[17] The Amish derived from the Reformation, which in itself was a liberating and self-determining movement. Amish life is permeated with the Christian tradition and its codifications of reality. The folk model demonstrates the structure of Amish society, its tradition-directed quality, and the variety of its interpersonal relationships. To understand the inner dynamics of Amish society, however, we must look elsewhere. The model that follows will attempt to illuminate some of the problems of social discourse between the Amish community and mainstream American culture.

16. Redfield, *The Little Community*, p. 4.
17. For a classification of folk types, see Elman Service, *Profiles in Ethnology* (New York: Harper & Row, 1963).

A HIGH-CONTEXT CULTURE

Cultural anthropologists have demonstrated enormous variations between cultures and a significant degree of elasticity within a single culture. Culture patterns determine what people pay attention to and what they ignore. What people feel, think, and do varies from one culture to another. Edward T. Hall has distinguished between "high-" and "low-context" cultures, illustrating different but legitimate ways of thinking and perceiving.[18]

A high-context culture is one in which people are deeply involved with one another. Awareness of situations, experience, activity, and one's social standing is keenly developed. Information is widely shared. Simple messages with deep meaning flow freely. There are many levels of communication—overt and covert, implicit and explicit signs, symbols, and body gestures, and things one may and may not talk about. Members are sensitive to a screening process that distinguishes outsiders from insiders.

The models created to explain nature are rooted in culture—are very much a part of life—but are unavailable for analysis except under very special circumstances. The nonverbal, or unstated, realms of culture are extremely important as conveyors of information. High-context cultures are integrated, for members are skilled in thinking comprehensively according to a system of the common good. Loyalties are concrete and individuals work together to settle their problems. If one person has a problem, others are expected to know what is bothering him.

Low-context cultures emphasize literacy and rationality. Highly bureaucratized segments of culture within American life are "low" in context because information is restricted primarily to verbal communication. Other levels of awareness are underdeveloped or dormant. Ways of perceiving are restricted primarily to a linear system of thought, a way of thinking that is considered synonymous with truth. Logic is considered the only road to reality. Low-context cultures use primarily mathematical models to explain nature and environment. People are highly individualistic and somewhat alienated in contexts that require little involvement with other people. Low-context culture is fragmented rather than integrated, and people live more and more like machines. The contradictions that compartmentalize life are carefully sealed off from one another. Persons in

18. Edward T. Hall, *Beyond Culture* (Garden City, N.Y.: Doubleday, 1976). Grateful acknowledgment is made for permission to use excerpts from pp. 74–77 and 91–93.

low-context cultures are prone to use manipulation to achieve their goals and are also prone to be manipulated. Failures are blamed on the system. In times of crisis, individuals expect help from institutions, not from persons.

High- and low-contexting cultures emerge not through conscious design or because people are not intelligent or capable but because of the way in which deep cultural undercurrents structure people's lives in subtle ways that are not consciously formulated. It is the hidden currents of culture that shape the lives of people living under its influence. These differences are rooted in how people express themselves, the way in which they think, how they move, how problems are perceived and solved, how transportation systems function, and how people arrange their time and space. Edward Hall does not discuss high- and low-contexting within a single culture (American culture as a whole), but his scheme appears to allow for such comparisons.

What are the consequences when the Amish (a high-contexting culture) and low-contexting segments within mainstream America come together? There is no indication that they cannot cooperate in certain ways, but there are likely to be structured misunderstandings. Two illustrations will suffice to indicate some possibility consequences. One is based on information systems and the other on methods of training the young.

Information overload is a technical term applied to information-processing systems in which the system breaks down because it cannot properly handle the large amount of information to which it is subjected. Hall illustrates this with the case of the mother who in trying to cope with the demands of small children, run a house, live with her husband, and carry on a normal social life is suddenly faced with the feeling that everything is happening at once and that everything seems to be closing in on her. This American mother is experiencing the same information overload that afflicts business managers, administrators, physicians, attorneys, and air controllers. How the Amish and persons in mainstream American culture cope with information overload has important consequences. Amish culture provides a highly selective screen between itself and the outside world. The flow of information into the Amish community is highly selective. Furthermore, the Amish are keenly aware of their own screening process. Direct exposure to mass communication systems is greatly reduced. This screening protects members, and their nervous systems, from information overload. What the Amish pay attention to (contexting) and what they ignore are different from the choices of low-contexting cultures. Information overload is handled differently in the two cultures. Most Americans are exposed to large amounts of information daily and are scarcely aware of a screening process between themselves and the outside world.

The way children are treated in school will vary according to high- and low-contexting cultures or settings. In high-context cultures like the Amish, the young are effectively prepared for adult life by the family and community, and formal schooling is a minor part of their lives. The Amish teach their children social cohesion, practical skills, and social responsibility. This is accomplished in small groups, in small country schools where persons learn to know one another well. Each recognizes and knows the talents of the others. Learning is always interspersed with liberal periods of work and play. Children form close and lasting friendships, and they communicate well with one another and are effective in group processes. Studies of children in small schools (in groups of from eight to twelve members) show that the children are absent less frequently, are more dependable and more articulate, and find their work more meaningful than children in large schools.[19]

In the large American public schools children are subject to massive learning situations. It is well known that in such large groups natural leadership patterns suffer and that it becomes necessary to choose leaders by manipulation and political process. Children in low-context cultures suffer from overstructuring, overbureaucratization, and the compulsive need to consolidate and coerce social structures to fit budgets. According to Hall, organized public education in the United States has managed to "transform one of the most rewarding of all human activities into a painful, boring, dull, fragmenting, mind-shrinking, soul-shriveling experience."[20]

Whether one accepts this judgment of the quality of learning in the public schools or not, it is clear that preparation for life is very different in these two contexts. Both social cohesion and technical competence are essential for any society. The Amish emphasize values that generally supersede the emphasis on facts. By design, Amish schools are not suited for training artists, musicians, painters, and actors. The Amish school does not function as an institution for upward mobility in the modern industrial complex. By design, public schools do not teach children simplicity, humility, and the fear of God. State regulations for the approval of schools in American society take for granted the practices important to verbal articulation (low-

19. Ibid., p. 183. See also Jonathan P. Scher, ed., *Education in Rural America: A Reassessment of Conventional Wisdom* (Boulder, Colo.: Westview Press, 1977), p. 96.

20. Hall, *Beyond Culture*, p. 96.

contexting situations). The long conflict between state departments of education and the Amish is rooted in these deep undercurrents of culture.

THE VIEW FROM THE INSIDE

The Amish are real people, not simply an ideal type of a theoretical construct. Like all human beings, they use signs and symbols to cope with everyday life in order to make their world more meaningful and desirable. They are engaged in a social discourse with reality, the meaning of which is revealed in the analysis of the "unconscious" structure of their religious ideology. Such an analysis takes into account the mythological, the ritual process, and the charter of the community, and thus opens doors that aid us in comprehending how the Amish view themselves as a people and how they regard their mission in the world.

The Amish view themselves as a Christian body suspended in a tension-field between obedience to an all-knowing and all-powerful Creator on the one hand and the fear of disobedience on the other. The setting is the story of Creation in the Genesis account. God made all things, including the physical world, the animals and plants, dry land and sea, and after God had made man and woman he placed them in a perfect garden as stewards. Satan, the evil one, who himself had been cast out of heaven for his "pride," in a cunning way tempted Eve into taking a position of "knowing better than God." Through the temptation, both Adam and Eve fell into the sin of disobedience, and consequently all mankind acquired a disobedient or carnal nature which is under the curse of death. Meanwhile, man must suffer the consequences of having to earn his living "by the sweat of his brow" and woman must suffer the pain of childbirth (Gen. 3: 16–19). God provided a way of escape, however, for the spiritual side of man. He took pity on man in his sinful plight and provided hope by offering his son as a gift. By becoming a human being and suffering crucifixion and death at the hands of disobedient men, the Son of God became the medium of escape from spiritual death. Whoever believes and lays claim to the gift (the substitutionary suffering and death of the Son of God) can be restored to a spiritual or right relationship with God—he can attain eternal life after death of the body. The individual must acknowledge his natural state of disobedience, declare his helplessness without the Son of God, and surrender his will to the community of the believing.

This basic religious mythology, so common to the Semitic tradition, is, however, very different from that of other Christian groups. The

Amish have retained certain elements from biblical tradition and have combined them into a system that is relevant for them. Let us examine two of the important paradigms: *pride vs. humility* and *love vs. separation*.

Pride leads to knowledge that is counterproductive to the knowledge of God. The knowledge that comes from disobedience to God comes from the "evil one" and will lead to the broad path of distruction. By contrast, the knowledge of God comes from obedience, and obedience leads to the narrow path of redemption. The Amish people's educational goals for their childen and their antipathy toward philosophical and worldly knowledge are grounded in this dialectic.

The love of God for sinful man requires an appropriate response. That response is "a brotherly community" living in obedience. The model for this "love community"—the life and teachings of the Son of God—emphasizes sacrificial suffering, obedience, submission, humility, brotherly love, and nonresistance. Not only is this community made up of surrendered members, but Christ himself is incarnated into the community, or "body." As a corporate offering to God, the brotherly community must be "without spot or blemish" (Eph. 5:27; I Pet. 1:19; II Pet. 3:14) and must be "a light to the world" (Matt. 5:14). Living in a state of unity and constant struggle to be worthy as "a bride for the groom" (Rev. 21:2), the community must be vigilant, living on the edge of readiness. Within the community the "gift" of God is shared and reciprocated among the members, for since God loves all, "we ought also love each other" (John 3:23). This reciprocation commits the members to an indivisible unity according to which each lives in harmony with all other members.

Separation must naturally exist between those who are obedient to God and those who are proud and disobedient. There is, therefore, a continuous tension between the obedient and the disobedient. The Amish are mandated to live separate from the "blind, perverted world" (Phil. 2:15) and to have no relationship with the "unfruitful works of darkness." The Amish are "in the world but not of it" and hence claim the status of "strangers" and "pilgrims" (I Pet. 2:11). As a believing community, the Amish strive to be "a chosen generation" (I Pet. 2:9), "a congregation of the righteous," and a "peculiar people" (Tit. 2:14) prepared to suffer humiliation or persecution.

Aside from the usual acts of admonition, indoctrination, and worship, ritual in the Amish community consists of maintaining the purity and the unity of the community. Unworthy members and those who are disobedient or cause disunity must be expelled, for they cannot be part of the "bride" offered to God. The "old leaven" must be purged from the group (I Cor. 5:7). Twice each year the church-community enacts the necessary ritual to cleanse and purify the corporate body through the observance of communion. The charter of the Amish community, insofar as it affects the behavior of individuals, has great significance in everyday life. Loyalty to God is judged by obedience and conformity to the community's rules of discipline. These rules, enacted by the church-community, stipulate the ways in which members may interact with worldly and disbelieving members. The overriding principle is that members must not be "unequally yoked with unbelievers" (II Cor. 6:14). On such grounds business partnerships or conjugal bonds with outsiders are forbidden. Strife, war, and violence have no place in the community or in the life of the member. Members of the community cannot function as officers or caretakers of the political or world society. The community is guided by the teachings of the Son of God, by the recorded stories of the people of God from the time of creation, and by the rules of discipline.

The structural implications of Amish mythology and religious ritual are discussed in greater detail under "The Charter" in Chapter 4. The relations between language, though, and social action lie within the scope of structural analysis. The same myth may have different meanings for different groups. The significance of symbols so pervasive in Amish life, e.g., soil, preparation and fertilization of the soil for planting, manual work, fertility, "plain" living, productivity associated with animals, and the ritualization of the calendar year, has yet to be fully analyzed.

Myth in Amish society serves as a charter for social action, i.e., it becomes a by-product of a living faith and hence takes on a sociological character requiring group consensus, moral rule, and sanction. Myth institutionalizes the behavior of a society by enforcing traditions and norms. Acting as a charter, myth endows the society's values with prestige and supernatural force. It is not only a conservative force, perpetuating the status quo with powerful integrative functions as indicated by Malinowski, but it is also a language of social discourse which provides the members with purpose.[21] In times of social conflict and change, myth provides a language of argument using signs and symbols to establish meaningful distinctions from those of other groups.

21. Bronislaw Malinowski, *Magic, Science, and Religion* (New York: Anchor Books, 1954), pp. 144–46. For insights on myth as a social discourse, I am indebted to Abdul Hamid M. el-Zein, *The Sacred Meadows: A Structural Analysis of Religious Symbolism in an East African Town* (Evanston, Ill.: Northwestern University Press, 1974), pp. 195–98.

The models introduced here are offered as aids for comprehending the whole of Amish life. It is hoped they will help to place in perspective the complexity of the society and serve as a benchmark for some of the more detailed analyses that follow. The effectiveness of these models must be judged on how well they encompass and explain the material.[22] The description of Amish society is not limited to one or any of these models. All such models are incomplete and most elicit answers to objective questions asked from the outside. The view from the inside is offered throughout the ethnography so that the reader may come to understand the logic of Amish society.

22. The Amish as an ethnic group and as a minority group are discussed elsewhere. See Calvin Redekop and John A. Hostetler, "The Plain People: An Interpretation," *Mennonite Quarterly Review* 51 (October 1977): 266–77.

CHAPTER 2

The Birth of Amish
Society

🌿

THE AMISH are direct descendants of the Anabaptists of sixteenth-
century Europe and were among the early Germanic settlers in Pennsylvania. As part of a widespread counterculture movement of religious
reform, the Anabaptist movement[1] produced three groups that survive
to this day: the Mennonites of Dutch and Prussian origin, the Hut-
terian Brethren of Austria, and the Swiss Brethren. Named after their
leader, Jacob Ammann, the Amish are a branch of the Swiss Brethren.
In order to understand the origins of the Amish it is first necessary to
understand the role of the Anabaptists in the social context of religious
reform.

THE SOCIAL CLIMATE OF REFORM

Fundamental changes had been taking place in European society
long before the outbreak of the Reformation in the sixteenth century.
This unrest was articulated by able and dedicated spokesmen. Among

1. The literature on the Anabaptists is voluminous. I recommend first the
magnum opus by the Harvard church historian George H. Williams, *The Radical
Reformation* (Philadelphia: Westminster Press, 1962); and then the shorter, more
readable accounts of Walter Klaassen, *Anabaptism: Neither Catholic nor Protestant*

25

the prophets of a new way were Peter Waldo in Italy (founder of the Waldensians), John Wycliffe in England, and John Huss in Bohemia (forerunner of the Moravians), all of whom helped to set the stage for popular reform. Discontent was widespread. Traders and peasants found themselves displaced by the growing commerce with other parts of the world. People who had lost faith in the traditional institutions were ready to become followers of radical religious movements. For them, the old church was legalistic, irrelevant, and exploitive. The Catholic church had become the scapegoat for the social ills of society.

The astonishing variety of nonconformists in the sixteenth century demonstrates the seriousness with which people sought solutions leading to a better life. Following the invention of the printing press, people began reading the Bible for the first time. Some turned to following the teachings of the Gospels literally: because Jesus taught that a person must become as a little child to enter the Kingdom of God, some people literally behaved like children, playing with toys and babbling like babies.[2] One source lists the heretics of the period, and among them were the Adamites, who ran naked in the woods; the Free-livers, who had wives in common; the Weeping Brothers, who held highly emotional prayer meetings; the Blood-thirsty Ones, who drank human blood; the Devil-worshippers, who praised the devil ten times daily; and the Hypocritical Ones, who were indifferent to all liturgical ceremonies.[3]

Rebellion against old systems of authority gave rise to religious wars, to new territorial boundaries, and to a general reorganization of religious groups ranging from "right" to "left" in their attitude toward social reform. When Martin Luther wanted to discuss some of the practices of the established church, the church took a rigid position against changes. Following Luther's excommunication from the church, he found himself the leader of a group that later became the Lutheran church. Reforms more liberal than those of Luther were instituted by Ulrich Zwingli and John Calvin, who founded the Reformed church in Switzerland. Both of these Protestant groups, however, retained the concepts of a united church and state and infant baptism, and Luther

---

(Waterloo, Ont.: Conrad Press, 1973); and C. J. Dyck, *An Introduction to Mennonite History* (Scottdale, Pa.: Herald Press, 1967). The idealism of the Anabaptists is described in Harold S. Bender's classic "The Anabaptist Vision," *Church History*, March 1944, also published in pamphlet form by Herald Press, Scottdale, Pa.

2. Klaassen, *Anabaptism*, p. 2.

3. Henry A. DeWind, "A Sixteenth Century Description of Religious Sects in Austerlitz, Moravia," *Mennonite Quarterly Review* 29 (January 1955): 44. For a longer history of revolutionary millenarianism, see Norman Cohn, *The Pursuit of the Millennium*, rev. ed. (New York: Oxford University Press, 1970).

retained the mass in a modified form. These changes were still unsatisfactory to those who wanted more far-reaching reforms. [Those seekers who wanted to take a more radical position and "reform the reformers" were called Anabaptists.[4]

The rejection of infant baptism became a symbol of the Anabaptist movement, a movement the authorities considered seditious. The term *Anabaptist* originated as a nickname meaning "rebaptizer." Rebaptizing was practiced by sincere seekers who felt that baptizing babies could not be supported by the Scriptures. They argued that sin entered the world with a knowledge of good and evil (Gen. 3). Since an infant does not have this knowledge, it cannot have sin. Thus, children do not need baptism for the removal of sin. Those who refused to baptize their infants were also seeking new ways of reforming the church. They expressed their displeasure with economic and social injustices.

Diverse groups of nonconformists flourished throughout Western Europe at this time, but the authorities did not distinguish between militant anarchists and pacifist believers. Both groups were labeled as seditious Anabaptists, as worthy of arrest, torture, exile, or death.] To its enemies Anabaptism appeared to be a cancerous growth that would destroy Europe's religious and social institutions. The Anabaptists' beliefs were regarded as devil-inspired; their practices, odd and antisocial.[5]

THE SWISS BRETHREN

A small group of dedicated persons in Zurich, Switzerland, began to study the Gospels seriously and to propose reforms to the heads of state churches. Conrad Grebel, a nobleman by birth, had attended the universities of Basel, Paris, and Vienna. Felix Manz knew Latin, Greek, and Hebrew and spent much of his time preaching without authorization from the state, an action for which he was often put in prison. George Blaurock was educated for the priesthood. These men came to believe that the name "Christian" should be applied only to those who truly practiced the teachings of Jesus, and not indiscriminately to all who observed such state church rituals as infant baptism and the mass. Their reforms were rejected first by Ulrich Zwingli, head of the Swiss state (Reformed) church, and later by the Zurich City Council, and they were ordered not to disturb the unity of the church. But the small

---

4. The nature of this radicalism is set forth by Franklin H. Littell in *Origins of Sectarian Protestantism* (New York: Macmillan, 1964). See also Williams, *Radical Reformation*, chap. 11.

5. Klaassen, *Anabaptism*, p. 1.

group continued to meet secretly for Bible study and prayer. With full knowledge that they might be brought to trial by state authorities, they baptized one another into a new church-community, and commissioned one another as missioners to proclaim their newly founded "believers' church."[6] This church was to be separate from the state and membership was to be voluntary, free from the hierarchy and coercive power of the old church. Strong emphasis was placed on obedience to the words of Jesus, his teaching of love and nonresistance, and the imitation of his life and character. Christ was present not in the sacraments, they said, but in the body of believers who lived redemptive lives and practiced his teaching.

The small group in Zurich was arrested, imprisoned, and banished. Manz was publicly executed by drowning for the crime of rebaptism, Grebel died of the plague at the age of twenty-seven in exile, and Blaurock was burned for his heretical beliefs.

Another important leader, Michael Sattler, left his post as prior of a Benedictine monastery to become an Anabaptist evangelist. He presided over a secret conference of Anabaptist leaders in February 1527. The conference issued a declaration of "Brotherly Union" (since called the Schleitheim Articles) which became instrumental in structuring the character of the movement.[7] Its seven articles (abridged below) embody the Swiss Anabaptists' view of a Christian brotherhood living in a viable community.

THE SCHLEITHEIM ARTICLES

1. *Adult baptism*

Baptism shall be given to all who have been taught repentance and the amendment of life, who believe that their sins are taken away through Christ, and who desire to walk in the resurrection of Jesus Christ. This excludes all infant baptism.

2. *The ban*

After taking baptism as a sign of commitment to the fellowship, if any inadvertently slip and fall into error and sin, the ban shall be employed. First they shall be warned twice privately, and the third time publicly before the congregation (according to Matthew 18). This shall be done before the breaking of bread, so that all may in one spirit and in one love, break and eat from one loaf and drink from one cup.

---

6. For a detailed account of the founding of the first Swiss Brethren congregation in 1525, see Fritz Blanke, *Brothers in Christ: The History of the Oldest Anabaptist Congregation* (Scottdale, Pa.: Herald Press, 1961).

7. The conference was held in the town of Schleitheim on the Swiss-German border. For the text and critical discussion, see John Y. Yoder, *The Legacy of Michael Sattler* (Scottdale, Pa.: Herald Press, 1973).

3. *Concerning the breaking of bread*

Those who partake of the bread (the Lord's Supper) must beforehand be united in the one baptism and one body of Christ. Those who desire to drink in remembrance of the shed blood of Christ, cannot be partakers at the same time of the table of the Lord and the table of devils. All who have fellowship with the dead works of darkness have no part in the light. We cannot be made one loaf together with them.

4. *Separation*

We have been united concerning the separation that shall take place from the evil and wickedness which the devil has planted in the world, simply in this; that we have no fellowship with them, and do not run with them in the confusion of their abominations. . . .

Thereby shall also fall away from us the diabolical weapons of violence—such as sword, armor, and the like, and all of their use to protect friends or against enemies—by virtue of the words of Christ: "You shall not resist evil."

5. *Shepherds*

The shepherd in the church shall be a person of good report according to the rule of Paul, who can read, exhort, teach, warn, admonish and properly preside in prayer and in the breaking of bread. If he has need, he shall be supported. If he is driven away or martyred, another shall be installed immediately.

6. *The Sword*

The sword [government] is an ordering of God outside the perfection of Christ. It punishes and kills the wicked, and guards and protects the good. . . .

Within the perfection of Christ only the ban is used for the admonition and exclusion of the one who has sinned—without the death of the flesh—simply the warning and the command to sin no more.

The rule of government is according to the flesh; that of Christians, according to the spirit.

7. *Rejection of oaths*

The oath is a confirmation among those who are quarreling or making promises. In the old law it was permitted in the name of God. Christ, who taught the perfection of the law, forbids all swearing. One's speech shall be yea or nay. Anything more is evil.

Within a few years most of the leaders of the Swiss Brethren had died or been martyred. But the seven articles on which they had agreed are still basic guidelines in the lives of the Swiss Brethren and the Amish today.

Several years after the Schleitheim meeting, a priest in the Netherlands began to doubt whether the bread he held in his hands turned into the flesh of Jesus every time he recited the mass. He soon had second thoughts about infant baptism. By 1536, Menno Simons felt he had to choose between the authority of church tradition and the authority of the Scriptures.[8] The courageous example of the suffering and death of the Anabaptists around him was so compelling that he joined them. He preached, admonished, argued, and wrote long explanations of the Scriptures for the rest of his life.)The high and learned doctors of the church, he said, were blinded to the simplicity and directness of the Gospels by many trappings: "legends, histories, fables, holy days, images, holy water, tapers, palms, confessionals, pilgrimages, masses, matins, and vespers . . . , purgatory, vigils, and offerings."[9] He felt that the observance of these matters was trivial and kept the people in ignorance of the real Christ. Menno Simons became the most important Anabaptist leader in the Netherlands in the sixteenth century. His followers were called "Mennists" or "Mennonites," and the name was later adopted by descendants of the Swiss Anabaptists who came to America.)

Among Menno's friends who had turned Anabaptist were two brothers, Dirk and Obbe Philips. Dirk, like Menno Simons, wrote many tracts. Trained as a Franciscan monk, he had had a good education and had an excellent command of classical languages. In the interest of strengthening the new brotherhoods he wrote eloquently on church discipline, the ban, spiritual avoidance, and order within the church. His lengthy volume *Enchiridion or Hand Book*,[10] as well as *The Complete Writings of Menno Simons*, is prized and read by Amish and Mennonites today in both German and English editions. The Anabaptists were not content with merely changing a few rituals or with surface reforms. The newly formed movement was concerned with restructuring the religious order and creating its own cosmos. The Catholic church had maintained a social-religious structure that was built on the observance of the sacraments. The grace of God, dispensed through the proper hierarchy, was necessary for salvation. The Protestants—the Lutheran and Reformed state churches—emphasized creed and doctrine. Both Catholic and Protestant churches closely coordinated their religious structures with the political structure of a territory or region. The Anabaptists rejected such an alliance as un-Christian. For the Anabaptists, being a Christian meant voluntarily yielding one's sovereignty to a committed community, a spiritual brotherhood

8. For an evaluation of the teaching of Menno Simons, see Franklin H. Littell, *A Tribute to Menno Simons* (Scottdale, Pa.: Herald Press, 1961).

9. Menno Simons, *The Complete Writings of Menno Simons*, ed. J. C. Wenger, trans. Leonard Verduin (Scottdale, Pa.: Herald Press, 1956), p. 165.

10. Dietrich Philip, *Enchiridion or Hand Book* (1910; reprint ed., Aylmer, Ont.: Pathway Publishers, 1966).

of believers. The process of redemption required not only personal repentance and yielding to God but also forsaking "the works of darkness": wrongdoing, self-assertiveness, greed, and the uses of retaliation. As Christ suffered and died, so his followers must be ready to suffer. The qualities taught by Jesus in the Sermon on the Mount (Matt. 5,6,7) were to become the model in this redemptive community.

The authorities perceived that the Anabaptists were building a new social order that was undermining their control. As Anabaptist groups sprang up in many places, imprisonment, torture, and harassment followed. The authorities argued that the Anabaptists refused to obey the constituted, God-ordained government. Protestant reformers, including Martin Luther, were disturbed by the irresponsible acts of the peasants, which culminated in 1525 in the Peasants' War and which were indeed a basic threat to a unified and orderly society. Panic provoked the Catholic and Protestant states to use military force against the peasants as well as the Anabaptists. For the Anabaptists, a martyr's death represented the supreme identification with Christ's "death on the cross."[11]

Living in a country dominated by the Reformed church, the Swiss Mennonites suffered persecution and oppression for at least two centuries. With the original leadership gone, succeeding generations settled into the hinterlands and valleys of the Jura and the Vosges Mountains and pursued an agrarian life. Here they managed to exist as conservative islands of sectarianism.[12]

THE AMISH BRANCH

The Amish division of the Swiss Mennonites owes its existence as well as its name to the elder of Markirch (Sainte Marie-aux-Mines), Jacob Ammann (Figure 1).[13] Little is known of him except that he was born in Switzerland and later migrated to Alsace, where he became an elder and spokesman for Anabaptists who had moved to that region.

11. See the enormous martyr book, *The Bloody Theatre; or, Martyrs Mirror*, comp. Thieleman J. van Braght (Scottdale, Pa.: Mennonite Publishing House, 1951). Originally published in Dutch (Dordrecht, 1660); also published in German.

12. For the agricultural and rural character of these communities, see Ernst Correll, *Das schweizerische Täufermennonitentum* (Tübingen: Mohr, 1925); and Jean Séguy, *Les Assemblées anabaptistes-mennonites de France* (The Hague: Mouton, 1977).

13. Ammann's role in the division is treated by Harold S. Bender in the *Mennonite Encyclopedia*, s.v. "Ammann, Jacob," and known facts about his person are discussed by Delbert Gratz in "The Home of Jacob Amman in Switzerland," *Mennonite Quarterly Review* 25 (April 1951): 137–39.

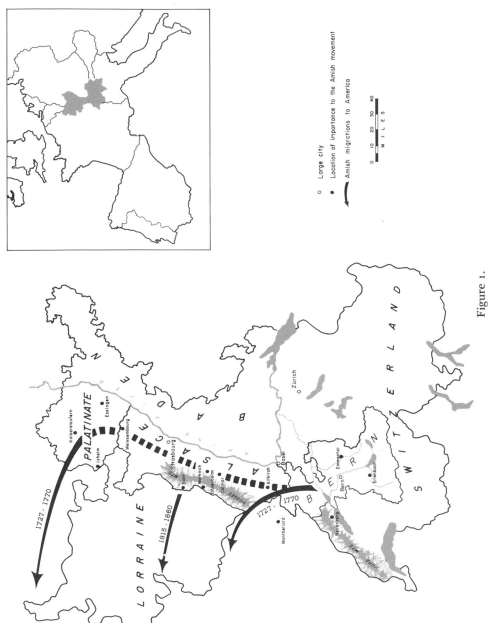

Figure 1.

He is presumed to have left Switzerland in 1693 or earlier.[14] In a state document of 1696 he is cited as the spokesman for a group of members in the Alsatian area who were seeking exemption from military service.

Compared with the major reforms that grew out of the Reformation, the division of the Swiss Brethren was a family squabble. The French sociologist Jean Séguy holds that the division grew out of certain tensions between the "mother" group in Switzerland and the "diaspora" in Alsace.[15] The chain of events leading up to the schism can be reconstructed from a number of letters that have been preserved, most of which were written after the events themselves had taken place.[16] According to the letters, the sequence of events was as follows:

Probably in July or August 1693, Jacob Ammann of Markirch advocated that communion should be observed twice each year instead of once as had been the custom. News of this innovation spread rapidly, and the majority of the congregations, including those in Switzerland, were faced with the question of whether to reprove or follow Ammann. When the issue was discussed in a meeting, the senior Swiss elders, Benedict Schneider and Hans Reist, did not squarely oppose the suggestion. They replied that the high priest in Old Testament times had entered the holy place yearly and that if anyone was worthy and could prepare himself twice, then twice was not too often. On the other hand, they said, if one is deserving, then yearly communion would seem to be sufficient.[17]

Ammann then turned from the observance of communion to the subject of social avoidance (*Meidung*). He insisted that members who had been excommunicated should also come under the censure of

---

14. An extant letter by Ammann states that he was in Alsace in 1693. See John B. Mast, ed., *The Letters of the Amish Division* (Oregon City, Ore.: C. J. Schlabach, 1950), p. 41.

15. Séguy, *Les Assemblées*, p. 256. I am indebted to Jean Séguy for important cultural insights, both from personal conversations in 1977 and from his comprehensive work, coming as they do from a prodigious scholar in the country where the Amish division occurred.

16. The letters are listed and discussed by Milton Gascho in "The Amish Division of 1693–1697 in Switzerland and Alsace," *Mennonite Quarterly Review* 11 (October 1937). The texts were published in German by Joseph Stucky in *Eine Begebenheit* (1871), by Johannes Moser in *Eine Verantwortung* (1876), and by the *Christliche Gemeinde Kalender* in 1908 (pp. 138–51), 1909 (pp. 134–41), and 1915 (pp. 121–24). L. A. Miller of Arthur, Illinois, published the Stucky edition with new material in 1936. English translations appear in John B. Mast, ed., *The Letters of the Amish Division* (Oregon City, Ore.: C. J. Schlabach, 1950). Several of the letters were translated into English (with comment) by C. Henry Smith in *The Christian Exponent* (April 11, May 9, June 6, and July 1, 1924).

17. Peter Geiger letters, in Mast, *Letters*, p. 69.

social avoidance. The Swiss Anabaptists had practiced excommunication in keeping with the Schleitheim Articles of Faith. But the Alsatians, unlike the Swiss, had accepted the Dutch or Dordrecht Confession of 1632, which in addition to excommunication also upheld social avoidance (*Meidung*) and the practice of foot washing. Articles 11 and 17 from the Dordrecht document[18] read as follows:

Article 11, Of the Washing of the Saints' Feet

We also confess a washing of the feet of the saints, as the Lord Jesus did not only institute and command the same, but did also Himself wash the feet of the apostles, although He was their Lord and Master; thereby giving an example that they also should wash one another's feet, and thus do to one another as He did to them; which they also afterwards taught believers to observe, and all this is a sign of true humiliation; but yet more particularly as a sign to remind us of the true washing—the washing and purification of the soul in the blood of Christ. John 13:4–17; I Tim. 5:9, 10.

Article 17, Of the Shunning of Those Who Are Expelled

As regards the withdrawing from, or the shunning of, those who are expelled, we believe and confess, that if any one, whether it be through a wicked life or perverse doctrine—is so far fallen as to be separated from God, and consequently rebuked by, and expelled from the church, he must also, according to the doctrine of Christ and His apostles, be shunned and avoided by all the members of the church particularly by those to whom his misdeeds are known, whether it be in eating or drinking, or other such like social matters. In short, that we are to have nothing to do with him; so that we may not become defiled by intercourse with him, and partakers of his

18. The Dordrecht Confession originated in Holland in 1632 as an ecumenical statement by a number of Dutch and Old Flemish Mennonite factions. (See *Mennonite Encyclopedia*, s.v. "Confessions of Faith," "Dordrecht Confession," and "Flemish Mennonites.") The document was printed and circulated widely outside the Netherlands in French and German. Thirteen of the Alsatian ministers and elders from eight congregations signed the Dordrecht Confession in 1660. (The document, with signatures, appears in J. C. Wenger, *History of the Mennonites of the Franconia Conference* [Telford, Pa.: Franconia Mennonite Historical Society, 1937], pp. 462–63.) Some signed it because they thought it was being universally accepted by their Anabaptist brethren (Jonas Lohr letters, in Mast, *Letters*, p. 18).

That it was signed by the Alsatian ministers does not necessarily indicate that they endorsed all its points, some of which differed from Swiss Mennonite practice. For example, Rudolph Egli signed it but spoke against social avoidance (Jacob Good letter, ibid., p. 58). Not all congregations that subscribed to the Confession practiced foot washing or social avoidance. Similarly, the Franconia Conference in America adopted the Dordrecht Confession in 1725 but never practiced social avoidance and began to practice foot washing only late in the nineteenth century. Because the document was printed and widely distributed, it was readily available for submission to governments that requested a statement of Mennonite beliefs. This fact may help to account for its popularity.

sins; but that he may be made ashamed, be affected in his ways. I Cor: 5:9–11; Rom. 16:17; II Thess. 3:14; Titus 3:10,11.

That nevertheless, as well in shunning as in reproving such offender, such moderation and Christian discretion be used, that such shunning and reproof may not be conducive to his ruin, but be serviceable to his amendment. For should he be in need, hungry, thirsty, naked, sick or visited by some other affliction, we are in duty bound, according to the doctrine and practice of Christ and His apostles, to render him aid and assistance, as necessity may require; otherwise the shunning of him might be rather conducive to his ruin than to his amendment. I Thess. 5:14.

Therefore we must not treat such offenders as enemies, but exhort them as brethren, in order thereby to bring them to a knowledge of their sins and to repentance; so that they may again become reconciled to God and the church, and be received and admitted into the same—thus exercising love towards them, as is becoming. II Thess. 3:15.[19]

Ammann advocated both avoidance and foot washing. Realizing that the congregations in Switzerland were not observing these practices uniformly, Ammann decided to visit their assemblies. He took with him three Alsatian ministers (Uli Ammann, Christian Blank, and Nicholas Augsburger). Ammann met with the Swiss elders rather hastily in a number of meetings. One of the senior elders, Hans Reist, had already decided not to practice *Meidung* and refused to take part in the meetings.

At each of the meetings the elders were asked to state their policies with respect to the practice of *Meidung*. If they agreed with Ammann's view, he demanded their attitudes on two other issues: whether true-hearted persons[20] would be saved, and whether persons who were guilty

19. J. C. Wenger, *The Doctrines of the Mennonites* (Scottdale, Pa.: Herald Press, 1950), pp. 80–83.

20. True-hearted persons were non-Anabaptist sympathizers called *Treuherzigen*, or "half-Anabaptist," and were nominal members of state churches. The controversy was whether these persons, because of their good deeds, would attain salvation. The German reads "Dass man die treuherzigen Menschen ausser Gottes Wort nich selig sprechen soll, die noch in den weltlichen Ordnungen stehen" (Ulrich Ammann letter, 1698). The true-hearted people aided the Anabaptists, giving them food and shelter, protecting them from the official "Anabaptist hunters," and in so doing endangered themselves, for Swiss mandates threatened and condemned these sympathizers. One observer wrote in 1690: "Great is the number of those who are suspended between heaven and earth, and know not what to do" (*Mennonite Encyclopedia*, s.v. "Half-Anabaptists"). Hans Reist composed several prayers for the true-hearted, "who love us and do good unto us and show mercy, but have little strength to come unto the obedience of God." See Robert Friedmann, *Mennonite Piety through the Centuries* (Goshen, Ind.: Mennonite Historical Society, 1949), p. 185; see also John Horsch, *Mennonites in Europe* (Scottdale, Pa.: Mennonite Publishing House, 1950), pp. 394–97. To Ammann, however, the true-

of telling a falsehood should be excommunicated. Ammann demanded unconditional answers, and he succeeded in polarizing the churches. At their first stopping place, Friedersmatt (near Bowil), minister Nicholas Moser agreed to the ban, but he advised Ammann to go and see Elder Schneider. Instead the delegation went to Reutenen (near Zaziwil), which was near the home of minister Peter Geiger. There Ammann called a meeting without notifying Geiger, who had retired for the night. When Geiger arrived later that evening, the meeting was about over. At neighboring Habstetten, minister Nicholas Baltzi was summoned and accused of teaching that true-hearted persons would be saved. Baltzi asked that the delegation be patient.

The investigating group then went to Eutigen, where it summoned Hans Reist to declare his position on *Meidung*. He answered, "What one eats is no sin; Christ also ate with publicans and sinners."[21] Avoidance at the table was wrong, according to him, for it is not what goes into a man's mouth that defiles him. His answers to this and other questions were unsatisfactory to Ammann.

At their next stop, Eggiwil, Ammann was informed by two elders that it would be best if the entire ministry would assemble and decide upon a general rule. Forthwith Ammann summoned the Swiss ministry to a meeting in Nicholas Moser's barn. Given such short notice, not all the ministers could be present, and when pressed for their attitudes on *Meidung*, some said they could not come to a decision until after the entire ministry had met. The only conclusion they reached was to call another meeting of all the ministers. Ammann wanted to hold the meeting in eight days, but Geiger wanted it in three weeks. Meanwhile, Ammann sent two men to visit Reist to ask him a second time about his stand on the *Meidung*. Reist stalled in giving a reply, but wrote a letter to several ministers saying he could not accept the *Meidung* and that "in matters concerning doctrines and church rituals, not too much attention should be given younger men."[22] He obviously meant Jacob Ammann.

While waiting for Reist to come to the second meeting in Moser's barn, Geiger again quoted the Scriptures: "What enters the mouth does not defile a man, but what goes out of the mouth."[23] Ammann replied that the quotation had nothing to do with the issue. Geiger then quoted another passage: "If ye bite and devour one another, see

---

hearted were "thieves and murderers" who were being admitted "by another way into the sheepfold, without the cross and without tribulation" (Mast, *Letters*, p. 38).

21. Mast, *Letters*, p. 69.
22. Ibid., p. 29.
23. Ibid., p. 71.

that ye be not consumed of one another."[24] He pleaded with Ammann not to bring about a division in the church. Meanwhile, some women were instructed to go and tell Reist and others to come to the meeting, but they returned saying that it was harvest time and these men could not come. Ammann interpreted their absence as an indication of their indifference.

Ammann, according to the account, became enraged. Taking a letter from his pocket, he read six charges against Reist, declaring him and six other ministers excommunicated. One of the women fell on her knees and in tears begged Ammann to be patient. He turned to Moser and asked his opinion of the *Meidung*, but Moser said he could not speak for his congregation since he had not asked their counsel. Ammann turned to Geiger for his opinion, but he replied that he could not give his opinion until all the ministers were present. Ammann then charged both of them with falsehood and took upon himself the task of excommunicating them. He next turned to Habegger, Schwartz, and Gul, and when they could not accept the *Meidung*, he excommunicated them. The meeting broke up and the Ammann party left without shaking hands. Geiger pulled Ammann by the shirt sleeve, saying, "Let me present my word also," but Ammann jerked his arm away and departed.[25]

Shortly after the dramatic meeting in the barn at Eggiwil, Ammann wrote a warning letter to the Swiss ministers demanding that by a certain date they appear and yield to his interpretations or prove them false. His warning letter in English translation follows:

JACOB AMMANN'S WARNING MESSAGE

Together with the ministers and bishops, I, Jacob Ammann, am sending this writing to everyone who is not already expelled by judgment and resolution [*durch Urteil und Rat*], both men and women, ministers and lay members, to inform you that you shall appear before us on or before February 20th to answer whether you can confess these controversial articles with us namely: to avoid those who are expelled, and the liars shall be expelled from the church, and that no one shall be saved, apart from the Word of God. Or if you can instruct us of a better way, from the Word of God, we shall lend you our ear. If you are unable to report by this appointed date, to confess these articles with us, or to point out to us another way from the Word of God, then we shall appoint another date, namely, March 7th, on which you may present your answer. But if you fail to appear, and answer at this appointed time, then you shall according

24. Ibid.
25. Ibid., p. 73.

Present-day Markirch (Saint Marie-aux-Mines), in Alsace, France,
near where the first Amish churches were formed

to my teaching and creed [*nach meiner Lehr und Glauben*], be expelled by
us ministers and elders, especially by me, Jacob Ammann, as sectarians
[*als sektische Menschen*], and shall be shunned and avoided [*gescheut und
gemieden werden*] until the time of your repentance according to the
Word of God. This paper shall be sent from one person to another to
make it known to all.

A.D. 1693[26]

In Alsace most of the congregations supported Ammann. On hearing
about the dissension, the elders across the Rhine River in the Palatinate
arranged for a meeting of both sides of the dispute. The meeting was
held on March 13, 1694, at "Ohnenheim (Alsace) in the mill." Despite
the willingness of the Palatines to negotiate their differences, no agreement could be reached. The Ammann party refused to compromise on
any of its demands and left the conference. The Swiss and Palatine
ministers issued a statement telling why they were unable to agree with
Ammann.[27] Ammann then excommunicated the Palatine ministers,
including numerous persons he had never seen. Thus the Mennonites
of Switzerland, Alsace, and southern Germany were divided into two

26. Ibid., p. 49.
27. Ibid., p. 50.

factions. Of the sixty-nine ministers who took sides in the division, twenty-seven sided with Ammann. Twenty of the twenty-three ministers in Alsace supported Ammann. One in Switzerland and five in Germany were sympathetic to Ammann.

In 1700 the Ammann or "Amish" party, as it was called, admitted that its methods were too rash and hasty.[28] The Amish party made an overture toward reconciliation by revoking its excommunication of the Reist group. Furthermore, its members "excommunicated themselves," anticipating that the Reist party would be humiliated into offering some gesture of reconciliation.[29] When the two parties met in conference, however, the Amish group was not willing to surrender the doctrine of *Meidung*. The Swiss Brethren contended that if the Amish group were to be restored into their fellowship, foot washing, as Ammann wanted it, would still be an issue. Some of the congregation doubted the motive of the Amish party and advised against reunification. With so many hurt feelings, animosity continued between the factions.

After the initial confrontations on social avoidance, it became evident that Ammann also attached great importance to the wearing of traditional, simple clothing, and to the avoidance of the grooming styles of the world. Ammann condemned the trimming of the beard and the wearing of fashionable clothing, and "anyone desiring to do so," he said, "shall be justly punished."[30] Although the use of hooks and eyes was not part of the initial controversy, it later symbolized their differences. The Amish were known as *Häftler* ("hook-and-eyers") and the Mennonites were the *Knöpflers* ("button people"). Such material differences provided members with a constant stimulus for social distance and consciousness of their differences.

In retrospect, what were the real causes of the Amish division? Personal ambition for leadership, perhaps even jealousy, has been suggested as the main cause.[31] Jacob Ammann appears to have been particularly inflexible, stubborn, and extremely sure of himself and his judgments. His signature, it has been pointed out, was that of a tough, pretentious, and headstrong man.[32] To understand the causes, however, we must place the controversy in wider perspective. As has been suggested, neither a purely psychological explanation nor a moral judgment is adequate.

28. Ibid., p. 89.
29. Ibid.
30. Ibid., p. 42.
31. Gascho, "The Amish Division," p. 51.
32. Séguy, *Les Assemblées*, p. 258.

The Alsatian Mennonites, immigrants of Swiss background, were experiencing tensions that were different from those they had known in Switzerland. When Ammann arrived in the valley of Markirch in Alsace, he found several practices that were dissimilar from those in the "mother" community. Certain demands were being made on the local Anabaptists. They had been pressed for but had refused service in the militia and in the *Heimburg*. A *Heimburger* was a local office-holder, a civil servant who acted in the name of the community for the common good, e.g., in the surveillance of roads and in the administration of the village. Whether the office was an elective one or was filled by local family heads taking turns is not clear. The Anabaptists had also refused the duties of watchman, which involved guarding against marauders. At any rate, Ammann was emphatic in declaring that the Anabaptists in that area "were not in a position to have one single member serve in the *Heimburg* in any area of the valley, or for their young boys to serve in the militia as some had previously done."[33] Ammann arranged for an exemption fee to be paid each year by the Anabaptists so that they would be relieved of the duties in *Heimburg* and in the militia. Thus Ammann found himself in the middle of severe tensions between his Alsatian members and the local authorities, and between the Alsatian and the Swiss Anabaptists.

The Alsatian immigrants and their children appear to have been a well-integrated social and self-contained religious community. There was, however, a tendency among them to be loyal to the local lords and princes who had provided land and a means of livelihood. This alliance represented certain dangers, not of persecution, but of compromise. Some had frequented Lutheran worship services. Lutherans also were a minority in this region, or tantamount to a free church, and there were fraternal associations between the two groups. It was in this context that the question about the salvation of true-hearted persons had arisen back in Switzerland. Ammann drew a sharp line, excluding from congregations those who attended state churches or who attributed salvation to the true-hearted.

Both foot washing and *Meidung* were practiced by the early Mennonites in Holland and were included in the Dordrecht Confession of 1632. Neither was practiced by the Swiss, nor were they included in the Schleitheim Articles of 1527. The controversy between the two groups reflected differences in their understanding of exclusion. The

---

33. Ibid., p. 130. Because of the exemption fee a list of family heads (presumably newcomers and residents) in Ammann's region has been preserved (*Archives Haut Rhin* E 2014, E 2808). See Jean Séguy, *Les Assemblées*, p. 130 and p. 163, nn. 69 and 70.

Swiss called the *Meidung* "a new doctrine," and the elders admonished their members not to adopt the new teaching.[34] Ammann argued with his colleagues: "If you want to look to the forefathers, then look to the confession of faith made in Holland in the town of Dortrecht."[35] The Reist group flatly denied that avoidance was practiced by Christ or his apostles, and called the articles in the Dordrecht statement "a statute of mortal origin."[36]

In taking a firm position, Ammann was attempting to teach an uncompromising gospel. He had no patience with the deliberations of those who would not make up their minds immediately. Aware of the dangers of compromise faced by the Alsatian congregations, Ammann demanded that all return to a stricter discipline. One result of this position was the creation of a cohesive group with a particular ethnic composition. By instituting communion twice yearly, the Alsatian congregations were able to exercise greater discipline over the lives of their members. Ammann's emphasis on orthodoxy and on more frequent practice of the rituals led to stronger cohesion but also to greater legalism. Ammann was able to win the Alsatian congregations to his views most likely because they sensed that their ranks needed to be firmly tightened if they were going to retain their distinctive identity.

JACOB AMMANN, FOUNDER

Jacob Ammann has remained a mystery with respect to his birth, family line, and date of death. Except for his role in the division of the Swiss Brethren, little is known about him. Archival sources have indicated that he lived at Erlenbach in the Simme Valley south of Thun.[37] Whether he was born here or only served as an elder at this place is not known for certain. He lived in Alsace from about 1693, when he began to serve the Anabaptist groups. His name appears as a co-signer on lists of Anabaptists (required by the authorities) who resided in the area of Markirch. One of his grown daughters was admitted into the state church by baptism at Wimmis, near Erlenbach, in 1730. According to this baptismal record in the archives at Bern, Jacob died outside the Republic of Bern before this date. A psalm

34. Mast, *Letters*, pp. 53, 54.
35. Ibid., p. 40.
36. Ibid., p. 19.
37. Delbert Gratz has summarized what has heretofore been known about Ammann, and dates reported in this paragraph are based on his work. See his article "The Home of Jacob Ammann," pp. 137–39. An inventory of Anabaptist property (most likely made between 1703 and 1708) shows that Ammann owned two cows and three goats (*Archives Haut Rhin* E 2089).

book that once belonged to Jacob Ammann contains a note written by Baltz Ammann saying that he inherited the book from his father. It is possible that Jacob was the son of Michael and Anna Rupp Ammann, born February 12, 1644, but it is not probable; he was called "a young fellow" by Hans Reist at the time of the division, and at that time he would have had to have been forty-nine years of age. In 1712 an order of expulsion disbursed the Anabaptist community in Markirch, although all its members do not seem to have left the area at that time. What happened to Jacob Ammann in those circumstances is not known.

The publication of an Ammann family genealogy in Zurich in 1975 provides the documentation for a new thesis about the lineage of Jacob Ammann.[38] A Jacob Ammann was born on February 19, 1656, and baptized as an infant as the third son of Jacob and Katharina (Leuenberger) Ammann, a farming couple, in Steingasse of Madiswil. Madiswil lies between Langenthal and Huttwil, also an area of Anabaptist activity in the canton of Bern. The compilers of the genealogy did not find marriage or death dates for Jacob, or any record of wife and children. They found a notation in the records that he had vanished from the community. The notation states that he had been a very diligent student in the village school, especially zealous in religion, and that he was so industrious that he completed his work a year in advance of his class. For this he was given a Bible and was advanced to the adult age group. It was noted that he later went to Alsace.

At the onset of the Amish division, this Jacob would have been thirty-seven years old. That age fits the description of Hans Reist, who referred to Ammann as one of the younger ordained men. Ammann is a common name in the canton of Bern, as is Jacob, but few Ammanns appear in Anabaptist records. Of the Ammann families who came to America, none are known to have been Anabaptists.[39]

Was Founder Jacob a convert to Anabaptism and not born of Swiss Brethren parentage? If born at Madiswil, we may surmise that after completing his schooling, he vanished from his community and became

38. Paul Ammann and Hans Ammann, *Aus der Sippe Ammann von Madiswil, Stammregister, 1612–1955* (Zurich, 1975). This work represents the combined efforts of father (Hans, 1874–1959) and son (Paul, b. 1901) over many years. I am indebted to Paul Ammann for genealogic date as well as for insights gained from a personal interview in 1977.

39. Several Ammann families came to Pennsylvania as well as to North Carolina after 1730. See Ralph B. Strassburger and William J. Hinke, *Pennsylvania German Pioneers*, 3 vols. (Norristown, Pa.: Pennsylvania German Society, 1934), 1: 417, 643, 665. See also A. B. Faust and G. A. Brumbaugh, *Lists of Swiss Emigrants in the Eighteenth Century to the American Colonies*, 2 vols. in 1 (1920; reprint ed., Baltimore: Genealogical Publishing Co., 1968), 1: 30, 45, 195; 2: 35.

an Anabaptist. To become an Anabaptist would have been a criminal offense, and therefore it would have been necessary for him to leave his native town. There would have been no recording of his marriage or the birth of his offspring in state church records, and therefore the information would be lost for future generations.

There are clues in the letters exchanged by the Ammann and Reist parties which suggest that Founder Jacob may have been a convert to the Swiss Brethren. This information provides insights into the psychological causes of the Amish division. Jacob was zealous, and perhaps ambitious, as stated earlier. He pressed for observance of communion twice yearly. New converts to religious movements are frequently more deeply committed to the observance of forms and are more sensitive to inconsistencies than are members of long standing. One wonders who in a frontier community (Alsace) other than a novice would have had the audacity to confront the old bishops in the home community (Switzerland) with radical changes in ceremonies and basic practices and to call these elders liars.[40]

The two extant letters written by Jacob Ammann reveal an authoritarian policy of church government more typical of the Reformed church than of the Anabaptists. This, too, hints that he may have been a convert. In his letter to the Palatine ministers, he addresses himself

40. Letters of Peter Lehman and Rudolph Huszer (Mast, *Letters*, p. 61). Animosity between Reist and Ammann is evidenced by name-calling. Reist "was an eminent man of considerable influence at that time" (ibid., p. 77). Ammann accused Reist of pride. Legal claim to a meetinghouse also was in dispute. Nevertheless, knowing what havoc the practice of social avoidance had wrought in Holland, the senior elders were unwilling to give Ammann a serious hearing. They had knowledge of its adverse effects (Jacob Good letter, 1699, ibid., p. 59). Menno Simons had supported not only excommunication but also social avoidance on the grounds of excluding the "Münster fanatics" and "the abominations of the perverse sect [polygamy, violence, apolyptic tendencies, and coercion]."
In Holland the early Mennonites practiced marital avoidance, whereby married partners were required to cease cohabiting when one was excommunicated. Leenaert Bouwens and Dirk Philips carried the practice to the extreme. Wives who were uncertain whether they should leave their husbands or stay with them were forcibly taken from their homes at night by the strict party. While innocent children screamed, the husband pleaded with tears that his wife should be permitted to stay with the needy children, but there was no pity. Some spouses lived all their lives without ever finding their mates. Married couples divided their money and children and went their separate ways. Menno Simons grieved deeply over this excessive discipline and disapproved of attempts to enforce marital avoidance in cases where the couple was not convinced by conscience that it should be observed (*Complete Writings*, pp. 1050, 1060–63). The South German churches emphatically rejected *Meidung* in the sixteenth century and many Dutch Mennonites joined the Reformed church as a result of the bitter factionalism.

as "I, Jacob" sixteen times,[41] a practice that is out of character for an Anabaptist letter writer. He attached great significance to the office of elder and to his convictions, and lesser weight to the counsel of the brotherhood. Decisions in the Reformed church were made by synods. In Anabaptist churches, major decisions were made by counseling first with the ordained and then with the assembled members.

Two other incidents suggest a difference from Anabaptist practice. When Benedict Schneider asserted that no one should be excommunicated except by unanimous counsel of the entire congregation, Jacob Ammann said sarcastically: "[It appears] as though the keys [of the kingdom] were entrusted to all lay-members."[42] In another exchange, Nicholas Moser stated that for the acceptance of a new doctrine by the whole brotherhood, "toleration will be required."[43] Ammann questioned this procedure, charging: "You are a minister and want to learn your faith from the congregation!"[44] Today there are no Ammanns among the Amish. We do not know when the name disappeared among them. In her adult life one daughter of Jacob returned to the Reformed church. If a convert to Anabaptism, it is possible that Jacob Ammann felt emotionally rejected by the ethnic character of the Swiss group. The facts are suggestive but inconclusive for this new thesis.

Our final source of information on Jacob Ammann is his own handwriting, his signatures, of which four have been found in archival sources (see Figure 2). At that time many people could not write their names, and signatures varied. Ammann's name occurs in many variations, and his signatures for the years 1701, 1703, 1708, and 1709 were, respectively, "Jacob Amen," "I. Amme," "Jacob Ami," and "I.A." In keeping with the German custom at that time, no distinction was made between "J" and "I," especially when capitalized. There was no "en" ending, in keeping with the custom of using a printed "E" (or a script capital "E") for "en." The encircled signature "I A" (1709) with the words "Marque Jacob Aman" in the handwriting of the scribe of the text assures the reader that it was indeed the mark of Jacob Ammann. Co-signers with Ammann in 1701 were Hans Zimmerman and Jacob Hostetler, and in 1703, Hans Zimmerman and Nikolas Blank. The signature of 1703 is distinct from the text of the manuscript, and since the writer was presumably Swiss, the signature is likely that of Jacob Ammann. Swiss names often end in "i," as distinguished from German ones, which typically end in "e" or "en." Jacob wrote his name both ways, Amen as well as Ami.

41. Mast, *Letters*, pp. 28–49.
42. Ibid., p. 32.
43. Ibid., pp. 102–3.
44. Ibid., p. 103.

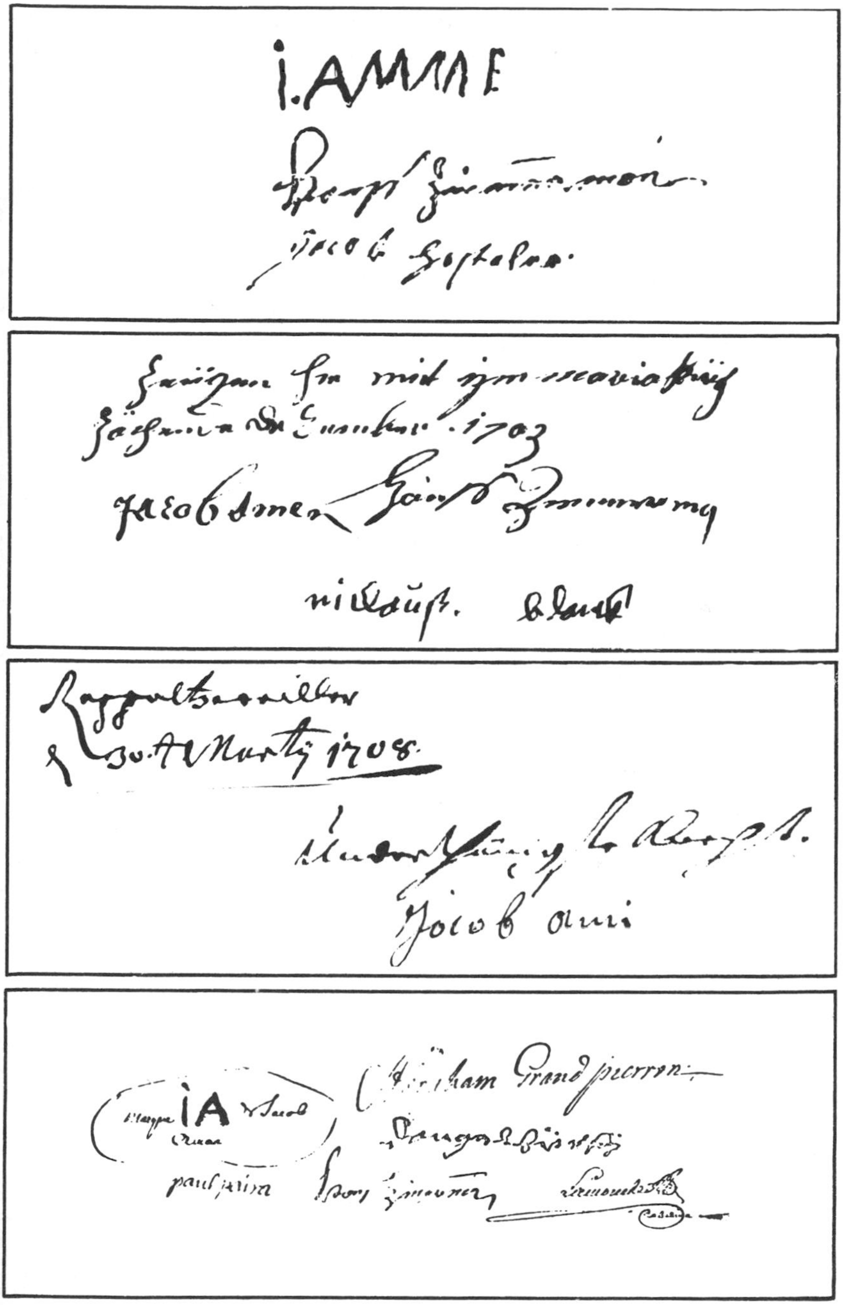

Figure 2.
Signatures of Jacob Ammann of Alsace

Jean Séguy, the French sociologist and researcher of Alsatian Mennonites, reviewed these signatures and offered the following comments in a letter: "Compared with the other signatures on the four documents, Jacob Ammann's own can be described as the most firmly written. Ammann makes his presence dramatically and theatrically felt in the way that he graphically manifests the consciousness he has of his own importance. He is a man who entertains outwardly no doubts as to his psychological and social identity. His signatures are of someone who claims leadership roles for himself, and tends to dominate over the people."[45]

Séguy also observed that only Ammann and the Alsatian officials used Latin. He says: "One cannot help asking the following question: Did not Jacob Ammann use the Latin rather than the Gothic script in order to convey the impression that he was culturally superior to his fellow Mennonites in Markirch, since he only could use the same script as the officials? Consequently, the use of Latin letters in his signature would mean that he was the man whom the local administration could trust. When he does use Gothic letters, as he partially does in the 1703 document, he still writes them in such a way as to make his signature appear in a class apart from that of the other Mennonite signers."[46]

With respect to the personality traits of Ammann, Séguy says: "The 1708 signature stands out as the least sophisticated." [Ammann is the only Anabaptist signer.] Could we say then, that when he did not feel competition around himself, Jacob Ammann could also be a simple, amiable person? It may have been the case after all. The variations and differences that can be observed in the four signatures of Jacob Ammann probably suggest that their author, on the one hand, was not a person given to the daily use of his writing pen; on the other hand, they also mean, I suppose, that the writer's personality was complex and contradictory."[47]

In view of the great emphasis placed on humility among the Amish, how do today's Amish regard the actions and innovations of Jacob Ammann? Some are frankly embarrassed by his harsh behavior and do not speculate further. Others regard him as a person who must have sensed the lukewarmness of his people and demanded a return to stricter rules. The social character of Amish life has much in common with the early Anabaptist practice of "brotherly love," which predated the Ammann era. This is evidenced by the books found in Amish homes today, e.g., the writings of Menno Simons and Dirk Philips, the *Martyrs Mirror*, and the *Ausbund*.

45. Personal letter, March 7, 1979.
46. Ibid.
47. Ibid.

Two Amishmen, Shem and David Zook, wrote in 1830: "The birth-place of Jacob Aymen we have not ascertained, nor yet the exact place of his residence—having never considered him a man of note, we do not deem the place of his nativity a matter of consequence."[48] In writing for his local newspaper in 1936, Eli J. Bontreger observed that the Amish church was observing its four hundredth anniversary.[49] The occasion was the year Menno Simons turned from the Catholic priest-hood to become an Anabaptist preacher.

The Amish people today regard themselves as Anabaptist, or *Wieder-täfer*, and most know nothing of Ammann. Through Ammann's influ-ence, however, they added foot washing, simple grooming styles, and social avoidance to the earlier basic Swiss tradition of brotherly love and brotherly union embodied in the Schleitheim Articles. The name given to the followers of Ammann was "Amish Mennonite" or "Amish," from the Swiss diminutive "Ami," though spellings vary in German and French sources. Early American usages such as "Aymennist" or "Aymeniten" were probably attempts to combine the phonetic features of "Amish Mennonite." The name "Old Order Amish" was never used in Europe but was a nineteenth-century label used in America to distinguish the traditional congregations from others.

THE DEVELOPMENT OF SEPARATISM

The Amish cleavage was not unlike the formation of other social movements. Certain characteristics are common to all leaders, prophets, or founders who establish dissenting movements.[50] Sectarian move-ments tend to emerge from the following conditions.

A *sectarian movement*[51] *must establish an ideology different from*

---

48. Letter dated November 26, 1830, in *Register of Pennsylvania*, ed. Samuel Hazard, vol. 7 (March 12, 1831), p. 162.

49. Eli J. Bontreger, "Amish Church Observes 400th Anniversary this Year," *Middlebury Independent*, June 8, 1936, p. 7. For a modern Amish view of Ammann, see David Luthy, "The Amish Division of 1693," *Family Life*, October 1971, pp. 18–20.

50. The natural history of dissident movements has been the concern of a number of social scientists. See Rex D. Hopper, "The Revolutionary Process: A Frame of Reference for the Study of Revolutionary Movements," in Ralph H. Turner and Lewis M. Killian, *Collective Behavior* (Englewood Cliffs, N.J.: Prentice-Hall, 1957), pp. 310–19. A more recent study is that of Ron E. Roberts and Robert M. Kloss, *Social Movements* (St. Louis: C. V. Mosby, 1974).

51. Sociologically defined, the sect is a movement of religious protest which tends toward perfectionism and exclusiveness from the dominant institutions of society. See the excellent treatment by Bryan Wilson, *Religious Sects* (New York: McGraw-Hill, 1970). For the distinction between "church" and "sect" as sociological types, see the classical work of Ernst Troeltsch, *The Social Teachings of the Christian*

that of the parent group in order to break off relations with it. Emergent beliefs tend to be selected on the basis of their difference from the parental group. They are essentially negative doctrines that state what the movement is against. Ammann succeeded in making *Meidung* a major issue that precipitated a cleavage.

The articulation of differences in belief by an enthusiastic leader claiming divine authority is an early condition necessary for the emergence of a sect. Beliefs are always articulated by persons who manifest leadership abilities. There is evidence that Ammann was both highly articulate and aggressive. Though Ammann had two other preachers with him on his tour of investigation, he was the main spokesman and relied upon his own inspiration rather than on authority shared by others who were with him.

A sense of urgency is vocalized by an authoritarian person who imposes negative sanction on opposing persons or groups. An appeal to patience and cautious deliberation made no sense to Ammann. In his view, the church was slipping farther and farther into worldliness, and could be salvaged only by immediate action. The founder of a movement acts on the basis of personal, charismatic authority, and not on authority delegated by the group. Ammann could not follow a middle course and he would not respond to those who fell on their knees to beg for patience.

The goals of a sect must be specific rather than general if they are to gain acceptance. Ammann's goals were specific and literal rather than general and philosophical. Most social movements are based on both kinds of motivation, but concrete goals are a vital ingredient in the initial stages of forming a movement. Broadly defined goals give room for personal interpretation, but specific goals demand uncompromising conformity. Ammann's specific and attainable goals defined a new order.

A sect must establish cultural separatism by invoking symbolic, material, and ideological differences from those of the parental group. The symbols of separation in Ammann's group took the form of different styles of dress, grooming, and physical appearance. For Jacob Ammann, doctrinal matters had to take on visible and explicit, not just "spiritual," character. *Meidung* was to be practiced not only at the communion table, or in spiritual matters, but in all areas of daily living and interaction. Nonconformity to the world meant not only a difference in thought and in the heart but also an outward material

---

Churches (New York: Macmillan, 1931). Such structural analyses are essential but are of limited value in explaining motivation and vision and how the subculture creates its own cosmos.

separation as characterized by Ammann's emphasis on the avoidance of "worldly" hair, beard, and dress styles. The example of Jesus washing the feet of His followers was to be taken not only spiritually but literally.

In the course of their natural history, the Amish have proved similar to other social movements in four ways: (1) they attempted to change or keep from changing certain beliefs or practices among existing groups; (2) they appealed to the people as a means of achieving their goals and thereby distributed responsibility among followers and leaders according to the vision or skill of the dominant leader, which resulted in (3) a geographical scope that transcended the local community and (4) persistence through time.[52] The Amish achieved all these features.

The persistence of custom, its slow response to change, is a distinctive feature of the Amish people. The pervasiveness with which the Amish literally adhere to their traditional religious practices is carried over into the social and economic aspects of their lives. Sociologists call this slow pace of change cultural inertia, cultural lag, or formalism. Through it we can observe how Amish society has remained relatively stable while the dominant society has changed radically.

52. C. Wendell King, *Social Movements in the United States* (New York: Random House, 1956), pp. 25–27.

CHAPTER 3

To America

THE AMISH CAME to America as part of a much larger movement of Palatine German-speaking people, including the Mennonites and other religious groups. The Amish of today derive from two peak immigration periods, one in the eighteenth century (1727–1770) and the other in the nineteenth (1815–1860) (see Figure 3). Before the Amish became a separate body in 1693, several groups of Mennonites from the Netherlands and northern Germany had already found their way to Pennsylvania. The first permanent settlement of Mennonites was founded in 1683 in Germantown, which is today a municipal division of Philadelphia.

THE TORMENT IN EUROPE

The Anabaptist groups in Europe had encountered severe persecution, and conditions arose that forced numerous migrations. Those of Swiss background migrated primarily to southern Germany, France, and Pennsylvania, but small groups also went to Holland, Prussia, and Polish Russia. The Anabaptists were highly valued within the German Empire as skillful and productive farmers, but they were not given legal religious status. They were completely dependent on the good will of lesser rulers for a peaceful existence.

The lands north of Switzerland along the Rhine were sought by the Swiss Mennonites as a place of refuge prior to 1620. Today this area is known as Alsace in France, and Rhineland-Pfalz (the Palatinate) and Baden in Germany. Between 1671 and 1711 several hundred Swiss Anabaptists left the canton of Bern to find homes in Alsace and the Palatinate. Although the Amish were largely of Swiss origin, many of them lived in Alsace or the Palatinate before crossing the Atlantic.

A secret police force of "Anabaptist hunters" was organized to spy, locate, and arrest Anabaptists for their nonconformist beliefs. A Commission for Anabaptist Matters was formed by the Swiss government (and sanctioned by the Reformed church) to confiscate the property of the Anabaptists, enforce the mandates, determine the length of prison sentences, and decide who should be banished. Finding an Anabaptist leader yielded a higher reward than finding a member or sympathizer. Children of Anabaptist parents were declared illegitimate because the parents had not been married by a Reformed minister, and were therefore disallowed the inheritance of their parents' estates. The expenses of imprisonment, the work of spying and arresting, and the rewards for the secret police were all paid for through the sale of the property confiscated from the Anabaptists. Considered a threat to the land because they refused to serve in the military, take oaths, or baptize their infants, the Anabaptists were punished for their non-conformity in a variety of ways. Some were imprisoned, others were sent to Italy as galley slaves. Men were taken to the border, branded with hot irons, and threatened with death if they returned, but in spite of the threats, they kept coming back to their wives, children, and relatives.

Although some Palatine lords provided farming opportunities for the Anabaptists, the area was politically unstable. Located as it was in the very heart of Europe, between France and many German states, the Palatinate was the battlefield for the major wars of the seventeenth century. During the Thirty Years' War (1618–1648) the armies of both Catholic and Protestant forces played havoc with the lives and possessions of the people in this area. The Treaty of Westphalia (1648) provided that each prince was to determine the religion of his people. But the religions were restricted to Catholic, Lutheran, or Reformed. This resulted in further chaos, for the Palatinate was fragmented into small principalities, and populations that were Protestant were required to become Catholic and vice versa.[1] Those people who refused

1. Karl Scherer, Director of Heimatstelle Pfalz, a provincial archives of the Palatinate, states that within an eighty-square-mile area there were forty-four different sovereign ministates, each having its own laws, administration, monetary system, and units of measures and weights. In addition, he says, "there had been for about a hundred years continuous religious quarrels." Address to the Pennsylvania German Society, May 4, 1974, published in "The Fatherland of the Pennsylvania Dutch," *Mennonite Research Journal* 15 (July 1974): 25.

membership in the approved religions—and they included the Anabaptists, Huguenots, and Walloons—were called "sectarians" and were driven from the country. Catholic princes turned against Protestants, and both Catholic and Protestant forces turned against the sectarians.

The devastation of war, plunder, and fire was followed by famine and pestilence. People ate roots, grass, and leaves. Some even resorted to cannibalism. The gallows and graveyards were guarded. The bodies of children were not safe from their mothers. Once flourishing farms and vineyards were now raided by hordes of hungry people. In the War of the Palatinate (1688–1697) Louis XIV ordered his generals to devastate the area once again. These conditions precipitated the great Palatinate emigration to America in the first half of the eighteenth century. The emigration movement encompassed many people of every known faith in the region. Most numerous were the Lutherans and Reformed, but there were Catholics, Schwenkfelders, and a variety of mystics, as well as groups of Mennonites and Amish. All these groups spoke the Palatinate dialect known today as Pennsylvania German or Pennsylvania Dutch. Related to these refugees in faith and culture were the Dunkards and Moravians, who also came to Pennsylvania in the eighteenth century.

Mennonite emigration began in 1709, a year that was unusually cold and severe throughout Europe, but the largest migrations of Swiss Mennonites to America took place betwen 1717 and 1732, when an estimated three thousand left the Palatinate to come to Pennsylvania.[2] Many Palatines came to London expecting help from the British to cross the Atlantic. Queen Anne had for several years been trying to obtain colonists for unoccupied possessions in America, and had even sent agents to the Palatinate for this purpose. William Penn had traveled up and down the Rhine inviting oppressed peoples to come to Pennsylvania. The Society of Friends in London helped some of the immigrants to pay for their passage, and the Mennonites in the

2. For an understanding of Mennonite and Amish emigration, see C. Henry Smith, *The Mennonite Immigration to Pennsylvania*, vol. 28 (Norristown, Pa.: Pennsylvania German Society, 1929); and idem, *The Mennonites of America* (Goshen, Ind.: By the author, 1909). For a general history of Swiss emigration, see A. B. Faust, "Swiss Emigration to the American Colonies in the Eighteenth Century," *American Historical Review* 12 (October 1916): 21–41. The latter was also published in A. B. Faust and G. M. Brumbaugh, *Lists of Swiss Emigrants in the Eighteenth Century to the American Colonies*, 2 vols. in 1 (1920; reprint ed., Baltimore: Genealogical Publishing Co., 1968). For an exhaustive bibliography on Pennsylvania German emigration, see Emil Meynen, *Bibliography on German Settlements in Colonial North America, Especially on the Pennsylvania Germans and Their Descendants, 1683–1933* (Leipzig: Otto Harrassowitz, 1937).

Netherlands organized the Commission for Foreign Needs to aid their Swiss brothers with a variety of problems.

By 1699 the prisons in Bern were full and the Swiss authorities had to take action, either to deport the Anabaptists or to permit them to emigrate. European governments generally looked upon emigration with disapproval in the eighteenth century.[3] To leave one's fatherland was considered a sin equivalent to desertion and a shirking of one's duties. Martin Luther's translation of the Psalms (37:3) commanded the young to remain in the land of their forefathers and make an honest living.[4] Those who departed were considered an undesirable class of people. Moreover, Switzerland feared the loss of its population through emigration as much as it feared such loss by war or pestilence because one of the country's primary sources of income came from furnishing the powerful nations of Europe with young soldiers. For a price, these mercenary soldiers were provided by the wealthy Swiss noblemen to the warring countries of Europe. Soldiers from Switzerland fought on all the major battlefields of Europe, serving on both sides of a conflict.[5] To permit a liberal emigration policy would have provoked the powerful nobles, and granting military exemption to the Anabaptists would have instigated rebellion of the common people against the autocratic military system, a system widely disliked.

At about this time a scheme to deport undesirables was promoted by two merchants who organized a marine company called the Ritter Company. The Bern government became interested in the matter. Here was an opportunity to rid itself of two classes of people, the paupers (the homeless *Landsassen*), who were squatters but not citizens, and the Anabaptists.[6] In 1709 the Ritter Company was secured to take a boatload of Anabaptists and paupers to the Carolinas in America. When the vessel reached the Netherlands, the Dutch government (influenced by Dutch Mennonites) refused to grant passage to a vessel carrying passengers who were being deported against their will. The passengers were set free and guards were prevented from harming their prisoners. The Anabaptists visited their Mennonite brothers in the

3. Faust and Brumbaugh, *Lists of Swiss Emigrants*, p. 5.
4. Ibid., p. 4. Psalms 37:3 (RSV) reads: "Trust in the Lord and do good; so you will dwell in the land, and enjoy security." Luther's translation of the latter phrase is in the imperative: "Bleib im Lande und nähre dich redlich . . ." ("Stay in the land of thy forefathers, and earn an honest living therein"). The *Züricher* and *Froshauer* Bible (1535), widely read by Anabaptists, reads: "So wirdst du im Land wohen [wohnen] und es wirt dich wailich [wahrlich] neeren [nähren]" ("So you will dwell in the land, and enjoy an honest living").
5. Faust and Brumbaugh, *Lists of Swiss Emigrants*, p. 7.
6. Ibid., p. 2.

Netherlands and then most returned to the Palatinate. The captain, who had been promised 45 thaler for each Anabaptist he deported to America, was left without money or friends. Three of the Anabaptists went to Amsterdam and gave a full report of their experiences to the Mennonite Commission for Foreign Needs. One of these was Benedicht Brechbühl, a minister and elder from Trachselwald who later became a leader in the Mennonite emigration to Pennsylvania.

EIGHTEENTH-CENTURY EMIGRATION

Meanwhile, negotiations continued between the Dutch government and Bern over the plight of the Bernese Anabaptists. After many discussions it was agreed that emigration rather than forced deportation was the solution. The question was, emigration to where? King Wilhelm I of Prussia invited all the Swiss Anabaptists to his country, and it was also suggested that the Anabaptists settle the swamp areas of the Bernese territory. Finally, Bern agreed to allow the Anabaptists to go to the Netherlands and choose a destination from there. Meanwhile, the Dutch began to collect money for the emigration and to plead with the Bernese government to grant certain conditions: (1) to permit the Anabaptists to choose whether they wanted to migrate to Holland or to Prussia; (2) to declare a general amnesty so that the Anabaptists could come out in the open and sell their goods before leaving; (3) to appoint someone to care for possessions not sold before leaving; (4) to release all Anabaptists in prison; (5) to allow those who were married to non-Anabaptists to take their spouses and children with them; and (6) to exempt the Anabaptists from the ordinary departure tax. Most of the conditions were granted. However, released prisoners were to pay for their stay in prison, and those who were not steadfastly Anabaptist were to pay the 10 percent departure tax.

Five boats were prepared by the Ritter Company. The day of departure was set for July 13, 1711, but there were still other complications. Some did not want to leave their homeland; Hans Gerber, who did not want to leave, was sentenced as a slave to the Venetian galleys.[7] The Ammann and Reist factions did not want to travel together on the same vessel. Since the number of Anabaptist emigrants did not reach the expected total of 500, other passengers (paupers) were taken along. After a stay of four days in Basel, four boats sailed down the Rhine. A description of the sadness that came over the group is pro-

7. Ernst Müller, *Geschichte der Bernischen Täufer* (Frauenfeld, Switz., 1895), p. 300.

vided by Ernst Müller.[8] It appears that in spite of the cruel persecution, few of them wanted to leave. Many were suspicious of plans and promises made by the government. At various points along the Rhine, dozens of passengers got off the boat to join their brethren in Alsace and in the Palatinate. Later some of them found their way back to Switzerland. The majority of the Anabaptists who arrived in Amsterdam were of the Amish faction. Most of the Reist group had left the boats at various points on their journey.[9] A large warehouse provided temporary shelter for the group in Amsterdam. The citizens of Amsterdam came to see the emigrants, and collection boxes were set up to receive voluntary contributions for the refugees.

Before an investigative delegation of Anabaptists had returned from a tour of Prussia, the emigrants were taken to several Dutch Mennonite communities. There they were taken into the homes of the Old Flemish and Waterlander Mennonite groups. Preferring Holland to Prussia, the leaders of the emigrant group soon began to earn a livelihood as farm workers and dairymen. The Amish formed congregations at Groningen, Sappemeer, and Kampen. The small Reist group went to Harlingen, and declaring that it was difficult to fellowship with the Amish, returned to the Palatinate in 1713. The approximately three hundred Amish who settled in Holland maintained a small cultural island for almost a century, but eventually they acquired a Dutch language and their congregations merged with the Mennonites of the Netherlands. After 1720 the Amish in Holland split into the "Old" and "New" Swiss.[10] From visits and reports written by Hans Nafziger of the Palatinate in 1781, much has been learned about their disintegration before they were assimilated into Dutch life in the Netherlands.[11] There is no evidence that any of the Amish who came to the Netherlands in 1709 ever reached America.

Just when the first Amish came to America remains unknown. There is a possibility that some may have arrived with the Swiss Mennonites in 1710 when they bought from William Penn ten thousand acres of land comprising an area in Lancaster County known as Pequea (pronounced *peck-way*) Colony, but documentation is lacking. However, the area is heavily populated by the Amish today. Some Amish indi-

8. Ibid., p. 304.
9. Ibid.
10. The cause of the division was a house, called the "large monastery," the preacher Hans Anken had purchased. Its architecture offended some as being too ostentatious. See *Mennonite Encyclopedia*, s.v. "Anken, Hans."
11. Published in John D. Hochstetler, ed., *Ein alter Brief* (Elkhart, Ind., 1916). For an English account, see "An Amish Church Discipline of 1781," *Mennonite Quarterly Review* 4 (April 1930): 150–48.

viduals likely arrived in America between 1717 and 1736.[12] Then, as now, the Amish did not formalize the movement of their members, and as a persecuted group they did not keep formal records. Families were not prevented by church rules from moving if they wished. The Amish as a whole were very reluctant to leave their native Switzerland, a fact which is borne out by a careful study of the sources. It may well be that the first to come to America were those who were least dedicated and most opportunistic.

Arriving in Philadelphia on October 2, 1727, the ship *Adventure* had on its passenger list several typical Amish names.[13] Ten years later, on October 8, 1737, the ship *Charming Nancy* brought numerous families whose residence and genealogy can be established as Amish. As the first "Amish ship," it brought enough Amish to make an assembly or congregation possible. In this group were Jacob Beiler, Christian Burki, Hans Gerber, Christian Hershberger, Christian Kurtz, Jacob Mueller, Hans Schantz, and Hans Zimmerman.[14] Others who likely were Amish were listed as Erb, Garber, Hertzler, Kauffman, Lehman,

12. The tradition that the first Amish arrived in America in 1714 (a widow Barbara Yoder, whose husband had died at sea, and nine children, according to C. Henry Smith, *The Mennonite Immigration to Pennsylvania*, p. 225) is not borne out by recent genealogical and historical research. The "widow Barbara" story has been verified by genealogist Hugh Gingerich, but he claims she was an immigrant of 1742.

Immigration records between 1717 and 1736 contain names typical of the Amish, either of those in Europe before the immigration or of those in America, but it is virtually impossible to prove that they were Amish. For a discussion of these names, see C. Henry Smith, *The Mennonites of America*, pp. 154, 210; and idem, *The Mennonite Immigration to Pennsylvania*, p. 155. The task of identifying Amish immigrants has been facilitated by the publication of ships' passenger lists. The heavy influx of Germans into Pennsylvania alarmed the English, so in 1727 the Provincial Council required all vessels to submit a list of passengers. A declaration of allegiance to the King of Great Britain also was required of passengers. These lists date from September 21, 1727, and continue to the Revolutionary War. See Ralph B. Strassburger and William J. Hinke, *Pennsylvania German Pioneers*, 3 vols. (Norristown, Pa.: Pennsylvania German Society, 1934); and I. D. Rupp, *Foreign Immigrants to Pennsylvania, 1727–1776* (Philadelphia, Pa.: Leary, 1898).

13. Strassburger and Hinke, *Pioneers*, pp. 15–16. These names were Beydler (Beiler), Kurtz, Leman (Lehman), Mayer, Miller, Pitscha (Peachey), Riesser, Snyder, Stutzman, and Swartz. Names typical of the European Amish were Bowman, Hess, and Histand. Arrival dates of other persons with Amish-like names were Peter and Ulrich Zug (Zook), September 27, 1727; Johannes Lap, Johannes Reichenbach, and Johannes Slabach, September 29, 1733; and Jacob Hostedler, Johannes Lohrentz, Peter Rupp, and Melchior Detweiler, September 1, 1736. When Amish-like names appear on ship lists in clusters, they are thought almost certainly to have been Amish. When such names appear infrequently among less typically Amish names, their affiliation is considered more doubtful.

14. Strassburger and Hinke, *Pioneers*, ship list 49A, pp. 188–91.

Lichty, and Mast. The period of heaviest immigration appears to have been 1737–1754. By 1770, with the dawn of the Revolutionary War, Amish immigration had almost ceased, and few new immigrants came until the nineteenth century.

During the colonial period the Amish formed several settlements in Berks, Chester, and Lancaster counties (see Figure 3). Through the use of land records, tax lists, wills, and the alms books of the Amish, it is possible to ascertain the location of the early communities.[15] Most were named after a watershed or valley.

The Northkill settlement was situated in what later became known as Tilden, Upper Bern, Centre, and Penn townships in Berks County, and is presently west of Hamburg between the towns of Shartlesville and Centre Point. Berks County had just been opened for settlers the year before the Amish arrived, which may help to explain why they chose this area. As the largest of several Amish settlements in the country, it may have accommodated from 150 to 200 persons. In the same year of their settlement, however, several families (Erb, Gerber, Kurtz, Tschantz) went to Lancaster County. An Amish cemetery and a historic marker on the old residence of Bishop Jacob Hertzler, an immigrant of 1749, are still maintained.[16]

The Tulpehocken Valley settlement, in what is now Heidelberg and North Heidelberg townships, was occupied by Amish families from about 1764. A few families lived west of the town of Womelsdorf. A small cemetery is located on the farm that was occupied by John Kurtz, the deacon.

A third settlement, Maiden Creek Valley, was located near the mouth of Maiden Creek and the Schuylkill River in Maiden Creek Township. A small cemetery is located near Leesport. Amish families were scattered southward along the Schuylkill River to Shillington in the borough of Reading. Whether Maiden Creek, and those families living around Reading, constituted more than one district is not clear.

15. Documentation for the early settlements was gleaned by the author from the work of Grant M. Stoltzfus, "History of the First Amish Mennonite Communities in America" (M.A. thesis, University of Pittsburgh, 1954), published with the same title in the *Mennonite Quarterly Review* 28 (October 1954): 235–62. Additional help from Amish persons who have mapped the early Amish homesteads is gratefully acknowledged. See the continued series by Joseph F. Beiler, "Our Fatherland in America," in *The Diary* (Gordonville, Pa.), beginning in 1972, and another by Amos L. Fisher, "To Recall a Few Memories of the Past."

16. Immigrant Jacob Hertzler has long been considered the first Amish bishop in America. This appears doubtful, however, in view of the many Amish who arrived in 1737 and who depended upon the services of a bishop for performing marriages and conducting communion. For a history of the Hertzler descendants, see Silas Hertzler, *The Hertzler-Hertzler Family History* (Goshen, Ind.: By the author, 1952).

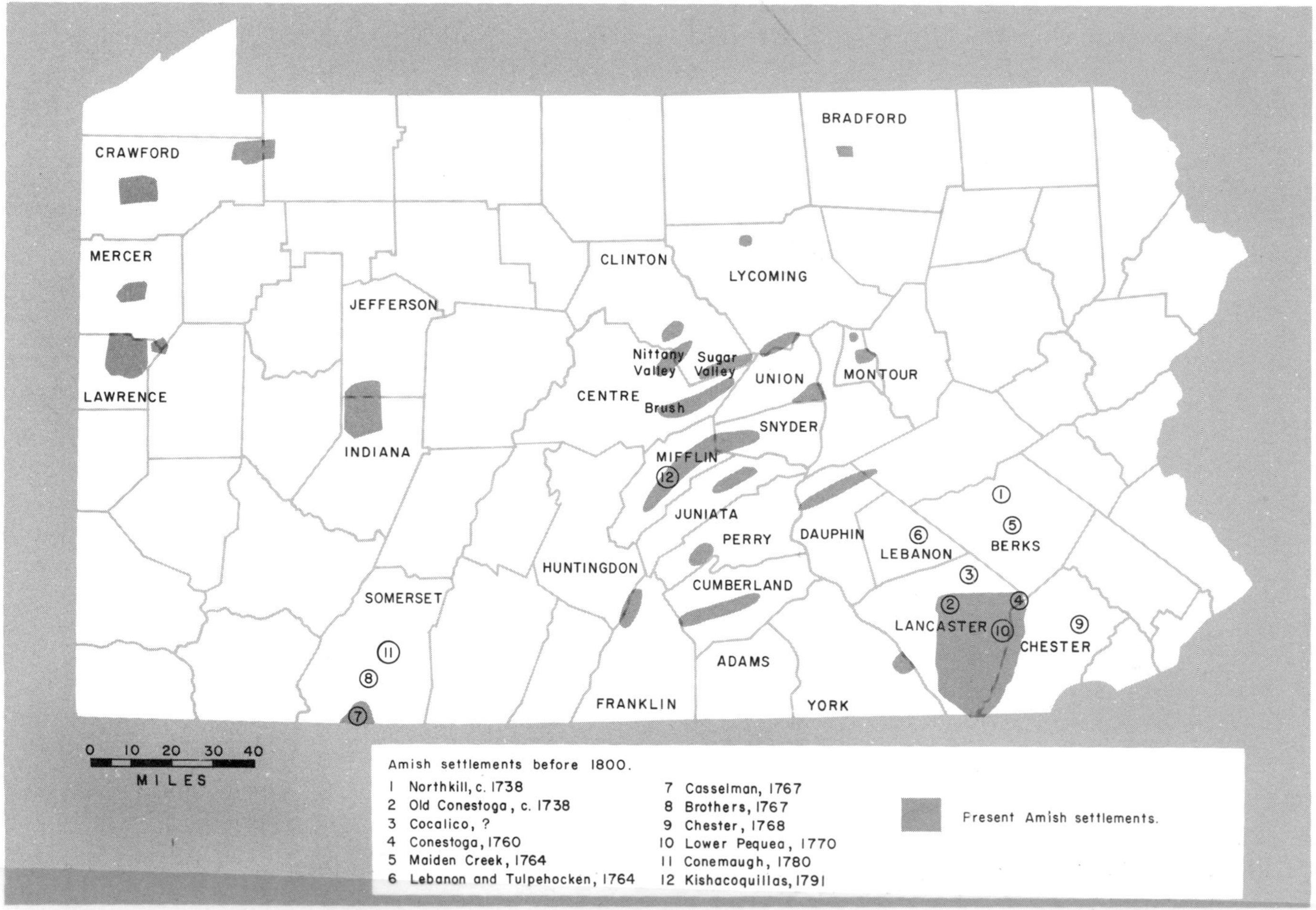
CRAWFORD
MERCER
LAWRENCE
JEFFERSON
INDIANA
SOMERSET
CLINTON
LYCOMING
BRADFORD
CENTRE
Nittany Valley
Sugar Valley
Brush
UNION
MONTOUR
SNYDER
MIFFLIN
JUNIATA
PERRY
HUNTINGDON
CUMBERLAND
DAUPHIN
LEBANON
BERKS
LANCASTER
CHESTER
ADAMS
FRANKLIN
YORK
0 10 20 30 40
MILES
Amish settlements before 1800.
1 Northkill, c. 1738
2 Old Conestoga, c. 1738
3 Cocalico, ?
4 Conestoga, 1760
5 Maiden Creek, 1764
6 Lebanon and Tulpehocken, 1764
7 Casselman, 1767
8 Brothers, 1767
9 Chester, 1768
10 Lower Pequea, 1770
11 Conemaugh, 1780
12 Kishacoquillas, 1791
Present Amish settlements.

Figure 8

The Conestoga Valley settlement, between Churchtown and Elverson, spans the corners of Chester, Berks, and Lancaster counties. From 1760 this region was occupied by families from the Northkill settlement who bought land from Welsh settlers. The region has been continuously occupied by the Amish since that time.

The Chester Valley settlement, located in Whiteland Township, Chester County, near Malvern, was founded by the Zook, Lapp, and Kauffman families in 1768 and continued until 1834. A cemetery and the ruins of an Amish meeting house remain near Malvern.[17]

Lancaster County, the location of the most densely populated Amish community in Pennsylvania today, contained three separate settlements in the eighteenth century. "Old" or "West Conestoga," mentioned in Amish writings and believed to have been occupied by some Amish as early as the founding of the Northkill settlement,[18] is located in Manheim and Upper Leacock townships. According to some accounts, there was also a Cocalico settlement, concentrated in East and West Cocalico townships and the nearby townships of Brecknock and Clay. This area is north of Ephrata and would have been near the Tulpehocken Amish in Berks County. The Amish may have settled here as early as 1742. In later years this area was occupied by Mennonite families. The "Lower Pequea" settlement around Whitehorse, Compass, and Honeybrook (largely in Salisbury Township) grew as the Berks County group declined before the close of the eighteenth century.

In addition to these communities, there is evidence from land records that many Amish families settled in Lebanon County in an area extending from the Tulpehocken community all the way to Dauphin County. The strong proselyting influence from other religious groups appears to have eventually destroyed the Amish in this area.

PROBLEMS OF THE EARLY COMMUNITIES

The early settlements were small, disbursed, and isolated from each other. Primarily agriculturalists, farm laborers, and tenants, most Amish emigrants had little means. There were, however, Amish people who bought land soon after they arrived. In Europe some had invested their resources in livestock-raising and in the improvement of their living houses. Some may have had savings until they were forced by war to leave.

17. See Maurice A. Mook, "An Early Amish Colony in Chester County," *Mennonite Historical Bulletin* 16 (July 1955). For photographs of the tombstones, see *Christian Living*, October 1956, p. 20.

18. Joseph F. Beiler, "Eighteenth Century Amish in Lancaster County," Mennonite Research Journal 17 (October 1976): 37.

Prior to the American War of Independence there were at least eight small settlements in Pennsylvania. The Amish probably came first to Lancaster County, but seeing that it was already settled by Mennonites, sought land in adjoining Berks County. They were soon faced with problems: assaults by the Indians, proselyting from other religious groups, and internal difficulties. Some Amish who were unable to pay for their passage came to America as redemptioners. Upon landing in Philadelphia, their services were auctioned to the highest bidder as payment for their passage from Europe. Canvassers, ship captains, and innkeepers tended to take advantage of simple and trusting emigrants. The traffic in redemptioners was profitable, and ship captains were prone to entice persons, including children, onto their vessels and to sell their services once they reached America. In this manner, Amishman Melchior Plank and his wife were brought to America. Philip Lantz, a boy of five, was kidnapped by a captain, brought to Baltimore, and indentured to Peter Yordy of Lancaster County.[19] Whether Yordy sought the services of the young man as a form of brotherly service is not known. According to tradition, Lewis Riehl (b. 1746), a boy of eight, was coaxed onto a boat and brought to America. Following a period of inhuman servitude in Philadelphia, he was attracted to "Germans" he saw on the street one day. They were Amish people. He later joined them.[20]

Little is known about the journeys of the Amish to America because few eighteenth-century diaries have been preserved. One fragment of a diary believed to have been written by Jacob Beiler, a passenger on the *Charming Nancy* (arriving October 8, 1737), speaks of tragedy:

The 28th of June while in Rotterdam getting ready to start my Zernbli died and was buried in Rotterdam. The 29th we got under sail and enjoyed only 1½ days of favorable wind. The 7th day of July, early in the morning, died Hans Zimmerman's son-in-law.

We landed in England the 8th of July remaining 9 days in port during which 5 children died. Went under sail the 17th of July. The 21 of July my own Lisbetli died. Several days before Michael's Georgli had died.

On the 29th of July three children died. On the first of August my Hansli died and Tuesday previous 5 children died. On the 3rd of August contrary winds beset the vessel from the first to the 7th of the month three more children died. On the 8th of August Shambien's (?) Lizzie died and on the

19. C. Henry Smith, *Mennonites of America*, p. 172.

20. "Pioneer Life of Our Ancestors" (mimeographed history by descendants and relatives of the Riehl families of Pennsylvania, n.d., 6 pp.). For the literature on redemptioners and indentured servants see Meynen, *Bibliography on German Settlements in Colonial North America*, pp. 83–84.

An artist's conception of the ship *Charming
Nancy*, which brought the first major
group of Amish to America in 1737

9th died Hans Zimmerman's Jacobi. On the 19th Christian Burgli's child
died. Passed a ship on the 21st. A favorable wind sprang up. On the 28th
Hans Gasi's (?) wife died. Passed a ship 13th of September.

Landed in Philadelphia on the 18th and my wife and I left the ship on
the 19th. A child was born to us on the 20th—died—wife recovered. A
voyage of 83 days.[21]

The journey was a frightful ordeal according to Gottlieb Mittelberger, a Württemberger who came to America in 1750 and returned
to Germany four years later.[22] He speaks of thirty-six different customs
houses between Heilbronn and Holland, each involving long delays
and additional expense. In Rotterdam, he observed that people were
"packed into the big boats as closely as herring." He describes the
stench of fumes, dysentery, vomiting, and scurvy. Filthy food and water

21. See S. Duane Kauffman, "Early Amish Translations Support Amish History,"
The Budget, February 22, 1978, p. 11; and "Miscellaneous Amish Mennonite Docu-
ments," *Pennsylvania Mennonite Heritage* 2 (July 1979): 12–16. The diary was
found among papers of the late Dr. D. Heber Plank, who had translated it into
English. Other diaries include those of Daniel Gingerich, an emigrant from
Waldeck, Germany; see David Luthy, "Sailing to America, 1833," *Family Life*,
March 1974, pp. 14–18; Jacob Swartzendruber, *An Account of the Voyage from
Germany to America* (N.p.: By the author, 1937); and Delbert Gratz, *Bernese
Anabaptists* (Goshen, Ind.: Mennonite Historical Society), pp. 147–50.

22. Gottlieb Mittelberger, *Journey to Pennsylvania* (Cambridge: Harvard University Press, 1960), pp. 7–12.

were a major source of misery, together with lice, disease, and severe storms. Overcrowding gave way to stealing, cheating, cursing, and bitter arguments between children and parents, husbands and wives. On arrival in America, those who could pay for their journey were released first. Those who lacked the money to pay, including the sick, were held on board until their future labor was auctioned to the highest bidder.

On the whole, Pennsylvania's Quaker government maintained peaceful relations with the Indians until about 1755. Under pressure from the British citizenry, a chain of forts was established along the Blue Mountains, Pennsylvania's frontier during the French and Indian War. The Jacob Hochstetler family was one target of the numerous Indian attacks on settlers in the Northkill area. On the evening of September 19, 1757, after the family had retired, there was a disturbance. One of the boys opened the door and was shot in the leg. He quickly reached for the rifle but his father objected, stating that it was against their principles to take human life. The house was set afire by the Indians, and when the family escaped through the cellar window, the mother, a son, and a daughter were scalped. Jacob and his sons Joseph and Christian were taken captive. After several years of living with the Indians they managed to return.[23] The encounter with the Indians, it has long been believed, was responsible for the decline of this Amish settlement. There likely were other reasons for the movement of families out of Berks County, however, such as the influence from proselyting groups.

The Amish families were neighbors to other immigrants of other religions, including German Reformed, French-speaking Huguenots, and various pietistic sects, especially Dunkards. As a result many Amish families joined the Dunkard or Church of the Brethren religion. The Methodist revival movement that swept through Pennsylvania attracted the Amish and some became leaders in that denomination.[24] An Amish minister, Abram Draksel (Troxell) of Lebanon County, was silenced for making "too much of the doctrine of regeneration" and became a

23. For an account of the attack, see Harvey Hostetler, *The Descendants of Jacob Hochstetler* (Elgin, Ill.: Brethren Publishing House, 1912), pp. 29–45. Peter Glick, an immigrant of September 15, 1748, came to Berks County with a large family, but all except a son John died when their house was burned by Indians. The Glick families trace their lineage to John, who escaped the Indians by hiding in a hollow tree.

24. Grant Stoltzfus, "History of the First Amish Mennonite Communities in America," p. 254. See also C. Z. Mast and Robert E. Simpson, *Annals of the Conestoga Valley* (Elverson Pa.: By the authors, 1942), p. 88; and Joseph F. Beiler, "Revolutionary War Records," *The Diary*, March 1971, p. 71.

leader in the revival movement.[25] When the young began m.
non-Amish, the most devout of the Amish leaders began to re;
By 1767 the Amish had begun three settlements in Somerset C
in southwestern Pennsylvania.[26] Mifflin County had attracted families
from most of the early small communities by 1791. The Stoltzfus family, immigrants of 1766, settled in Berks County but soon moved to
the Conestoga Valley.[27]

To the Amish community the Revolutionary War was more disruptive than the assaults of the Indians. Amish genealogist Joseph F.
Beiler writes: ". . . most of our initial ancestor families in America have
not raised more than one son to remain in the old faith. Some have
not kept any sons in the church, some have kept a few. . . . After the
war there was a steady flow of Amish converts to the Tunkers or
Brethren, German Baptists and even to the Lutherans as well as the
Moravians."[28] Before the Revolution, Beiler states, not one family
pedigree showed that all the children had remained with the Amish
church.

Had the early Amish settlers not relocated in order to solve their
problems, such as finding adequate and productive land, stability and
unanimity in church discipline, and leaders who were committed to
Amish principles, it is doubtful that they would have survived at all.
The early settlements are illustrative not of failure but of the trial-and-
error process integral to ongoing community-building.

During the War of Independence from Great Britain, the Amish
and Mennonites retained the principle of nonresistance. Their opposition to taking the oath of allegiance and joining the militia was
interpreted by patriots as an alignment with the British. The Amish,
unlike the Quakers, generally paid the war tax but disclaimed any
responsibility for its use.[29] In refusing to take the Oath of Renuncia-

25. C. Brane, "Landmark History of United Brethren in Pennsylvania," *The
Pennsylvania German* 4 (July 1903): 326.

26. The three settlements were (1) Conemaugh, including Johnstown, Pa., named
after Amishman Joseph Schantz (see Maurice A. Mook, "The Amishman Who
Founded a City," *Christian Living*, July 1955, pp. 4–7); (2) Brothers Valley (also
called Glades), near Somerset, Pa.; and (3) Casselman, centered near Meyersdale
and Elklick, Pa. The backgrounds of these settlements are discussed by Sanford
G. Shelter, *Two Centuries of Struggle and Growth* (Scottdale, Pa.: Herald Press,
1963). See also Ivan J. Miller, "The Amish Community at Grantsville," *Tableland
Trails* 2 (Summer 1956): 91–94.

27. See Wilmer D. Swope, *The Genealogical History of the Stoltzfus Family in
America, 1717–1972* (Seymour, Mo.: Edgewood Press, 1972).

28. Joseph F. Beiler, "Revolutionary War Records," p. 71.

29. Wilbur J. Bender, "Pacifism among the Mennonites, Amish Mennonites, and

tion and Allegiance they were told that they would be disqualified from serving on juries, suing at law, holding public office, or buying and selling land. The Amish, along with the Mennonites and Quakers, refused the oath not only on religious grounds but also because they had promised allegiance to the Crown and feared perjuring themselves.[30] Several Amish people were charged with treason and were held in jail at Reading, Pennsylvania.[31]

The first communities were made up of clusters of families, most of whom were related by kinship ties. There was no overall or master plan of settlement. In fact, individualism and strong family autonomy seem to have had greater reign than church control. The behavior of some Amish was inconsistent with the tradition of the Amish as we know it today. Some married non-Amish neighbors, the color of their wagon tops was not yet uniform, and in Chester County the Amish built a meeting house. The long, intense voyages across the ocean may have resulted in alliances and friendships with persons who were not Amish. For many years a single bishop, traveling by foot and horseback, performed marriages and offered communion to scattered clusters of families. The Lancaster Amish settlement was not divided until 1843, nearly a hundred years after the first Amish families arrived in America. With the growth of settlements, the Amish ordained resident bishops, and thus church control began to be exercised over family and kinship rule. A new identity began to emerge as Amish were distinguished from non-Amish, and with this major trend, both religious and secular controversies began to plague the Amish people.[32] Families began to move to other settlements or regroup on the basis of a stricter or milder discipline.

Schwenkfelders of Pennsylvania to 1783, Part II," *Mennonite Quarterly Review* 1 (October 1927): 26, 46 n. 127.

30. It appears that the Amish petitioned the Provincial Assembly for exemption from the oath in securing naturalization. The Provincial Council passed a bill on November 11, 1742, naturalizing Protestants not of the Quaker faith (*Pennsylvania Archives*, p. 626). A copy of the petition appears in *Register of Pennsylvania*, ed. Samuel Hazard, vol. 7 (1831), p. 151; it was submitted for publication by Redmond Conyngham, who stated that it was written for the Amish by Emanuel Zimmerman and was submitted to William Penn on May 20, 1718. The date may have been in error, as C. Henry Smith writes in *The Mennonite Immigration to Pennsylvania*, p. 232 n. 35.

31. Richard K. MacMaster, Samuel L. Horst, and Robert F. Ulle, *Conscience in Crisis: Mennonites and Other Peace Churches in America, 1739–1789* (Scottdale, Pa.: Herald Press, 1979), chap. 7.

32. The trend toward church over family control was noted by James E. Landing, "Amish Settlement in North America: a Geographic Brief," *Bulletin of the Illinois Geographical Society* 12 (December 1970): 65–69.

NINETEENTH-CENTURY EMIGRATION

The second wave of emigration to North America from Alsace, Lorraine, Bavaria, Waldeck, Hesse-Darmstadt, and the Palatinate began in 1816 and continued until 1860, with a few latecomers arriving in 1880.[33] These settlers formed communities in Butler, Stark, Wayne, and Fulton counties in Ohio; Adams, Allen, and Daviess counties in Indiana; Woodford and Tazewell counties in Illinois; Henry and Washington counties in Iowa; Lewis County, New York; Somerset County, Maryland; and Waterloo and Perth counties in Ontario. Altogether there were possibly three thousand Amish Mennonite immigrants during the nineteenth century, in contrast to an estimated five hundred in the eighteenth century.[34]

Precipitating this migration were the unsettling conditions in Europe, the French Revolution (1789–1799), followed by the Napoleonic Wars until 1815, and various economic hardships. The European Amish learned that the Amish in America were not being molested but were prospering.

Most of the Amish immigrants of this period formed contacts with Amish groups upon their arrival in America. However, most never affiliated with the descendants of immigrants of the pre-Revolutionary period. The nineteenth-century immigrants found the American Amish more traditional than themselves. Several regional conferences were founded by the nineteenth-century immigrants, and many of their congregations later merged with the Mennonite Church.[35]

Today Old Order Amish descendants of the nineteenth-century immigrants live in Adams, Allen, and Daviess counties, Indiana, and in Perth County, Ontario. Although these groups maintain fellowship with the early Pennsylvania churches, they also perpetuate unique and distinguishing material cultural traits. The Amish of Adams County, Indiana, who came from Switzerland and from Montbéliard, speak a Swiss dialect. Families here still sing Swiss yodels that were common in Switzerland in the nineteenth century. The family names of those

33. No better description of the emigration of this period exists than that of C. Henry Smith, *The Mennonites of America*, pp. 275–92.

34. The estimate of five hundred is based on the ship lists and the first tax assessments in Berks County. Married family heads who appeared on the ship lists (from 1737 to 1749) and who also appeared on the first tax lists (1754) numbered approximately 102. Estimated at five persons per household, the total population would have been about five hundred. Estimated with the assistance of Joseph F. Beiler, 1978.

35. *Mennonite Encyclopedia*, s.v. "Amish Mennonites." See also Jean Séguy, *Les Assemblées anabaptistes-mennonites de France* (The Hague: Mouton, 1977).

who emigrated to North America during this period are distinct from those who came in the eighteenth century.

The Ontario Amish community began with the coming of Christian Nafziger of Bavaria. He landed in New Orleans in 1822 and after going to Lancaster County in Pennsylvania, was directed to Ontario. Here he secured a large tract of land for his congregation, which was still in Bavaria.[36]

The Amish port of entry in the eighteenth century had usually been Philadelphia. In the nineteenth century many of the Amish came to New Orleans and Baltimore in order to take advantage of low-cost transportation. When French ships came to New Orleans to obtain large amounts of cotton, they brought with them many German-speaking people who were eager to come to the United States.[37] The Germans continued their voyage up the Mississippi River. When the Germans began to trade with the United States they came to Baltimore for tobacco cargo, and they, too, sought out passengers for their westbound voyages.

THE FATE OF THE EUROPEAN AMISH

Today there are no Amish congregations in Europe that have retained the name and practices of the original group. The group's descendants in Europe have reunited with the Mennonites or have otherwise lost their Amish identity.[38] Some of the families and churches are aware of their Amish background, but it is only in North America that the name and distinctive practices of the Amish have survived.

The Amish in Europe were scattered and were unable to live in compact settlements because of economic and social factors such as the scarcity of land and the general intolerance for Anabaptists. Individuals and families who were either exiles or fugitives from the countries where they had been persecuted accepted asylum wherever they were tolerated. In Europe the Amish lived in Switzerland, Alsace, France, Germany, Holland, Bavaria, Galicia (Poland), and Volhynia (Russia). Geographic distance made association between families extremely difficult. Worship services, held in their own farm homes, took place monthly or every two weeks, but always at different places. Those who

36. Orlando Gingerich, *The Amish of Canada* (Waterloo, Ont.: Conrad Press, 1972).

37. Barbara K. Greenleaf, *America Fever: The Story of American Immigration* (New York: The New American Library, 1974), p. 57.

38. For assimilation in Europe, see *Mennonite Encyclopedia*, s.v. "Amish Mennonites." See also John A. Hostetler, "Old World Extinction and New World Survival of the Amish," *Rural Sociology* 20 (September/October 1955): 212–19.

lived within a short distance could attend the services, but they found it possible to come only once or twice annually. Under such conditions the scattered Amish families associated more with local non-Amish persons than with people of their own affiliation. The Amish who became renters or managers of large estates employed many laborers whose families also lived on the estate. The laborers, who were usually of a different religious affiliation, lived side by side with Amish families on the same estate. The Amish made no attempt to gain converts other than their own offspring.

With the passing of long years of suppression, the descendants of the Anabaptists changed their goals from reforms to ways and means of physical survival. It was under these conditions that they learned the disciplines of mutual aid, intensive agriculture, thrift, and toil, qualities for which they were later sought by emperors and princes to transform wastelands into productive soil. Thus the Swiss Brethren, including the Amish, became "the quiet people of the land" and formed agrarian cultural islands.

In Switzerland there were two settlements of Amish, one in the Emme Valley and one in the Lake Thun area. The Amish founded two other congregations, La Chaux-de-Fonds and Neuchâtel (Neuenburg), when there was a general emigration from the canton of Bern to the bishopric of Basel in the eighteenth century. There were still two Amish congregations in Switzerland as late as 1810, but they have since gradually lost their distinctiveness. In 1886 these groups still practiced foot washing, but by about 1900 they no longer called themselves Amish. They affiliated with the Swiss Mennonite Conference. The present Mennonite congregation in Basel (Basel-Holeestrasse) dates from 1777 and is of Amish background.

In southern Germany, Amish families lived in scattered places, but especially in the vicinity of Kaiserslautern. An Amish group from Alsace also settled at Essingen, near Landau. The Amish never developed large communities in the Palatinate, but emigrated in large numbers from the Palatinate to other points in Germany and to North America. In 1730 a group settled in middle Germany in the Hesse-Cassel region at Wittgenstein (later Waldeck), and in 1800 some settled in the Lahn Valley near Marburg. Small groups found their way to the vicinity of Neuwied and the Eiffel region. The groups from middle Germany, known as Hessian Amish, left for North America, and by 1900 all traces of the Amish had vanished from that area. A group from Hesse settled in Butler County, Ohio, beginning in 1817. The Waldeck and Marburg groups came to Somerset County, Pennsylvania, and Garrett County, Maryland.

Another group of Amish from the Palatinate, along with others

from Alsace and Lorraine, moved to Bavaria near the towns of Ingol-
stadt, Regensburg, and Munich. Descendants of the Amish still live at
Regensburg. The Amish who settled in Bavaria overcame many of the
prejudices against them through diligent work and agricultural inven-
tiveness. Because they were excluded from village life, they became
tenants on large estates. Here they had more opportunity to experiment with farming methods than did the peasants with their few plots
of ground and their deeply regimented economic routine. Their marginal nonconformity and marginal acceptance motivated them to work
harder and produce more than non-Amish tenants, and this gave them
the incentive to adopt new methods. Some of the descendants of the
Bavarian Amish are today superior farm managers. Their distinct
Amish organization was lost before the advent of the present century,
but a few practices, such as foot washing, the wearing of the cap by
women, and congregational autonomy, persisted longer.

In 1791 small groups of Anabaptists from the Palatinate and from
Montbéliard, France, emigrated to Galicia (Poland) and to Volhynia
(Russia), having been attracted to these areas by liberal offers from
progressive noblemen who sought their agricultural talents.[39] They
were few in number, and through intermarriage and close association
with the Swiss Mennonites they lost most of their Amish consciousness
before emigrating to Moundridge, Kansas, and Freeman, South Dakota, in 1874.

In the Palatinate, the Amish congregation that maintained distinctive practices the longest, including the use of lay preachers, strict
shunning, foot washing, and the wearing of beards and hooks and
eyes, was Ixheim, near Zweibrücken. Some of the older members practiced foot washing until 1932, but hooks and eyes were discarded before
1880. The congregation also served scattered families in the Saar. The
Ixheim Amish were long called *Häftler* (hookers), while the nearby
Ernstweiler Mennonite members were known as *Knöpfler* (buttoners),
but consciousness of their differences largely disappeared in the twentieth century. The two churches were officially merged in 1937 and
the Ixheim meeting house still stands as a private dwelling.[40]

In Alsace and its neighboring principality Lorraine, there are about
three thousand Mennonites today who are descendants of the Amish.
The Amish were formally expelled from the valley of Markirch in
1712. The natives complained that they did not have to bear arms.

39. *Mennonite Encyclopedia*, s.v. "Volhynia." See also Martin H. Schrag, *European
History of the Swiss Mennonites from Volhynia* (North Newton, Kans.: Mennonite
Press, 1974).

40. *Mennonite Encyclopedia*, s.v. "Ixheim."

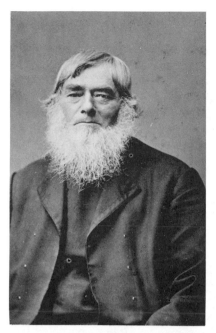

Amish of Alsace and Bavaria. *Upper left*: Bishop Peter Hochstetler (1814–1885), born in Alsace, died in Bavaria. *Upper right*: Maria (Hage) Hochstetler, wife of Peter Hochstetler, in work garments. *Lower left*: Magdelena (Roggy) Güngerich (1815–1879), wife of Johannes Güngerich (1808–1886). *Lower right*: George Guth (1811–1897), deacon at Ixheim Amish Church, Zweibrücken.

A large farm estate in Altkirch occupied
by descendants of the Amish

The industry, thrift, and prosperity of the Amish Mennonites was
related to the vigorous protest the natives made to authorities. King
Louis XIV gave orders that only the Lutheran and Reformed religions
were to be tolerated, and the Anabaptists were ordered to leave without
exception. Many migrated to Montbéliard, Lorraine, Zweibrücken,
and the German Palatinate. The Amish organized a strong community
in the small province of Montbéliard,[41] where they lived on farms,
many of which belonged to Duke Leopold-Eberhard. In spite of the
displeasure of the native population, the duke gave them full protection, granting them exemption from the swearing of oaths, as well as
permission to have their own cemetery and their own schools. Following the French Revolution, many of the Anabaptists in this area were
able to become landowners.

41. Jean Séguy explains the background of this expulsion (*Les Assemblées*, pp.
133-37). See also Gratz, *Bernese Anabaptists*, p. 87. The *Gemeindebuch*, or church
record book, from 1750 remains the property of the Mennonite congregation at
Montbéliard.

The Amish Mennonites developed special farming techniques in France. Their industry and prosperity, together with their practice of magical healing, led to the notion among the French people that they had powerful secrets or gifts others did not have.[42] Their honesty, thrift, hard work, and productive capabilities made them all the more desirable to the landed nobility.

If all the Amish had remained in Europe, it is doubtful they would have survived at all as a cultural group. When they came to America in the eighteenth century, they found conditions favorable for growth and development. Land was available in unlimited quantities. They could live adjacent to one another on family farms and maintain relatively self-sufficient and closely knit communities. Under these conditions an integrated folk culture could develop and maintain an identity. Thus the Amish survived in the New World, emerging as distinctive, small, homogeneous, and self-governing communities.

42. Séguy, *Les Assemblées*, pp. 509–15.

Part II

Stability and Fulfillment

· CHAPTER 4

The Amish Charter

THE AMISH have lived in America for approximately two and one-half centuries. During this time span they have formed unique communities, communities that differ from those in their European homelands. With privileges of landownership in America and freedom to move about at will, they have been virtually unrestricted in the develpment of their ideals. The Amish communities of today have syncretized many traditional elements of their material culture with elements in the New World.

We turn now to the organizing principles that support Amish community life. From the viewpoint of the Amish people themselves, we will describe the major elements in their world view and their view of themselves. The fundamental values and common ends recognized by the people and accepted by them have been designated as the charter.[1] The charter encompasses basic beliefs and a body of tradition and wisdom that guide the members in their daily lives.

The Amish view of reality is conditioned by a dualistic world view.[2] They view themselves as a Christian community suspended in

1. Bronislaw Malinowski, *A Scientific Theory of Culture* (Chapel Hill: University of North Carolina Press, 1944), pp. 48, 162. In a little community like the Amish one, the charter need not be reduced to writing to be effective.

2. For an elaboration of the Anabaptist "Doctrine of the Two Worlds," see Robert Friedman, *The Theology of Anabaptism* (Scottdale, Pa.: Herald Press, 1973), pp. 36–48.

a tension-field between obedience to God and those who have rejected God in their disobedience. Purity and goodness are in conflict with impurity and evil. The Amish view, however, differs from classic dualism, in which matter is set in opposition to spirit. The Creation account, as revealed in Genesis, encompassing a garden with animals, plants, and marine life, is viewed as good and for the benefit of mankind. The Amish are suspended between pride and humility (*Demut und Hochmut*), stewardship and greed, submission and disobedience. The Amish sanction marriage, family, and children, and a disciplined life in a disciplined brotherhood. The Amish rejected the European monastic system, which emphasized celibacy and a disciplined life expressed in a hierarchy. Monastics renounced personal property, although the wealth of the community was lavishly and symbolically expressed in great cathedrals and in elaborate altars. The Amish view personal property, expressed in farms and family dwellings, as a form of stewardship, but they carefully avoid any ostentatious display of wealth. The fruits of their labor are used to perpetuate community life through sharing, hospitality, stewardship, and underwriting the cost of an expanding population.

The rejection of worldly structures and the creation of their own cosmos is manifest in all phases of the Amish charter. The following description of the Amish charter will focus on *Gemeinde* as a redemptive community, separation from the world, the vow of baptism, *Ordnung* and tradition, excommunication and social avoidance, and closeness to nature.

GEMEINDE AS A REDEMPTIVE COMMUNITY

Amish fraternity is based upon the understanding of the church as a redemptive community. To express this corporateness they use the German term *Gemeinde* or the shorter dialect version pronounced *Gemee*. This concept expresses all the connotations of church, congregation, and community. The true church, they believe, had its origin in God's plan, and after the end of time the church will coexist with God through eternity. The true church is to be distinguished from the "fallen church."[3] Like numerous other Christian groups, the Amish hold that at some point in Christian history the established church became corrupt, ineffectual, and displeasing to God.

The church of God is composed of those who "have truly repented, and rightly believed; who are rightly baptized . . . and incorporated

3. Franklin H. Littell, *The Origins of Sectarian Protestantism* (New York: Macmillan, 1964), p. 55.

into the communion of the saints on earth."[4] The true church is "a chosen generation, a royal priesthood, an holy nation," and "a congregation of the righteous."[5] The church of God is separate and completely different from the "blind, perverted world."[6] Furthermore, the church is "known by her evangelical faith, doctrine, love, and godly conversation; also by her pure walk and practice, and her observances of the true ordinances of Christ."[7] The church must be "pure, unspotted and without blemish" (Eph. 5:27),[8] capable of enforcing disciplinary measures to insure purity of life and separation from the world. These definitions and conceptions of the church are ideals, the recognized purposes toward which the members strive. Community-building is central to the redemptive process; salvation is not an individualistic effort to be practiced when convenient or in keeping with one's personal definition. The aim of the Amish is to incarnate the teachings of Jesus into a voluntary social order.

SEPARATION FROM THE WORLD

The individual Amish member is admonished to keep himself "unspotted from the world" and separate from the desires, intent, and goals of the worldly person. Amish preaching and teaching draw upon passages from the Bible that emphasize the necessity of separation from the world. Two passages, perhaps the most often quoted, epitomize for the Amishman the message of the Bible. The first is: "Be not conformed to this world, but be ye transformed by the renewing of your mind that ye may prove what is that good and acceptable and perfect will of God" (Rom. 12:2). To the Amish, this means among other things that one should not dress and behave like the world. The second is: "Be ye not unequally yoked together with unbelievers; for what fellowship hath righteousness with unrighteousness? What communion hath light with darkness?" (II Cor. 6:14). This doctrine forbids the Amishman from marrying a non-Amish person or entering into a business partnership with an outsider. It is applied generally to all social contacts that involve intimate connections with persons outside the ceremonial community. This literal

---

4. *The Dordrecht Confession*, art. 8.

5. Ibid.

6. Dietrich Philip, *Enchiridion or Hand Book* (Aylmer, Ont.: Pathway Publishers, 1966), p. 86. This work by a sixteenth-century Anabaptist represents a comprehensive scriptural interpretation of the meaning of being Christian and the meaning of the redemptive process as understood by the Anabaptists.

7. *The Dordrecht Confession*, art. 8.

8. King James Version.

emphasis upon separateness explains the Amish view of themselves as a "chosen people" or "a peculiar peole."[9]

The principle of separation conditions and controls the Amishman's contact with the outside world; it colors his entire view of reality and being. By the precepts of Christ, the Amish are forbidden to take part in violence and war. In time of war they are conscientious objectors, basing their stand on biblical texts such as "My kingdom is not of this world: if my kingdom were of this world, then would my servants fight" (John 18:36).[10] The Amish have no rationale for self-defense or for defending their possessions. Like many early Anabaptists they are "defenseless Christians." Hostility is met without retaliation. The Amish farmer who is in conflict with the world around him is admonished by his bishop to follow the example of Isaac: after the warring Philistines had stopped up all the wells of his father, Abraham, Isaac moved to new lands and dug new wells (Gen. 26:15–18). This advice is taken literally, so that in the face of hostility, the Amish move to new locations without defending their rights.

Both the Amish and the Mennonites practice adult rather than infant baptism, nonresistance and the refusal to bear arms, the refusal to take oaths, and both generally refrain from holding public office. Religion is a total way of life, not a compartmentalized activity. The Amish today differ from the the main body of Mennonites in the extent to which external changes have affected the groups. Most Mennonites are more willing to accept changes and to incorporate them into their religious values.[11] Most are technologically modern, and they generally accept higher education. Furthermore, during the nineteenth century they founded their own institutions of higher education.

The Amish show little interest in improving the world that is outside their immediate environment. They profess to be "strangers and pilgrims" in the present world. The Amish interpretation of salvation differs in emphasis from that of modern fundamentalism. Belief in predestination is taboo, as is the idea of assurance of salva-

9. This concept was present in the Old Testament in the case of the Jews (Exod. 19:5; Deut. 14:2), and the Amish tend to apply the concept to themselves using New Testament passages I Pet. 2:9 and Titus 2:14. Max Weber observed that the notion of the "chosen people" comes naturally with ethnic solidarity and is a means of status differentation ("Ethnic Groups," in *Theories of Society*, ed. Talcott Parsons, 2 vols. [Glencoe, Ill. The Free Press, 1961], 1: 305).

10. The teaching of nonresistance implies not only refusal to bear arms but an exemplary life that is not revengeful. See *Dordrecht Confession*, art. 14.

11. Excepted are the Old Order Mennonites, some of whom, like the Amish, use horses for farming and transportation.

tion. A knowledge of salvation is complete only after the individual hears the welcome words at the last judgment, "Come, ye blessed of my Father, inherit the kingdom prepared for you from the foundation of the world" (Matt. 25:34). Furthermore, the commands of obedience and self-denial are given more emphasis than is the teaching on "grace through faith alone." To assert that "I know I am saved" would be obnoxious because it smacks of pride and boasting. Humility (*Demut*) is highly prized but pride (*Hochmut*) is abhorred. Among the highly traditional Amish, Christ becomes a *Wegweiser*, "One who shows the way," and not merely one who has atoned for the sins of mankind.

Amish preaching and moral instruction emphasize self-denial and obedience to the teaching of the Word of God, which is equated with the rules of the church. Long passages from Old Testament are retold, primarily the crucial events in the lives of Abraham, Isaac, Jacob, Joseph, and Moses. The escape of the Israelites from Egyptian bondage and Moses's giving of the law are sermon themes. The choice put before the congregation is to obey or die. To disobey the church is to die. To obey the church and strive for "full fellowship"—i.e., complete harmony with the order of the church—is to have *lebendige Hoffnung*, a living hope of salvation. Thus an Amish person puts his faith in God, obeys the order of the church, and patiently hopes for the best.

Although separation from the world is a basic tenet of the Amish charter, the Amish are not highly ethnocentric in their relationships with the outside world. They accept other people as they are, without attempting to judge or convert them to the Amish way of life. But for those who are born into the Amish society, the sanctions for belonging are deeply rooted.

THE VOW OF BAPTISM

Membership in the Amish church-community is attained by becoming an adult and voluntarily choosing instruction and baptism. Baptism signifies repentence, total commitment to the believing church-community, and admission to adulthood. This vow embodies the spiritual meaning of becoming an Amish person, an acceptance of absolute values, and a conscious belief in religious and ethical ends entirely for their own sake, quite independent of any external rewards. This orientation to *Wertrational*,[12] or absolute values, makes

12. Max Weber, *The Theory of Social and Economic Organization*, trans. A. M. Henderson and Talcott Parsons (Glencoe, Ill.: The Free Press, 1947), p. 165.

In summer, worship services are often held in barns
rather than in houses. Here members
gather for a funeral.

certain unconditional demands on the individual. Members are required to put into practice what is required by duty, honor, personal loyalty, and religious calling, regardless of the sacrifice.

When young people reach late adolescence, they naturally think about becoming members of the church. In their sermons, ministers challenge young people to consider baptism. Parents are naturally concerned that young people take this step. In most cases, persistent parental urging is not necessary, since it is normal for young people to follow the role expectation of their peers. No young person can be married in the Amish church without first being baptized in the faith.

After the spring communion, a class of instruction is held for all who wish to join the church. This is known as *die Gemee nooch geh*, or literally, "to follow the church." The applicants meet with the ministers on Sunday morning at worship service, but separately. The Confession of Faith (Dordrecht) is used as a basis for instruction. The ministers very simply acquaint the applicants for baptism with the incidents in the Bible that suggest the right relationship with God and the right attitudes toward the community. After six or eight periods of biweekly instruction, roughly from May to August, a day is set for the baptismal service. The consent of the members is obtained to receive the applicants into fellowship. Baptism occurs prior

to the fall *Ordnungsgemee* ("preparatory service"), which is followed
by *Grossgemee* ("communion"). Great emphasis is placed upon the
difficulty of walking the "straight and narrow way." The applicants
are told that it is better not to make a vow than to make a vow and
later break it; on the Saturday prior to baptism they are asked to
meet with the ministers and there they are given the opportunity to
"turn back" if they so desire. The young men are asked to promise
that they will accept the duties of a minister should the lot ever fall
to them. The following account of a preaching and baptismal service
will serve to illustrate both the nature of the individual commitment
and its community context:

It is a beautiful September morning. The sun shines brightly into
the faces of the audience through large, swinging, red barn doors. The
huge doors are propped open with sticks on the barn's sloping banks.
The rows of benches on the barn floor are almost filled—men on one
side and women on the other—except for two rows in the middle. To
the right, behind the women, alfalfa bales are stacked high. A curtain
of binder canvas is tacked along the side to prevent the stubble from
scratching the women's backs and to improve the barn's appearance.
To the left is a long granary, on the side of which the men have hung
their large-brimmed black hats.

As the *Vorsinger* ("song leader") begins to sing the first song, the
ministers, bishops, and deacons retire to a room in the house for
consultation and to meet with the baptismal applicants for the last
time. Here they will also agree on the order of the service for the day.

Between hymns there is a deep silence in the audience. The aroma
of the haymow and the sounds of the birds and insects penetrate the
consciousness of the audience. One can hear the horses munching
hay below. While waiting for the next hymn to begin, the farm
owner notices that it is too warm, and with some difficulty opens a
second barn door on the side where the women are seated. The
ventilation taken care of, he returns to his seat.

Several hymns are sung and the applicants for baptism—on this
occasion six girls aged eighteen and upward—file up the barn bank
and take their seats in the center section near the minister's bench.
Both young and old intently watch the six young women who are ready
to make their vows to God and the church, to say "no" to the world
and "yes" to Jesus Christ and his *Gemein* here on earth. Each sits with
bowed head, as though in deep meditation and prayer for the lifelong
vow about to be taken. None dare to risk a glimpse at the audience or
to gaze about, for it is a solemn occasion. Their clothing is strictly
uniform: black organdy caps, black dresses, white organdy capes, long

white organdy aprons, black stockings, and black oxfords. The fabric of the dresses and the color of ribbon bows at the left shoulder, faintly showing through the organdy capes, are the only evidence of personal taste.

The ministers now enter, quietly removing their hats. All seven, including several visiting deacons and bishops for this special service, offer handshakes to those nearby as they slowly make their way to the ministers' bench. They take their seats. The one who will make the *Anfang* ("opening address") sits at the head of the bench; the bishop who will give the longer message sits next in line. As soon as the ministers are seated the assembly stops singing.

Sitting silently in anticipation, the audience listens to two sermons. Two hours of intense waiting finally give way to the climax of the day as the bishop turns to the applicants with a personal admonition. The deacon leaves the service and returns with a small pail of water and a tin cup. The bishop reminds the applicants that the vow they are about to make will be made not to the ministers or to the church but to God. He requests the applicants to kneel if it is still their desire to become members of the body of Christ. All six kneel. The bishop asks a few simple questions[13] and each gives an affirmative answer.

After the applicants respond to the preliminary questions, the bishop asks the assembly to rise for prayer. He reads one of the simple prayers from *Die Ernsthafte Christenpflicht*, a prayer book of the Swiss Anabaptists.

The assembly is seated, but the applicants continue to kneel. The bishop, a deacon, and the deacon's wife proceed with the baptism. The three stand at the head of the line while the deacon's wife unties the ribbon of the first applicant's cap and removes the cap from her head. The bishop then lays his hands on the girl's head and says: *Auf deinen Glauben den du bekennt hast vor Gott und viele Zeugen wirst du getauft in Namen des Vaters, des Sohnes und des Heiligen Geistes, Amen* ("Upon your faith, which you have confessed before God and these many witnesses, you are baptized in the name of the Father, the Son, and the Holy Spirit, Amen"). The deacon pours water into the bishop's hands, cupped above the young woman's head, and it drips down over her hair and face.

Overhead, the pigeons flap their wings and fly from one end of the

13. The method of baptism is pouring, not immersion. Two sets of baptismal questions appear in *Handbook für Prediger* (Arthur, Ill.: L. A. Miller, 1950). An English translation appears in Harvey J. Miller, "Proceedings of Amish Ministers Conferences, 1826–1831," *Mennonite Quarterly Review* 33 (April 1959): 141.

barn to the other. A gentle breeze from the open door of the straw shed stirs up a cloud of fine particles of chaff and dust. An airplane roars in the distance.

When the rite of baptism is completed, the bishop takes the hand of each kneeling applicant in turn and greets her: *In Namen des Herrn und die Gemein wird dir die Hand geboten, so steh auf* ("In the name of the Lord and the Church, we extend to you the hand of fellowship, rise up"). The applicant stands up and the bishop then gives her hand to the assisting wife, who greets the new member with the Holy Kiss. All applicants remain standing until the last one is greeted, and then the bishop asks them to be seated. A few tears are brushed aside as they retie their covering (cap) strings. They will now be considered members of the church and will enjoy full privileges as members of the *Gemein*.

The bishop takes his former speaking position and admonishes the congregation to be helpful to the new members. He instructs those just baptized to be faithful to the church and to the ministry. To illustrate the importance of obedience, he retells the story of the idolatry committed by the children of Israel while Moses was up on the mountain praying, comparing Israel to the young people who throw parties and engage in other sinful activities while parents are away from home. He concludes the long sermon with the reading of Romans 6. Other ministers are invited to give testimony to his sermon, and three of the remaining six give brief statements of approval. After four hours the service ends in the usual way: everyone kneels for prayer, a short benediction is given, and a hymn is sung.

The text of the Amish vow is not significantly different from that required by Christian churches generally. What is significant is the promise to abide by implied rules not explicitly stated in the vow. By inference or otherwise, the strict Amish churches include in the vow the promise to help maintain the *Regel und Ordnung* ("rules and order") and the promise not to depart from them in life or death. "That's the way we have it in our church," explains one bishop. "It seems to me that every person should stay in church where he is baptized. He should never leave that group if he once makes a vow."[14] A more moderate view of the vow requires commitment to the true church of Jesus Christ, but does not imply a lifetime commitment to the particular rules and regulations of a given district. For instance, the late Bishop John B. Peachey said, "It is not right

14. John B. Renno of Mifflin County, Pa., in a personal interview.

to make the young people promise to stay with the *Ordnung* for life, but rather with the teachings of the Bible."[15]

The difference in these two views can become very important in case of excommunication. Social avoidance is implied in the former but not in the latter. As a young man considering baptism in the Amish church, I remember the above two opposing views being expressed by two ministers. I did not want to take a vow I could not keep, nor take a vow that implied social avoidance in case I could not live by Amish standards. Consequently, on the day my chums began their instruction for baptism, I drove my horse and buggy to the nearby Mennonite church.

ORDNUNG AND TRADITION

The process of social ordering is embodied in the *Ordnung* (in the dialect pronounced *Ott-ning*). These regulations represent the consensus of the leaders and the endorsement of the members at a special meeting (*Ordnungsgemee*) held semiannually, before communion Sunday, and are considered necessary for the welfare of the church-community. All members know the *Ordnung* of their congregation, which generally remains oral and unwritten. Most rules are taken for granted, and it is primarily borderline issues that call for discussion at the *Ordnungsgemee*.

Two kinds of regulations must be distinguished—those made at special conferences in history from the sixteenth century onward, and the contemporary *Ordnung* of each church district. The former rules have been printed,[16] but most contemporary rules governing the district have not. The older rules clarify the basic principles of separation, nonresistance, apostasy, and exclusion. The contemporary *Ordnung* guides members in the application and practice of the principles.

The *Ordnung* clarifies what is considered worldly and sinful, for to be worldly is to be lost. Some of the rules have direct biblical support; others do not. Regulations that cannot be directly supported

15. John B. Peachey of Mifflin County, Pa., in a personal interview.

16. For published disciplines, see Harold S. Bender, "Some Early American Amish Mennonite Disciplines," *Mennonite Quarterly Review* 8 (April 1934), which covers the conferences of 1809, 1837, and 1865. For the conferences of 1779 and 1781, see ibid. 4 (April 1930) and 11 (April 1937); for "An Amish Bishop's Conference Epistle of 1865," see ibid. 20 (July 1946). See also *Christlicher Ordnung or Christian Discipline* (Aylmer, Ont.: Pathway Publishers, 1966), and Miller, "Proceedings of Amish Ministers Conferences, 1826–1831." Other published tracts and manuscripts are known to exist.

by biblical references are justified by arguing that to do otherwise would be worldly.[17] The old way (*das alt Gebrauch*) is the better way. A father who tried living in a newly formed Amish settlement "without the rigid traditions, where everything was figured out according to the Bible (or the understanding of the Bible)," found that "it didn't work." Following this experience he said, "I have a healthy respect for the traditions in the larger communities."

To be separate from the world is to be different from the world. Being different is more important, within limits, than specific ways of being different. The Amish, for example, feel some affinity to other Anabaptist groups (viz., Hutterite and Old Colony Mennonites) that differ from them in specific ways, but that maintain separation from the world. The strong commitment to the principle of separation from the world also helps to explain why the Amish are not disturbed by slightly different rules in other Amish communities.

The congregation must agree on *how* to be different from the world, for the body of Christ must be "of one mind." Twice each year the members must express their unity before communion. This unanimous expression of unity implies satisfaction with the *Ordnung*, peace among all the members, and peace with God. Unless there is a group expression of unity, the Lord's Supper is not held.

The rules of the Amish church cover the whole range of human behavior. In a society where keeping the world out is a primary goal, there are many taboos, and customs become symbolic, although they vary from one community to another. The most universal Amish norms in the United States and Canada are: no high-line electricity, telephones, central heating systems in homes; no automobiles; no tractors with pneumatic tires; beards are for all married men, but moustaches are not allowed. Required are long hair (covering part of the ear for men, uncut for women), hooks and eyes on dress coats, and the use of horses for farming. No formal education beyond the elementary grades is a rule of life, but there are infrequent exceptions to this rule.

Besides a means of separation, the *Ordnung* provides a communal means of managing the natural human tendency toward self-exaltation (*Hochmut*) and manipulative power. Through individual submission (*Gelassenheit*) to the community's will, members are able to contribute to a network of community relationships. Tendencies viewed as disruptive and dangerous—such as self-seeking, personal power, wealth,

17. For insights on the Amish practice of separation, I am grateful to Gertrude Enders Huntington, "Dove at the Window: A Study of an Old Order Amish Community in Ohio" (Ph.D. diss. Yale University, 1956), pp. 109–18.

and status—are channeled into a social order of love and brother-hood. Order and tidiness characterize the physical Amish community. Witness the well-tended gardens and fields, the well-kept buildings and lawns, and the laundry hanging out on the line in rows according to size and color.[18]

A contemporary Amish minister says of the *Ordnung*: "A respected *Ordnung* generates peace, love, contentment, equality and unity. It creates a desire for togetherness and fellowship. It binds marriages, it strengthens family ties to live together, to work together, to worship together and to commune secluded from the world." Concerning those who disobey, he explains: "We will always have members that, when they fall prey to sin, will blame the *Ordnung*. A rebelling member will label it 'a man-made law with no scriptural base.' We have a minority who resist the *Ordnung*. Obedience is a close associate to *Ordnung* for it is a symbol informing us whether the member loves the church or if he does not. One is either in the church or on the outside. There is no happy medium. In spite of an outsider's view that *Ordnung* is a law, a bondage of suppression, the person who has learned to live within a respectful church *Ordnung* appreciates its value. It gives freedom of heart, peace of mind, and a clear conscience. Such a person has actually more freedom, more liberty, and more privilege than those who would be bound to the outside."[19]

EXCLUSION: EXCOMMUNICATION
AND SOCIAL AVOIDANCE

In keeping with Anabaptist practice, to assure the purity and un-blemished character of the church the wicked and the obdurate members must be excluded from the group. According to Menno Simon, who vigorously taught that exclusion must apply to all without respect to persons, three classes of persons must be expelled from the believers' church: those who live in open sin, those who cause divisions, and those who teach a false doctrine.[20]

The German term *Bann* means excommunication. Social avoidance

18. I am indebted to Sandra Cronk for insights on the relationship of communal control of manipulative power through the ritual process ("Gelassenheit: The Rites of the Redemptive Process in Old Order Amish and Old Order Mennonite Communities" [Ph.D. diss., University of Chicago, School of Divinity, 1977], pp. 14–21). The emergence of an "Old Order" type in America on the basis of a search for *Gelassenheit* is a useful concept. There are some problems, however, in explaining the Ammann-Reist division with the *Gelassenheit* model.

19. Comments by Joseph Beiler, Lancaster County, Pa.

20. *The Complete Writings of Menno Simons* (Scottdale, Pa.: Herald Press, 1956), p. 94.

(*Meidung*), also called shunning, is the practice of restricting member associations with persons who have been excommunicated. The biblical instruction is that one neither "eat" with such a person nor "keep company" (I Cor. 5:11). The term *avoidance* is taken from Romans 16:17, where the apostle instructs the believer to "avoid" those who work against the peace of the church. The believer is advised in II John 10 neither to "receive into the house" nor to greet a person who advocates anything but a true doctrine.

In the sixteenth century social avoidance was exercised by the Anabaptists against fanatical groups such as the Munsterites, Baden-burgers, and Davidians.[21] Jacob Ammann introduced the practice to the Swiss churches, and as explained in Chapter 2, the result was the Amish division. The Amish today practice *Meidung* as taught by Ammann. According to Matthew 18:15–17, excommunication from membership is exercised after the offender has been properly warned and remains unwilling to desist from his transgression, divisive teaching, or rebellion. The ordained leaders attempt to be loyal to every instruction of the Word, to avoid offending the weak believers, and to cause the sinner to examine himself and repent. According to Matthew 18:18, the church of Christ has the authority to "bind" and to "loose" and to exercise the "keys of the Kingdom."

The affect of shunning on the life of the individual is illustrated in the life of a young man whom we shall fictitiously name Joseph. Joseph grew up in a very strict Amish home under the influence of parents who were known for their orthodoxy. He was baptized at the age of twenty. Three years after his baptism Joseph was excommunicated and shunned. Charges laid against him included the following: he had attended a revival meeting, associated with excommunicated persons, bought an automobile, and began to attend a Mennonite church.

Joseph was excommunicated in the presence of the assembled congregation after a series of warnings. At home, the young man could no longer eat at the family table. He ate at a separate table with the young children who were not church members. Joseph was urged by parents and ministers to mend his ways, to make good his baptismal promise. Several times he attended preaching services with his family. Since members may not accept services, goods, or favors from excommunicated members, he could not take his sisters to church, even if he used a buggy instead of his offensive automobile, but they could drive a buggy and take him along. It was not long

21. John Horsch, *Mennonites in Europe* (Scottdale, Pa.: Mennonite Publishing House, 1950), pp. 328–35.

until Joseph accepted employment with a non-Amish person and began using his automobile for transportation to and from home. When shunned friends came to his home for conversation, Joseph's parents met them at the gate and turned them away. It was not long until his father and mother asked him to leave home. He explained: "I had to move away from home or my parents could not take communion. My parents were afraid that younger persons in the family would be led astray. They didn't exactly chase me off the place, but I was no longer welcome at home."

Persons who acknowledge their sins and wish to make amends are received back into the fellowship usually within two or three weeks. For minor offenses, such as flaunting the dress codes or exchanging hostile words with another person, the offender makes a formal apology to the church. For major offenses such as adultery, fornication, or teaching heresy, the offenders must confess their error while kneeling, and are only then restored into the church by the welcome hand of the bishop.

Among Amish communities today, differing views on shunning have led to numerous divisions. The moderate interpretation, taken by many of the "milder" groups, holds that moral transgressors should be excommunicated and shunned, but if the offender is restored to some other congregation or branch of the pacifist Anabaptist faith, then shunning should be discontinued. But this, according to the adherents of "strict" shunning, is a departure from Ammann's teaching. In speaking of a former Amish member who joined the Mennonites, a bishop explained: "The only way for us to lift the ban is for him to make peace with the Old Order church, going back and living his promise made on his knees before God and the church."[22] According to this view, an excommunicated person must be shunned for life unless he restores his previous relationship with the group. By shunning him in all social relations, the community gives him a status that minimizes the threat to other members of the community. This perpetuation of the controversy undoubtedly helps the Old Order group to remain distinct and socially intact.

The Amish make no effort to evangelize or proselyte the outsider. It is their primary concern to keep their own baptized members from slipping into the outer world, or into other religious groups. With greater mobility and ease of travel and communication, Amish solidarity is threatened. Members who may wish to have automobiles, radios, or the usual comforts of modern living face the threat of being excommunicated and shunned. Thus the ban is used as an instrument

22. John B. Renno, letter of October 19, 1950.

Farming is a moral directive and is generally a meaningful experience
for the entire family. This farm is located
in Holmes County, Ohio.

of discipline not only for the drunkard or the adulterer but for the
person who transgresses the *Ordnung*. It is a powerful instrument for
preventing involvement in outside loyalties.

CLOSENESS TO NATURE

The Amish have a strong affinity for the soil and for nature. Working with the soil was not one of the original issues that gave rise to
the Anabaptist movement or the Amish group, but was a basic value
acquired during the process of survival. As persecuted people, the
Amish found it possible to survive in the hinterlands, and there they
developed unique skills for crop production and livestock-raising.[23]

23. For the ingenious agrarian development of the Anabaptist groups in Europe,
see especially Ernst Correll, *Das schweizerische Täufermennonitentum* (Tübingen:
Mohr, 1925); and Jean Séguy, *Les Assemblées anabaptistes-mennonites de France*
(The Hague: Mouton, 1977).

Harvesting wheat in the traditional way. Farming requires
commitment and cooperation among family members.

In America the Amish perpetuated the skills they had acquired in
the valleys of Switzerland, France, and Germany.

The physical world is considered good, and in itself is not cor-
rupting or evil. Its beauty is apparent in the universe, in the orderliness of the seasons, the heavens, in the world of living plants as well
as in the many species of animals, and in the forces of living and
dying. It is not uncommon to see an Amish family visiting the zoo
in a large metropolitan area. Animals are considered part of the
Creation, and those not found on Amish farms are of great interest.

The charter of Amish life requires members to limit their occupation to farming or closely associated activities such as operating a
saw mill, carpentry, or masonry. The Amishman feels contact with
the material world through the working of his muscles and the aching

of his limbs. In the little Amish community, toil is proper and good, religion provides meaning, and the bonds of family and church provide human satisfaction and love. In Europe the Amish lived in rural areas, always in close association with the soil, so their communities were largely agrarian in character. It is in America that they have found it necessary to make occupational regulations for protection from the influence of urbanism.

The preference for rural living is reflected in attitudes and in informal interactions rather than in an explicit dogma. For the Amish, God is manifest more in closeness to nature, in the soil and the weather, and among plants and animals than in the man-made city. Hard work, thrift, and mutual aid find sanction in the Bible. The city, by contrast, is held to be the center of leisure, of nonproductive spending, and often of wickedness. The Christian life is best maintained away from the cities. God created Adam and Eve to "replenish the earth, and subdue it; and have dominion over the fish of the sea, and over the fowl of the air, and over every living thing that moveth upon the earth" (Gen. 1:28). In the same way, man's highest calling in the universe today is to care for the things of creation. One Amishman said, "The Lord told Adam to replenish the earth and to rule over the animals and the land—you can't do that in cities." Another said, "While the Lord's blessings were given to the people who remained in the country, sickness and ruination befell Sodom. Shows, dances, parties, and other temptations ruin even the good people who now live in cities. Families are small in cities; in the city you never know where your wife is, and city women can't cook. People go hungry in the cities but you will never starve if you work hard in the country."[24]

The Amish have generally prospered on the land more often than their neighbors. Lancaster County, Pennsylvania—a center of Amish life—has long been distinguished as the garden spot of the nation. The product of an intensive kind of farming on relatively small holdings, it reflects long experience with agricultural practices of the Old World and a philosophy of work and thrift. Some Pennsylvania landowners occupy farms that were acquired directly from William Penn or his land agent. As farms have been handed down from father to son, so have the experiences and the wisdom associated with the care of livestock and farming. The Amish attribute their material success in farming to divine blessing.

24. Quotation is from Walter M. Kollmorgen, *Culture of a Contemporary Community: The Old Order Amish of Lancaster County, Pennsylvania,* Rural Life Studies no. 4 (Washington, D.C.: U.S. Department of Agriculture, 1942), p. 23.

The main objective of their farming, as Walter Kollmorgen has pointed out, "is to accumulate sufficient means to buy enough land to keep all the children on farms. To this end the Amish work hard, produce abundantly, and save extensively."[25]

Farming is a subject of Amish conversation and their concern for it is reflected in their publications. Topics customarily covered in *The Budget*, a weekly newspaper, are the weather, seeding, planting activity, and harvest. In springtime we read that "farmers were busy in the fields last week." "Some are sowing wheat." "Wheat and alfalfa fields look nice." In summer we read that "farmers are busy threshing oats and picking tomatoes." "People are starting to make hay and are picking strawberries." "The women are picking wild berries and putting up peas." "Most of the beans are harvested and some people are beginning to pick corn." During the winter months reporters normally comment about livestock, sales, farm accidents, and construction work. The farm provides a space in which the family can function independently of the larger society. A farm of sufficient size may include several dwellings, a diversity of enterprises, and meaningful work for all family members.

The Amish charter is strongly supported by the myths and beliefs of the society. In this context, the beliefs perform a conservative function in maintaining the social order. Acting as a charter, the beliefs justify the norms of Amish society. When supported by beliefs, deeds, and a living faith, the Amish charter performs an integrative function in keeping the society together.

25. Ibid., p. 30.

CHAPTER 5

The Community

AMISH COMMUNITIES may be found in various geographic locations but not as discrete villages, counties, or compounds. In any region where there are Amish farmers, their families live on either side of the highway, around small rural towns, and they are interspersed among "English" farm families. The Amish are not a social class or a caste, a commune or a monastic order, but a religious community constituting a subculture in America. As a corporate group in the United States and Canada, the Old Order Amish celebrate communion and break bread together; they represent a community of "one mind," one discipline, and "one body." The Amish community attempts to be "in the world, but not of the world" (John 17:16).

SETTLEMENT PATTERNS

The Amish have developed a unique community structure in America. In addition to the household, which is comprised of the married couple and their offspring, the community consists of the *settlement*, a *church district* or districts, and the *affiliation*. These terms characterize the basic social groupings.

A *settlement* consists of Amish families living in a contiguous relationship, that is, households that are in proximity to one another. A settlement may be small, consisting of a few families and their or-

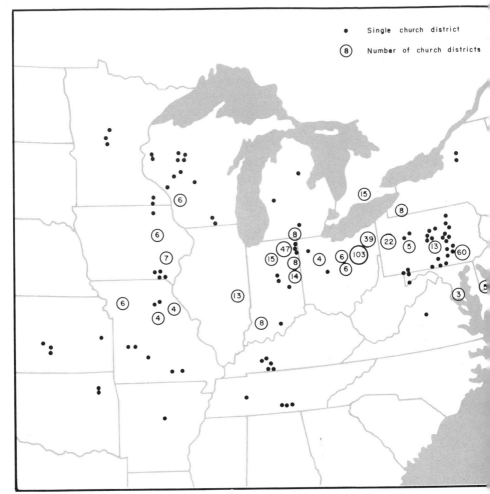

Figure 4.
Location of Amish church districts,
United States and Canada

dained leaders, or it may embrace several counties. The largest
settlement of Amish is located in Holmes and several adjoining
counties in Ohio. The two next largest are Lancaster County and
vicinity in Pennsylvania and Elkhart and Lagrange counties and
vicinity in Indiana. No specific limits are imposed upon the size of
a settlement. The location and density of the settlements in the
United States are indicated in Figure 4.

The *church district* is a congregation, a ceremonial unit encompassing a specific geographic area within a settlement. The size of
the church district is determined by the number of people who can

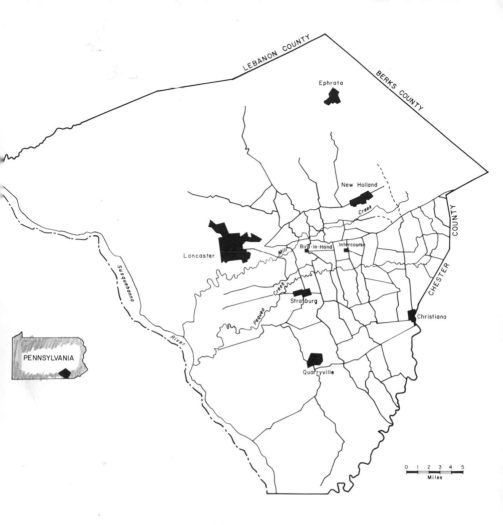

Figure 5.
Amish church districts, Lancaster County,
Pennsylvania

be accommodated for the preaching service in one farm dwelling. The
church district is a self-governing body with ceremonial and institutional functions reinforced by the preaching service. Baptisms, marriages, ordinations, and funerals are functions of the district. The
boundaries of the church districts are agreed upon by the leaders
and members, and they constitute such guidelines as roads, creeks,
cable wires, or small mountain ranges. Districts on the fringes of the
settlement are not assigned physical boundaries but encompass all the
Amish households in that general area. The curved and oblong shapes
of the Lancaster districts contrast sharply with the Elkhart and La-

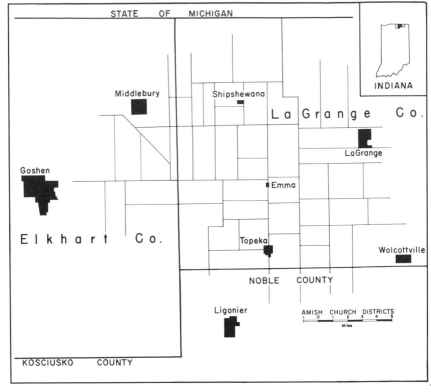

Figure 6.
Amish church districts, Elkhart
and Lagrange counties, Indiana

grange settlement in Indiana, where the districts are measured by square miles. (Compare Figures 5 and 6.) In the Lancaster settlement each district encompasses an area of about four square miles. In Indiana, where farms are larger, the districts average about six square miles in total area. Amish members and their children are obliged to attend the preaching services in the church districts in which they reside.

The church district is the "home church" for all the members who live within its borders and who observe communion together. A member can be disciplined only by his own church district, not by an outside authority. Likewise, a member who is disciplined has no recourse outside his home district. Members may attend other church district services on "off" Sundays when there is no service in their home district. Young people may date and marry persons in other districts. The Old Order districts attempt to keep their discipline fairly uniform. The ordained leaders themselves attempt to maintain uniformity, and for the sake of "peace" and of being an example, they often adhere to regulations more strictly than do lay members.

Through its kinship and many informal contacts, the district is an integral part of the wider settlement. The older settlements, for example, that have spawned new communities experience a high degree of informal association. Amish families have relatives in various settlements or in neighboring districts. The frequent visiting back and forth not only between relatives but also among friends makes a formal relationship between districts unnecessary. Some of the important life rituals, including weddings and funerals, reach across church district boundaries, as do economic and social activities such as barn-raisings and mutual aid.

An *affiliation* is a group of church districts that have a common discipline and that commune together. In other words, it is an exclusive ceremonial group. A clear separation is maintained between the Amish church and the world. But what about other groups that have broken away from the Old Order discipline, or churches that are altogether worldly? The Old Order Amish tend to classify groups according to their degree of worldliness, from "low" to "high" church. A low church (the most simple and humble) is one that observes strict discipline, teaches separation from the world, and practices social avoidance. A high church is one that has relaxed its discipline. Between the extremes many affiliations are recognized. The degree of interaction with other groups is governed by the social distance between them. Districts that are generally said to be of one mind are "in fellowship" with one another. They reciprocate with one another in maintaining discipline, so that if a member is excommunicated in his home district, the other districts will respect the action and will practice social avoidance.

Affiliations arise most frequently from liberal-progressive interpretations of the discipline. The various Amish affiliations have their analogues in the numerous subdivisions within most Protestant denominations. Because minor symbolic traits distinguish one affiliation from another, differences in affiliation among the Amish are not apparent to the outsider. All the large Amish settlements have several affiliations. In Lancaster County there are the Old Order Amish and two more progressive groups known as the "Beachy Amish" and "New Amish." The Beachy Amish permit the ownership of automobiles, the use of a meeting house for preaching services, and the use of English in ceremonial functions. The New Amish began when a group of families wished to relax the restrictions on the use of telephones, electricity, and tractor-driven farm machinery. They formed a separate affiliation in 1966. In Ohio and Indiana there are several affiliations of Amish in the same settlement with the Old Order Amish. The different affiliations add to the complexity of community organization, for the geographic boundaries of each affiliation overlap the boundary lines of other affiliations. Old Order Amish, who do not associate ceremonially with other Amish groups, simply say, "They are not in fellowship with us." Full fellowship means, in addition to common agreement in discipline and communing together, that ordained persons are permitted to preach during exchange visits.

In addition to the varied Amish affiliations within a single region, there are often different groups of Mennonites in the larger settlements. The Mennonites also have a spectrum of liberal-to-orthodox groupings ranging from the horse-and-buggy Old Order Mennonites, who speak the dialect, dress, and farm like the Amish, to those who are indistinguishable from "worldly" people. Their separate subdivisions include the Wisler, Stauffer, Wenger, Burkholder, and "Black Bumper" Mennonites. All these orthodox-type Mennonite groups, together with still others such as the Reformed Mennonite, Old Order River Brethren, Church of the Brethren (Dunkards), and Old Colony Mennonites, are affiliations apart from the Old Order Amish but in some instances exist in the same region.

GROWTH AND EXPANSION

The Amish themselves do not keep precise records of their membership beyond the number of families in a district and the number of children in school.[1] The names of the districts and their ordained leaders are published annually in *The New American Almanac* at Baltic, Ohio, by an Amish bookseller. The number of original Amish immigrants remains unknown. The 1890 U.S. *Census of Religious Bodies* reported twenty-two Old Order Amish congregations with 2,038 baptized adult members in nine states.

1. The Amish distaste for keeping an exact membership count is based upon the ill-advised example of King David, who, after "numbering the people" against the wishes of Jehovah, suffered a disastrous pestilence (II Sam. 24). Although the Amish may indirectly benefit from the work of non-Amish investigators who conduct demographic studies (namely, for medical genetic purposes), they lay no claim to the consequences. For many years (from 1905 to 1967) the *Mennonite Yearbook* reported memberships of the Old Order Amish. Four periods of Amish settlement are discussed by W. K. Crowley in "Old Order Amish Settlement: diffusion and Growth," *Annals of the Association of American Geographers* 68 (June 1978): 249–64.

Table 1
Old Order Amish church districts and population by decade

Year	Total number of districts	Estimated population	Lancaster County	Holmes County	Elkhart County
			Districts in vicinity of		
1890	22	3,700	5	6	4
1900	32	5,300	6	7	6
1910	57	9,500	9	8	8
1920	83	14,000	11	13	10
1930	110	18,500	12	16	12
1940	154	25,800	18	24	18
1950	197	33,000	25	40	25
1960	258	43,300	38	49	29
1970	343	57,600	47	70	37
1979	526	85,783	60	103	47

Sources: *Mennonite Yearbook* (Scottdale, Pa.), 1905–1967; *The New American Almanac* (Baltic, Ohio), 1930–1979; U.S., *Census of Religious Bodies, 1890*; and Amish informants.

The Amish population has grown steadily since 1890 (Table 1). Each decade the population has increased from 30 to 48 percent. The total population is estimated as accurately as possible from published sources and informants. There are generally more children (non-baptized persons) than baptized persons in a district. The districts vary in size, but each group is kept small by horse-and-buggy transportation and by the number of people who can gather for worship in either the farmhouse or barn. The three largest settlements average about 35 households per district. The largest settlement (in Ohio) averages 86 baptized members and 113 nonmembers in a district, or a total of 199 persons per district.[2] (For every 100 baptized persons, there are at this rate 131 unbaptized persons [or children] in the Amish population.)

The present population by state (and province) is shown in Table 2. The total population is estimated at 85,783, with Amish settlements existing in twenty states and one Canadian province. There have been many attempts to form communities in the Great Plains, and in such faraway states as New Mexico, Mississippi, and North Dakota, as well as in Mexico, Paraguay, and Honduras, but those families have

2. Harold E. Cross, "Genetic Studies in an Amish Isolate" (Ph.D. diss., The Johns Hopkins University, 1967), p. 42.

Table 2

Location and characteristics of the Old Order Amish by state and province

Location	Estimated population	Number of districts	Number of settlements	Date of settlement
Ohio	29,137	160	14	1808
Pennsylvania	22,570	125	25	1737
Indiana	16,628	99	12	1839
Missouri	2,560	22	9	1947[a]
Iowa	2,280	18	5	1846
Wisconsin	2,280	18	8	1925
Ontario	2,040	15	9	1824
Illinois	1,690	13	1	1864
Michigan	1,290	11	6	1900[a]
New York	1,120	10	3	1949
Maryland	970	5	2	1850
Delaware	775	5	1	1915
Minnesota	610	5	5	1972
Kentucky	550	5	3	1958
Tennessee	410	5	3	1944
Kansas	520	4	3	1883
Oklahoma	180	2	1	1892
Florida	40	1	1	1927
Montana	60	1	1	1970[a]
Arkansas	55	1	1	1976[a]
Virginia	18	1	1	1942[a]
Totals	85,783	526	115	

Sources: *The New American Almanac, 1972* (Baltic, Ohio); Amish directories; and correspondence with Amish informants. Estimates are based on mean district size within each settlement.

[a] Date of present settlement, not of extinct, earlier settlement.

either returned to the large "mother" communities or have associated with more modernized affiliations.[3] Approximately 75 percent of the Amish are located in three states: Ohio, Pennsylvania, and Indiana. Also indicated in Table 2 are the dates of settlement in each of the states (or province) and the approximate number of settlements. With the formation of many new settlements in recent years, we may expect the number to vacillate within each of the states.

3. For a discussion of settlements on the Great Plains, see John A. Hostetler, "The Old Order Amish on the Great Plains: A Study in Cultural Vulnerability," in *Ethnicity on the Great Plains,* ed. Fred Luebke (Lincoln: University of Nebraska Press, forthcoming).

POPULATION CHARACTERISTICS

The Amish have large families, a low rate of infant mortality, increasing longevity, and prohibitions against birth control. Thus they have experienced a much greater net population gain in recent years than have non-Amish people. In an intensive study of the Amish population, several Amish population growth patterns have been ascertained.[4] The highlights of these findings, with comparisons to the population of the United States and the Hutterites (the fastest-growing U.S. subpopulation on record), are discussed in the following sections.

Age at marriage. The median age at first marriage for Amish women is just under twenty-two years.[5] The median age for men at first marriage is slightly more than twenty-three years. Amish women marry at about the same age as other women in the United States. The age difference between husband and wife for the U.S. population as a whole is about 2.5 years. Among the Amish the age difference is about 1.5 years.

There are differences between the three largest regions—Pennsylvania, Ohio, and Indiana. Amish women in Pennsylvania marry at a slightly younger age than do those in Ohio or Indiana, where their age at marriage is very similar. Amish men tend to marry later in Ohio and Indiana than they do in Pennsylvania.

Not only are there variations between the three largest Amish settlements but there have been variations during the past forty years as well. Amish women today tend to marry at a younger age in Pennsylvania and Ohio than they did forty years ago. Only in Indiana do they marry at a slightly older age than they did in previous years. Amish men in Indiana get married at about the same age as they did forty years ago.

4. John A. Hostetler et al., "Fertility Patterns in an American Isolate Subculture," Final Report of National Institutes of Health Grant (NICHHD) No. HD-08137-01A1, 1977. For a substantial publication based on this report, see Julia A. Eriksen et al., "Fertility Patterns and Trends among the Old Order Amish," *Population Studies* 33 (July 1979). The study is one of several projects resulting from collaboration between Victor A. McKusick and his associates at The Johns Hopkins University School of Medicine and the author. The demographic aspects of the study incorporate the three largest settlements of the Old Order Amish in the United States, one each in Pennsylvania, Ohio, and Indiana.

5. These findings support those of earlier investigators, but this study for the first time measures fertility trends over time. Earlier works include Harold E. Cross and Victor A. McKusick, "Amish Demography," *Social Biology* 17 (June 1970): 83–101; and "Pockets of High Fertility in the United States," *Population Bulletin* 24 (December 1968).

Family Size. The average number of live births per Amish couple is seven. The Ohio Amish have the lowest average number of live births, while the Pennsylvania and Indiana Amish groups have the highest (Table 3). Since the Ohio Amish marry at a slightly older age, one would expect the number of live births among them to be smaller. Over a span of forty years, Amish family size has increased. The influence of modern medicine and better health care would seem to account for this trend. The percentage of childless couples has declined over the forty-year period, particularly in Pennsylvania and Ohio. As medicine has improved, infecundity has declined generally among the Amish as it has among all American women. It is not surprising that the rate of childlessness for the Amish is lower than that for the United States as a whole (4.4 percent compared to 7.5 percent),

Table 3
Trends in family size in the three largest Old Order Amish settlements

Births	Pennsylvania (Lancaster County and vicinity)	Ohio (Holmes County and vicinity)	Indiana (Elkhart County and vicinity)	Total
Number of live births (mean)				
Pre-1899	7.1	6.3	6.7	6.6
1899–1908	8.2	6.2	7.0	6.8
1909–1918	6.9	6.4	6.7	6.6
1919–1928	7.2	6.8	7.2	7.0
Percentage of childless couples				
Pre-1899	7.6	7.8	4.3	6.6
1899–1908	2.8	6.7	3.2	5.0
1909–1918	6.6	5.1	5.2	5.5
1919–1928	2.9	5.3	5.2	4.4
1929–1938	0.9	3.1	3.9	2.6
Percentage of couples with ten or more children				
Pre-1899	28.7	21.0	21.8	22.7
1899–1908	33.5	14.7	25.6	21.2
1909–1918	25.2	19.1	16.7	20.0
1919–1928	25.7	19.4	24.5	21.8

Note: Includes first marriages only; number of live births is for women married before the age of forty-five.

since among the Amish there is no divorce and children are wanted. Hutterites have an even lower rate, 2.9 percent.[6]

The consistently high growth trend among the Amish is indicated by the proportion of couples who have ten or more children: 21.8 percent. The percentage is higher in Pennsylvania than in Ohio or Indiana, probably in part because of the younger age of women at marriage in Pennsylvania. This rate is still only half that reported for Hutterites, 48.2 percent.[7]

The Marriage Season. Among the Amish, as in many agrarian societies, it has been the custom to marry after the crops are harvested. The marriage involves a two-day period of preparation and festivity for both sets of relatives, to say nothing of the longer period of preparation on the part of the bride's family. Weddings are accommodated into the community's schedule most suitably after the summer's work is over, from October to December.

The preferred months for marriages are November and December. The tendency to marry in these two months is most marked in Pennsylvania. Here 92 percent of all marriages occur during these months as contrasted to 41 percent in Ohio and 34 percent in Indiana. Marriages in Ohio and Indiana also take place in January, February, and March. Second marriages or remarriages often occur during the "off season" because they do not require the same degree of community involvement and festivity as do first marriages.

By observing the marriage calendar over time, one can see that the Pennsylvania Amish have consistently concentrated their marriages in November and December. Marriages in Indiana have occurred consistently in January, February, and March. Marriages in Ohio have declined in number in January but have tended to spread into March, April, and May.

Variations between Communities. Reasons for the differences among the three largest settlements (Ohio, Pennsylvania, and Indiana) with respect to age at marriage, family size, and marriage season are not obvious without some knowledge of the customs of each community. These differences can be explained in part by economic and cultural factors. The Ohio and Indiana Amish have much in common. Penn-

6. Joseph W. Eaton and Albert J. Mayer, *Man's Capacity to Reproduce: The Demography of a Unique Population* (Glencoe, Ill.: The Free Press, 1954), p. 31, where the figure is erroneously given as 3.4.

7. Ibid. Amish persons having the largest number of living descendants have been noted. Moses Borkholder of Indiana (d. 1933) had 554 living descendants. Eli S. Miller of Delaware (d. 1977) had 494.

sylvania stands out consistently as distinct from the Midwestern settlements. The Pennsylvania Amish have a long tradition of living on highly productive soils. They also have smaller acreages than the Midwestern Amish, but they farm more intensively.

Work organization and the motivations for work may be other factors associated with family size. The Lancaster County Amish people, it is recognized, are more aggressive and work with greater rigor than the Midwestern Amish. Their horses, for example, reflect better breeding and trot faster than those in other Amish communities. Motivation for high economic productivity may not have a direct relationship to family size, but there appears to be an indirect one.

The discipline that limits the kind of modernization in the three communities is different. Although the three are in "full fellowship" with one another, and visiting officials may preach in the others' communities, the *Ordnung* that restricts farm technology is different in each region. The Lancaster churches have allowed some technological concessions, thereby permitting their young, aggressive farmers to stay on the farm. Power-driven farm implements are permitted if they are horse drawn. Dairy barns are equipped with milking machines, bulk tanks, and diesel-powered cooling systems. Incentives for hard work and motivation for staying on the farm appear to be maintained in this manner. The Midwestern Amish communities have relaxed some restrictions that symbolize greater individual convenience, such as the use of bicycles and store-bought clothes, but have been firm in opposing farm technology, which would yield greater profits and motivation for staying on the farm. In some Ohio regions where the districts have not permitted milking machines and improvement of farm technology, the younger men have given up farming. Instead, they have become carpenters, construction workers, or employees in small factories. Although they are still Amish members, the social structure and character of the Amish community have changed.

Population Growth and the Loss of Members. There is no indication that the Old Order Amish are reducing their growth rate by birth control. There has, in fact, been a slight increase in the rate of population growth over the past seventy years. The land area occupied by the Amish in Lancaster County, Pennsylvania, in 1940 was 150 square miles, compared to approximately 525 square miles in 1980 (see Figure 7). The number of church districts has increased dramatically (see Table 1). There were six districts in 1900, twenty-five in 1950, and sixty in 1979. The slow growth rate from 1910 to 1930 is accounted for by the formation of a division in 1911 that is today known as the Weavertown Amish Mennonite church.

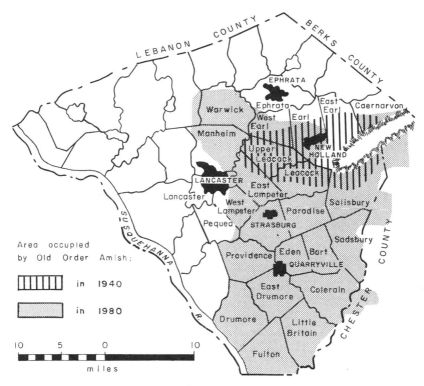

Figure 7.
Area occupied by the Amish in Lancaster County,
Pennsylvania, 1940 and 1980

What is the extent of membership loss and what influence does it have on population growth? In a comparative study of Old Order Amish and former Amish family size, it was found that the number of children born per former Amish family was significantly reduced.[8] For example, the average number of live births among Old Order Amish (using the birth cohort for 1900–1909) was 7.2, but among former Amish who had Amish parents it was 4.0, and among former Amish whose parents were not Amish, 3.9. We have evidence, therefore, that leaving the Amish is coupled with a reduction in family size. To be Old Order Amish is to have a large family.

What proportion of the children born to Amish parents do not remain with the Amish church? With genealogical records and the

8. Eugene P. Ericksen, Julia Ericksen, and John A. Hostetler, "The Cultivation of the Soil as a Moral Directive," *Rural Sociology*, in press.

help of Amish informants this information was computed for Lancaster County, Pennsylvania. The overall rate of loss to the Old Order from 1880 to 1939 was 22.4 percent (Table 4). There is considerable variation, however, when ten-year birth cohorts are examined. The rate of loss was high prior to 1880, had declined by 1919, and rose again by 1939. It is impossible to compute a comparable loss rate for the current period because persons born since 1939 have not yet completed their families. The land pressures in recent years, it appears, are making an impact, but not to the extent that a high rate of population increase is impossible.

The decision to remain or leave the Amish church is related to the economic problems of setting up a farm or Amish business. Leaving often occurs after marriage and at the beginning of the child-bearing stage. Buying land for the adult children, or loaning them money or collateral, visiting them frequently—in short, aiding them in a variety of socially supportive ways—is recognized by the parents of married children as an important obligation. In a study of dropouts it was found that instead of occurring at random, they were clustered in certain families. Generally, the fathers of sons who left the Amish were themselves not earning money from farming. Where the fathers were physically disabled, the children frequently did not learn farming and thus did not remain Amish.

Other Unique Characteristics. Several unusual features of the Amish population have been revealed in studies of genetic diseases among the

Table 4

Proportion of Old Order Amish offspring who are not members of the Old Order Amish church, Lancaster County, Pennsylvania

Birth cohort	Number of cases	Percentage not Amish
Pre-1880	612	28.1
1880–1899	599	19.5
1900–1909	400	22.0
1910–1919	645	17.9
1920–1929	917	21.7
1930–1939	450	23.7
Total	3,623	22.4

Note: The percentages are based on the number of offspring who were born Old Order during specified periods but who are not members of the Old Order Amish. The percentages do not indicate the trend for the present population or for those born after 1939. I wish to thank Eugene P. Erickson for assistance in compiling these data.

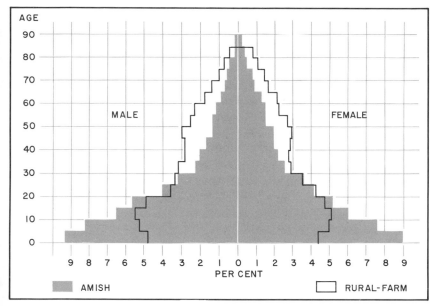

Figure 8.
Age and sex profiles of Amish and rural-
farm populations, Elkhart and Lagrange counties,
Indiana

Amish.[9] The Amish have the highest twinning rate of any known
population (15.3 per 1,000 live births among the Ohio Amish families,
21.1 among the Indiana Amish). The natural rate of population
increase per year for the Ohio settlement has been computed to be
3.019 percent, or a doubling of the population every twenty-three
years.[10]

As seen in Figure 8, the age and sex composition of the Amish
population is strikingly different from that of the rural-farm population of the rest of the United States.[11] The differences reflect the

9. Victor A. McKusick, *Medical Genetic Studies of the Amish: Selected Papers,
Assembled, with Commentary* (Baltimore: The Johns Hopkins University Press,
1978); see especially chap. B1, "Amish Demography," by Harold E. Cross and
Victor A. McKusick (pp. 29–47).

10. The reported rate for Hutterites is 4.1265, or a doubling every sixteen years;
see Eaton and Mayer, *Man's Capacity to Reproduce*, p. 44.

11. Based on the U.S. Census of 1970 and the *Indiana Amish Directory* (1970).
Adapted from and published with the permission of Richard F. Hamman, "Pat-
terns of Mortality in the Old Order Amish" (Ph.D. diss., The Johns Hopkins
University, 1979).

social and cultural patterns of Amish life. A comparison of Amish to non-Amish rural-farm populations shows that the Amish population has only half the proportion of people over the age of sixty-five that the non-Amish population has, and that for persons under twenty years of age, the Amish proportion is double that of the rural-farm population. The age distribution of a society has important economic and social consequences. As long as the Amish population over the age of sixty-five remains relatively small, the financial problems at retirement are less acute than in the general population. Although the Amish are opposed to receiving Social Security payments from the government, the difference in age structure is a sound reason why benefits payments are more critical to the general population in America than to the Amish. The profile for the Amish does not reflect a low birth rate during the Depression, just before the sudden increase in the birth rate of 1940, as does the profile for the non-Amish population.

LEADERSHIP

Among the Amish—who have rejected coercive powers as worldly, and who cultivate humility, obedience, and simplicity—the selection of leaders is a delicate process. One who is chosen to lead must not seek either authority or power, but in reality he is placed in a position where he must exercise both. In selecting candidates for office, members look for humility and evidence of good farm and family management. Any forwardness or idiosyncratic tendencies are quickly detected. An Amishman would never prepare himself for the vocation of preacher, nor would he announce that he felt called of God to prepare for the ministry, as members of evangelical groups do. Attending a seminary would be a sure sign of worldliness and reason for excommunication, for it would indicate a loss of humility and the development of ego. The Amish method of using nominations for election and selection by lot helps to prevent manipulative power and personal ambition. Authority is widely distributed among all members so that no single leader or subgroup will have all the power. Leaders are expected to help the community in the redemptive process but never to stand in the way. We will return to the method of selecting leaders after their functions have been described.

The organization of the Amish community is focused in the church district. The elected officials are called *Diener* (literally, "servants", and each district has three kinds. Traditionally they are the *Voelliger-Diener* ("minister with full powers" or "bishop"; *Diener zum Buch* ("minister of the book" or "preacher"; and *Armen-Diener* ("minister to the poor" or "deacon"). These three positions in the dialect are *Vellicherdiener, Breddicher,* and *Armediener.* Each district ideally has one bishop, two ministers (also called preachers), and one deacon.

The bishop is the leader of the congregation and its chief authority. He administers the rites of communion, baptism, marriage, and excommunication, and reinstates "backsliders" to membership in the church. He supervises the choice of ministers by lot and performs ordination services. He announces disciplinary action against violators of the church *Ordnung.* The bishop is responsible for obtaining "the voice" or vote of the church in decision-making processes where such unanimity is required. The bishop also takes his turn at preaching *es schwere Deel* "the main sermon" at regular meetings for worship. Upon his ordination, the bishop is given the following lifetime charge:

(1) So in the name of the Lord and of the church the complete ministry or bishop's office is entrusted to you (2) that you shall declare the Lord's bitter suffering and death and observe the breaking of bread and wine (3) and if there are people who wish to unite with the church then you shall teach them the Christian faith and baptize them (4) and, with the counsel of the church, you shall punish the disobedient and sinners and when they manifest repentence and conversion you shall receive them again with the counsel of the church (5) and when there are brethren and sisters in the church who wish to marry you shall unite them according to the godly ordinance (6) and you shall also ordain ministers with full authority [i.e., bishops] whenever it is necessary and requested in the church (7) and when you become old and weak you are to ordain a man after you in your place (8) and may the Lord strengthen you with his holy and good spirit through Jesus Christ Amen.[12]

In addition to the bishop there are typically two preachers in every district who are expected to preach when their turn comes. The bishop and preachers must be able to stand before the congregation, without notes or the aid of books, and admonish the people in the ways of God. On those Sundays when there is no preaching in his own district, an ordained person may, if he wishes, visit other districts. Very frequently visiting preachers are called to preach if they are "in full fellowship" with the host district. Preachers also assist the bishop in distributing the wine and bread at the communion service, held twice each year. Upon ordination, the preacher is given the following

12. The passage is a translation from German sources; see John Umble, "Amish Ordination Charges," *Mennonite Quarterly Review* 13 (October 1939): 236.

charge: "So in the name of the Lord and of the church the ministry to the book is committed to you that you shall preach [expound the Word], read, and pray with the church, help protect good and help punish evil."[13]

A deacon is given the following charge at the time of his ordination:

So in the name of the Lord and of the church the ministry to the poor is committed to you that you shall care for widows and orphans and receive alms and give them out with the counsel of the church and if there are brethren and sisters who wish to enter the marriage state then you shall serve them according to the godly order and read the scriptures for the ministers when it is requested and shall serve with water in the baptismal ceremony if you are requested to do so.[14]

The deacon assists regularly in the worship service by reading a chapter from the Bible. The reading is usually prefaced by voluntary admonitions on his part. As his title (*Armen-Diener*) implies, he is charged with looking after any needy members or widows by disbursing funds collected for that purpose. At the special service for baptism he pours the water into the cupped hands of the bishop over the applicant's head. He looks after the cups, bread, and wine for the communion service and keeps the chalice filled during the service. He assists in the foot-washing service, which accompanies the communion, by preparing the pails of water and the towels. He becomes a kind of housekeeper working behind the scenes on ceremonial occasions. Two other important functions are assigned to the deacon: he is often sent by the bishop to secure information about transgressors, and he conveys messages of excommunication. As an adjuster of difficulties between members, he has the most difficult task of the three ordained officials. This distasteful task is perhaps offset by the more pleasant function of the *Schtecklimann*, or "go-between," in the arrangements for marriage. When a couple wishes to be married, the deacon is so informed by the prospective bridegroom. The deacon then inquires whether the bride's parents approve. *Wann nix im Weg schteht* ("if nothing stands in the way"), he informs the bishop, who announces the intended marriage to the congregation about two Sundays before the wedding.

In some instances, a bishop must supervise two or three districts. This is usually considered a temporary arrangement until the additional district becomes large enough to warrant its own bishop or

13. Ibid., p. 237.
14. Ibid.

until the right person is found for the position. A bishop generally may not move from one district to another if dissatisfaction has been expressed within his district. Preachers and deacons are perhaps freer to do so, but in any event, not without prior consultation with the districts involved. The ordained positions of bishop, preacher, and deacon are appointments for life unless persons holding them are "silenced" for misbehavior or transgression.

Each church district is a small, face-to-face human group, a self-government unit. There is no central organization or conference to interpret policy for the local group. The bishop is the chief authority figure within his district. In large settlements of Amish, however, there is informal consultation among the different bishops in the area. In Lancaster County the ordained officials meet for consultation before communion in the spring and fall. At these meetings questions of discipline or causes for disunity also are dealt with. The oldest bishop generally is the one who calls these ministers' meetings and presides at them.

Each district conducts its own business and deliberations following the preaching service after nonmembers, including children, have been dismissed. The decision-making processes are of the patriarchal-democratic type. While a bishop may exercise considerable power in making a decision, he is subject to *der Rat der Gemein* ("the counsel or vote of the church"). For example, a member is excommunicated and put under the ban only by the vote of the baptized members, men and women. He is reinstated by vote. The deacon assists poor members only when authorized by the vote of the congregation. Although the ideal of congregational rule is maintained, the ordained persons usually bring a suggested course of action to the assembly for a vote. The ordained persons meet for the *Abrot* ("ministers' council") at every preaching service. This regular meeting provides occasion for any of the ministers to discuss circumstances that they feel should be brought to the attention of all. Any matter brought before the congregation must first be discussed by the ministers. Furthermore, a plan of procedure must be agreed upon by all the ministers before the problem can be brought before the members' meeting.

The selection of leaders is a serious occasion and is marked by an orderly sequence of communal rites.[15] As stated earlier, the individual

---

15. An insightful treatment of the ideal patterns of Old Order leadership is that of Sandra Lee Cronk, "Gelassenheit: The Rites of the Redemptive Process in Old Order Amish and Old Order Mennonite Communities" (Ph.D. diss., University of Chicago, 1977), esp. pp. 77–92. Amish practices and exceptions to the rule are discussed by David Luthy in "A Survey of Amish Ordination Customs," *Family Life* (March 1975): 13–17.

does not determine whether God is calling him to a position. Instead, the "voice" of the church, followed by the lot, constitutes the call. Admonitions to lowliness of mind are assured, but there is no provision for training or education, and no pay. All candidates are selected from within the district; no outsider is ever brought into the congregation and ordained to be bishop, preacher, or deacon. A bishop is selected from among the ordained preachers. Once chosen by lot, it would be a bad omen for him to refuse the calling. For most preachers it is a traumatic experience. A few have suffered mental relapses. In speaking of the newly ordained, a preacher's wife observed that "it makes them sickly, for as long as five years sometimes."

In anticipation of an ordination the congregation is urged to examine its corporate life. If there is a feeling of unity among the members, the signs are right for an ordination. If there is a spirit of friction or misunderstanding, an ordination may be delayed. Once an ordination is considered appropriate, the bishop will announce the proposal and set a two-week period for serious deliberation and prayer, usually prior to the biannual preparatory service (*Attningsgmee*). All members must agree to an ordination.

Most bishops try to have the ordination service on the day of communion. Since communion is a high point of the group's spirituality, the selection and installation of a leader is fitting for this time. Following the communion service the assembly remains for the ordination. The presiding bishop reminds all of the seriousness of the occasion and reads a Biblical passage dealing with the qualifications of the ministry (I Tim. 3). He may comment on the qualifications but will likely not mention what is taken for granted, that the nominee for the office must be married and must be a man. The ordained men go to an adjoining room. All the members file past a door (or window) that is slightly open, and whisper the name of a person qualified for the office to the deacon. The deacon relays the name to the bishop, who writes down the name and keeps an accounting of the votes. In order to be a candidate, a person must receive at least two votes. In some districts three votes are required. Those who support the rule of three votes hold that trickery can be eliminated. (A husband and wife or two persons cannot plot to nominate a certain person out of spite.) Members, including husbands and wives, are not to discuss among themselves whom they will nominate. The ministry does not make nominations.

In the event that only one person receives all the votes, that person will be ordained without using the lot. There have been as many as sixteen names in the lot, but typically there may be from four to eight nominations. Once nominated, a person may not withdraw his name for any reason. In Lancaster County, Pennsylvania, candidates for bishop must have children who are members of the Amish church, or at least one child must be a member, and all the children must be in good Amish standing. One consequence of this rule is that there are no young bishops. Among the Swiss settlements of Adams and Allen counties in Indiana, only two nominees for minister, those with the most votes, are placed in the lot.

Using the lot as a method of selection is based upon the example of the apostles in selecting a successor to Judas (Acts 1:23–26). The instrument used in the lot, a small piece of paper, frequently contains a Bible verse. Two verses used are: "The lot is cast into the lap; but the whole disposing thereof is of the Lord" (Prov. 16:33). "And they prayed and said Thou, Lord which knowest the hearts of all men, show whether of these two thou hast chosen" (Acts 1:24). The piece of paper is placed in a hymnbook. Additional hymnbooks are selected to equal the number of candidates. The books are rearranged and placed on a table or bench. Following a prayer by kneeling, the candidates are asked to select a book. The bishop then examines the books until he finds the one containing the lot. When he finds the book containing the slip of paper, he repeats the man's name so all can hear.

The man "struck" by the lot is asked to stand for the charge placed upon him by the bishop. If it is a bishop who is chosen, he is asked to kneel and the hands of two presiding bishops are placed on his head as the charge is given. The bishop greets the newly ordained man with a handshake and the Holy Kiss. Noticeable at these services are sobbing and weeping, a ritual mourning, expressing deep sympathy for the heavy burden placed on the chosen servant. All the members are enjoined to encourage and pray for the newly ordained brother as the assembly is dismissed. Even though the community might view the man chosen as less qualified than another nominee, the members are satisfied with the result because the choice was God's.

PATTERNS OF INTERACTION

As indicated earlier, the charter requires that a definite line of separateness be maintained between the Amish church and the world. Complete geographic isolation is neither sought after nor considered desirable. There are necessary and preferred patterns of interaction. Interaction patterns are governed by the way in which the Amish

classify groups according to their shades of worldliness. Thus interaction with other Amish, with Mennonite and related groups, or with
other religious groups is different from interaction with the world. In
his home district the individual member is surrounded by a series
of "fences" or lines of separation which must be learned and observed
with great discretion. Since the interaction within the Amish community was discussed earlier, we will consider here the social and
economic aspects that require interaction with the world.[16]

Separation from the world has some practical consequences. By
keeping the clock either slower or faster than worldly time, the Amish
effectively stay out of step with the world. When daylight-saving time
first went into effect, the Amish resisted it, saying "the world is
changing too fast anyway." Thus, when the world changes to daylight-
saving time, the Amish keep "slow" time. When the world changes
to standard time, the Amish set their clocks a half-hour ahead. Not
only is this puzzling to the outsider, but it introduces an ambiguous
element between the Amish community and the rest of the world.
Whether practiced consciously or unconsciously, it is an effective
means of insulating the Amish from the activity and structures of
the world. In keeping appointments with an Amish person the outsider must make sure whether the appointment is for "slow" or "fast"
time. Within the Amish community the time frame is understood, but
when interacting with the outside world the Amishman abides by
worldly time.

The Amish community is knit together by community patterns of
consumption, employment, and the sharing of capital and mutual
aid. In order to survive, the Amish must have a strong economic
base, and this base must attract and hold the children. Many of the
farms today are not completely self-sufficient, and additional income
is necessary. The family members are the labor force. An Amish boy
will work on his father's farm until he is trained. After this he may
hire out to relatives, or if he works outside the Amish community, in
construction work or in a small factory, he will typically work with
other Amish persons. After the age of twenty-one, his earnings are
his own, and he will save money for a down payment on a farm.

Amish girls tend to hire out at a younger age than boys, and a girl
will typically live with the Amish family she works for. Her earnings
are returned to the family. The family will then return some to her
for spending money and clothes, spend some for family needs, and

16. For insights on interaction patterns, I am indebted to Gertrude E. Huntington, "Dove at the Window: A Study of Old Order Amish Community in Ohio"
(Ph.D. diss., Yale University, 1956), pp. 230–396.

save some for her until she reaches the age of twenty-one. An Amish girl will occasionally work for an English family or in a small business, frequently as domestic help or as a cleaner, and in a capacity where she will not meet the public. Working away from home is usually enjoyed, and being a hired girl is considered part of growing up.

There is a certain amount of neighboring with rural people who are not Amish. An English neighbor may invite the Amish housewife to a kitchenware "party." She may or may not accept. The Amish will assist English neighbors with harvest or in an emergency when they are not likely to visit socially. Attending movies, farm conventions, banquets, or fairs is off limits, but parents and children will often plan a trip to the city to visit the zoo; since the animals are creations of God, they may be seen and enjoyed. The visiting schedule of the Amish is always full, and most complain that they are behind in their visiting, so that there is no time left to visit with the English people.

The Amish do not send representatives to interchurch gatherings or conferences. Individuals may contribute to various non-Amish causes such as the local volunteer fire company or send contributions to agencies for the relief of human suffering, but they do not meet with other churches to discuss common problems or programs of action.

Almost every Amish family knows and interacts with English friends on a long-standing basis. These meetings occur at random. They are cherished by the Amish as well as by the English. Because the interaction is so infrequent, and the physical distance between them so great, the rule of separation is not violated. A German-speaking tourist, for example, halted an Amish carriage and asked for directions. The German-speaking couple was invited to the Amish home and later visited the Amish preaching service. The tourist was a physician from New York City and supplied the couple with medical advice and prescriptions. The two couples enjoyed each other's company over a period of fifteen years.

The Amish turn to the outside world for markets for their farm products. All their grain and hay is fed to livestock. They are sensitive to price fluctuations and follow market reports carefully. They produce far more than they can consume or sell to other Amish people, and their major income is from dairy, livestock, and other products sold to outside markets. They will ship their produce to a distant place if the market is better there.

They buy staple foods such as sugar, salt, and flour and other groceries in village stores. They will not buy canned goods, for many Amish families preserve up to 500 quarts of fruit, meat, and vegetables yearly. Some Amish will buy yard goods and other items regularly from mail-order catalogs and from salesmen who come to their door. Various farm magazines subscribed to by the husband may influence dairy or poultry production and ways of marketing, but they have little influence on the home. Needless conveniences, luxuries, and fancy clothing bear the stigma of worldliness.

CHAPTER 6

Agriculture and Subsistence

Soil has for the Amish a spiritual significance. As in the Hebrew account of Creation, the Amish hold that man's first duty is to dress the garden. That is, he is to till it, manage it, presumably for pleasure and fulfillment (Gen. 2:15). Second, man is to keep the garden, protecting it from harm through the use of his labor and oversight. Ownership is God's (Ps. 24, "the earth is the Lord's . . ."), while man's function is looking after it in behalf of God. The parables in the New Testament also indicate to the Amish that man is the steward of an absentee landlord. His stewardship is continuous, ending in a day of reckoning when man will be called to give an account.

This view of land implies not only sustenance but to a certain extent pleasantness, attractiveness, and orderliness. Man has limited dominion. He has power over animals and vegetation, but land also must receive proper toil, nourishment, and rest. If treated violently or exploited selfishly, it will yield poorly, leaving mankind in poverty. The Amish view contrasts sharply with the so-called western world view, which sees man's role as an exploiter of nature for his own advancement and progress. To damage the earth is to disregard one's offspring.

The primary occupation in Amish society is farming, and if farming is not possible, then occupations of a rural or semirural character are preferred. The Amishman does not farm to make money. On the contrary, he works and saves so that he can farm and support himself and his family with minimum interference from the world. The advice

117

of Menno Simons in the sixteenth century expresses the sentiments of the Amish people today: "Rent a farm, milk cows, learn a trade if possible, do manual labor as did Paul, and all that which you then fall short of will doubtlessly be given and provided you by pious brethren."[1]

This description of Amish agriculture will focus on three elements: agricultural skills in the Amish tradition, the differences in resources and soil productivity among Amish settlements (especially between Lancaster County, Pennsylvania, and the other settlements), and farm management strategy within the bounds of Amish values. The involvement in nonfarming enterprises will conclude the chapter.

THE EUROPEAN AGRICULTURAL HERITAGE

Distinctive Amish and Mennonite agricultural practices began when the Anabaptists were disfranchised politically in their homelands and were forced to devise new farming methods in previously unproductive regions and climates. In the seventeenth century they practiced rotation of crops, the stable feeling of cattle, meadow irrigation, used natural fertilizers, and raised clover and alfalfa as a means of restoring soil fertility.[2] Instead of "mining the soil" and moving away when fertility declined, they devised ways of restoring productivity.

Model Farmers. The Anabaptists' reputation for skilled farming was established as a result of their success in Alsace. Soon after the Amish were expelled from the valleys of Markirch (Sainte Marie-aux-Mines) in 1712, the local rulers wrote to the French authorities complaining about the economic setback caused by the expulsion. The Anabaptists, they said, "apply themselves with extraordinary care to agriculture, an occupation for which they have admirable knowledge."[3] They transformed "sterile and dry lands" into "tillable lands and the most beautiful pastures of the province," the report said. The Anabaptist farmers cleared land, created meadows and pastures, and combined farming with cattle-raising. In addition, what the princes liked was that they paid their taxes "with utmost exactness and without compulsion."[4]

1. Menno Simons, *The Complete Writings of Menno Simons* (Scottdale, Pa.: Herald Press, 1956), p. 451.
2. Ernst Correll, *Das schweizerische Täufermennonitentum* (Tübingen: Mohr, 1925), p. 101.
3. Jean Séguy, "Religion and Agricultural Success: The Vocational Life of the French Anabaptists from the Seventeenth to the Nineteenth Centuries," trans. Michael Shank, *Mennonite Quarterly Review* 47 (July 1973): 182.
4. Ibid.

Contemporary observers claimed they could identify Anabaptist farms by taking a look at the cultivated hills and fields. This favorable image of the Anabaptist farmer persisted well into the nineteenth century.

Having been denied the ownership of land, the Anabaptists combined animal husbandry with intensive cultivation on the farms they rented. The family occupied a farm, and the entire household worked there. Married children sometimes lived with the family in anticipation of renting the farm. The parents would retire early and help their children financially, spending their later years assisting the young couple to take over. In this manner all the generations of a farming family were integrated by agricultural labor. Improvement of the soil and the dwellings was made feasible by long-term leases. The principles of family occupancy, family entrepreneurship, continuity, and motivation for labor were combined in the management of the farms.

Tenants in Europe, Owners in America. In Europe the Amish acquired the skills of clearing the land and methodically improving the soil by using manure from their herds and by using mineral fertilizers. Deposits of gypsum were mined and processed in kilns for spreading on the land. A three-year system of crop rotation typically consisted of (1) wheat; (2) rye, barley, and clover; and (3) potatoes, carrots, and turnips. Livestock farming was one of the most distinctive features of Anabaptist farmers. Additional pastures were rented, some in the high mountains of the Jura and Vosges ranges. The Bernese Anabaptists are credited with introducing many varieties of clover to France and Germany, as well as with cross-breeding new strains of cattle. Milk provided a good income, and in the eighteenth century the Anabaptists were renowned for making cheese. In the nineteenth century, Jacques Klopfenstein, a successful Amish-Mennonite farmer of Belfort, was awarded a gold medal by the Agricultural Society in France for his outstanding achievements as a model farmer. He was also the founder of an almanac, *The Anabaptist Farmer by Experience.*[5] The tradition of good farming took shape in Europe.

The Amish who came to Pennsylvania showed a strong preference for family-sized holdings on soils that were suited to relatively intensive kinds of cultivation. Furthermore, they wanted to combine agriculture with a preferred way of life, and not farm primarily for commercial

5. Séguy, *Les Assemblées anabaptistes-mennonites de France* (The Hague: Mouton, 1977), pp. 503–7. See also John H. Yoder, "Mennonites in a French Almanac," *Mennonite Life* 7 (July 1952): 104; and Ernst Correll, "Master Farmers in France," ibid. 6 (July 1951): 61. Klopfenstein's almanac was issued from 1812 to 1821.

The Anabaptist farmer (cover
of an Alsatian almanac, 1841)

gain. The Amish, like other Germans, sought limestone soils, which
they believed to be superior. The Amish presence on nearly all the
limestone soils in southeastern Pennsylvania today is due not to the
original land selection but to a process of resettlement. Although
the Amish located on large acreages, ranging from 100 to 400 acres at
the outset, they gradually reduced their holdings to what could be
managed with family labor. Plantations or large-scale farms did not
interest them.

The agricultural practices of the two major immigrant groups of
the colonial period—the English-speaking Scotch-Irish and the Swiss-
Germans—were very different.[6] The Scotch-Irish were more mobile,
"forever changing," and were inclined to move to cheaper land.[7] The
Swiss-Germans, who settled in communities, soon made the land valu-
able. Pennsylvania's famous physician and citizen Benjamin Rush
observed that the German farms were "easily distinguishable from

6. For a discussion of the different traditions, see Richard H. Shryock, "British
versus German Traditions in Colonial Agriculture," *Mississippi Valley Historical
Review* 26 (June 1939): 39–54.

7. Walter M. Kollmorgen, "The Pennsylvania German Farmer," in *The Pennsylvania German*, ed. Ralph Wood (Princeton: Princeton University Press, 1942),
p. 33.

those of others, by good fences, the extent of orchard, the fertility of soil, productiveness of the fields, and luxuriance of the meadows."[8] This observation is still apt today, for the Amish have maintained these characteristics, as can be seen when driving through the Amish farmlands. Moreover the Germans (and Amish) tended to secure the farms of the Scotch-Irish after they had moved and to improve and restore the depleted land.[9]

SOIL PRODUCTIVITY AND MANAGEMENT

In the upkeep of the soil, equipment, and buildings, and of themselves as well-groomed persons, there is diversity among Amish communities. The public image of the Amish as "picturesque Americans," or as "a solid culture that produces happiness as well as abundance," appears to be based upon the Lancaster group. No Amish communities excel this group in outward appearance: newly painted farm buildings, abundant gardens, and tidy children. Other settlements that reflect fine farm upkeep are those in Somerset and Mifflin counties in Pennsylvania. Settlements in the Midwest vary a great deal from farm to farm and from one settlement to another.

Lancaster County, Pennsylvania, is the oldest continuously occupied farming area of the Amish in the United States. The soils in Lancaster and Chester counties in Pennsylvania are considered among the most productive in the United States, indeed in the world.[10] There is a long-established belief among Pennsylvania Germans that limestone soils are superior to other types of soil. Many Amish today prefer limestone, believing that the soil has greater depth and will hold moisture better than other soil types. It appears that eighteenth-century settlers found native limestone and alluvial bottom lands superior in fertility. Through experience, however, it has been found that high productivity does not depend on limestone soils. Soil types that were earlier considered inferior are today as productive as limestone lands.[11] The

8. Benjamin Rush, *An Account of the Manners of the German Inhabitants of Pennsylvania, Written in 1789*, with notes added by I. Daniel Rupp (Philadelphia: Samuel P. Town, 1875), pp. 11–12.

9. According to Fletcher there were many farms with depleted soil in Pennsylvania by 1730. See S. W. Fletcher, *Pennsylvania Agriculture and Country Life, 1640–1840* (Harrisburg: Pennsylvania Historical and Museum Commission, 1950), p. 124.

10. James T. Lemon, *The Best Poor Man's Country: A Geographical Study of Early Southeastern Pennsylvania* (Baltimore: The Johns Hopkins Press, 1972), pp. 39–40.

11. Ibid.

Newly cut grain on an Amish farm in Lancaster
County, Pennsylvania

application of humus and fertilizers in recent years, and the uniform
climate and vegetation pattern over a long period of time, have reduced the differences in fertility among soil types. Wheat, one of the
most profitable crops in the eighteenth century in Lancaster County,
has been largely replaced by corn.

Diversity Preferred. Amish farmers today, as in earlier periods, prefer
general farming or a diversity of crops. They do not raise one crop to
the exclusion of other crops, nor do they cultivate a single crop for
cash income. The Amish raise corn, oats, rye, a variety of hay crops
for feeding, and a great number of vegetables for home consumption.
Where possible, their farms incorporate woodlands and pasture lands.
They maintain a careful plan of crop rotation, usually a three- or
four-year system including a corn, grain (oats, wheat, or barley), and
hay crop, often alfalfa or clover. An abundance of animal manure,
crop rotation (especially the use of a clover or hay crop), and lime
and commercial fertilizers are used to maintain soil fertility and
conservation.

The Amish farm typically maintains livestock of various kinds—

horses, dairy cattle, beef cattle, hogs, poultry, and sheep. Orchards earlier occupied an important place on most farms. A diversified vegetable garden and the production of milk and cheese, fruit, cereals, and meat have aided the Amish in maintaining a high degree of self-sufficiency. Farming is a means whereby the Amishman has maintained himself and members of his family on the land while supporting the religious community of which he is a part.

Land Pressure. With the passing of each decade and the invention of new machines, farm management has not been easy. Population pressure has forced the Amish to have smaller farms, to engage in specialized farm enterprises, and to carefully assess the influence of technology on their community life. These changes are accentuated in Lancaster County, Pennsylvania, where land prices have skyrocketed.[12] In 1850, farms in the county averaged 92.1 acres. The average size declined to 62.7 acres by 1954 but increased to 84 acres by 1978. Today Amish farms range from 30 to 120 acres. The Amish subdivided their farms in order to keep the young generation on the farm and they also bought farms from the non-Amish as they became available. When land prices fluctuated in the Midwest, the Amish in the East remained calm and were not inclined to speculate with their homesteads. As the Lancaster Amish community expanded, land prices in the center of the community rose consistently.[13] One reason for this is that the Amish (and other plain people) prefer to live together in reasonable proximity, and their horse-and-buggy mode of travel limits the distance they wish to travel from their own kin.

Diminishing farm size and the high price of land, together with price fluctuations during critical periods (in times of war and depression), have forced the Amish into more intensive land use. The result is an increase in specialized farming, raising crops for cash (e.g., tobacco, potatoes, tomatoes, peas), and the production of fluid milk and poultry. The Amish in Lancaster County prepare their seedbeds more intensively than do the Amish in the Midwest. With the rapid adoption of herbicides there has been a great reduction in cultivation for the purpose of weeding.

12. For historical data on Amish agriculture, I am indebted to Walter M. Kollmorgen, *Culture of a Contemporary Community: The Old Order Amish of Lancaster County, Pennsylvania,* Rural Life Studies no. 4. (Washington, D.C.: U.S. Department of Agriculture, 1942), pp. 23–55. See also Ira D. Landis, "Mennonite Agriculture in Colonial Lancaster County, Pennsylvania," *Mennonite Quarterly Review* 19 (October): 254–72.

13. Prices in the center ranged from $300 to $400 per acre and on the margin about $200 in 1938. The highest price paid for farmland in 1978 was $6,400 per acre for 47.5 acres.

Cash Crops. It appears that the Amish in Lancaster County started raising tobacco soon after the tobacco industry was established there, probably about 1838.[14] They, along with a group in Saint Mary's County, Maryland, are the only Amish in the nation who grow tobacco. In 1929, 85 percent of the Amish farmers in Leacock Township, Lancaster County, grew tobacco. It is estimated that about one-third of the Amish farmers raise tobacco today. A good crop will yield 2,000 pounds per acre. Tobacco has helped to maintain the high land values. In more recent years whole milk and tomatoes have replaced tobacco as the main source of cash income. When a new silo is built, it frequently signifies a change from tobacco to milk production. Agricultural reports show a striking correlation between the areas occupied by the Amish (and Mennonites) and the regions where tobacco is grown. Experts do not regard the Lancaster County soil as superior to adjacent lands for raising tobacco. The explanation for this correlation is that the Amish have the necessary labor and realize substantial returns. In winter, when there is little other farm work, stripping tobacco is a way to keep the family occupied with a good income-producing activity.

Raising potatoes is a potential source of cash income but is difficult for the Amish. Although potatoes grow well and yield from 400 to 450 bushels per acre in Pennsylvania, raising potatoes requires special machinery and heavy labor input and presents marketing problems. Large wholesale outlets will not bother with growers who have small acreages. Harvesting, processing, and delivering potatoes requires speed, and farmers without a telephone have a poor chance of competing with the automated market.

Amish in the Cornbelt. The Midwestern Amish communities have larger acreages than do the Lancaster County Amish.[15] They too have been compelled to develop more intensive land use and specialized farming. The Indiana Amish supplemented their income with mint

14. Fletcher, *Pennsylvania Agriculture*, p. 165. For additional discussions, see J. Winfield Fretz, "The Growth and Use of Tobacco among Mennonites," *Proceedings of the Seventh Annual Conference on Mennonite Cultural Problems* (1949), pp. 87–100; and idem, "Plain People Grow Big Tobacco," *Farm Quarterly*, Autumn 1951, p. 60.

15. Average acreage of the Nappanee, Indiana, Amish farms is reported to be 104, and for the non-Amish in the same region 261 acres. See Alice Rechlin, "The Utilization of Space by the Nappanee, Indiana, Old Order Amish: A Minority Group Study" (Ph.D. diss., University of Michigan, 1970), p. 89. In Illinois the acreage differences are greater: Amish, 85; non-Amish, 500. See John A. Dukeman, "Way of Life of Illinois Amish-Mennonite Community and Its Effects on Agriculture and Banking in Central Illinois" (The Stonier Graduate School of Banking, Rutgers—the State University, New Brunswick, N.J., 1972), p. 43.

farming until it was no longer profitable.[16] The presence of Amish in the center of a rich corn- and soybean-producing area in central Illinois brings into focus the values of the Amish farmers in contrast to highly mechanized farmers. Here the economic costs of remaining Amish become obvious. In central Illinois, one man with modern machinery and a small amount of part-time help can operate a 600-acre farm. Because of high labor costs he does not raise livestock. The Amish farmer, who has on the average 85 acres, concentrates on livestock production, and raises a diversity of crops, does not fit into this intensive, single-crop income-producing activity. A banker who compared the financial trends of the Amish with those of commercial grain farmers concluded that the Amishman is "reaching a serious financial crisis which can be traced to his way of life."[17] He pointed out that over a ten year period the non-Amish farmer had increased his net worth 48 percent over the Amish farmer, and predicted that with continued large families, the Amishman's plight "cannot improve, and will gradually worsen."[18] From an economic point of view, commercial grain production calls for large units, competitiveness, high production, low labor costs, and access to large amounts of capital and management expertise. Some economists would argue that the Amish are "holding back the economy of the area" and therefore are a liability to the economic growth of the region.[19]

Although the Amish may be reproved for holding down their income potential by refusing to increase the scale of their operations, they cannot uniformly be held accountable for low unit yields. When the Amish were urged by a U.S. government spokesman following World War II to use tractors to produce "more grain for starving peoples of the world," Amish bishops issued a firm response. They asserted that they were growing more food with horse power than their neighbors were with tractors. Every member of their group had already plowed every square inch of his farm (by April), they said, while the neighbors with tractors were just starting to plow. "Our hearts go out to hungry

16. For further reading, see James E. Landing, "An Analysis of the Decline of the Commercial Mint Industry in Indiana" (M.A. thesis, Pennsylvania State University, 1963); and Melvin Gingerich, "Mint Farming in Northern Indiana," *Mennonite Life* 4 (October 1949): 40–41, 46.

17. Dukeman, "Way of Life of Illinois Amish-Mennonite Community," p. 52.

18. Ibid. These views are those of a banker and appear to lack solid supporting data. The Amish realize many noneconomic values.

19. Ibid., p. 57. It is reasoned that if the Amish (in Illinois) would produce on their 20,000 acres at the same rate as the non-Amish farmers, the economy would rise. "This would also put more funds in the area for the banks to loan which would in turn increase the GNP of the area" (ibid., pp. 57–58).

Natural sources of energy. *Left*: Water wheel in a meadow stream generates power for the family farm. *Right*: A single water wheel provides power for five nearby farms.

people wherever they are," they stated, and plowing and planting take place "right under the fences."[20]

Moderate Energy Demands. Crop yields vary among Amish communities. One study reports that for some farm enterprises the Amish use less energy than the other farmers to achieve the same yields.[21] It also appears that Amish farmers have more moderate yields than fully mechanized farmers. In Illinois the Amish corn yield ranges from 70 to 130 bushels per acre in contrast to mechanized farmers, who report 150–170 bushels.[22] The Illinois Amish do not use commercial fertilizer, use much less nitrogen, and maintain wider rows in the field than do non-Amish farmers.

20. The spokesman was Clyde A. Zehner, Chairman of the Pennsylvania Agricultural Adjustment Administration; see *New York Times*, April 28, 1946, p. 12. Before "factories in the field" made some average county figures so high, average farm incomes in counties where large proportions of "plain people" lived were the highest in the nation, according to Charles P. Loomis, former Senior Social Scientist, U.S. Department of Agriculture.

21. W. A. Johnson, Victor Stoltzfus, and Peter Craumer, "Energy Conservation in Amish Agriculture," *Science*, October 28, 1977, pp. 373–78. The study appears to be inconclusive, but the variations among Amish communities are impressive. In this study energy is defined as "the amount of food energy produced per unit of energy spent to produce it."

22. Victor Stoltzfus of Eastern Illinois University, Charleston, provided the data on yields.

The Amish are moderate consumers of fossil energy. They make limited demands, using natural power resources to support their way of life. In many communities the Amish use windmills. In Lancaster County they harness streams in their meadows by constructing water wheels. In other regions the water supply is piped from a reservoir in the mountains. The Amish purchase less fuel, fertilizer, feed, and equipment than do commercial farmers. To buy an automobile, one Amishman said, would mean milking five more cows. One wonders how many more cows it would take to maintain and operate an automobile and a farm truck or to furnish the farm dwellings with electrical appliances. While the Amish have worked out a satisfactory way of life with simple technology and have avoided major financial crises, their experience can scarcely serve as a model for wide application in the modern world. Farmers of today would not appreciate the constraints of manual labor and the austere consumption pattern.

When tractors were first introduced on American farms, the Amish rejected them with the comments, "They don't make manure" and "They ruin the land." Most outsiders accepted the comment as a harmless rationalization, and yet no in-depth study has ever been made of the conservation factor in Amish horse-powered farming as contrasted to tractor farming. Even with horse power, the Amish with few exceptions are first to have their fields plowed and seeded. Tractor farmers have greater convenience, more choice as to when they will till the land, and can get the job done faster than the Amish. Tractors, Amish farmers say, compact the land, which results in reduced yields. Amish farmers who have bought land from the non-Amish have noted that the soil begins to work easier after the third year. The land also begins to drain better, so it is ready for plowing earlier in the spring. Plant roots penetrate the soil better and crops survive better during periods of drought where the soil structure has not been destroyed by compacting. The Amish are more systematic than commercial farmers in getting waste plant material back into the soil.

Amish farmers must make a concerted effort a maintain adequate horse power for field and road. Normally a farm operator will have six draft horses and one or two light horses for road transportation. In every large Amish settlement there are several horse dealers, both Amish and non-Amish, who either raise or deal in horses. Amish farmers make it a point to attend auction sales to transact business. Those who do not buy or sell will nevertheless attend in order to keep abreast of trends, prices, and the thinking of their respected peers. The joking, storytelling, intense sharing, and comradeship among those who buy and deal in horses is a coveted experience. Belgian and Persian horses are common breeds among the Amish.

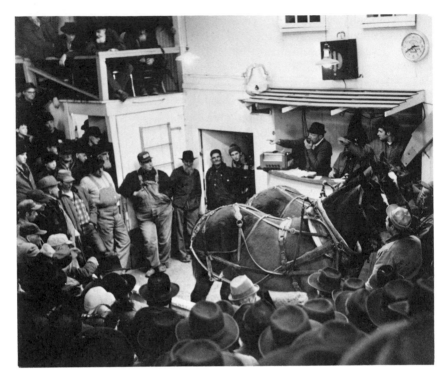

Each spring Amish farmers assess the adequacy
of their horse power for the agricultural season.
Horse auction, Kidron, Ohio.

Young horses are shipped from the Western states to the eastern
regions, but the Amish also maintain breeding stock. Many farmers
in Lancaster County prefer mule power for field work, believing that
mules eat less and have greater endurance. Such preferences appear
to vary among farmers, as others consider mules to be more obstinate
than horses. In Ohio, raising mules was forbidden by an Amish
Ministers' Conference in 1865 on the grounds that it was "improper
to mix the creatures of God such as a horse and donkey by which mules
arise, because the Lord God did not create such in the beginning."[23]

Modernization and Amish Rules. Many Amish dairy herds produce
well, but according to experts the Amish are not the highest producers.
The names of many Amish farmers do not appear on the published

23. Harold S. Bender, "Some Early American Amish Mennonite Disciplines,"
Mennonite Quarterly Review 8 (April 1934): 97.

lists of producers, because they do not wish "to be advertised." Although they may have pure-bred herds that produce well, and may use artificial insemination, the Amish are not permitted to have registered livestock. Members are discouraged from belonging to dairy herd associations. Not only would membership "draw too much attention from the world," but there are more informal reasons. Excessive record-keeping and "paper work" is one deterrent. The kind of manipulation required for competitive production appears unethical to the Amish.

The Amish have made some adaptations to modernization, but they will not allow technology and convenience to run away with their family and community. The Old Order Amish try to maintain a balance between the discipline of the Amish community and modernization. The more the rules are believed to be incompatible with survival, the greater the likelihood of a high rate of membership loss or the breakup of the community. Lay leaders know the costs of being Amish, and the sacrifices of maintaining the simple life and loyalty to the church-community. Those who are unwilling to make the sacrifices will accommodate, and most large settlements have several progressive Amish (Mennonite) churches with which former Amish members affiliate. The pressures for greater economic gain imply more modernized machines, and these impulses are felt by the bishops. Bishops moderate the sentiments for and against change and may propose a course of action, but not all, as outsiders think, dictate the rules. Should disagreement occur among the ministers on how much modernization should be permitted, a new settlement may be formed. The most orthodox groups will typically disallow hay bailers, bulk tanks, and milking machines.

During the past twenty years the Amish have introduced many changes in their farming practices.[24] The agitation for tractors that was keenly felt twenty years ago has subsided. Today, the Amish say, farms in Lancaster County, Pennsylvania, are too small for tractors. Improved production also has relieved the pressure for tractor farming. With better seed and greater productivity, corn cribs are too small, even though the acreage is only half that of years ago. The traditional method of crop rotation has changed. Today corn is grown on the same soil in successive years. Crops are planted in contoured terraces to conserve the soil and moisture, a practice scorned by the Amish as "book farming" thirty years ago.

24. Gideon L. Fisher, *Farm Life and Its Changes* (Gordonville, Pa.: Pequea Publishing Co., 1978). In this book a Lancaster County Amish farmer discusses changes in farming over a period of a century or more.

In Midwestern settlements, where tractors with steel wheels are allowed for field work, Amish farmers are faced with additional problems. Local laws forbid vehicles with lugs on asphalt- or oil-surfaced roads. Several Iowa Amish attempted to solve this problem by outfitting their tractors with pneumatic tires. They were excommunicated and soon formed a Beachy Amish congregation. The Old Order Amish kept their tractors off the surfaced roads or secured detachable rims that covered the steel lugs.

Although the Lancaster County Amish have often been considered very conservative and a trusted source of authority in religious matters by other Amish communities, they have also been the most innovative in economic affairs. They have been more exposed to industrial life and are keenly aware of the pressures of worldly economic competition. Ordained leaders from all the districts in Lancaster County meet twice annually to discuss the welfare of the community. Many divisions have undoubtedly been avoided by this moderation of some of the more delicate pressures felt by the separate districts. Lancaster County Amish farmers are permitted to have milking machines and bulk milk tanks operated by diesel engines, but pipes connecting the milkers to the bulk tank are not accepted.[25] These adaptations allow farmers to realize a stable income from selling whole milk. Also permitted are gasoline-driven motors on horse-drawn farm implements. Amish repair shops will buy old tractor equipment, adapt it for horse-drawn use, and mount a gasoline motor on the chassis for operating a hay mower, rake, crimper, baler, corn picker, and stalk shredder. Although self-propelled grain combines are used by the Kansas Amish, the Pennsylvania Amish have not adopted any combines.

Whether the Lancaster Amish can have it both ways (conservative in doctrine and enterprising in farm management) may be an open question. In the past this appears to have been the case. When the Midwestern churches needed ministerial advice in doctrinal matters, they called upon the Lancaster Amish. The Lancaster Amish often felt that the Midwesterners were too lax in shunning. The Midwestern Amish chided the Easterners for raising tobacco and for their modern farm machinery. Presently the Lancaster Amish are seldom called upon in matters pertaining to arbitration, for their bulk tanks and farm practices symbolize for the very conservative Western Amish a credibility gap.

25. A period of experimentation with bulk milk tanks, cooled by diesel and air power, resulted in their adoption in Illinois in 1972 when the bishops informally agreed not to oppose or endorse the innovation. See Victor Stoltzfus, "Amish Agriculture: Adaptive Strategies for Economic Survival of Community Life," *Rural Sociology* 38 (Summer 1973): 196–206.

Mules are preferred by many Amish in Pennsylvania,
for they are capable of enduring hot weather
and are believed to eat less than horses do.

Amish communities that have firmly opposed milking machines and
the modernization that is required if one is to sell fluid milk have
probably declined in their economic capabilities as well as in their
ability to provide an incentive for the young men to remain on valu-
able farms. In Geauga and Trumbull counties in Ohio, the young
who saw no prospect of securing a farm started working in local
factories in large numbers. Many Amish farmers who cannot meet the
standards for selling fluid milk sell their milk at a reduced price to
cheese factories. The cheese industry is well developed in certain Amish
communities.

One difficulty encountered with the commercialization of the farm
has been the traditional observance of Sunday as a holy day. Believing
that Sunday is a day on which there should be no business transactions, the Amish have consistently refused to allow their milk to be
picked up by trucks on Sunday. Most firms agree to pick up the Sunday
milk on Monday morning if proper cooling and storage are assured.
Even so, milk companies in most instances will not take on producers
unless they agree to sell milk seven days per week. This has often
resulted in a serious problem for the Amish. They have sought other

Gardens and roadside markets, common in most
Amish communities, help supplement
the family income.

ways to solve the problem, some by separating the milk and selling
cream, and some by taking an inferior price. The adoption of bulk
tanks and cooling systems has alleviated this problem in communities
where they are permitted. Government subsidy checks, whether for
milk or other parity purposes, are refused on the grounds that money
not earned in honest toil cannot be accepted in good faith. Some feel
that the acceptance of such checks would lead to complications and
perhaps binding obligations to the government.

Saving for a Farm. The Amish save their money to buy additional
farms for their sons and daughters, and they spend much on the upkeep and improvement of their farm dwellings. Many forms of assistance are given to young married couples who are struggling to establish themselves as farmers. Lending money at a low interest rate to
fellow members is common. Land is nearly always kept in the family.
Although Amish inheritance practices differ little from those of other
people, a son is more likely to get the home farm than is a daughter,
and a younger son is more likely to get the family farm than is an

older son. The aging parents usually reserve the privilege of domicile on the farm as long as they live.

Many farm households receive a modest income from selling their products at roadside stands. Often the sales go to regular or favorite customers. A sign at the end of the lane announces goods and produce for sale: potatoes, violets, lawn chairs, dry goods, honey, lumber, brooms, home-baked bread, greenhouse plants, and vegetables in season. For many years the Moses Stoltzfus family sold ice cream cones on their farm. When the sign at the end of the lane brought too many customers, it was removed, but the flow of traffic scarcely diminished. The farm also became a distribution center for Amish-made rugs, quilts, hand-painted dishes, and other handicrafts. This practice, however, is hardly typical of Amish farms.

Traditionally, a young Amishman who climbed the agricultural ladder in Lancaster County began as a laborer or farm hand on an Amish farm, then became a one-third-share tenant, then a one-half-share tenant, next a cash tenant, and finally a farm owner.[26] This has changed somewhat because fewer farms are available. It is now possible to go from laborer to owner very quickly when a farm does become available. Amish boys do not go to high school and therefore may begin as farm hands at the age of sixteen. Their accumulated savings are invested in livestock or machinery. Renting usually precedes buying a farm. Amish boys who receive considerable assistance from their parents will obtain a farm in their own name a few years after they are married. Securing enough land for farming has been a continuous problem in most Amish communities. With many non-Amish youth leaving the rural community for the city, however, there has been a tendency for the Amish to buy the "English" farms as they become available. The Amish have also founded new settlements when land has become difficult to obtain in the older settlements.

Moderation and Austerity as a Life Style. The Amish make a reasonable living with horse-drawn implements and limited acreages. At the same time, they refuse to accept direct cash subsidies from the government for any reason. How do they manage? Artificial income would introduce dangers for them in several respects. They fear the moral consequences of accepting government aid, which is for them an erosion of conscience and motivation. This rejection is also related to their desire to avoid the spiral of rising income, rising costs, and an even higher standard of living. Having achieved a certain plateau of

26. Based on the Kollmorgen study with revisions; see Kollmorgen, *Old Order Amish of Lancaster County*, pp. 42–45.

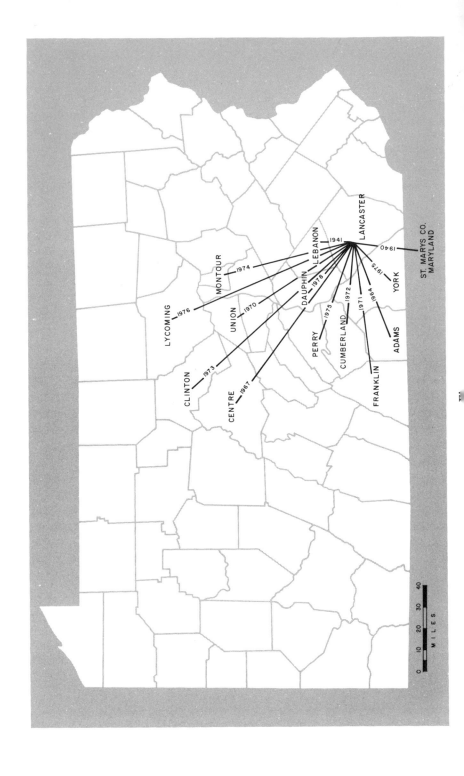

LANCASTER

1941

1940

1975

YORK

ST. MARYS CO.
MARYLAND

1964

ADAMS

1971

FRANKLIN

1972

CUMBERLAND

1973

PERRY

1978

DAUPHIN

LEBANON

MONTOUR

1974

UNION

1970

LYCOMING

1976

CLINTON

1973

CENTRE

1967

MILES

0 10 20 30 40

living, the Amish do not want to be forced to live on a higher standard than what they feel comfortable with. In a recent election year when presidential candidates were promising a higher standard of living, an Amish patriarch remarked: "Striving for such a high standard of living is nothing more than the worship of the golden calf." The Amish simply want to avoid unrealistic inflation of their income-producing capacity.

Moderation and contentment are only part of the secret of survival. Making a reasonable living also involves knowing how to teach children to work and to enjoy the positive aspects of family labor in various contexts—among members of the farm family, within the extended family and religious community, and between the generations. Stable social traditions support this type of resource, which the Amish are quick to point out "cannot be bought with money." Fertile soil with proper intensive cultivation, good seeds, and adequate fertilizer is an important asset. Even after all these techniques are used, barnyard manure still makes a difference in getting the highest possible yields.

Given their high rate of population growth and the limited supply of land in their larger settlements, the Amish face three basic choices. One is to establish new settlements where farming can be realized, but where the land is less productive than that in the larger settlement. The response of the Lancaster settlement in forming new settlements elsewhere in the state has been dramatic since 1967 (see Figure 9).[27] A second alternative is to find nonagricultural occupations while maintaining the Amish pattern of living. This is not easy, and many recognize that it is not a satisfactory solution. A third alternative is to continue to subdivide existing acreages and farm the land more intensively. This might mean expanding dairy and poultry enterprises, but at the cost of buying rather than growing most of the feed. Some Amish sons have persuaded their fathers to sell them small plots of ground on which they have built mechanized poultry or hog barns. This arrangement permits the father to be at home with his children, a necessary element in Amish family life. Those who buy farms at a high price and pay a high interest rate (from $20,000 to $40,000 per year) also find it necessary to construct mechanized hog, poultry, and dairy barns to assure an adequate overall income. All these alternatives are developing in the larger settlements. Some farms are beginning to appear like agrifactories, and the traditional image of a peaceful, quiet countryside is disappearing.

27. For a history of this development, see Rachel K. Stoltzfus et al., *History and Directory of the Old Order Amish of Brush, Nittany, and Sugar Valleys in Centre and Clinton Counties, Pennsylvania* (Gordonville, Pa.: Pequea Publishers, 1979).

WORK AND SEASONAL ACTIVITIES

Generally speaking, the Amish set high standards of work for themselves. Work patterns take on the characteristics of ritual. Communities will differ, however, in the tempo of work and in motivation. Few Amishmen will hire an outsider to do farm work. Outsiders, they say, "do not know enough and they don't work hard enough." When Amish boys were drafted as conscientious objectors during wartime, the Amish said, "If we must hire outsiders, who want to work short hours and do things in a slipshod way, we'll all go broke."[28]

The Work Day. The day begins between four and five o'clock in the morning with milking and other chores. Depending on the number of adults and the number of cows, this daily chore may take from one to two hours. Breakfast may be served at five-thirty during the busy season of the year. During plowing, seeding, and harvest, field work receives the major amount of attention. In the wintertime, feeding the livestock and hauling manure are the most important tasks. The noon meal is served in some areas as early as eleven o'clock. After a short rest period the teams again go into the fields. Supper is served between four and five o'clock. The daily chores of feeding and milking must then be done, if not by the working men, by the women, who often help out during the busy season. This permits the men to go back to the fields and work until dark. Bedtime comes at nine o'clock or a little later.

The Amish workweek ends abruptly on Saturday evening. Outside of the busy season, Saturday is reserved for stable-cleaning and preparing for Sunday. Only the animals and the essential routine chores are taken care of on Sunday, which is a day of rest. On Sunday the major activity is the preaching service, except on alternate Sundays, when visiting is common.

The Yearly Work Cycle. Not only are the agricultural activities of sowing and reaping reflected in the annual calendar, but so too are leisure activities and customs, which tend to become associated with the different seasons of the year. Such seasonal activities vary from one settlement to another. The account that follows is based upon the yearly cycle of the Lancaster County, Pennsylvania, Amish and with the exception of the raising and harvesting of tobacco, would apply generally in other areas.[29]

28. Kollmorgen, *The Old Order Amish of Lancaster County*, p. 43.
29. Ibid., pp. 45–46.

In January the few farmers who have not finished stripping their tobacco complete this work. If steers are being fed, they receive considerable attention at this time so that they will be ready for market whenever prices seem favorable. January, like December, is a popular month for the slaughtering of meat animals. If the winter is mild, apple trees may be trimmed. Frequently visiting is done during this month.

Harnesses are mended and greased in February. If there is little frost in the ground, the farmer begins to plow. During February and March, when the curtain is about to rise on the farming season, farmers who wish to retire or to restrict their operations hold farm sales. Items offered for sale are usually confined to farm machinery, stock, harnesses, household items, and stored grains and feeds, but the farm itself may also be sold. These sales are not only business occasions but also important social events, providing men, women, and children with an excellent opportunity for visiting. School teachers find it expedient to dismiss youngsters when sales take place in the neighborhood. Many sales are attended during March even if there is no need to buy anything.

Manure is hauled during the winter months when the ground is frozen and dry. When the ground is in the right condition, the fields are plowed. Clover or alfalfa seed is sown in the wheat field. Liming requires the attention of some farmers during March. Tobacco beds are sterilized with steam, and some vegetables are planted in the garden.

Potatoes are planted as early in April as possible. Tobacco seed is sown in the sterilized tobacco bed. Farmers who raise oats seed the crop during this month. The ground is well prepared for corn planting. The garden receives much attention and is prepared with manure from the barn.

Corn is generally planted during the last week in April or early in May. Toward the end of May, the young tobacco plants are transplanted into the field. More vegetables are planted in the garden. If the growing season begins early, the cultivation of corn and potatoes is begun in the last part of May.

The transplanting of the young tobacco plants continues until some time in early June. These plants are transplanted at intervals so that the crop will mature over a period of time and can be harvested properly at the right moment. Corn and potato cultivation begins or continues in June, and the operation is repeated from four to six times. Potatoes need to be sprayed about once a week.

In early June, alfalfa is ready for the first cutting. A week later, the mixed clover and timothy hay may be ready to cut. This crop is generally cut only once, whereas alfalfa is usually cut three times in the season. As soon as the hay is dry it is baled in the field and stored in the barn. None of it is stacked outside. Barley is generally ready to be harvested by the middle of June. Wheat, if it matures early, is ready to be harvested late in June. The grain is shocked in the field after it is cut so that it will dry thoroughly. After a few days it is threshed in the field or in the barn. The straw, however, is nearly always stored in the barn, whether baled or unbaled.

In July, the cultivation of corn and potatoes continues. The whole tobacco patch is thoroughly hoed early in the month and this work engages the entire family. The threshing of small grains begins early in July and may continue into August. Threshing is accompanied through work exchanges with extended families or neighbors.

August is often a slack month, and family members may travel to visit distant relatives. Sometime in August, tobacco-cutting gets into full swing and the alfalfa is ready to be cut the second time. Some early potatoes are dug in the latter part of this month.

September and October are very busy months. In September the silos are filled and the cutting and storing of tobacco is completed, safely ahead of an early frost. During the latter half of the month potatoes are dug and the corn is harvested. Each of these tasks generally requires several days of work. Farmers begin to buy steers for winter feeding. The digging and marketing of potatoes may well last until the middle of October.

The corn harvest may continue until November. Generally the corn stalks are shredded during November to be used as feed. In this month some farmers will remove loose stones from the fields. December is the month for stripping tobacco, and the feeding of steers may receive attention. A good deal of butchering is done. Visiting is frequent and perhaps prolonged. With few exceptions, weddings are reserved for November and December.

THE NONFARMING AMISH

Although the Amish excelled as agriculturalists in Europe, not all made their living from the land. On early American tax lists some were listed as operators of grist mills, sawmills, and quarries, and others were tanners, brewers, and blacksmiths. It appears that the sturdy farming tradition emerged in America with the second generation of Amish. When some of the family members worked as hotel-keepers, clerks, and merchants, the conservative elements of the Amish regrouped and clung to farming as the approved form of occupation. Other occupations were extremely limited from about 1830 to 1950.

In the wintertime, sleighs are used to transport families
to church and social gatherings.

Every newly married couple of able body and mind was expected to
operate a farm.

Squeezed Off the Farm. With the increasing cost of farmland, the
diminishing availability of good farmland, decreasing farm profits,
and the increase in costs of farm machinery and supplies, the occupational pattern has changed. Prior to 1954, Amish fathers in Lancaster
County, Pennsylvania, who sought employment in factories were
excommunicated. Today many are forced to work off the farm or to
move to areas where cheaper farmland can be secured. The proliferation of nonfarming employment occurred very rapidly after 1960. The
economic pinch the Amish find themselves in today is different from
that of a half-century or more ago. The old assumption that "if you

Home of an Amish factory worker. Only a small barn
is needed, for the horse and carriage.

work hard you can survive" is no longer true. No matter how hard a
family works, today man and wife cannot assure their sons and daughters that they will be able to start housekeeping on a farm.

This conclusion is based on a series of interviews with two generations of Amish farmers who were asked, "What are the most serious
problems confronting a young Amishman wishing to enter farming?"
The overwhelming responses from the younger men were "money
problems," "finding a farm," "high interest rates," and "the high cost
of equipment."[30] Responses from the older farmers were no different.
They stressed the important function of a father, as in this comment:
"The only way he can start is if his father helps him, moves on and
works, and maybe he can buy it for half of what his daddy paid. If he
hasn't a daddy to help he just can't get started."

Today roughly half of the Amish households are engaged in farming
(Table 5). Of the three main settlements, Ohio has the largest per-

30. Eugene P. Ericksen, Julia A. Ericksen, and John A. Hostetler, "The Cultivation of the Soil as a Moral Directive: Population Growth, Family Ties, and the
Maintenance of Community among the Old Order Amish," *Rural Sociology*, in
press.

Table 5
Occupations of Amish household heads in the Pennsylvania,
Ohio, and Indiana settlements

Type of occupation	Pennsylvania (%)	Ohio (%)	Indiana (%)
Farming	49.5	41.3	49.0
Farming and second occupation	0.7	2.3	9.1
Farm laborer	1.7	0.1	—
Nonfarming	34.6	44.8	36.0
Retired	7.9	9.5	3.2
No information	5.6	1.1	2.7
Number of household heads	2,034	2,680	1,360

Sources: Pennsylvania Amish Directory (1973); *Ohio Amish Directory* (1973); *Indiana Amish Directory* (1970).

centage of nonfarmers. Very few of the Amish household heads work as farm laborers. Single men, if they are the sons of farmers, typically work on the farm of their father or on another Amish farm.

Diverse New Occupational Patterns. A large proportion of the non-farming Amish work in shops and trades within the Amish community as carpenters, cabinet-makers, carriage-makers, blacksmiths, harness-makers, and lumber workers. Traditional occupations that are useful to the Amish community but do not involve group participation are butcher, sheep-shearer, shoe repairman, broom-maker, beekeeper, plumber, horse-trainer, bookbinder, tool-sharpener, orchard-grower, and carpet-maker.

Since about 1960, newer occupations have emerged, as indicated in the Amish *Shop and Service Directory*, which covers the major communities.[31] The listings include accountants, appliance stores, bake shops, bee supplies, butcher shops, cabinet shops, canvas products, carpentry supplies, casting and foundry work, chair shops, cheese houses, clocks and watches, country stores, dry goods, engine shops, farm equipment and repair, farm markets, farm wagons, feeds, furniture shops, greenhouses, hardware, harness shops, hat shops, health food stores, machine shops, locksmiths, print shops, refrigeration, shoe shops, silos and silo equipment, sporting goods, tailor shops, tomb-

31. *Old Order Shop and Service Directory of the Old Order Society in the United States and Canada*, 1st ed. (Gordonville, Pa.: Joseph F. Beiler, Compiler, November 1977). The publication is, in effect, a "yellow page directory" without telephone numbers.

stones, upholstery, and woodworking shops. The shops are generally located on farms and are neither obvious nor advertised. On many farms such activities supplement farm income. It may well be that modest yields and a limited scale of farming are maintained by income from commercial activity.

The above list does not reflect some of the more specialized types of farming such as broiler-, chicken-, turkey-, and hog-raising. Another is raising trout fish. Many specialty shops and services have sprung up. They support the diverse needs of the community and also provide economic support and employment within the Amish community. The multiplication of these small enterprises, commensurate with the growth of the Amish population, is one of the most important changes that have taken place in Amish society in the twentieth century. Now that the Amish can buy and sell to members of their own faith and community, they are less dependent on the outside world for their survival. Interaction with the non-Amish is also thereby greatly reduced.

Work in Small Industries. Amish breadwinners who work for non-Amish employers constitute a small percentage in some Amish settlements and a large percentage in others. In 1970, less than 5 percent of the Amish household heads in Lancaster County, Pennsylvania, were employed by "English" employers. In the Nappanee community of Indiana 71 percent were employed by non-Amish.[32] The Amish prefer to work close to their homes, and with the trend toward ruralization of industry, they have begun to work in mobile-home industries or boat factories. Some of these industries locate near Amish communities in order to recruit the Amish as workers. Employment is seen as an opportunity to save money toward the purchase of a farm. Often an Amish father will work as a laborer until there are several children under the age of six in the family, and then he will make serious efforts to locate on a farm. There are, however, an increasing number who have no intention of locating on a farm.

A marginal occupation may be tolerated by the Amish community for good reasons, or as long as it does not constitute a direct threat. However, when an individual takes his marginal occupation seriously and wishes to excel by outside standards, the distress to the community may exceed toleration limits.

Amish Industries and Professions. When Amish enterprises become large—successful by worldly standards—they also constitute a liability

32. Rechlin, "The Utilization of Space," p. 79.

An Amish carriage shop

to the Amish way of life. The determination to maintain a small-scale operation dictates that if the business becomes "too large," it must be sold to an outside company. One Amish plant employs twenty-eight people, which is considered exceptionally large. Steel-fabricating plants or machine shops require large sources of energy, the movement of large quantities of raw material, and transportation. These plants may employ a diesel-powered generator as an energy source. For the delivery of their products they will hire non-Amish trucks and drivers. One Amish company makes, delivers, and installs farm silos, often within a radius of 200 miles. Another makes steel grain bins and delivers and installs them according to specification. The delivery and installation of these products requires a crew of several persons and from one to five days of labor. These firms typically hire trucks with non-Amish drivers and single Amish boys as laborers.

One of the new professions is school teaching. Most Amish children went to the public school thirty years ago, and thus the Amish did not train their own people for this vocation. Teaching is learned by apprenticeship and is normally done by single girls, never by a wife and mother of small children, and rarely by a married man who depends on teaching as a source of income. There are no Amish physicians, and there will be none so long as college training is forbidden. A few Amish girls have become practical nurses. Again, this activity is regarded as a calling to a community need and is not pursued as a means of livelihood.

Amish Prestige and Management Patterns. The measures of social class in terms of income, education, and material possessions have little relevance in Amish society. The goals of an Amish person are obedience, humility, and brotherly love, and thus are very different from those in a competitive and consumer-oriented society. Persons having the highest prestige in Amish society are those retired couples who have trained their children well, have remained with the Amish church, and have provided their children with farms. Such a retired couple will have very modest savings, a small income, but will have earned great respect in the Amish community. In a study of Amish fertility patterns no relationship was found between income and family size.[33] The best indicator of Amish prosperity is the labor-force activity of the male household head. The highest prestige activity is farming, the second highest is self-employment in a nonfarm business, and the lowest is day labor.

Among young Amish couples today, farming is a highly cooperative enterprise between husband and wife. Wives are frequently book-keepers and are in close control of the flow of information on finances. Farm schedules of harvesting, meal preparation, and sleeping often require adjustments involving a high degree of understanding and commitment. In this respect the Amish are a stable asset for land invest-ment firms. The Farm Credit Service in some areas regards its loans to Amish customers as a sound investment. If the crops are poor in one year, the Amish are not inclined to quit the farm, but will expect a better crop the next year. They will have family help, for farming is made into a family enterprise. A loan from a young operator's father or a relative, combined with a mortgage, will often make the differ-ence. Amish farm enterprises are not suddenly disrupted by divorce.

Good management is an important differentiating quality in Amish life. By "good management" the Amishman means acquiring a whole complex of attitudes and resources, including the following: willing-ness to start the day early, working cooperatively within the family, knowing how to include children in family work, maintaining punc-tuality and orderliness, having equipment and tools in place and in good repair, maintaining good livestock and horses, working the soil and harvesting at times when the weather is right and the labor is available, learning to preserve food and conserve material supplies and

33. Julia A. Ericksen et al., "Fertility Patterns and Trends among the Old Order Amish," *Population Studies* 33 (July 1979).

An Amish blacksmith replacing the shoes
on a road horse

energy, and not shrinking from the demands of hard work. When the members nominate persons for church leadership and ordination, they choose persons who they believe have practiced these values, and they invariably choose farmers rather than laborers and business persons.

The Amish themselves recognize differences in style and tidiness among family lines. Amish genealogists refer to a "classy style of life" and "an extraordinary trim impulse" in the Lapp family line in the Pequea Valley and the Mast family in Conestoga Valley.[34] This finery is manifest in well-bred horses, spacious and well-ordered farm dwellings, many varieties of flowers in the garden and at the windows in the home, regular sweeping of the walks and driveways with a broom, and decorative china in the cupboards. There are also family lines that have a reputation for being slothful. However, since unity and brotherly love are the overriding goals, these differences are deliberately minimized and generally not vocalized.

How do the Amish justify living on some of the highest-priced agricultural land in the nation? To them the land is a trust to be shared and to be made productive for the needs of many, and to be passed on to generations to come. By exercising a variety of skills, they attempt to improve the land before passing it on to the next generation. An enormous variety of practical skills is needed on their part

34. *The Diary* 10 (April 1978): 32.

to maintain this goal. Although the Amish might be classed as small-scale capitalists, they differ greatly from Max Weber's description of the Protestant ethic as expressed in Calvinism, Pietism, and Methodism.[35] As in Weber's thesis, manual labor, frugality, industry, and honesty are valued and may be useful, but unlike his thesis, such moral virtues do not give assurance of salvation for the Amish. Wealth does not accrue to the individual for his enjoyment, or for the advancement of his social standing, but rather enhances the well-being of the community. The Amishman is, in fact, embarrassed by outward signs of social recognition. Similarly, the Amish calling is not that of seeking worldly success, for the Amishman does not depend on material success for his sign or assurance of salvation. The ascetic limitations on consumption, combined with the compulsion to save, make possible an economic base for a people "in the world, but not of it."

35. Max Weber, *The Protestant Ethic and the Spirit of Capitalism* (New York: Charles Scribner's Sons, 1958), pp. 144–54.

CHAPTER 7

The Amish Family

❧

PROCREATION, nurture, and socialization are the major functions of the Amish family. The central role that the family is given in Amish culture can be illustrated in many ways. The family has authority over the individual not only during childhood but also during adolescence and later life. Certain loyalties to parents, relatives, and grandparents may change, but they will never cease. The size of the church district is measured by the number of families (households), not by the number of baptized persons. It is the families that take turns having the preaching service. Maps and directories of settlements made by Amish persons list the households and often the names of the parents, their birth and marriage dates, and the birth dates of the children as well. After marriage it is recognized that the most important family function is childbearing. Parents stress not their own individual rights but their responsibilities and obligations for the correct nurture of their children. They consider themselves accountable to God for the spiritual welfare of their children.

MATE-FINDING

The young Amishman's choice of a wife is limited or conditioned by his value system. He must obtain a partner from his own Amish faith, but not necessarily from his own community. Because of minimum contact with Amish young people of other communities and states, marriages in the large settlements have for the most part taken place within the immediate community. The choice of a mate is also governed by the rules of the church. First-cousin marriages are taboo, while second-cousin marriages are discouraged but do occur infrequently. Forbidden in Lancaster County is marriage to a "Swartz" cousin—that is, to the child of a first cousin.[1]

There are certain exceptions to the rule that marriage must be endogenous with respect to group affiliation. It is always permissible to marry into a more orthodox affiliation if the more liberal party joins the conservative group. Young people intermarry freely among Amish districts and settlements that maintain fellowship with one another.

The occasion that provides the best opportunity for young people to meet is the Sunday evening singing. The singing is usually held at the same house where the morning preaching was held. The youth from several districts usually combine for the singing. This occasion provides interaction among young people on a much broader base than is possible in the single district.

On Sunday evening after the chores are done, the young folks make preparations for the singing. The young man puts on his very best attire, brushes his hat and suit, and makes sure that his horse and buggy are clean and neat in appearance. He may take his sister or his sister's friend to the singing, but seldom his own girl friend. If he does take his own girl, he will arrange to pick her up about dusk at the end of a lane or at a crossroad.

A singing is not regarded as a a devotional meeting. Young people gather around a long table, boys on one side and girls on the other. The singing is conducted entirely by the unmarried. Only the fast tunes are sung. Girls as well as boys announce hymns and lead the singing. Between selections there is time for conversation. After the singing, which usually ends formally about ten o'clock, an hour or more is spent in joking and visiting. Those boys who do not have a date usually arrange for a *Mädel* ("girl") at this time.

Although there are other occasions when young folks get together, such as husking bees, weddings, and frolics, the singing is the primary occasion for boy-girl association. Both the boy and the girl look upon each other as a possible mate. A boy or girl may "quit" whenever he or she pleases. The usual age for courtship, called *rumspringa* ("running around"), begins for the boy at sixteen, and for the girl between fourteen and sixteen. Secrecy pervades the entire period of courtship

---

1. The nickname "Swartz cousin" originated with Jacob Swartz, who was excommunicated for marrying Magdalena Stoltzfus (b. June 18, 1832). She was his "first cousin once removed" (the offspring of his first cousin).

Friendship groups offer the opportunity for meeting prospective mates. Courtship requires a spirited horse and usually an open (topless) buggy.

and is seldom relaxed, regardless of the length of the association. If a boy is charged with having a girl friend, he will certainly be very slow to admit it. Courting that cannot be successfully disguised becomes a subject for teasing by all members of the family.

Among themselves, young people seldom refer to their boy or girl friends by first name. The pronoun "he" or "she" is used instead. The terms *beau* and *Kal* ("fellow") are used in general conversation. The term *dating* is used, but has no dialect equivalent.

Besides taking his girl home after the singing on Sunday evening, the young man who has a "steady" girl will see her every other Saturday night. When Saturday evening comes, he dresses in his best; he makes little ado about his departure and attempts to give the impression to his younger brothers and sisters that he is going to town on business.

Before entering the home of his girl, he makes sure that the "old folks" have retired. Standard equipment for every young Amishman of courting age is a good flashlight. When the girl sees the light focused on her window, she knows that her boy friend has arrived, and she quietly goes downstairs to let him in. The couple may be together in the home until the early morning hours on such occasions. The clatter of horses' hoofs on hard-surface roads in the early hours of the morning is evidence of young suitors returning home.

The old way of spending time together was for a boy and girl to lie on the bed fully clad. The Amish have no uniform word in their speech for this practice, which to them in earlier times was very ordinary. *Bei-schlof* ("with sleep") is the term used in one area. In English this behavior pattern is known as bundling. It is an old custom, having been practiced in Europe and in early American colonies, especially in large, unheated houses. Unfortunately the subject has been exploited by pamphleteers and story writers. The practice has been sharply condemned by most Amish leaders, though it is defended by some. In the nineteenth century new settlements were started by families that wanted to get away from the practice. Those communities that assimilated most to the American society have sensed the misinterpretations of outsiders and thus tend to oppose the practice of bundling. Those groups that have consistently retained their traditional culture with its very rigid sex codes have been least opposed. The practice has disappeared without argument in other areas with the influx of modern home conveniences (living-room suites, etc.) and a wider range of social contacts with the outside world.

Mate-finding takes places in the confines of the little community rather than outside it. Conflict and casualties resulting from mismating are absorbed by the culture. Conflicts are less obvious here than in the

Newlyweds receive many gifts and substantial help
from their families in the process of establishing
a new home.

greater society. The wedding is a climactic experience for family and
community, and the families of both bride and bridegroom take an
active part in helping the newlyweds to establish a home.

It is an important task of the family to provide a dowry. Homemade
objects and crafts are the usual items. Furthermore, it is understood
that each person invited to a wedding will bring a gift for the new
couple. These tokens of friendship, which are usually displayed on the
bed in an upstairs bedroom, consist of dishes, kerosene lamps, bed-
spreads, blankets, tablecloths, towels, clocks, handkerchiefs, and small
farm tools.

The parents of the bride and bridegroom also provide furniture, livestock, and sometimes basic equipment when the couple moves into their home. For instance, one bridegroom, an only son, had the farm deeded over to him together with the farm machinery and livestock. The bride received from her parents a cow, tables, chairs, a new stove, dishes, bedding, and many other items. The dowry of the bride was in this case not unusual. All mothers by tradition make a few quilts and comforters for each child. These are usually made years in advance so that they will be ready when needed. One housewife made three quilts and two comforters for each child; she had seven boys and three girls. The wedding ceremony will be discussed in Chapter 9.

MARRIED-PAIR LIVING

Social roles are well defined within the Amish family. The force of tradition, religious teaching, and emphasis on the practical help to make it so. Family organization is strictly monogamous and patriarchal. Overall authority tends to belong to the father, but there are varying degrees of practice in specific families. In keeping with a biblical teaching (I Cor. 11:3), the man is the head of the woman just as Christ is the head of the church. The wife has an immortal soul and is an individual in her own right. Although she is to be obedient to her husband, her first loyalty is to God. In marriage husband and wife become "one flesh," a union which is terminated only with death. There is no provision for divorce. The wife follows her husband's leadership and example but decides as an individual whether she is ready for communion. In church council she has an equal vote but not an equal "voice." Should her husband sin to the extent that he is placed under the ban, she, like all members, will shun him. The husband would do the same if his wife were under "the ban." Important family decisions typically are joint decisions. The Amish wife participates actively in any decisions to move to a different locality, which may not be true of today's "corporation wife."[2]

Cooperation between husband and wife prevails in differing degrees, depending somewhat on the make-up of the personalities and their adjustment. The line of authority is not rigid, however, as an example will indicate. A man and his wife called at the home of a neighbor to see a bed that was for sale. He remained seated in the

2. An observation made by Gertrude E. Huntington in "The Amish Family," in *Ethnic Families in America*, ed. Charles H. Mindel and Robert W. Habenstein (New York: Elsevier Scientific Publishing Co., 1976), p. 307. I am indebted to Gertrude E. Huntington for assistance in clarifying the nature of family structure and roles in Amish society.

The married pair upholds community rules
and sets an example for the children.

buggy while she entered the house and inspected the bed. Undecided, and not willing to commit herself without the encouragement of her husband, she called him. After both had looked at the bed and pondered over the price, she said, "What do you think?" He replied, "You are the boss of the house." After a few gestures that indicated she approved of the purchase, he wrote out a check for the amount asked. ⌐ The wife is often consulted when family problems arise, and she exercises her powers in rearing the children, but her husband's word is regarded as final in domestic matters. She is her husband's helper but not his equal. An Amish woman knows what is expected of her in the home, and her attitude is normally one of willing submission. This is not to suggest that there are no exceptions, for the writer has known families where the wife exerted influence out of proportion to the usual pattern. In practice, the farm is the Amishman's kingdom, and his wife is his general manager of household affairs.

Property, whether household goods or farm equipment, is spoken of as "ours" within the family. In actuality, however, any transaction involving the sale or purchase of property is made through the husband or has his approval. Farms are usually owned jointly by husband and wife to ensure legal ownership in case of the death of the husband. In public affairs men are regarded as more fit than women for leadership. Banking, writing checks, and depositing money are done by both in many households. Women and men bid for household items at public sales. The experienced housewife generally has the authority to make decisions pertaining to the house, but husband and wife usually confer with each other before making any large purchases, and the considerate husband will consult his wife before purchasing any household item. The wife generally has a purse of her own that is replenished periodically by her husband for the purchase of household supplies, groceries, and clothing. When her supply of money is exhausted, she asks for more.

Major household expenses or anticipated medical expenditures are usually discussed mutually, and if the wife decides she would like to patronize a certain doctor, her husband is likely to consent. The husband, on the other hand, may purchase farm equipment or livestock without seeking the advice of his wife. The wife often keeps the income from vegetables or produce sold on the farm.

The extent to which the farmer aids his wife in household tasks is nominal. He helps on special occasions such as butchering and cooking apple butter, but he does not help in the routine preparation of food, nor does he wash dishes. At weddings, the men serve as cooks and table waiters with their wives. Guests at an Amish table are often addressed by the husband: "Now just reach and help yourselves."

The wife's duties include care of the children, cooking and cleaning, preparation of produce for market, making clothes for the family, preserving food, and gardening. Typically, washing will be done on Monday, ironing on Tuesday, baking on Friday, and cleaning on Saturday. There are no special shopping nights, as purchases are made in the village store during weekdays. Women and adolescent girls frequently help with the harvest of crops, especially cornhusking. In one family, each of the older girls manages a team of horses during the summer months. They plow the fields, cultivate the soil, and do the work of adult males. This is exceptional, however, since women are not generally called upon to help with the heavier jobs in farming. It is the woman who sees that the fences, posts, grape arbors, and frequently the trees about the farm buildings are whitewashed in the spring. The appearance of the lawn and the area surrounding the house is largely the responsibility of the wife, and she feels obligated to keep the inside as well as the outside clean and neat in appearance.

The wife aids the husband in chores that are not usually considered household tasks more than the husband helps his wife in household work. In one home, while the men and carpenters were remodeling the barn in anticipation of the oldest son's marriage, the mother arranged to have neighbor women and relatives come for a day to paint the barn's window sashes.

Gardening, except perhaps for the initial spading in the spring, is the sole responsibility of the wife. The Amish wife usually raises a large variety of edibles, often as many as twenty kinds of vegetables. She makes sure that there are plenty of cucumbers and red beets because they are part of the standard lunch at Sunday services. Typical Amish gardens abound with flowers. Some gardens have as many as twenty varieties. Order and cleanliness tend to be distinctive features of Amish gardening. Orchards are a part of the typical Amish landscape, and spraying, if done at all, is the man's job. More often than not, fruits are purchased from commercial sources because expensive equipment for spraying is considered too costly for a small orchard.

Almost all women's and children's clothing is made at home by the wife or her relatives. Food-processing consumes a large part of the wife's time. Meat-curing may be done by the husband, often at the suggestion and according to the plans of the wife.

With regard to the woman's role in religious services, the teaching of the Apostle Paul is literally obeyed: "Let the woman learn in silence with all subjection." In leadership activities, the woman is not "to usurp authority over the man." At baptismal service, boys are baptized before girls. Women never serve as church officials.

Amish parents try to be of one mind when dealing with their children and to discuss any differences between themselves privately and prayerfully. Marriage partners are taught to be considerate of each other and never to disagree in public.

PERSONAL RELATIONSHIPS

The personal relationship between husband and wife is quiet and sober, with no apparent displays of affection. The relationship is in striking contrast to the expectation of a romantic ideal expressed in popular American culture. Patterns of conversation vary among Amish mates, but terms of endearment, or physical gestures of affection, are conspicuously absent.

The husband may address his wife by her given name, or by no name at all. He may merely begin talking to her if he wants her attention. In speaking about his wife to others he may use "she" or "my wife," but rarely her given name. The mother of the family in like manner may refer to him simply as "my husband" or "he."

Irritation between mates is expressed in a variety of ways, but is conditioned by informally approved means of expressing dissatisfaction. As a rule, institutional patterns override personal considerations. Little irritation is observable among the Amish. Displeasure or disapproval is expressed by tone of voice or by gesture. The husband may express disapproval by complete silence at the dinner table, in which case the wife is left to guess what is wrong. The usual conversation may lag for several days before it is completely restored to a normal level. Harsh and boisterous talk between mates is rare.

Roles of the parents are defined in terms of traditional familial patterns and to some degree by kinship ties. The husband and wife are not only individuals connected by personal sentiments, but as members of a group must maintain the standards and dignity of that group. This tendency toward the consanguineal system compares favorably with the findings of Thomas and Znaniecki in their study of the Polish peasant family, in which, they say, "the marriage norm is not love, but 'respect.'" As they explain:

The norm of respect from wife to husband includes obedience, fidelity, care for the husband's comfort and health; from husband to wife, good treatment, fidelity, not letting the wife do hired work if it is not indispensable. In general, neither husband nor wife ought to do anything which could lower the social standing of the other, since this would lead to a lowering of the social standing of the other's family. Affection is not explicitly included in the norm of respect, but is desirable. As to sexual love, it is a purely personal matter, is not and ought not to be socialized in any form; the family purposely ignores it, and the slightest indecency or indiscreetness with regard to sexual relations in marriage is viewed with disgust and is morally condemned.[3]

The Polish pattern of marital relationships compares favorably with the Amish. The Amish are in addition very conscious of the biblical pattern: "Wives, submit yourselves unto your own husband, as unto

3. William I. Thomas and Florian Znaniecki, *The Polish Peasant in Europe and America* (New York: Alfred A. Knopf, 1927), 1: 90.

the Lord. . . . So ought men to love their wives as their own bodies. . . . and the wife see that she reverence her husband" (Eph. 5:22, 28, 33).

The Amish are strongly opposed to premarital sex and extramarital affairs, and any transgression among members must be confessed to the church assembly whether or not pregnancy occurs. Males and females have equal responsibility to confess. After a period of punishment (by excommunication), repenting individuals are received back into the church. They are completely forgiven. Pregnancy is not always considered sufficient reason for the offending couple to marry, but if the couple decides to marry, the wedding is held before the birth of the child. If there is no marriage in such cases, the mother may keep the baby or the baby may be adopted by an Amish couple.

CHILDREN AND PARENTS

Amish children appear innocent and unspoiled by the things of this world. The birth of a child brings joy to the family and community, for there will be another dishwasher or woodchopper, and another church member. Thus, children are wanted. At no time in the Amish system are they unwelcome, for they are regarded as "an heritage of the Lord."

The first two years of life are happy ones. Baby obtains what he wants. He is given permissive care with great amounts of love from mother, father, brothers, sisters, aunts, uncles, grandfathers, grandmothers, and cousins.

After about the second year, restrictions and exacting disciplines are continuously imposed upon the child until adolescence. He must be taught to respect the authority of his parents and to respond properly to their exactness. The child is considered sinless since he does not know the difference between right and wrong. It is the duty of parents to teach him this difference so that he will realize his moral inadequacy and choose the "right way" of the Amish religion.

The Amish home is an effective socializing agent that is directed at making the child a mature person in the Amish way of life. Early in life the child learns that the Amish are "different" from other people. Thus, he must learn not only how to understand to play the role at home and in the Amish system but also how to conduct himself in relation to the norms of his "English" neighbors. He cannot have clothes and toys just like the "English" people have. He soon learns to imitate his parents, to take pride in the "difference," and appears no longer to ask "why" until adolescence.

Amish children are raised so carefully within the Amish family and community that they never feel secure outside it. The faces of many

Strong ties are maintained
between generations.

Amish boys and girls reflect pure intent, a sincere, honest, cordial, and well-bred disposition. The extraordinary love and discipline they get prepares them well for Amish womanhood and manhood.

The family is expected to transmit to the child a reading knowledge of German. The Amish school also aids in this process. The family members may gather about the sitting-room table, each with a German Testament, and take their turns spelling, enunciating the alphabet, and reading. In some families, this exercise is carried out daily in connection with morning and evening prayers. Even preschool children, ages four and five, take their turns by repeating words or syllables as they are pronounced by the family head.

Amish children do not receive regular allowances from their parents. A young person who works a day or half a day for a neighbor is often permitted to keep the earnings, but is expected to save the money. When parents take their children to town they may give them a small sum for buying candy. Early in life parents may provide a "bank" in which to save pennies. The necessity of taking good care of one's clothing and other personal items is strongly emphasized to the child.

Just as the parents are to be examples to their children, so the older children must be good examples to the younger ones. Among children in the family, age is more important than sex in determining authority, accountability, and work. The older ones care for and help the younger children, but they do not punish them physically. Normally they persuade and wheedle them into obedience. In late adolescence masculine dominance becomes more evident in brother-sister relationships.

Teaching the child to work and accept responsibility is considered of utmost importance. The child begins to assist his parents at the age of four and is given limited responsibility at the age of six. The boy learns to feed the chickens, gather eggs, feed the calf, and drive the horses. The girl is trained to perform small jobs for her mother and to learn early the art of cooking and housekeeping. Some parents give a pig, sheep, or calf to each child with the stipulation that he or she tend the animal and take care of it. In this way the child is motivated to take an interest in the farm.

The role of children and the work performed by each is well illustrated in the following description of a family of six children, five boys and one girl, between the ages of three and twenty-two.

The girl (aged twelve) enjoys helping her mother with the household duties, especially setting the table and preparing meals. She and her younger brother (aged eight) help their mother with the garden. When the time comes to do the chores, each has a specific assignment, but their duties also overlap. The four oldest children and the father milk fifteen cows regularly. The oldest son feeds and beds the horses, hogs, and calves. The second feeds the laying hens, and the third tends the pullets on range and carries wood for his mother. The girl milks three cows, feeds the rabbits, and gathers the eggs. The eight-year-old boy has no regular work assignment but assists his mother or one of the older members of the family. The two older sons frequently help on washday with heavier tasks such as carrying water. The third son has a decided dislike for housework.

In many farm families each child will be given an animal, usually a calf or heifer, which will become exclusively his. The boy or girl will choose and name the animal. Typically this may occur as early as the seventeenth birthday, and the family may gather to watch the young person choose his animal from among the herd. When the animal matures and has a young calf, the calf may be sold and the proceeds will go into the savings account of the child. The fate of the animal is linked to the care and attention it is given by the owner. The child as owner learns the consequences of feeding, neglect, growth, birth, sterility, disease, or death. After the young person marries, the animal is taken to the farm home of the new couple.

In the Amish family, sons who reach the age of twenty-one are paid

Young children acquire familiarity with farm animals and the natural environment while learning Amish rules of behavior.

monthly wages if they are unmarried and continue to work at home. A young man may hire out for the summer, but this practice has almost completely disappeared among those Amish who farm with tractors. Farmers who need assistance frequently request help from a neighbor or a relative for a few days. Single girls occasionally work as maids in other Amish homes. A *Maut* ("maid") among the Amish enjoys the same privileges as a family member would.

The ability of the family to act as a unit in an emergency is illustrated by what happens when the livestock breaks out. Charles P. Loomis, who worked at an Amish place as a farm hand, describes such an incident. As the family was seated at the suppertable,

Mattie got up to get some milk and saw that the cows were getting through the gate. She screamed and the whole family dashed to the door. Mother hurriedly put the baby into the carriage. We ran after the 22 cows. The big family encircled them, one girl having run over a mile on plowed ground. We got them back in. They had not been out this spring and were wild. Mother said she had read in books about stampedes in the west. Chris and I put them back in their stanchions after supper. He fed them grain first, but still we had a job. He said, "They're out of practice. When they get to going to the meadow each day they will do better."[4]

Strict obedience to parents is a profound teaching stressed over and over by Amish parents and by the preachers and is a principle based upon several passages in the Bible. An Amish lad who runs away from home, or even an adult who leaves the Amish church, is held guilty of disobedience to his parents.

Amish children, like all children, manifest resentments by pouting or by responding negatively. But when these manifestations are overt, "smackings" are sure to follow either with the palm of the hand, a switch, a razor strap, or a buggy whip. Temper tantrums, making faces, name-calling, and sauciness among youngsters are extremely rare, for the child learns early that his reward for such rebellion is a sound thrashing.

Disputes between boys are perhaps as frequent in Amish as in non-Amish families. The manner of expressing dissatisfaction is mostly verbal, especially among youngsters, but noses occasionally do get broken. Profanity is not permitted, and if discovered by the parents, is usually promptly treated with punishment. Resentment toward a brother or sister is expressed only mildly in the presence of older

4. Charles P. Loomis, "A Farmhand's Diary," *Mennonite Quarterly Review* 53 (July 1979): 248.

persons. In the presence of parents, a quarrel may be expressed by silence, hesitancy, or by completely ignoring the situation.

The subject of sex in Amish life is regarded as a purely personal matter. Adults purposely ignore any mention of the subject, especially in the presence of children. Very little sex instruction is given to the ordinary Amish child. In spite of this suppression, the child acquires gradually, piece by piece, an elementary knowledge of the process of biological reproduction. The Amish child most certainly does ask questions about the sexual behavior of animals on the farm. To satisfy his curiosity, the child more often than not talks such matters over with associates his own age. The jokes of young men show that sexual interests have developed long before courtship and marriage. Any remark about sex in private conversation between a boy and girl of courting age is inopportune, but an indecent joke is not uncommon among a group of men.

FOOD AND TABLE

In the Amish home a "place at the table" is symbolic of belonging. When a place is vacant due to death, marriage, sickness, father's having gone to town, the discipline of the ban, or a runaway child, all are deeply aware of the empty place. The seating is traditionally arranged with father at the end of the table and the boys to his right from youngest to oldest. Mother is seated just to the left or right of father with the girls on her side of the table. Figure 10 shows the seating arrangement of a typical family—father, mother, and children, with their ages—before the marriage of any of the nine children.

The family table becomes the scene for the evaluation of behavior, for expressing personal likes and dislikes before the group, and for group participation and decision-making. Conversation for its own sake is not encouraged. Conversation at breakfast is typically about the work that needs to be done, how and who should do it. The mother may indicate that certain decisions need to be made relative to preparing the brooder house for the chicks, or about the apples that need to be picked. The father may delegate such a task to one of the sons, directing that it be done after school or when there is time. At noon, the absence of the school-age children makes possible a more intimate conversation between parents and older children. A progress report on the work accomplished thus far is often the topic of conversation. Father and mother may evaluate the products of a salesman who called during the morning hours. In the evening the entire family gathers about the table. Silence during this meal is often interrupted by an occasional belch, a question from a child, or the bark of a dog.

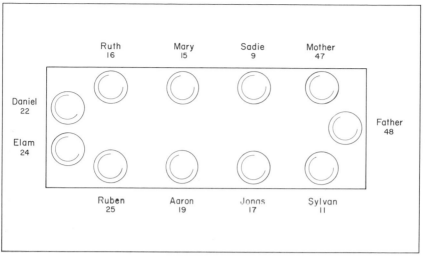

Figure 10.
Seating pattern at the Amish family table

Amish women spend much time cooking, baking, and canning foods. They take advantage of the growing season by serving vegetables from the garden and fruits and berries when they are ripe. They used canned foods when necessary and convenient. They also shop in small supermarkets for specific kinds of food. The old-fashioned Amish maintain ice boxes for cooling in the summer. Others have kerosene-operated refrigerators. At the table their portions of food are generous and the flavor is often excellent.

The Amish work hard and eat accordingly. The standard breakfast in Pennsylvania may include eggs, fried scrapple or cornmeal mush, cooked cereal, and often fried potatoes. Bread, butter, and jelly or apple butter are served with every meal. The standard diet is rich in fats and carbohydrates, consisting of potatoes, gravy, fried foods, and pastries. There are traditional foods like home-cured ham, chow-chow, pickled beets, shoo-fly pie, apple dumplings, bean soup, rivel soup, green tomato pie, and stink cheese. The Amish diet is also influenced by contemporary foods like meat loaf, bologna, and pizza. Cakes, pies, and puddings are numerous. Amish gardens are a good source of fresh vegetables, but the Amish tradition of overcooking and oversweetening probably cancels out much of the natural vitamins and minerals. In recent years health foods, vitamins, and food supplements have been much in evidence. Some Amish operate health-food stores.

The outdoor bake oven has disappeared in most Amish communities. Earlier it was preferred for drying fruits and vegetables and for baking

The family garden is an important economic and cooperative enterprise. Some families preserve as many as 800 quarts of fruits and vegetables each year.

pies in large quantities for the preaching service. Field corn is dried and browned in the oven before it is ground into cornmeal. Amish cooks prefer winter wheat for making pies and pastries and ·spring wheat for baking bread. Ground cereals—cornmeal, wheat hearts, and whole wheat flour—are still available in some village stores.

Among outsiders, especially tourists who flock to Lancaster County, there are many myths about Amish foods. There is the legend of "seven sweets and seven sours" on Amish tables. The only place I have ever eaten the seven sweets and sours is in a tourist hotel. The tourist industry has done well in capitalizing on myths, judging by the number of restaurants that cater to "Amish" foods. Advertised items such as "Amish soda," "Amish highball," or some kinds of pastries are obviously an outsider's capitalization on the tourists' determination to find something distinctively Amish. Over fifty "Dutch" restaurants have emerged in Amish localities. Some of them have Mennonite or former Amish cooks in their kitchens. Most outsiders are not able to distinguish between restaurants that serve "real" Amish dishes as opposed to "fake" ones. There are forty Amish-type cookbooks. Although many are small and localized, a few have enjoyed extensive distribution.[5]

Family ceremony is minimal, for social order and social roles are clearly defined and effective. According to older Amish informants, the only religious rite observed by a family in bygone days was silent prayer before and after meals. Bedtime prayers were repeated silently in bed. This is the traditional pattern still practiced by the most orthodox groups. Some families kneel together before retiring while the father reads a prayer from the prayer book.[6] Rarely is there a spontaneous audible prayer. The Amish have retained some of the ceremonial practices of the Reformation, such as the use of prayer formularies and prayer books, silent prayer, and Luther's German translation of the Bible.

Ritual

At mealtime each member at the table repeats silently his memorized meditation. Children, upon reaching the age of puberty or earlier, are expected to say their own prayers. These prayers are memorized, in German, and they may consist of the Lord's Prayer or a prayer of about the same length taken from a prayer book. The following are examples.

Gebet Vor Dem Essen

O Herr Gott, himmlischer Vater, Segne uns und Diese Deine Gaben, die wir von Diener milden Güte zu uns nehmen werden. Speise und tränke auch unsere Seelen zum ewigen Leben, und mach uns theilhaftig Deines himmlischen Tisches durch Jesus Christum. Amen. Unser Vater, etc.

Prayer before Meal

O Lord God, heavenly Father, bless us and these the gifts, which we shall accept from thy tender goodness. Give us food and drink also for our souls unto life eternal, and make us partakers of thy heavenly table through Jesus Christ. Amen. Our Father, etc. [Lord's prayer is repeated].

Gebet Nach Dem Essen

O Herr, wir sagen Dir Lob und Dank für Deine heilige Speis und Trank, für Deine vielfaltige grosse Gnaden und Gutheiten; Herr, der Du labest und regierest, ein wahrer Gott bis in Ewigkeit. Amen. Unser Vater, etc.

5. *Amish Cooking* (Alymer, Ont.: Pathway Publishers, 1977) is the major publication of the Amish themselves. (The original collection of recipes for this volume was compiled by Joseph N. and Sylvia Peachey of Belleville, Pa., under the title *Favorite Amish Family Recipes*.) See also Bill Randle, *Plain Cooking* (New York: New York Times Book Co., 1974).

6. The standard prayer book is *Christenpflicht*. Prayers on pp. 124 and 126 of the book are typically used in the morning and evening.

Prayer after Meal

O Lord, we give praise and thanks for your sacred food and drink, for your manifold great grace and goodness; Thou who livest and reignest, a true God till eternity. Amen. Our Father, etc. [Lord's Prayer is repeated].

The Amish home is the center of life and place of belonging for all the family members. Home is a place of security. It is a center for decision-making with respect to work, play, and exposure to the wider community and to the outside world.

RECREATION AND LEISURE

Recreation and leisure are informal and related to work; they are not entered into as pursuits in themselves. Homemade rather than store-bought toys are typically provided. There are certain games which Amish children and young people play. Clapping games are a common form of indoor play among adolescent girls and they are frequently played at informal family visits. It is called "botching." There are several ways of playing the game. Two people, seated on chairs and facing each other, clap the palms of their hands together alternately, then alternately strike each other's lap until there is a decided loud clap. The feet may be used to keep proper timing. If several are efficient, a vigorous contest will ensue to see who can go the fastest. These clappings are sometimes played to the tune of "Darling Nellie Gray" or "Pop Goes the Weasel."

Much of the leisure time of the Amish is spent visiting relatives, the older members of the community, and the sick, and attending weddings in the fall. Easter and Pentecost, observed not only on Sunday but on Monday as well, provide long weekend occasions for visiting. In large settlements where distances to be traveled are as great as forty miles, a family may start early on a Sunday morning and attend church in a neighboring district. They will drive still further in the afternoon, stop for Sunday evening supper with a family, and continue their journey after supper until they reach their destination.

Weekly auction sales and household auctions are a common form of recreation for many family members. For some boys and men, hunting is a favorite sport in season. Softball is rarely played on Sunday. Young people of courtship age play ball on special weekday holidays such as Ascension Day or Easter Monday. Hiking is a common activity among boys.

The use of tobacco can be classed as another form of pastime. Its use varies from one area to another and with *Ordnung*. Many districts have officially discouraged its use and will excommunicate a persistent smoker, but conservative groups have tended to have few or no scruples against its use. Among the Lancaster County Amish, who themselves raise tobacco as a cash crop, single and married men, including preachers, use it. In those districts where it is permitted, there is no effort to conceal smoking, except in the case of cigarettes, which are viewed as "worldly." Where forbidden, it is often done secretly. Older men appear to have more of a "right" to chew or smoke than young men. Pipe and cigar smoking is the accepted practice. Modern lighters are used by some. Older informants among the very orthodox Amish say that as far back as they can remember the people have used tobacco.[7] It was formerly common for older women to smoke a pipe and a few of them still do, but this is not done openly.

THE MATURE YEARS

Respect for the elders, already obvious among children, is even more pronounced with regard to mature Amish people. All age groups in both sexes revere parents, grandparents, and great-grandparents. The duty to obey one's parents is one of the main themes in Amish preaching. Perhaps the verse most often repeated on this point is one of the Ten Commandments: "Honor thy father and thy mother, that thy days may be long upon the land which the Lord thy God giveth thee" (Exod. 20:12; Eph. 6:2; Col. 3:20).

Not only is there respect for the aged, but authority is vested in the old people. This arrangement naturally lends itself to control of life by the aged. Preservation of the religious ideals and mores is thereby ensured, and the younger people who are inclined to introduce change can be held in check.

A strong consciousness of kinship is peculiarly favorable to gerontocracy, or social control by the older members of society. This control is informal rather than formal, but is, nevertheless, "closer to us than breathing, nearer than hands or feet."[8] The part that old people have "in drawing forth and molding the character and life-policy of every younger person in the kinship group makes the necessity for direct control much less frequent in isolated culture than in more accessible communities."[9] The relatively integrated community is associated with effective rules imposed by the aged, be they parents or church leaders.

---

7. Additional sources on the use of tobacco appear in John Umble, "The Amish Mennonites of Union County, Pennsylvania. Part I: Social and Religious Life," *Mennonite Quarterly Review* 7 (April 1933): 71–96; and in the *Mennonite Encyclopedia*, s.v. "Tobacco."

8. Howard Becker and Harry E. Barnes, *Social Thought from Lore to Science*, 3rd ed. rev., 3 vols. (New York: Dover, 1961), 1: 11.

9. Ibid.

Thus deference to age pervades not only familial relationships but also the religious leadership of the group. Furthermore, the counsel of the older bishop or minister carries more authority than that of younger ones.

The Amish farm typically contains two dwellings, one of which is the *Grossdaadi Haus*, which houses the grandparents. At retirement the older couple moves into this house and a married son or daughter falls heir to responsibility for the farm. The grandparents may retain some type of control of the farm until the younger couple demonstrate their ability to manage the farm. The grandparents have not only a separate household unit but a horse and buggy of their own. Instead of two houses, many farms have one dwelling that is large enough to accommodate two separate household operations. When there are no grandparents to occupy these quarters, they are sometimes rented to other Amish people, or occupied by the hired man and his wife. Some of the Amish who retire in or near a village will erect a small barn beside their dwelling so that they can feed and maintain a horse.

By the time they are sixty, many Amish have accumulated enough wealth for a satisfactory retirement. Traditionally, the Amish do not accept old-age assistance or public assistance of any kind. Neither do they buy life insurance. Needy older persons are aided by relatives. Should such close relatives be incompetent or unwilling, the church will come to the assistance of the elderly.

The retirement of father and mother from active life on the farm stabilizes the social organization of the entire Amish community. While the young man is free to make his own decisions, the very presence of the parents on the farm influences the life of the younger generation. The young couple is not obligated to carry out the wishes of the parents, yet an advisory relationship stimulates not only economic stability but also religious integrity.

The final stages of life are characterized by integrity rather than despair. Amish attitudes and practices with respect to aging constitute a sound system of retirement.

Age at Retirement. The age at which Amish retire is not rigidly fixed. Health, family needs, and the inclination of the individual are all considerations in determining the proper time. A couple may retire anytime between the ages of fifty and seventy. Moving "off the farm" provides opportunities for the young who need a farm. By providing a farm for their offspring, the older couple advances their standing in the community. They also do not have to choose between full-time work or doing nothing. They continue to work at their own pace,

Many Amish farms have double or triple dwelling units,
one of which serves as the "grandfather" house
for the grandparents.

helping their married children to become established on the farm.
Many continue to work in small shops of their own.

Prestige. In community and church activities older men and women
keep their right to vote, and their influence or "voice" increases.
Ordained leaders never retire from their positions. Wives have an
important influence on their husbands. Long periods of visiting friends
and persons of the same age, and exchanges before and after the
preaching service, help to form an informal consensus on any subject.

Housing and Transportation. Private housing is provided in the
"grandfather" house, the dwelling unit adjacent to the main farmhouse. This arrangement allows for independence without sacrificing
intergenerational family involvement. By having their own horse and

Older Amish people usually gain respect and status
with age and are remarkably independent.

buggy, both couples may travel at will. There is no fear of losing a
driver's license.

Functional Traditions. By living in their own house, a retired couple
can maintain personal customs and living arrangements. This includes
furnishings, guest rooms for visitors, shop tools, facilities for making
toys for children, quilts, and rugs, and maintaining Amish standards.
Old-fashioned ways are preferred and perpetuated voluntarily. The
slow rate of technological change allows social bonds to take priority.
In an institution for old people or in an apartment, the same sense of
living comfortably with an unchanging social structure would not be
possible.

Economic Security. Amish retirees are with few exceptions not wealthy.
Income, however, is not a serious problem. Economic subsistence is
maintained without government aid of any kind. Life earnings, rentals
from farms, carpentry, or part-time work provides some income. They
do not seek or need counsel with respect to maintaining their human
rights. The community's sensitivity to sharing and practicing mutual
aid and its abiding interest in the well-being of those in need are
great assets to older people.

Social and Family Continuity. Transgenerational contacts are maintained with relatives. There is little problem with loneliness. Older

people are assured of meaningful social participation, in work and in community activities, in seasonal frolics, auctions, and in the activities of weddings and holidays. Travel to distant places may also constitute a significant pastime for older people. Contentment with helping the married children, whether in work, in times of sickness, or in crisis, constitutes a basic attitude and expectation. The young ask their parents about farming methods or for advice on rearing children. This does not mean that their advice is accepted, but their views as parents are recognized and respected.

Health and Medical Care. Good nutrition and health care are readily at hand. Years of physical labor and exercise have kept the body active. When health fails, relatives and friends come to visit frequently. There is no stigma attached to being sick. In case of financial need, either the relatives or the church will pay unmet medical bills.

CHAPTER 8

Child Nurture and Training

🌿

TRUE EDUCATION, by Amish standards, is "the cultivation of humility, simple living, and submission to the will of God." The single most important goal is eternal life. The Amish do not believe in predestination—that some persons are born to be saved and others are born to be damned. Children are believed to have an inherited sinful nature through no fault of their own, and they are therefore lovable and teachable. Given the proper environment, they are capable of assuming right conduct by the time they become adults. Parents are responsible for training their children, and they are morally accountable to God for teaching them right from wrong. Obedience to parents and ultimately to God is a fundamental virtue. Children are taught to be well-mannered, quiet, and humble in the presence of others. Children must not be idle. They must learn useful manual skills, learn to read and write, and acquire some knowledge of the Scriptures.[1]

1. Gertrude E. Huntington provided assistance in the development of this chapter. Amish socialization is discussed in greater detail in John A. Hostetler and Gertrude E. Huntington, *Children in Amish Society* (New York: Holt, Rinehart & Winston, 1971). The material in this chapter is based on our joint publication, with revisions, and is used with the permission of the publishers.

THE GOALS OF EDUCATION

The family, and to a lesser extent the Amish school, are believed to have the primary responsibility for training the child for life. The child also has an explicit relationship to a wide social fabric within his culture—his parents, siblings, extended relatives, church, community, and the school—all of which help to equip him for adult life. Schools are expected to teach the children literacy, cooperation, and the skills needed to live productive lives in keeping with values taught in the home and in the church. On reaching physical and social maturity and demonstrating sincerity and a knowledge of Amish religion, the young people are baptized into the believing community, where they will choose their spouse. Their willingness to suffer persecution or death in order to maintain their faith is made explicit in baptism.

AGE STAGES

From birth to death the Amish person passes through a series of stages in keeping with his age and sex. The social functions of each age group are delineated and determined by the Amish culture. These age groups or stages are: babies, little children, "scholars," young people, adulthood, and retirement. To become an Amish person, the individual must learn the appropriate attitude and behavior patterns in each of these stages. School is only one of many influences in the life of the individual. The socialization patterns of the first four stages will be discussed here; adulthood and retirement have been described previously.

Babies—from Birth to Walking. Babies are regarded as a gift from God and are welcomed with pleasure into the family and community. A baby is considered blameless, can do no wrong, and if he cries he is in need of comfort, not discipline. Babies are rarely fed on a strict schedule but are fed when hungry. The baby is included at the family table during mealtime, for the attitude of the family is one of sharing. Eating is an important social activity.

During the first year the baby receives solicitous care from persons of all ages. Babies are enjoyed, they are believed to be gentle and responsive. A baby can be spoiled by improper handling, especially by nervous, tense handling, but that is not the fault of the baby. The infant is secure within the home and the Amish community, and this equips him to trust himself and those around him. At this age babies are not scolded or punished. Although a baby may be difficult, he is not considered bad. The baby stage ends when a child begins to walk.

Children are included in important farm activities
after school hours and on Saturdays.

Little Children—from Walking to Entering School. Parents create a safe environment for their children, protecting them from physical and moral danger. The preschool child learns to respect and obey those in authority, to share with others and help others, to do what he is taught, and to enjoy work and perform it pleasantly.

Respect for authority is shown through obedience. The relationship between authority and responsibility is learned very early. Although the younger children must obey the older ones, the older children may not make arbitrary demands on the younger. The four-year-old is expected to hand over his toy to a younger child if he cries for it, but in the absence of the parents the younger one must obey the older.

Parents teach obedience by being consistent and firm. The use of a switch may be used, but not harshly. Parents vary in their handling of the disobedient child, but they will not tolerate stubbornness or defiance. Generally the Amish are matter-of-fact rather than moralistic in dealing with their children. Work is viewed as helping others, and children are trained to help one another rather than to be independent. There is little difference in the tasks done by preschool girls and boys. Children are not thanked for carrying out responsibilities

expected of them. Crying and deep emotion are not discouraged except in the case of physical pain or self-pity.

Amish children experience great freedom of movement as they accompany older persons around the farm. They are encouraged to be useful but are not pushed to perform tasks beyond their ability. Initiative in the physical world is encouraged, but asking questions of an intellectual nature is strictly channeled. Instead of asking how or why, the child learns to observe and imitate on a behavioral level. The presence of a father is considered necessary for the proper up-bringing of the preschool child. Little children sit through the long preaching service, girls with their mothers, and boys with their fathers. Here they learn to be quiet and patient. The Amish do not sanction kindergartens, believing that the child should be under the care of the parents in the home. Small children are kept away from the outside world as much as practical. They are not usually intro-duced to non-Amish people.

"Scholars"—Children between the Ages of Six and Fifteen. During the school years the family continues to be the primary agent of a child's socialization. The family protects the child, supports the

A young "scholar." Amish children receive strong support from their families in learning basic educational skills and acquiring the attitudes of humility, forgiveness, and appreciation.

training given in school, and punishes and forgives the transgressions of the child. Punishment is for the safety of the child—for physical, cultural, moral, and legal safety. School children are motivated primarily by concern for other people and not for fear of punishment. Rewards are used to develop the attitudes of humility, forgivenesss, admission of error, sympathy, responsibility, and appreciation of work. Parents are responsible for seeing that the children stay within the discipline of the church. The school supports the parents who teach their children by example to become Christians, and who teach them the work skills they will need to live in the Amish community.

The function of the school is to teach the children the three R's in an environment where they can learn discipline, basic values, and how to get along with others. There is concern that the home, school, and church teach the same things. Most children attend Amish schools. Here the teacher is an Amish person, and emotionally the school belongs to the Amish community. Amish children must learn to understand something of the world in order to reject it selectively. They are expected to master the English language and to learn the skills that will enable them to transact business with outsiders.

During his school years, the Amish child spends most of his non-school time with his family. The family attends church and visits many friends and relatives as a unit. The child spends much time with a mixed group when he chooses. In addition to his parents, he knows many adults who have an interest in him and his development. When not in school, girls learn to cook, bake, sew, and make things for their playhouses. The boys help with the farm work, but they also build toys or birdhouses, and they trap fur animals or fish in streams. Boys and girls are rewarded for the work of their hands and for their sense of industry. The child has many role models and informal teachers.

Young People—from Adolescence to Marriage. At the end of the school years, the peer group, rather than the family and the church, become the young person's reference group. The individual chooses his "crowd" or "gang" of friends. If a youth makes friends with outsiders and is governed by an alien peer group, he is likely in danger of leaving the Amish faith. Earlier in life the young person accepted being Amish as part of his identity. He must strive to determine what it means to be Amish. By working at various jobs—for other Amish families or away from the community—both boys and girls gain a knowledge of the wider community and the world outside their home. Some adolescent rebellion is to be expected. During working hours the young people are respectful of community standards. During free time with their peers there may be considerable testing of boundaries. But if the young Amish person is physically removed from the community, he may become susceptible to alien religious influences.

During this period the young person must come to terms with two great decisions: whether he will join the Amish church, and whom he will marry. To make these decisions, the individual must establish a certain degree of independence from his family and his community. The family relaxes some of its control. The church has no direct control over the young person who has not voluntarily become a member. Sampling the world and testing the boundaries may take the form of owning a radio or camera, attending movies, wearing non-Amish clothes, having a driver's license or owning an automobile— all more or less in secret. If these deviations are managed discreetly, they may be ignored by the parents and community. The young person is thereby allowed some freedom to taste the outside world he is voluntarily expected to reject when he becomes a church member.

Generally Amish young people discover continuity between what they were taught as children and what they experience as adolescents.

Intense play and group cooperation are part
of growing up.

What the young person learns about himself as a person, a worker, a member of a peer group, and a member of a family, he is able to integrate with who he is, where he has come from, and where he is going.

SCHOOLING

Today most Amish children attend Amish schools, though a few in rural areas still attend public schools. A half-century ago all Amish children attended public schools. The Amish built their own schools and staffed them with their own teachers in response to state consolidation of small country schools. In the one-room country schools, children were taught largely by oral means and by example; discipline and basic skills were stressed. Those aspects of schooling that were not considered relevant were tolerated. With consolidation, all this changed. The Amish have struggled to retain a human rather than an organizational scale in their schools, to make them complementary to their way of life.[2] In 1972, thirty-five years after the Amish first opposed the consolidation of schools, the Supreme Court upheld the validity of Amish schools.

2. The school conflict is discussed in Chapter 12.

Setting and Organization. The Amish have two types of schools—the elementary school, consisting of the first eight grades, and the vocational school.[3] The latter, not held uniformly in all settlements, is on-the-job training that combines instruction and farm work for pupils who have completed the elementary grades but are not old enough to obtain a working permit. Amish schools are built and operated by the parents of a local church district or districts and not by a centralized organization.

Most school buildings consist of one or two classrooms, often with an entrance room, sometimes a bookroom, and newer schools may have a finished basement where the children play during inclement weather. In earlier times rural one-room schoolhouses were purchased from the state when they became available. They were remodeled extensively. The high ceilings were lowered to create a cozier, more homelike atmosphere. Today most school buildings are built by the Amish themselves. Building committees have their blueprints approved by state fire and health officials. The land for the building is often donated by an Amish farmer. The schoolhouse is well constructed, made of glazed tile, cinder block, brick facing, stucco, or aluminum siding. The Amish schools do not have electricity. They are built in such a way as to take full advantage of available natural light. In certain communities schools have indoor lavatories, but in most areas outhouses are preferred. Many schools have old-fashioned rope-pulled school bells. Inside, colorful drawings and charts made by the "scholars" may be found on walls and windows. Every schoolyard has a ball field. A few have swings or seesaws. Sledding and ice skating are considered when a site is located for a school.

Most Amish pupils walk to school. In those settlements where distance is a problem, the Amish hire a school bus to transport their children. They are opposed to accepting transportation services or school subsidies from the government.

Elementary schools are administered by a school board. In most communities each school has its own board, but in some places several schools are administered by a single board. Members are elected by the patrons or appointed by the church. A board consists of from three to six members, one of whom serves as president. There is usually a clerk or secretary who keeps records, and a treasurer. The treasurer collects the funds for the operation of the school, issues the teacher's pay check, and is responsible for the bills. An attendance officer is responsible for seeing that attendance records are forwarded

3. The vocational school is described in Hostetler and Huntington, *Children in Amish Society*, pp. 71–79.

to state officials, although in some schools the teacher performs this function. To the outsider these slight variations and overlapping responsibilities may be confusing, but to the Amish such local diversities are respected. Where children from different Old Order affiliations (noncommuning churches) attend one school, the members of each different affiliation may elect one board member.

The school board meets as a unit with the teacher, ideally once a month. These are open meetings, and parents and other church members are encouraged to attend. The school board is responsible to the patrons and the local church district for the smooth functioning of the school. The board hires and fires the teacher, pays the teacher's salary, and keeps the building and playground in good condition. It must also set the tuition fee and assess the school tax. For patrons who cannot pay their share, the church may be asked to eliminate any debt at the end of the school year.

Statewide Amish board meetings are held annually for members of the school boards, committeemen, church officials, and others, including teachers and parents who are interested. Statewide committee members are elected at these meetings. These occasions attract from six to eight hundred people, who usually meet in a large barn. State committees may appoint several subcommittees. When vital issues are at stake, a small committee meets with public education officials to exchange views. The Pennsylvania "Amish Church School Committee," established in 1937, has attempted to clarify the Amish position on education to state education officials. The Old Order Book Society (Gordonville, Pa.), which was organized to print books suitable for use in Amish schools, reports to the several statewide annual meetings. This committee also functions as a treasury to help provide funds for the establishment of new schools.

Schedule. The school day consists of four major periods of about an hour and a half each, a pattern typical of rural schools a half-century ago. There is a recess between periods, including a noon break. During each period there is class recitation, generally about ten minutes for each class. The children who are not reciting know when it will be their turn and what subject they should prepare for.

School typically starts at 8:30 and is dismissed at 3:30. All schools have an opening period that includes the singing of hymns, Bible reading without commentary, and the recitation of the Lord's Prayer. Many schools have a song and silent prayer before dismissal for lunch. In the afternoon session the teacher may read to the children for a few minutes, occasionally from a completely secular book like a Nancy Drew story. The hardest or most important subject is frequently

Sledding and ice-skating are favorite sports
among Amish school children.

scheduled for the first hour of school. Spelling, generally considered
an easy subject, is usually scheduled for late in the afternoon. Spelling
matches are often held at this time. Singing has an important function
in Amish schools, and teachers encourage the children to learn new
songs and to enjoy this group activity.

Curriculum. Local preferences and different state rulings on school
curricula result in slight variations in subject matter taught. The

children learn English (including reading, grammar, spelling, penmanship, and, to a limited extent, composition) and arithmetic (addition, subtraction, multiplication, division, decimals, percentages, ratios, volumes and areas, conversion of weights and measures, and simple and compound interest). Amish schools do not teach "new math." Most schools teach some health, history, and geography; some teach a little science and art. Some substitute agriculture for history and geography. The children learn the letters and sounds of the alphabet phonetically before they begin reading.

Textbooks are chosen by the school board, with or without the consultation of the teacher. The Old Order Book Society publishes a list of books suitable for Amish schools. A special journal for Amish teachers, the *Blackboard Bulletin*, published monthly by Pathway Publishers (an Amish-owned-and-operated company with headquarters in Aylmer, Ontario, and LaGrange, Indiana), contains a variety of aids for teachers. Some of the discarded books from public schools may be used, and are sometimes donated to the Amish by public school teachers and administrators. The old books are preferred because they have less science, fewer references to television, and less discussion of sex education. The Amish are opposed to sex education and to health books that stress how to make oneself attractive.

Finding suitable reading material for Amish pupils has been a difficult problem. Those books that support conspicuous consumption, are superficially patriotic or militaristic, or contain illustrations supporting these values are unsuited for a nonresistant group that tries to live "separated from the world." The classic *McGuffey Readers* have been accepted in a few communities, especially in Ohio. This is not surprising, for they were written by one of the founders of the common-school system in Ohio at a time when the schools stressed proper morality and character development. This philosophy of education coincides with the Amish attitude. The brand of patriotism promoted in the *McGuffey Readers* is also shared by the Amish, for it stresses the beauties of the nation, and not its technological pride and superiority.

In response to the need for good reading books, Pathway Publishers has undertaken the task of producing a series of suitable readers for Amish schools. The Amish have also produced two history books: *Seeking a Better Country* (1963), by Noah Zook; and *Our Better Country: The Story of America's Freedom* (1963), by Uria R. Byler. The Amish do not want their children to read fairy tales, stories in which animals talk and act like people, or stories that involve magic. The stories selected and written by Amish authors are set in rural

America and stress the Christian virtues of honesty, thrift, purity, and love, but without a heavy religious vocabulary.

Amish schools use a limited amount of material in the classroom, but the children learn it thoroughly. The Amish stress accuracy rather than speed, drill rather than variety, proper sequence rather than freedom of choice. The Amish school aids the child to become a part of his community and to remain within his community. The school emphasizes shared knowledge and the dignity of tradition rather than progress. The Amish assume that individuals are weak, that they need help—from one another, from a higher power, and from individual effort—in order to improve. In short, Amish children are presented with certain appropriate facts that they are encouraged to learn thoroughly rather than question critically. These facts form a part of the community's shared knowledge and thereby help the community to remain of one mind. The schools function effectively to maintain the bounds of Amish culture, to prepare the young to live simply, with minimum reliance or middle-class values and the mass communication systems of modern society.

Amish schools support the religion taught in the family and church but do not attempt to interpret or teach religion in the classroom. Only those who are ordained of God should explain the Scriptures to an assembled group. Parents teach their own children within the family, but they do not teach the children of other families. Amish religion tends to be ritualistic and nontheological. Christianity is to be lived and not talked about. The Amish are critical of persons who show off their knowledge of the Bible by frequently quoting passages from the Scriptures. This is considered a form of pride. Although German verses are memorized in school, teachers do not teach religion or induce the children to be "scripture-smart for religious show." Teaching is by example. Self-denial, humility, and forbearance are the approved form of religious behavior.

The Teacher and Teaching Methods. Amish teachers are selected on the basis of their aptitude for and interest in teaching children. They have no formal training beyond the elementary grades. This fact is appalling to public school administrators, but the Amish feel that certified college teachers are "unsuitable" as teachers in their schools. If we compare the role of the teacher in two cultures, the Amish and a typical suburban school, the very different functions of the teacher become apparent.[4] Middle-class teachers are too far removed from

4. Ibid., pp. 107–8.

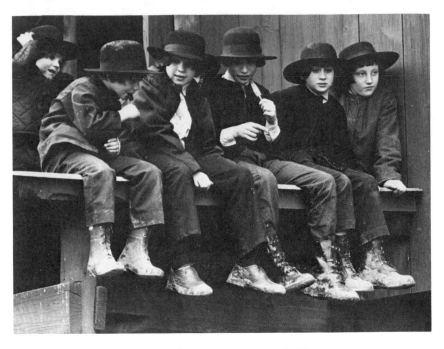

Young people progress toward adulthood
in an orderly pattern. Loyalty to a peer group
is an essential stage.

the oral tradition to identify with the Amish, and in most cases they
are unsuitable as examples.

The Amish teacher teaches with his whole life. He must be a
person who has integrated his life with that of the community, for
every aspect of behavior and personality is related to teaching. He
must be well grounded in his religious faith, exemplifying the Amish
traits of steadfastness and love of fellow man. In addition, he must
be interested in education and have sufficient factual knowledge to
keep ahead of the scholars. One becomes a teacher by being asked
to teach, by serving as an apprentice for a specified period. After
three years of teaching, a person is considered qualified by Amish
standards.[5] Teachers attend annual statewide teachers' meetings and
local meetings in their community for the purpose of lending one
another support and advice. The *Blackboard Bulletin* provides stimu-

5. *Guidelines in Regards to the Old Order Amish or Mennonite Parochial
Schools* (Gordonville, Pa.: Gordonville Print Shop, 1978), p. 29.

lation and discussion of school projects. Teacher-training is primarily informal and personal.

The school has the atmosphere of a well-ordered family. The teacher represents a parent or an older sibling. The pupils and teacher call each other by their first names. The classroom typically runs smoothly, for the teacher does not pretend that the children make the decisions. Orderliness, supported with appropriate biblical mottoes on the wall, is stressed. The Golden Rule, "Do unto others as you would have others do unto you," is to be followed. The children encourage one another's good performance so that the whole class or school may do well. Individual responsibility, not individual competition, is encouraged. Since a person's individual talents are God-given, no one should be praised if he is a fast learner, nor should he be condemned if he is a slow learner. There is a place for each person God has created. Such differences are acknowledged and respected by the teacher and children.

Teachers are not confronted with a room full of waving hands competing for the chance to give an answer. Grades conform to an absolute rather than a relative system of grading. Grading on the curve, where one child's good grade depends on another child's poor grade, is unacceptable. Grades are not manipulated to motivate the student. Rather, scholars are taught to accept the level of work they are able to do and always to work hard to do better. The discussion method is not considered appropriate for academic subjects, for every child is expected to learn and to be able to recite the facts.

Teachers use encouragement and rewards much more than punishment. The child in need of discipline is usually first spoken to in private. A teacher may ask a child to apologize to the group, or to remain in his seat during recess or at noon. Corporal punishment is sometimes used for serious or repeated offenses. Teachers aim never to belittle their scholars or to use sarcasm or ridicule as a means of controlling them. They try to make the offending child understand the transgression and to accept punishment willingly because it is deserved. Teachers feel emotionally very close to their scholars and the children in turn admire and want to please their teachers.

THE AMISH PERSONALITY

Amish schools stress social responsibility rather than critical analysis. Factual material, though somewhat circumscribed, is learned thoroughly. The children are taught both by practice and by example to care for and support the members of the school and community. Typically the Amish personality may be described as "quiet, friendly, responsible, and conscientious."[6] The model Amish person is loyal, considerate, and sympathetic. The Amish person "works devotedly to meet his obligations," and although careful with detail, "needs time to master technical subjects." How other people feel is important to him. He dislikes telling people unpleasant things.

When asked about their vocational preferences, Amish school children generally name occupations requiring service and manual labor.[7] Boys prefer farming or farm-related work. Girls prefer housekeeping, gardening, cooking, cleaning, caring for children, or some type of humanitarian service such as nursing or teaching. Their vocational aspirations are realistic and attainable within the limits of Amish culture. An analysis of drawing exercises done by Amish children reveals a strong awareness of other people. Work apart from play is not sharply delineated, nor are there rigid differences between the sexes in the leisure-time preferences of the children. Amish children show a remarkable ability to conceptualize space at an early age, and the inclusion of others in their drawings suggests the importance of the family and of group activities.

On several standardized tests, Amish children performed significantly higher in spelling, word usage, and arithmetic than a sample of pupils in rural public schools.[8] They scored slightly above the national norm in these subjects in spite of small libraries, limited equipment, the absence of radio and television, and teachers who lacked college training. The Amish pupils were equal to the non-Amish pupils in comprehension and in the use of reference material. They had lower scores in vocabulary. In those aspects of learning stressed by the Amish culture, the Amish pupils outperformed pupils in the control group.

Children of both sexes identify with the goals of their parents and generally accept these role models for themselves. Several studies of parent-child relationships support these conclusions. Sons identify closely with their fathers;[9] the child "knows exactly who he is and

6. The descriptions of Amish personality are based on the results of the Myers-Briggs Type Indicator (Isabell Briggs Myers, Educational Testing Service, Princeton, N.J.) as reported in Hostetler and Huntington, *Children in Amish Society*, pp. 80–81.

7. Hostetler and Huntington, *Children in Amish Society*, pp. 85–88.

8. Ibid., pp. 91–95.

9. Joe Wittmer, "Homogeneity of Personality Characteristics: A Comparison between Old Order Amish and Non-Amish," *American Anthropologist* 72 (October 1970): 1063–68.

Saturday work includes cleaning and refilling the kerosene lanterns.
© National Geographic Society.

Harvesting corn. With other members of the family,
young adults learn to work with machines
adapted to scale.

where he is going to fit when he grows up."[10] Amish children in the
eighth grade rate their families more positively than do non-Amish
children.[11]

By outside standards Amish culture provides an environment that
is limiting and restrictive. To the Amish child it provides reasonable
fulfillment and a knowledge of what is expected of the individual.
Learning is directed toward conformity with what is right, not
toward discovering new knowledge. The wisdom of the ages is for
the Amish more important than the pronouncements of modern
science. It is more important to do what is morally right than to
win acclaim, popularity, or riches, or to survive physically. Within
the clearly defined boundaries of the culture, there is a certain richness

10. M. L. Lembright and K. Yamamoto, "Subcultures and Creative Thinking: An
Exploratory Comparison between Amish and Urban American School Children,"
Merrill-Palmer Quarterly of Behavior and Development 11 (January 1965): 49–64.

11. Mervin R. Smucker, "Growing Up Amish: A Comparison of the Socialization
Process between Amish and Non-Amish Rural School Children" (M.S. thesis,
Millersville State College, Pa., 1978).

and diversity of experience in the small Amish school where long-term intimate relationships are formed.

The Amish Dropout. It is extremely rare for a child who has completed the Amish elementary grades to enter high school and continue formal schooling. The child who continues his formal schooling will not remain Amish and hence is a "dropout" from the Amish way of life. By not entering high school, Amish children are all classed as dropouts in public school statistics. If a family changes church affiliations by joining a liberalized group, the children are more likely to continue formal schooling. Some Amish resume their formal education in their late teens or after the age of twenty-one. An insatiable motivation for learning is manifest in a few. The belief advanced by some educators, that the Amish should be forced to complete more years of schooling so that in case they should leave the faith they would not be disadvantaged educationally, has no foundation. Lack of formal schooling is no problem for the Amish person who seeks employment. In many communities, both Amish and former Amish persons are in great demand as farm tenants, carpenters, painters, builders, housecleaners, and baby-sitters.

CHAPTER 9

The Life Ceremonies

🌿

BIRTH, coming of age, marriage, career achievements, and death
are marked by appropriate ceremonies or rites of passage in most
societies. Such major changes "are not accomplished without troubling social and individual life, and it is the purpose of a certain
number of rites of passage to check their noxious effects."[1] This
chapter examines Amish ceremonies as they relate to three major
turning points—birth, marriage, and death.

BIRTH

In many societies the ceremony associated with birth is formal and
elaborate, but in Amish society it is barely visible. Some folk beliefs
about pregnancy and birth exist, but birth is marked by neither
sacred nor kinship ceremonies. The addition of children to the
society is not "troubling" in any way, and their coming is not regarded
as an economic burden. In fact, the birth of a child enhances the
standing of the parents in the community. An Amish couple may
expect to have several, possibly many, children, for children are
wanted.

The majority of babies are born in the hospital because most

1. Arnold van Gennep, "On the Rites of Passage," in *Theories of Society*, ed.
Talcott Parsons, 2 vols. (Glencoe, Ill.: The Free Press, 1961), 2: 951.

doctors will not make home deliveries, but with the help of a few sympathetic doctors and midwives, some of the Amish are able to have their children at home. One obstetrician in Pennsylvania observes that she is making more and more home deliveries and that the present ratio is about three to one in favor of home deliveries. There are no taboos against good medical care, but home births are preferred. Amish women view birth not as a threat but as an experience that affirms them as part of the community. No social ceremony is needed to "check any noxious effects," because there are none.

Secular rituals such as baby showers, with their consumer orientation, have no place in the Amish family. Infants are dressed functionally, as are adults, and they are not lauded with fancy or expensive clothing or equipment. And because the Amish family is so effective in socializing the child for adult life, there is scarcely any need for a religious rite. The Amish believe in adult baptism; there is no occasion for infant baptism. Godparents are not assigned; the care and concern of the community for the children is assumed. It is only after the child has been raised to "a way of life" that he is brought into formal relation to the religious community through baptism. Baptism is, of course, a very awesome experience and admits one to a new state. It logically belongs in a discussion of the life ceremonies, but because of its religious significance I have treated it earlier as part of the Amish charter.

MARRIAGE

A wedding is an elaborate affair, for the whole community has a stake in marriage. It means a new home, another place to hold preaching services, and another family committed to rearing children in the Amish way of life. Marriage also means that the young man and young woman are ready to part with their sometimes wild adolescent behavior, to settle down and become respectable members of the community. Marriage is a rite of passage marking the passing from youth to adulthood.

Amish courtship is secretive, and the community at large is not informed of an intended wedding until the couple is "published" in church, from one to four weeks before the wedding. Signs of an approaching wedding, however, provide occasion for joking and teasing. Since there is nothing among Amish traditions that corresponds to the engagement period, other signs of a wedding are sought. An overabundance of celery in the garden of the home of a potential bride is said to be one such sign, since large quantities are used at weddings. Another cue may be efforts on the part of the father of the potential bridegroom to obtain an extra farm, or to remodel a vacant dwelling on one of his own farms.

Weddings are usually held in November and December, since this is a time when the work year allows community-wide participation. The great amount of preparation involved requires that weddings be held during the week, traditionally on Tuesday or Thursday.[2] Second marriages involving widows or widowers may be held anytime during the year and do not involve such elaborate preparations.

Shortly before a young man wishes to be married he approaches the deacon or a minister of his choosing and makes his desire known. The official then becomes the *Schtecklimann*, or "go-between." His task is to go secretly, usually after dark, to the home of the bridegroom's fiancée, verify her wishes for marriage, and obtain the consent of her parents. The girl and her parents have by this time already given formal consent, so the duty of the intermediary is little more than a formality.

The deacon reports his findings to the ministers and announces or "publishes" the intent of the couple at the preaching service in the girl's district. If the bridegroom-to-be is from the same district, he leaves immediately after the important announcement, just before the last hymn is sung. He hitches his horse and is off to the home of his fiancée, where she is awaiting the news that they have been "published." The bridegroom then remains at the bride's home until the wedding day. They are busy during this time with the innumerable preparations that must be made. Walnuts and hickory nuts need to be cracked, floors scrubbed, furniture moved, silverware polished, and dishes borrowed.

The bridegroom's first assignment is to invite personally all his relatives to the wedding. The parents of the couple also do some inviting. Relatives at a distance are notified by postcard or letter. No printed wedding invitations are mailed. Invitations are addressed to entire families or to certain members of the family, such as the husband and wife only. Some invitations are for the evening festivities only. Honorary invitations are extended to uncles, aunts, and special friends to serve as cooks and overseers. Both men and their wives serve in this capacity. The parents of the bridal party decide who will have the honor of serving the meal; on the wedding day they themselves do not work.

Wedding customs vary from one ceremonial and ecological com-

2. The practice of holding weddings on Tuesdays and Thursdays, according to William I. Schreiber, is a vestige of ancient peoples that predates the Christian Era. See *Our Amish Neighbors* (Chicago: University of Chicago Press, 1962), p. 186.

munity to another, especially in menu, physical arrangements, and social activities. The following are observations made by the author at a wedding in central Pennsylvania.

Food preparations began on the day before the wedding. The cooks—married couples numbering thirty persons in all—began arriving at the bride's home at seven o'clock in the morning. Custom required that the bridegroom cut off the heads of the fowl. Men picked the chickens, ducks, and turkeys. The women washed and dressed them. The women prepared the dressing, stuffed the fowl, washed dishes, baked quantities of pies, peeled two bushels of potatoes, and cracked nuts. The men cleaned celery, supplied plenty of hot water from large kettles, emptied garbage, and constructed temporary tables for the main rooms in the house. Six tables, made of wide pine boards and trestles, were set up around three sides of the living room, in the kitchen, and in one bedroom, to create a seating capacity of one hundred (see Figure 11). The dressed, stuffed fowl were placed in a large bake oven outdoors on the evening before the wedding.

The wedding day itself was a great occasion, not only for the bride and bridegroom, but for the kinship community and guests, especially the young people. Before daylight on the day of the wedding the bride and bridegroom and their two attending couples went to a neighbor's place a mile from the bride's home where the preaching and ceremony were to take place. This service was open to the public, but was attended chiefly by those who were invited to the wedding.

As wedding guests arrived for the service the bridal party was already sitting in the front row. At nine o'clock, when the house was filled, the singing began, and the ministers proceeded to the council room and the bride and groom followed. Here they were given instructions concerning the duties of marriage while the assembly below sang wedding hymns (*Ausbund*, selections 97, 69, 131). Upon returning to the assembly the bridal party (holding hands) took their seats near the ministers' row, the three young men facing their partners. Their clothes were new, but in the style of typical Sunday garb. The main sermon delivered by the bishop focused on marriages in the Old Testament: the story of Adam and Eve; the wickedness of mankind after the Flood, in that wives were chosen foolishly; the uprightness of Noah's household in not intermarrying with unbelievers; the story of Isaac and Rebekah, and the adulterous plight of Solomon. The sermon was concluded with a recounting from the Apocrypha (Tobit, chapters 1–14), indicating how Tobias carefully obeyed his father's instructions in obtaining a wife of his own tribe in spite of enormous stumbling blocks.

Near the hour of twelve noon and at the end of his long sermon, the bishop asked the couple to come forward. The marriage ceremony was carried out without the aid of a book or written notes. It consisted of a few questions and responses and concluded with the bishop placing his hands on the clasped hands of the couple as he pronounced a blessing upon them. The vows appeared to be similar to those of other Protestant groups, but no special prayer was offered. The vows, in translation, were as follows:

"You have now heard the ordinance of Christian wedlock presented. Are you now willing to enter wedlock together as God in the beginning ordained and commanded?"

"Yes."

"Do you stand in the confidence (*Hoffnung*) that this, our sister, is ordained of God to be your wedded wife?"

"Yes."

"Do you stand in the confidence that this, our brother, is ordained of God to be your wedded husband?"

"Yes."

"Do you also promise your wedded wife, before the Lord and his church, that you will nevermore depart from her, but will care for her and cherish her, if bodily sickness comes to her, or in any circumstance which a Christian husband is responsible to care for, until the dear God will again separate you from each other?"

"Yes."

"Do you also promise your wedded husband, before the Lord and his church, etc."

"Yes."[3]

The couple then clasped their right hands together and the bishop continued: "So then I may say with Raguel (Tobit 7:15), the God of Abraham, the God of Isaac, and the God of Jacob be with you and help you together and fulfill his blessing abundantly upon you, through Jesus Christ. Amen." The bishop pronounced them husband and wife. Many, including the bishop, wiped away their tears, for all understood that the marriage would remain unto death.

Near the end of the ceremony several close relatives and table-waiters left the service. The bridal party remained a full half-hour for the closing formalities and then left, walking briskly in couples to the yard gate, where they were met by three hostlers, each with a buggy ready to go. Each hostler remained in the buggy and sat on the lap of the couple as he drove them to the bride's home for the wedding dinner.

At the bride's home the couples alighted from their buggies and

3. Translated from a nineteenth-century source; see *Mennonite Quarterly Review* 33 (April 1959): 142.

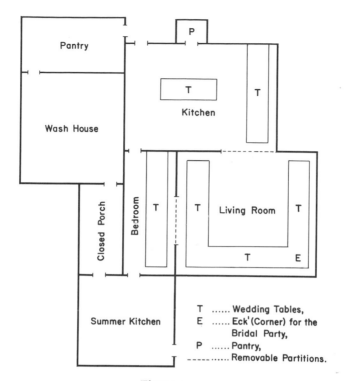

Figure 11.
Floor plan showing arrangement of tables
for an Amish wedding

walked quickly to an upstairs room. Their mood was most serious;
no shouting or handshakes of congratulations greeted them. The
tables were loaded with food, ready for the large crowd that began
to gather about the house and barn. The cooks had already eaten, so
that they would be ready for the afternoon's work of serving tables.
Two couples were assigned to serve each table.

Guests were seated under the supervision of the bride's father, who
ranked all but the young people of courting age according to kinship.
The bridal party sat at the *Eck* ("corner table") located in the most
visible part of the living room. The bridegroom sat to the right of
the bride, with attendants on either side. The unmarried girls (cousins
and friends), with backs to the wall, filled the wedding table(s)
around three sides of the living room. The young men sat on the
opposite side facing the girls. In the kitchen and bedroom the married
women took seats in similar fashion at the table(s) around the wall
and the men sat opposite. Facing the bride and bridegroom sat the

Schnützler ("carver"), who was to carve the fowl for the *Eck* and see to it that the bridal party was well served.

When the places at the tables were filled the bishop gave the signal for silent prayer. *Wann der Disch voll is, welle mir bede* ("If the tables are full, let us pray"). All bowed their heads in silent prayer. The wedding dinner consisted of roast duck and chicken, dressing, mashed potatoes, gravy, cold ham, cole slaw, raw and cooked celery, peaches, prunes, pickles, bread and butter, jams, cherry pie, tea, cookies, and many kinds of cake. The meal was a jolly occasion with plenty of opportunity for visiting. All were expected to eat well. Some brought tablets and mints to aid digestion.

The *Eck* did not contain flowers, but fancy dishes, cakes, and delicacies were abundant. No less than six beautifully decorated cakes (baked by friends) and numerous dishes of candy were displayed there. One large bowl of fruit was in the center of it all. An antique wine flask (containing cider) and matching goblets were used by the bridal party.

When the first group had finished eating, the dishes were quickly removed, washed in portable laundry tubs, and replaced for a second sitting. The bridal party did not leave the table. When most of the people were through eating, a hymn was announced by one of the singers. All heartily joined in singing except the bride and bridegroom, who by custom do not sing at their own wedding since it is considered a bad omen. Each guest had brought his own song book, the small *Lieder Sammlungen*. There was a considerable amount of singing until about five o'clock in the afternoon, when many older people went home. Some slow tunes were used, but most of the hymns were sung to the fast tunes. Women, who ordinarily do not assume leadership in religious services, frequently announced hymns and also led the singing. During the afternoon the young people left the tables to gather outdoors and in the barn for their own visiting and festivities.

It is the custom at the wedding supper for the young people to sit in couples; thus each boy was forced to bring a girl to the supper table whether he wanted to or not. The older boys who had "steady" girls had no difficulty in pairing off, but young boys with little or no experience in courtship showed great timidity in finding a partner. Those who refused to find partners were seized and dragged to the door, where they were placed beside a girl. Once in line, all resistance ceased and each couple went to the table holding hands, following the example of the bridal party. The supper included roast beef, roast chicken, noodles, beef gravy, chicken gravy, mashed potatoes, cole slaw, prunes, fruit salad, potato chips, cookies, pies, cakes, and for the bridal group and cooks there were, in addition, baked oysters and ice cream.

Hymns were sung during the supper hour, which continued until ten o'clock. The bride and bridegroom during this time sent plates of extra delicacies—cakes, pie, and candies—from the *Eck* to their special friends seated in various parts of the house. The final selection sung after the evening meal was *Guter Geselle* ("good friend"), a religious folk song. This selection cannot be found in any of the Amish song books. It is largely sung from memory, although it has been printed in leaflet form. The first verse reads:

Guter Geselle, was sagest du mir?	Good friend, what do you say?
O guter Geselle ich sage dir,	O good friend I tell you—
Sage dir was eins ist.	I tell you what one thing is;
Eins ist der Gott allein,	One is God alone,
Der da lebet und der da schwebet,	He who lives and He who soars,
Und der den wahren Glauben führet	And He who leads the true Faith
Im Himmel und auf Erden.	In Heaven and on Earth.

After supper the young folks again went to the barn, where they played games until midnight. At this point most of the married people returned to their homes, but the cooks stayed to wash dishes and take care of the remaining food.

The bride and bridegroom spent the night at the bride's home, but no pranks were sprung on the couple. Although there is no immediate honeymoon, the custom of visiting uncles, aunts, and cousins for a few weeks following the wedding is expected.

The parents of the bride and bridegroom were not present at the ceremony, nor were they given special recognition at the celebration. They were constantly supervising and managing the kitchen and entertaining, seeing that the supply of food was adequate and that the serving was progressing according to schedule. They ate with the cooks and played a subordinate role.

The bride and bridegroom were highly esteemed as they sat at the *Eck*. The occasion was geared for their full enjoyment. However, when they mixed in the crowd separately, between meals, they were treated as ordinary individuals. There was no expression of best wishes. This seems to have been taken for granted. The wedding gifts displayed on the bride's bed consisted chiefly of kitchenware and farm tools.

Barn games are commonly played at weddings, and husking bees take place in some of the most conservative groups. In some settlements games have "gotten out of hand," so that there are weekly hoedowns or "hops." The traditional games played include "Bingo" (not the conventional game but the singing and marching game), "Skip to Ma [My] Lou," "There Goes Topsy through the Window," "O-Hi-O," and "Six-Handed Reel." These and the following games have on occasion been played at weddings: "Little Red Wagon Painted Blue," "Granger," "Charlie Loves to Court the Girls," "We Will Shoot the Buffalo," "The Needle's Eye," and "Six Steps Forward-I-do-I-do." These games, also known as party games, involve holding hands and swinging partners.

Many families and church leaders are opposed to barn games, not because they are wrong in themselves, but because they have led to excesses, and often attract nonmembers with musical instruments. Their opposition is based upon the conviction that it is unnecessary, hilarious conduct, and does not conform to the Christian standard of good behavior. These party or "ring" games were characteristic not only of the Amish but of settlers in the colonial period in America. The Amish kept them alive in their traditions.[4] Although the Amish are opposed to dancing, they never reasoned that the "singing games" were a form of dancing.

The "infair," a distinctive institution in Lancaster County, is an event that formally recognizes the relationships formed between two new kinship systems. A few weeks after the wedding the parents of the groom entertain the bride's parents and all their married and unmarried children on a special day of visiting. The day is celebrated by a large, family-style dinner.

In summary, marriage in Amish life is not simply a romantic affair. The preoccupation with personal taste that is so common in Protestant weddings, where the ceremony and the content of the sermon are dictated by the couple, is not a factor in Amish weddings. The clothes of the bride and bridegroom are made in traditional styles. Marriage is bonded by the community and symbolizes the couple's acceptance of mature values. Community and personal expectations allow no room for divorce, and separation is almost unknown. The ceremony is elaborate because much is expected in the way of community conformity and responsibility.

DEATH

Death is a sober occasion. In some respects, however, it is taken as a matter of course, as the Amish person lives his life in the shadow

---

4. Several games played by the Amish appear in an album entitled *Colonial Singing Games and Dancing* (No. WS 107), produced by the Colonial Williamsburg Foundation, Williamsburg, Va.

of death and in conscious submission to the forces of nature. The Amish community is very sensitive to sickness among its members, and if someone is seriously ill, a sense of religious duty compels members of the church and community to visit the sick person's home, though it may be only a five- or ten-minute call.

When my father's cousin, "one-arm" Joe Byler, was on his deathbed with cancer, I visited his home with my sister. His children were all present. The women, dressed in black, were washing dishes and seemed busy with work. Evening callers entered the house without knocking, whereupon they were invited to enter the sitting room. The visitors, consisting of neighbors, friends, and relatives, extended the usual handshake with all the others in the sitting room and quietly found seats. Only a word or two was exchanged with the wife of the sick man when she came out of his room. She, as spokeswoman concerning the current condition of her husband, conversed with one of the women seated in the circle of visitors. All others, particularly the men, were quiet and resigned. An air of seriousness prevailed during the long periods of silence.

The Amish die in the hospital only when it is necessary or unavoidable; they prefer to die at home.[5] News of a death spreads throughout the Amish community very rapidly. Following a death a list is immediately made of persons who are to be notified personally and invited to the funeral. Next, nonrelatives are appointed to take full charge of all the work and arrangements. Relatives who live at a great distance are notified from the telephone of a non-Amish neighbor.

When death overtakes a family member, few decisions need to be made for which tradition has not provided. Neighbors and nonrelatives relieve the bereaved family of all work responsibility. The family is not confronted with the numerous decisions faced by the typical American family at such a time. Community responsibility relieves the Amish family of the tension and stress of such decisions as choosing a coffin and a place of burial, as well as the financial worries associated with death.

Young men take over the farm chores and an older married couple takes on the honorary position of managing the household. They appoint as many other helpers as they need for cleaning, food preparation, and burial arrangements. The closest kin spend their time

5. For observations on death and dying in Lancaster County, I am indebted to Kathleen B. Bryer, "Attitudes toward Death among Amish Families: Implications for Family Therapy" (M.A. thesis, Hahnemann Medical College, Philadelphia, Pa., 1978). For Iowa customs, see Melvin Gingerich, "Custom Built Coffins," *The Palimpsest* 24 (December 1943): 384–88.

in quiet meditation and in conversation in the living room. The bier is located in an adjacent or back room. Still other friends come to the home, and a few sit up all night while the closest kin retire. Some Midwestern Amish still observe the old custom of the wake by sitting up all night around the deceased, and young people gather at the home in the evening to sing. Generally, funerals are held on the third day following death.

Traditionally the dead are dressed in white. For a man this includes a white shirt, trousers, and socks. A woman is clothed in a white dress, cape, and organdy cap. The cape and apron are frequently those that were worn by the deceased on her wedding day.

Amish coffins and wooden vaults are made by an Amish carpenter or by an undertaker catering to Amish specifications. Formerly they were made of walnut, but due to the scarcity of this lumber, pine is now used. A coffin consists of a plain-varnished, stained and oiled wooden box without side handles. The coffin design varies among Amish settlements. The inside is lined with white cloth by some groups, but a lining is not used by the more traditional Amish. Some groups prefer to have the lid all in one piece; for viewing the body, the lid is slid back about two feet. Other groups have a two-piece lid, and the upper part of the lid is fastened with hinges and is opened for viewing. In both types the lid is fastened with wooden screws.

Most Amish groups have the body embalmed, though a few very strict groups do not. The undertaker never sees the body of the deceased person in the latter case. In some communities the body is not taken away from the home until the day of the funeral. The undertaker executes the burial permits. From four to six pallbearers, depending on the need, are selected by the family. One pallbearer may assist with the seating arrangements at the funeral and open and close the coffin for viewing at the funeral. All help to close the grave.

The funeral and burial are strictly "plain." There is no modern lowering device, artificial grass, carpet, or tent at the grave, nor are there flowers. The expenses of an Amish funeral would hardly exceed the cost of a wooden coffin and embalming fees. Simple obituaries, if requested by the local newspaper staff, are sometimes published in the village newspaper.

In Lancaster County, Pennsylvania, the Amish use several funeral directors. One is a native of the area and speaks the Amish dialect, and all provide the funeral wagon, the team of horses, and the driver for transporting the body to the cemetery. In such a densely populated Amish area certain customs are unique as well. During the

On the death of a member, many Amish come to the aid
of the bereaved family. The grave is prepared
by members who are not close relatives.

wedding "season," November and December, weddings take prece-
dence over the dates set for funerals. Inside the burial grounds the
coffin is again opened for a brief viewing.

When a death occurs the funeral director is notified by telephone
by a neighbor. Upon his arrival at the home, the funeral director
often finds forty or fifty people who have gathered to see the deceased
person just as he or she was when death occurred. These gatherings
are an expression of sharing and of support for the family. The body
is then brought to the funeral home for preparation, dressed in appropriate undergarments, placed in a coffin, and returned to the
home. The work of the funeral director does not involve contacting
the ministers or pallbearers, or preparing the grave. Young men called
leicht-ah-sager go from place to place extending invitations to the
funeral. Members within the church district of the deceased are welcome to attend without an invitation. But relatives must be invited,
and the cutoff point for relatives is usually cousins of the same age
as the deceased.

Great respect is shown for the dead in many ways. The burial
garments are made by the family. Members dress the body and comb
the hair. Manners and comments all indicate great respect, love, and
concern. Traditional mourning garments also indicate such respect.
Black (among women) will be worn for one year when there is a loss
in the immediate family, for six months for a grandparent, three
months for an uncle or aunt, and six weeks for a cousin.

The following is an account of the funeral of an Amish patriarch that was held at nine o'clock in the morning on a February day at his old homestead in Mifflin County, Pennsylvania:

On our arrival the barnyard was already full of black carriages. People were gathering slowly and silently in the large white house, first removing their overshoes on the long porch. Inside there were three large rooms. The wall partitions had been removed so that the speaker could be seen from any part of the three rooms. Benches were arranged parallel with the length of each room. About three hundred people were present. The living room held sixty-two persons, including the fourteen ministers (many of them guests) seated on a row of chairs down the center of the room. The large kitchen seated probably eighty persons, and the third room held about fifty persons, including children. Of the remaining people, some were upstairs, others were standing in the summer kitchen, and more were outdoors.

The third room, ordinarily the master bedroom, had been used as the living quarters of the deceased grandfather. It was in this room that the body of the deceased was resting—in a coffin that had been placed on a bench against the wall. Relatives sat facing the coffin, with the next of kin closest to it. They had their backs to the speaker.

The house gradually filled. The head usher was a friend of the family but not a close relative. With hat on his head, he seated incoming people and reserved special space for relatives. When every bit of available bench space was full, and chairs had been crowded in at all possible odd corners, the audience waited in silence for the appointed hour.

After the clocks in all three rooms struck nine the minister at the head of a long line of preachers removed his hat. At once all the other men removed their hats in perfect unison. The first minister took his position at the doorway between the kitchen and the living room. His message, similar to an ordinary introductory sermon at a regular worship service, was full of biblical admonitions, largely from the Old Testament. This gathering, he reminded his hearers, was special. God had spoken through the death of a brother.

He made reference to the life and character of the deceased, but these remarks were incidental to the sermon, which continued: "The departed brother was especially minded to attend worship services the last few years of his life, in spite of his physical handicaps. Those who ministered to his needs have nothing to regret because they have done their work well. His chair is empty, his bed is empty, his voice will not be heard anymore. He was needed in our presence, but God needs such men too. We would not wish him back, but we should rather prepare to follow after him. He was a human being and had weaknesses too, but his deeds will now speak louder than when he lived."

After thirty minutes the first speaker sat down. He was followed by a second minister, a guest in the community, who delivered the principal address. He too reminded his hearers that a loud call from heaven had come to the congregation, and that the Scriptures warn every member to be ready to meet death. "We do not know when 'our time' will come, but the important thing is to be ready," the minister warned. "Death is the result of Adam's sin. Young people, when you are old enough to think about joining the church, don't put it off." (Such direct admonitions to the young, linked with intense emotional appeal, provide motivation for conformity to traditional Amish values.)

Two passages were read, one near the beginning and one near the close of this second address. The readings were from John 5 and Revelation 20. The sermon was far from a eulogy. The emphasis was personal and direct. It was an appeal to the audience to live righteously, inasmuch as a day of reckoning comes for all people. The minister said he did not wish to make the sermon too long because the weather was unpleasant for the horses standing outside in the rain. After speaking for forty-five minutes, he read a long prayer as the congregation knelt. At the conclusion of the prayer the audience rose to their feet and the benediction was pronounced.

At this point the audience was seated and a brief obituary was read in German by the minister who had preached the first sermon. In behalf of the family he also thanked all those who had shown kindness during the sickness and death of the departed one and invited all who could to return to the home for dinner after the burial. The assisting minister read a hymn. There was no singing.

The minister in charge announced that the boys could retire to the barn. The reason was apparent, as rearrangement was necessary to provide for the viewing of the body. Except for the ministers, the living room was entirely vacated. Next, the coffin was moved to a convenient viewing place into the main entrance. Eveyrone present formed a line and took one last look at the body of the departed brother. Sorrow and tears were evident, but there was little weeping. The closest relatives stood in back of the coffin during the viewing and followed it to the grave.

Meanwhile friends and helpers had prepared the hearse for transporting the body to the graveyard. The hearse consisted of a one-horse springwagon with the seat pushed forward. Because of the

After the funeral service, relatives and friends drive in procession
to the burial grounds. Most then return to the home
of the deceased for a meal.

rainy weather, a canvas was placed over the coffin to keep it dry. The
horses of the mourners were hitched to their carriages by the many
helpers. Relatives of the deceased entered their buggies and formed
a long line to follow the body to the *Graabhof* ("graveyard"). The
procession traveled very slowly, seldom faster than the ordinary walk
of the horses.

Upon arrival at the graveyard the horses were tied to the hitching
posts. The coffin, supported by two stout, rounded, hickory poles, was
immediately carried to the open grave and placed over it. Relatives
and friends gathered near. Long, felt straps were placed around
each end of the coffin. The pallbearers lifted the coffin with the straps
while a bystander quickly removed the supporting crosspieces. The
coffin was then slowly lowered into the grave and the long straps
were slowly removed. Standing in the grave on the frame that surrounded the casket, a man placed short boards over the casket as they
were handed to him. Nearby a father clutched his four-year-old son
and whispered something into his ear, hoping that some recollection
of his grandfather would remain in his consciousness. With shovels
the four pallbearers began to fill the grave. Soil and gravel hit the

rough box with loud thumps. When the grave was half filled the shovelers halted as the minister read a hymn. As is their custom, all the men tilted or removed their hats. They filled the grave and mounded the soil. Family members turned from the scene, slowly got into their buggies, and returned to the home of the deceased to share a meal together.

Death and its associated ceremonies are conditioned by the beliefs and attitudes of the Amish community. In death the deepest emotions of community are engendered. The act of dying, which is the most private act that any person can experience, is transformed into a community event. Death, like the marriage announcement, is conveyed in person. In this way the most intimate sentiments are guarded with personal dignity. While death may shake the emotional foundations of the individual, it does not threaten the moral foundations of the society. Community organization is not adversely affected by the death of individual members. The reasons for death are understood within the context of the meaning of life.

The custom of sharing a meal following the burial is one that helps the mourners resume their normal roles and responsibilities. Here the bereaved experience a sense of belonging and togetherness. Conversational and interaction patterns are restored to their normal functions. The family is quickly reintegrated into the community, in sharp contrast to the typical American family, where even close neighbors often do not know of a death, and where sympathies are expressed over long periods of time in awkward and anonymous contacts.

Burials during earlier periods were frequently on farms, but this is rarely the practice today. In large, well-established Amish communities there are separate Amish cemeteries with plain headstones. In other places the Amish bury their dead in a community cemetery with various Mennonite or related groups. Married persons and their children are usually buried side by side.[6] In Illinois the Amish bury their dead in rows in the order of the deaths without regard to kinship or marriage. The respect of the Amish for their dead is reflected in the excellent attention they give to their cemeteries. Century-old cemeteries in extinct settlements are cleaned by groups of men who organize a frolic during the summer months.

6. For a study of burial and descent, see Gary Unruh and John M. Jantzen, "Social Structure and Burial Symbolism among the Kansas Amish," in *Conference on Child Socialization*, ed. John A. Hostetler (Philadelphia: Temple University, 1969), pp. 167–92.

For all people who cling to life and enjoy it to the fullest, death is the greatest menace. The Amish, who profess not to have conformed to this world, turn to the promise of life beyond death. Their belief in the divine order of all things, including immortality, is a source of comfort to the mourning family and community.

CHAPTER 10

Ritual Integration of the Community

FOR PURPOSES of analysis, Amish ritual behavior consists of two types, the social and the ceremonial. The social is concerned with the routine activities of work, dress, family relations, childrearing, kinship duties, and visiting. The ceremonial rituals are those performed in the narrower sense when the group gathers for worship, baptism, marriages, communion, and funerals.[1] Both types are in a very real sense sacred, for the Amish make no sharp distinction between sacred and secular activities. As activities that symbolize the fundamental "needs" of the society, ceremonial rituals help to revitalize and integrate the community. Such collective sentiments support the individual member in his beliefs. The ceremonies of the church district tie all families together in a common sense of destiny.

The whole disciplinary process of living "the Amish way" may be viewed as a redemptive process. Ritual allows the group to come into contact with the source of power which gives orders to their world view. Collective worship incorporates adequate myth recitation and

1. The distinction is developed by Sandra L. Cronk in "Gelassenheit: The Rites of the Redemptive Process in Old Order Amish and Old Order Mennonite Communities" (Ph.D. diss., University of Chicago, School of Divinity, 1977), pp. 8–14. I am indebted to her for important insights on ritual and *Gelassenheit*.

interpretation (the story of Creation) to sustain their cosmos, but primary emphasis is placed on interpersonal relationships within the *Gemeinde* ("community") itself. The Amish, like all Anabaptist groups, look to the life and teachings of Jesus and the character of the early Christian church for models of behavior.

For the Amish, sacred power is found within the community pattern, and not outside it. The Amish do not conduct pilgrimages to a holy place, nor do they encourage attendance at religious conventions of other denominations. The Amish have no class of legal scholars who concern themselves with the meaning of a sacred book or revelation. Their leaders exhort, admonish, and correct by using examples from the Bible and the teachings of Jesus. Ceremonial participation, as in all human groups, dispels personal anxiety, gives members confidence, and disciplines the social patterns. A description of some of the important ceremonial rituals follows.

THE PREACHING SERVICE

The most pervasive ceremonial activity in Amish life is the preaching service held every other Sunday at the home of various members on a rotating basis. The service involves most of the day, beginning at about 9:00 o'clock in the morning and often continuing until after 12:00 noon. It is followed by a common meal and visiting, which lasts until midafternoon.

Much preparation on the part of the host household is necessary prior to the Sunday meeting. The mundane work takes on ritual significance as stables are emptied of manure and carpets are removed from the house. The burden of the work falls on the woman, since the house must be cleaned, the furniture rearranged, the stoves blackened, and the ornamental china washed. On Saturday, neighboring women come to bake pies and prepare the other food that will be served after the preaching service. The man of the house secures the church benches, supervises the seating arrangements, and during the service performs the functions normally assumed by an usher.

Sunday is a day of anticipation in Amish society. It makes no difference whether it is a warm, sunny morning or a blustery, winter day; the Amish father, mother, and all the children in the family hustle around, get the cows milked, and by eight o'clock are on their way to the preaching service.

Father always drives the horse and buggy, with mother and baby beside him and the young children in the back seat. In winter, mother and baby may be tucked in the back seat of the carriage, where the air is not so sharp and raw. The sight of a dozen carriages turning

Walking to the preaching service on Sunday morning

single-file into the long farm lane, and the sound of still other horses trotting on the hard-surface road over the hill, evokes deep sentiments among the gathering community. Neighbors and those nearby usually walk to the service. No driver would think of passing another "rig" on the way to the service.

On arriving at the place of worship, the carriage halts in the barnyard, where the mother and girls dismount. Father and sons drive to a convenient stopping place, where they are met by hostlers, often sons of the host household, who help unhitch the horse and find a place for it in the stable. The horse is given hay from the supply in the barn. Meanwhile the men cluster in little groups in the stable and under the forebay of the barn, greeting one another with handshakes and in subdued voices.

Finally the preachers observe that it is time to withdraw to the house. In winter the men remove their heavy overcoats and hang them in the barn, frequently on the same hooks where the harness is hanging; there are no closets in Amish houses, and thus there is no place to hang so many clothes. In summer the service may be held in the barn. The order in which worshipers gather is determined by sex and age, a principle that is evident in the entire social life of the society. First the ordained men enter, followed by the oldest men. They are leisurely followed by the middle-aged. The last to enter the assembly are the unmarried boys, who come in single file according to seniority. The age grouping holds also for the meal that follows the service.

The women and girls place their shawls and bonnets in the wash-house or the woodshed. In summertime the girls remain here until it is time to join the assembly. In winter they gather in the kitchen. They usually take their seats before the boys come in from the barn; the latter, incidentally, in some districts remain in the barn until the service has begun. The girls also enter single file, generally according to age, shaking hands with the ministers as they enter. The baptized single women head the line as a rule. Visiting young people who are members are frequently given the privilege of following the lead person in the procession.

Amish houses are specially built to accommodate the many people, often 200 or more, who gather for worship. The houses have wide doors, and in the Eastern states there are removable partitions so that people seated in almost any part of the main floor can observe the preacher. Each church district owns benches and hymnals, which are transported from one meeting place to another. The furniture is removed or stored in such a way that rooms can be filled with benches.

The seating space consists of backless benches, which occupy the kitchen, sitting room, and main bedroom. A center row of chairs is reserved for the ordained. Older men take benches next to the wall, but the feeble ones are given rocking chairs. Chairs are frequently given to the ministers' wives and the oldest women. The preacher, who stands at the doorway between the two largest rooms, has no pulpit, but occasionally a chair upon which to lean. Women and men are seated separately, though they are not in separate rooms. Several rows of unmarried women occupy the sitting room with the men, and men who arrive late remain in the kitchen with mothers and infants. Preschool boys sit with their fathers and girls with their mothers. Infants, a month or six weeks old, also are brought to the service. Being present is important.

The customs of one district or settlement may differ slightly from those of others. The symbols that bind a group into a unified whole differ from Pennsylvania to Kansas, and even within the state of Pennsylvania. While the order of service is almost uniform, the manner of informal behavior, as well as the extent to which informal behavior is ritualized, differs. For instance, men in some districts leave their hats on in the house until the hymn is announced. Then, with one uniform swoop, off they come; they are put under the bench, piled on empty benches, or hung on hooks. In other districts hats are taken off as the men enter the house. The boys may pile them on the porch. In some groups men leave their hats on during the meal, taking them off only for the silent prayer at the beginning and at the end of the meal.

The preaching service may be three hours long and there are a variety of forms which the order of service may take.

ORDER OF AN AMISH PREACHING SERVICE

1. Hymns (several) are sung while the ministers retire to an upstairs room for counsel. The *Loblied* (*Ausbund*, p. 770) is always the second hymn. (The singing of a hymn may take from twenty to thirty minutes.)
2. *Anfang*, or "introductory sermon"
3. Prayer (assembly kneeling, and in most localities silent)
4. The assembly stands while the *Armen-diener* ("deacon") reads a chapter from the Bible.
5. *Es schwere Deel*, or "main sermon," which is concluded by the reading of a chapter from the Bible.
6. *Zeugniss*, or "testimonies," to the main sermon are given by other ministers present as requested by the one who preached. Other lay members are frequently asked to give *Zeugnis*.
7. Closing remarks by the minister who preached
8. All turn and kneel while the minister reads a prayer from *Die Ernsthafte Christenpflicht*. (The prayer on p. 55 is commonly used.)
9. Benediction (assembly standing)
10. Announcement: where the next meeting will be held; whether members should remain after dismissal for a members' meeting.
11. Closing hymn
12. Dismissal, with the youngest leaving first, followed by the older ones in the order of their ages.

After the rooms have been occupied and everyone is waiting for the service to begin, an elderly man announces a hymn number. The old man begins to sing what seems like a solo, but after the first syllable the whole assembly joins in unison. The *Vorsinger* or *Vorstimmer*, the one leading the singing, may be any male member who has had the informal training required. He is not formally appointed, nor does he stand or sit in any special place. The *Vorsinger* continues to sing the beginning of each new line of a hymn in a trembling falsetto. The tunes are extremely slow, with the voices of the old joining those of the young in unison.

With the singing of the first hymn, the ordained men withdraw (oldest first) to a room upstairs for *Abrot* (*Abrath*, or "counsel"), for prayer, and to arrange who will preach the sermons. When there are applicants for baptism, they appear before the ministers upstairs. On entering, the oldest applicant says, "It is my desire to be at peace with God and the Church." Each of the others in his or her turn says, "That is my desire too." After instruction they are dismissed and the ordained proceed with their business.

While the preachers are in the council room, the assembly continues to sing hymns, which are interspersed with long periods of silence. With a nod the elderly *Vorsinger* passes to another the responsibility for leading the next hymn, and frequently a young man is nudged by an older one to take over in the middle of a familiar hymn. Should a young man lose the melody and his courage, an older member will come to his rescue. Considerable talent is demanded of the song leader to sing the tunes from memory.

When the preachers descend the stairway the singing stops at the end of the verse. The preachers shake hands with latecomers and with any whom they had not greeted earlier in the morning. After the ministers are seated, one of them rises and stands between the two large rooms to deliver the first sermon. With hands folded beneath his full-grown white beard, a preacher typically begins to mumble in a low tone, gradually building up to an audible and rhythmic flow of words in mixed Pennsylvania German, German, and English:

Liebe Brüder und Schwestern und alle die womit versammelt sin, zum erschde will ich eich die Gnade Gottes winsche und die mitwirkente Graft des heiligen Geistes, un wie Petrus sagt, "Gelobet sei Gott und der Vater unsers Herrn Jesu Christi, der uns nach seiner grossen Barmherzigheit wiedergeboren hat zu einer lebendigen Hoffnung, durch die Auferstehung Jesu Christi von Toten, zu einem unverganglichen und unbefleckten und unverwelklichen Erbe." (I Pet. 1:3–4)

Dear brothers and sisters and all who are assembled here, first of all I wish you the grace of God and the accompanying power of the Holy Ghost. As Peter says, "Blessed be the God and Father of our Lord Jesus Christ, which according to his abundant mercy hath begotten us again into a lively hope by the resurrection of Jesus Christ from the dead, to an inheritance incorruptible, and undefiled, and that fadeth not away, reserved in heaven for you." (I Pet. 1:3–4)

In a typical opening sermon, the minister reminds the congregation of the purpose of their meeting—to listen once again to the Word of God. He brings to the attention of all some Scriptual teachings, pointing out the importance of obeying the commandments. For instance, he admonishes the worshiper: "schaffet, das ihr selig werdet, mit Furcht und Zittern" ("Work out your own salvation with fear and trembling" (Phil. 2:12). This is a favorite quotation. Before bringing his half-hour introduction to a close, he mentions the importance of prayer and of trust in God. Appreciation for freedom of worship is typically expressed. After a few words of apology for his weakness, he informs the congregation that he does not wish to take the allotted time away from the brother who is to bring the main message: "Auch ich will die Zeit net lang verbrauche in mein grosse Armut und Schwachheit und die Zeit wegnehmen von der Bruder wo es schwere Deel hat." He asks the hearers to pray for the minister who is to bring the main message and then quotes a favorite verse: "Kommt, lasst uns anbeten, und knieen, und niederfallen vor dem Herrn, der uns gemacht hat. Denn er ist unser Gott, und wir das Volk seiner Weide, und Schafe seiner Hand, Heute, so ihr seine Stimme horet, so verstocket euer Herz nicht." (For translation, see Ps. 95:6–8.) He then closes with the words, "Und wann dir einig sind lasset uns bede" ("If you are all agreed, let us pray"). All kneel together for a period of silent prayer.

The signal to rise from prayer may not be apparent to the visitor. When the preacher feels that enough time has been allotted for individual prayer, he gets up from his knees. Those who hear his foot scraping the floor as he rises know that it is time to stand.

All remain standing while the deacon reads the Scripture. The deacon may offer several remarks, after which he admonishes the congregation to be obedient to the Lord. The entire chapter is read in a singsong, chantlike fashion. After the last verse of the chapter, the deacon concludes: "So weit hat die Schrift sich ersteckt" ("Thus far extendeth the Scripture"), and all are seated. The Scriptures read at the preaching services follow a seasonal pattern.[2] The register of Scriptures begins at Christmas time with the birth of Christ and concludes with the New Testament account of the judgment and end of the world. Selections from the hymnal (*Ausbund*) are integrated with the register of Scriptures and hymns.

Now the time has come for the main sermon. The preacher begins with the usual greeting: "Gnade sei mit euch und Friede von Gott unser Vater. Wir sin schon viel-feldich vermanhnt wore auf dem meiget Stund bei dem Bruder." ("Grace be with you and peace from God our father. We have been admonished many times this morning hour by the brother.") He reminds his hearers of the importance of obedience to the vow of baptism, of obedience to the Bible and par-

2. Registers have been published on many occasions. Aside from pamphlets and those published by J. A. Raber in his *Der Neue Amerikanische Calendar*, a few have appeared in the *Mennonite Quarterly Review* 15 (January 1941): 26–32, and in Joseph W. Yoder, *Amische Lieder* (Huntington, Pa.: Yoder Publishing Co., 1942), p. xii.

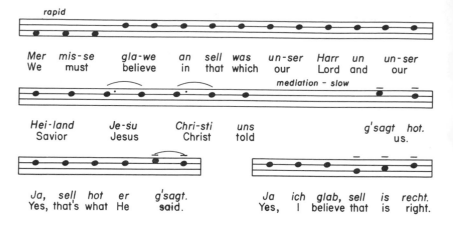

rapid

Mer	mis-se	gla-we	an	sell	was	un-ser	Harr	un	un-ser
We	must	believe	in	that	which	our	Lord	and	our

mediation – slow

Hei-land	Je-su	Chri-sti	uns	g'sagt hot.
Savior	Jesus	Christ	told	us.

Ja,	sell	hot	er	g'sagt.		Ja	ich	glab,	sell	is	recht.
Yes,	that's	what	He	said.		Yes,	I	believe	that	is	right.

Figure 12.
Intonation of an Amish sermon

ents. *Das alt Gebrauch* (equivalent to "the old way of life") sums up a major aspect of moral emphasis. This phrase embodies the principle of separation from the world, the *Regel und Ordnung* ("rules and discipline") of the church, and the idea of strangers and pilgrims in an evil world. Innovations that are unacceptable are labeled *eppes Neies* ("something new") and are met with the force of *das alt Gebrauch*.

Delivery of the sermon falls into a stylized pattern.[3] Somewhat like a chant, the preacher's voice rises to a rather high pitch; then, at the end of each phrase, it suddenly drops (see Figure 12). Babies who fall asleep in their mothers' arms are carried, sometimes directly in front of the preacher, into the next room and up the stairway, where three or more may sleep on the same bed. Other children lean on the arm of the parent, or pass the time with a handkerchief, making such objects as "mice" or "twin babies in a cradle." In the kitchen, mothers are nursing their new babies. Not only do the babies tire; the singsong sermon and the stuffy atmosphere and warmth of the packed room frequently put many of the hard-working men to sleep. Some who appear to be nodding or swaying in sleep are just changing their posture, since there are no backrests.

The service is orderly and reverent. On rare occasions humorous incidents occur, like the forgetful mother who put her baby to sleep and upon descending the stairway had the baby's little white cap on her own head.

3. Although characteristic of the traditional Amish preacher, chanting is not unique to the Amish. See Bruce A. Rosenberg, *The Art of the American Folk Preacher* (New York: Oxford University Press, 1970).

Meanwhile, as the preacher goes on with his singsong sermon, the backless benches seem to get harder and harder. The children begin to get restless. The mother of the house may pass a dish of crackers and cookies to all the mothers and fathers having youngsters at their side. The dish is passed down the aisle, across, and over to the next room so that no child misses this treat. Moments later a glass of water is passed for the same youngsters. The long sermon has just started and there may be two more hours of sitting still. The host of the house may bring a glass of water for the preacher.

The preacher relates first the Old Testament story from Adam to Abraham, and second the account from John the Baptist to the end of Paul's missionary journeys. The earnestness with which he speaks produces drops of sweat on his face, and every few minutes it is necessary for him to reach to his inside coat pocket and draw out a handkerchief to wipe his forehead. He holds the white handkerchief in his hand and occasionally waves it through the air as he illustrates a point.

He concludes the long sermon with the reading of a chapter from the Bible, but interrupts the reading with comments. Then, with a long sigh the preacher sits down and asks other ordained men to give *Zeugnis* ("testimony") to the message and to "bring anything up which should have been said," or to correct any mistakes. Those offering comments (ranging from three to five minutes in length) remain seated.

After the testimonies are completed, the main preacher rises to his feet for some closing remarks. He is thankful that the sermon can be taken as God's Word and he further admonishes the congregation to give praise to God and not to man: "Ich feel dankbar dass die Lehr hat erkannt sei kenne fer Gottes Wort. Gewet Gott die Ehr nicht Mensche." He thanks the congregation for being quiet and attentive. As a guest, he admonishes all to be obedient to the home ministry, and in speaking to the ministers he advises them to visit other districts. This, he says, strengthens and builds up the church. He asks the congregation to kneel for the closing prayer. Except for three or four mothers who are holding sleeping babies, all kneel while the minister reads in chant style from the prayer book.

When the minister is through chanting the long prayer, everyone rises for the benediction, which he recites from memory:

Zuletzt, liebe Brüder, freuet euch, seid vollkommnen, trostet euch, habt einerlei Sinn, seid friedsam; so wird Gott der Liebe und des Friedens mit euch sein, grüsset euch unter einander mit dem heiligen Kuss. Es grüssen euch alle Heiligen. (II Cor. 13:11–13)

So befehle ich noch mich, mit euch, Gott und seiner Gnadenhand an, dass er uns walte in dem seligmachenden Glauben erhalten, darinnen stärken, leiten und bewahren bis an ein seliges Ende, und das alles durch Jesum Christum, Amen.

Finally, dear brethren, rejoice, be perfect, be comforted and be of one mind; be peaceful, and the God of love and peace shall be with you. Greet each other with the Holy Kiss. You are greeted by all the saints. (II Cor. 13:11–13)

So I submit myself, with you, to God and his gracious hand, that He please to keep us in the saving faith, to strengthen us in it, to guide and lead us until a blessed end; and all this through Jesus Christ. Amen.

When the minister says the words "Jesum Christum" at the very end, all in complete uniformity bend their knees. This genuflection may come as a surprise to the visitor, but to the member it is an intense experience indicating full obedience and reverence. It symbolizes unanimity with the group.

When the assembly is again seated, the deacon announces the place of the next meeting. In the event that business pertaining to discipline is to be taken up, the deacon also asks that after the singing of the closing hymn, members remain seated: "Was Brüder und Schwechdre sin, solle wennich schtill sitze bleiwe." On such occasions, all the unbaptized boys and girls and nonmembers are dismissed.

When a members' meeting is not scheduled, the congregation is dismissed with the closing of the hymn. The youngest leave the service first, with the men and women marching out separately.

The men remove some of the benches, passing them through a window and the door, to make room for tables, which are formed by setting benches together. Soon the women and girls have set the tables with pies, bread, butter, jam, cheese, pickles, red beets, and coffee—a a standard menu that varies slightly with local custom. Each place setting consists only of a knife, cup, and saucer. The pies are baked firm enough so that each person can cut his own piece and eat it while holding it in the hand. This meal is not supposed to be a feast, but just a "piece" to hold one over until he returns home. The ordained, regardless of their age, always eat at the first sitting, and visitors are often asked to come to the first table. Otherwise age determines who should come to the table. It is usually necessary to set the tables three or four times, with the boys and girls and youngest children eating last. When preaching was held in my home, my brother and I hid some "half-moon pies" in the barn (with mother's permission) and with our best buddies ate them right after the dismissal.

The afternoon is spent in conversation about religion and other matters of mutual interest. To rush away from the service or to leave immediately following the meal is considered somewhat rude. The men congregate informally about the house or barn. In some of the larger districts there are well-developed age-interest groups that function after church, and on such occasions the young men scarcely converse with the older men.

Status among the young men is attained either by showing special interest in the church and Amish religion or by the opposite, namely, by being a nonconformist to the established religious folkways and mores. All young men tend to polarize between the two informal groups. Interest in religious matters is manifested in a variety of ways, chief of which is obedience to parents. Other means of gaining good standing are: being punctual in attending services, listening to the preacher instead of sleeping, helping to sing, showing some initiative in maintaining a conversation with older and more serious-minded men, conforming to the rules of dress to the letter, and appearing neat without ornamentation. On the other hand, those who gain status as nonconformists do precisely the opposite.

The afternoon fellowship breaks up by two or three o'clock when many families load into their buggies to go home and do the evening chores. Young people who are not needed to help with chores may go to a friend's home until the evening hymn singing, which takes place at the same farm where the preaching was held. Friends and neighbors, as many as fifty persons, are often invited to remain for the evening meal at the place of preaching.

VISITING PATTERNS

There are two kinds of Sundays among the Amish: those observed by going to a preaching service, as described above; and "off" Sundays, observed by staying at home and resting or by visiting relatives.

The *Gemeesunndaag*, or "church Sunday," structures the life of the individual. Individual desire must conform to group expectations. There are no alternatives but to do the usual milking and feeding in the morning and prepare to go to the preaching service. No member is allowed to stay at home unless he is sick. Father harnesses the horse before breakfast, but hitches up the horse only when the family is about ready to leave the house. A young man old enough to "run around" (being of courting age) has his own "rig," a one-seated buggy, topless in Pennsylvania but not so in Indiana and Iowa. If he has sisters of courting age, he takes them to the preaching service in his buggy. To be old enough, or to have the permission of parents, to attend the Sunday evening singing, becomes the cherished goal of adolescents. Upon returning home the Amish family spends the remainder of the day doing the usual farm chores and passes the evening in leisure. From the standpoint of the adolescent and the child, Sunday is an intense, rigorous experience.

The off Sunday is spent in a much more informal manner. This Sunday is a relief from the long, preaching Sunday. Of course, it is permissible to attend preaching in another district if the family or part of the family wishes to do so. It is not compulsory, and preachers more frequently than lay families tend to visit districts other than their own.

Among some districts in Iowa and Indiana the alternate Sundays are spent in Sunday School during the summer months. This represents a departure from the Amish tradition in the Eastern states. The Sunday School is held in an abandoned schoolhouse. Attendance is voluntary, and no lunch is served. The school elects its own lay leaders, a superintendent and an assistant, who in turn appoint teachers for the classes. The teachers of the classes stand up and see that the group takes turns in reading assigned passages from the German Bible. A major function of the school is to learn the German language. Teachers in the classes make little or no comment. The interpretation of difficult passages is left to the general superintendent and the preachers before dismissal. Young children are given rewards for completing reading assignments at the end of the Sunday School year. Each family generally returns home after the school, which lasts from about 9:30 in the morning until noon. Young people of "running around" age may gather with "the crowd" in a home. Here a lunch is served and the afternoon is spent in visiting and in the enjoyment of one another's company. It is also here that the young people gather to go to the evening singing.

But most Amish communities do not have Sunday Schools, and families enjoy spending the day at home. After a week of hard work in the field, a day of rest is welcome. When the farm chores are done, the family may dress in clean clothes and spend the time reading and learning the German language. Some families make this a regular time for gathering around the family table with German Bibles and primers. Mothers frequently read Bible stories to the younger children, in English as well as in German. This day is also made delightful with a delicious noon meal at home in an environment that is more relaxed than the weekday meals. The afternoon may be spent in reading or visiting. The young man usually catches up on sleep lost the previous night, for he may have stayed at his girl friend's home until the wee hours of Sunday morning. But Saturday evening courtship is restricted (traditionally) to every other Saturday, to those weekends when the girl has an off Sunday.

On Sunday an attitude of reverence prevails. No loud noise is per-

In some Midwestern communities, members meet on alternate Sundays
for "Sunday School." Shown here is the Iowa Amish institution
known as "Dutch College."

mitted on the farm. The use of a hammer or other tools is forbidden
to Amish boys on Sunday. The cracking of hickory nuts was tolerated
among the children in my home, but no whistling was allowed on
Sunday. Children may invite other Amish children to their home, or
ask to play at the home of another family. Hiking, and playing in
haystacks and in and out of the barn, also are common. Occasionally
the parents visit old or sick people, and the children are left at home
alone. In our home it was special to have visiting playmates and even
more special to be left at home without our parents. Though fishing
was forbidden, hiking to the top of the nearby mountain or wading in
the creek was not. We played many games and enjoyed these long
periods of uninterrupted play when our parents left us alone. We
seldom got into real mischief, though things did happen that could
not have taken place when adults were about: harnessing up the
neighbor's cow; teasing the rooster or the ram; or taking a trip to the

village dump, where we "drove" old automobiles. In the dump we learned how to shift gears, even though we could not get the motor to run. Our parents took some misbehavior in stride and were satisfied to leave us alone at home if one or two in the group acted reasonably responsibly.

Families that go visiting on Sunday enjoy a diversity of age groups similar to their own. It is customary to arrive at the friend's house in the forenoon, often an hour before lunch. Three or four families may be present for the occasion. The men unhitch their horses and talk as they find their way to the house, where the women have been setting a long table with delicious foods. The sitting room fills with people who seat themselves in a circle and wait until the women call the men to dinner. Men gather around the table first, and the women stand back and take the unoccupied seats. A second seating is often necessary. The noon meal is the highlight of the day. An outdoor picnic or eating in cafeteria style, practiced by some Midwestern Amish families, is not considered good hospitality by the most formal Amish groups, to whom sitting at the table is important.

The adults spend the afternoon talking in the living room, where the men are joined by the women after the dishes are done. Candy or popcorn may be passed around the circle. Topics discussed are the weather, crops, machines, sickness, recent events in the secular world, moving, farm transactions, journeys taken, and local folklore that borders on the awesome or mysterious. The women may vacillate between listening to the talk of the men and engaging in conversations on topics of interest to themselves, such as sewing, quilt patterns, household hints, and the diagnosis and treatment of illness. In late afternoon parents interrupt their children's play and gather the family into the buggy to go home and do the chores.

It is customary to visit relatives without invitation. The mother of every home expects to have Sunday guests, and she prepares accordingly. Short visits are often made to the sick after the preaching service. Sunday evening visits to the neighbors also are common. My own family often got into the buggy after supper on Sunday evening and drove to a neighbor's place. If they were not at home, we drove to another home. Visitors from distant states often circulate in one settlement among many families during the course of a one- or two-week stay. Of all the topics in the weekly Amish newspaper, *The Budget*, visiting is given the most coverage.

THE CEREMONIAL CALENDAR

Ritual behavior is governed by the days of the week, by season, and by the calendar. Baptism comes only once each year, preceding the fall communion service. Weddings are held in November and December. Council meetings and communion are held twice each year, in the spring and fall. Preaching services are held every second Sunday. Ordinations to office and funerals are the only rituals not governed by the seasons.

Special days observed as holidays are Christmas, Good Friday, Easter, Ascension Day, Pentecost, and Thanksgiving Day. The intensity with which they are observed differs among Amish communities, especially in the case of the last two. Amish preaching services are sometimes held on weekdays to accommodate preachers visiting from far-distant communities. Weddings provide additional holidays—not only the wedding day itself, which by tradition occurs on a Tuesday or a Thursday, but also the day of preparation preceding the wedding and the day of cleaning up after it.

Christmas is probably the most celebrated holiday, but is observed as a family and kinship, rather than as a ceremonial, holiday. The Amish observe it in their own way without a Christmas tree and without Santa Claus. However, children are exposed to such customs if they attend public school, and some Amish parents come to the annual parochial school Christmas program. Some Amish have adopted the practice of drawing names among themselves for buying presents. On Christmas Eve in my home, each child set a dish at his place at the table. Our parents filled the dishes with many kinds of candy and nuts after we were asleep. Children who want a specific toy usually get it, but toys are generally simple and inexpensive. Married couples may buy surprises for each other, usually something they need, such as a new bed or a chair. Girls may receive decorative dishes from their parents. Gifts are frequently left on display in the sitting room until after New Year's Day.

On Christmas Day it is customary for the relatives of the husband (and/or the wife) to meet for a feast. If the family is too large, the wife's siblings are invited one year and the husband's the following year. The two-day observance of Christmas by some Amish groups is a survival of European custom. Some observe New Year's Day by visiting. Old Christmas or second Christmas, on January 6, otherwise known as Epiphany, is observed by the older Amish people in Pennsylvania and in some other settlements.

Fasting is observed before the spring and fall communions. Good Friday is a fast day. Easter, like Christmas, is observed for two days in some areas. There is no special celebration on Easter, but some practices among the children are survivals of ancient European customs. For two or three weeks before Easter, some children go to the henhouse daily and get a few eggs, which they hide in a secret place in the barn. On Easter morning the eggs are brought to the house to see who has collected the most. Colored Easter eggs are common. Some children are permitted to eat as many eggs as they wish on Easter morning. Ascension Day is observed as a day of rest or visiting, but on this day young people, or whole families, go out into the woods for picnics and the boys may go fishing. Young men may gather together for a ball game. On weekday holidays hunting is generally not taboo, but such prohibitions vary with regional folkways and mores. Good Friday was never observed very strictly in my family in Pennsylvania, but when we moved to Iowa our neighbors were greatly perturbed when my father permitted his sons to do field work on that day.

COMMUNION AND FOOT WASHING

The semiannual communion and its associated rituals are the most important rituals in reinforcing the commitment of Amish church members. Communion service is held twice each year among the Amish, and it will be remembered that the frequency of this service was one of the points on which Jacob Ammann differed from the Swiss Brethren, who held communion only once each year.

Communion binds the Amish members within a district together with sacred ties. Communion symbolizes the unity of the church, and for a district not to have communion means that there has been serious difficulty in getting unanimous opinion on important issues. Communion means entering into the experience of the suffering and death of Jesus Christ, and to emerge with gratitude and remembrance for his death.

The personal examination process begins prior to or with the *Attnungsgemee* ("preparatory service"), which is held two weeks before communion. Every member must be present. The service usually takes most of the day, as the sermons are longer than usual, and the meeting is not dismissed until late afternoon. At this service the ministers present their views on the *Attnung* (*Ordnung*, in High German) and mention practices that are forbidden or discouraged. Each member is asked whether he is in agreement with the *Ordnung*, whether he is at peace with the brotherhood, and whether anything "stands in the way" of his entering into the communion service. Faults must be confessed and adjustments made between members who have differences to settle. In this respect, preparation for communion is a cleansing ritual.

Great emphasis is placed on the importance of individual preparation for this holy service. No person is to partake unworthily or with hate in his heart. The Scripture is made plain to all: "For let a man examine himself, and so let him eat of that bread, and drink of that cup. For he that eateth and drinketh unworthily, eateth and drinketh damnation to himself" (I Cor. 11:28–29).

Members who are known to be guilty of minor offenses but who do not confess are punished by "getting set back from communion"; they are excluded from participation in the communion ceremony. Those who have been excommunicated are sometimes received back into the fellowship at this service if they kneel and acknowledge their faults and receive the right hand of fellowship of the bishop. This service is therefore of utmost importance for evaluating personal behavior, achieving unanimity of opinion, and bringing deviating persons back into conformity with the community.

Another form of introspection prior to communion is fasting, which consists of eating no breakfast and spending the morning in quiet meditation. Fast day is generally Good Friday in the spring and *Michaelstag*, or "St. Michael's Day" (October 11), in the fall (in Lancaster County).

Children typically do not attend the strenuous *Attnungsgemee* and *Grossgemee*, as they are all-day affairs, and much of the meeting is closed to nonmembers. Amish children look forward to these occasions because they may spend the whole day with children of the neighborhood and be free from adult supervision. The children of several families often gather where they can be supervised by single young adults. Parents also look forward to these occasions, because they are a change from the usual routine. Parents enjoy the liberty of attending services without squirming youngsters by their side. Every church member anticipates the quietness of this most holy occasion. The Amish church is, after all, Anabaptist—i.e., an adult affair. These rites are not for children and certain not for entertainment.

Both *Attnungsgemee* and *Grossgemee* are attended by guest ministers and bishops, who are frequently needed to help preach the especially demanding long sermons on these occasions. Their presence also lends emotional support to the local group. The sermons on these two all-day meetings test the physical endurance and capacity of those who preach as well as those who listen. The sermons preached on these occasions are known as the *Altväter-Geschichten* ("the history of the old fathers or patriarchs") and must cover biblical history from the Creation to the suffering of Christ. The second sermon on these two occasions is usually the longer, lasting sometimes as much as three hours.

At the preparatory service the sermons begin with Abraham's call to leave his homeland. What follows is the drama of human conflict, guilt and reconciliation, in the lives of Abraham, Isaac, Lot, Jacob and his twelve sons, Moses, and the Pharaoh, and in the dramatic deliverance from Egypt. This history illustrates good and evil examples in dealing with human affairs and thus prepares members to make reconciliations in their own lives prior to communion. Some of the Bible stories are told with a great deal of suspense and emotion.

The communion sermons appear to be more relaxed than those preached at the preparatory service. They begin with the Genesis account of Creation, the Fall and curse of man, the Flood, the sinful condition of mankind, and many of the same accounts as were given at the preparatory service. This time, events are selected and reviewed which symbolize the coming of the Messiah. The second sermon, conducted by the bishop, ends with *das Leiden Christi* ("the suffering of Christ").

The long sermon continues through the noon hour as members leave the assembly in small groups (in no particular order) and find their way to another part of the house to eat. In some settlements, on these special occasions members eat while standing at a table. Those who have eaten return to the service so that everyone but the main preacher will have a chance to lunch. (The main preacher generally eats an early lunch.)

Near the end of the long sermon two ministers leave and bring bread and wine. While they cut the loaf on a table by the bishop's side, he talks about the origin of bread (and wine), the sowing, harvesting, milling, and baking processes. He recounts the growth of the grapes, the need for pruning, and the purifying of the wine. The meanings are, of course, symbolic for the life of the people of God. The bread is always home-baked, made by the hostess. The wine has been made by the wife of the bishop.

After concluding the sermon, the bishop receives a slice of bread from the deacon and asks the members to stand for prayer. After the prayer, all remain standing while the bishop and one of the ministers break and distribute the bread to the members. Each member bows his knees in reverence, eats the small piece of bread, and is seated. The same procedure is followed with the cup of home-made wine, or in some communities, grape juice. After the bread and wine are passed, the bishop proceeds by asking for *Zeugnis* in the usual manner, and then offers a prayer.

Following the prayer, a minister reads the account of the washing of the disciples' feet (John 13), while the deacon and lay members bring in towels and pails of water. The bishop admonishes members not to be partial but to wash the feet of the person nearest. As a symbol of complete humility, stooping, not kneeling, is required of the one doing the washing. A hymn is announced and the men begin to remove their shoes and stockings and to wash each other's feet in pairs. Women follow the same pattern in a different room. After each pair has finished, they clasp hands, kiss each other, and the oldest says, *"Da Herr sei mit uns"* ("the Lord be with us"), and the other responds, *"Amen, zum Frieda"* ("Amen, in peace"). As in the early church, the Holy Kiss is a symbol of love and fellowship between believers. The kiss is also exchanged between ordained men as they meet each Sunday for preaching, but is practiced less among the laymen. After all have washed feet, the service concludes with a hymn. As members leave the service, they contribute to the *Armengelt* (the "poor fund" of the district). In this final act of communion, each person places his contribution in the hand of the deacon, who without looking at the amount, immediately places it in his pocket.

MUSIC AND INTEGRATION

Singing is an integral part of worship, though secondary in importance to the preaching of the Word. The basis for singing is supported by the biblical instruction to "admonish one another . . . in hymns and spiritual songs, singing with grace in your hearts to the Lord" (Col. 3:16), and by the examples of Jesus and his disciples singing a hymn. Music is entirely *a cappella*. Instruments are not used in worship, for that would be considered ostentatious and contrary to the spirit of humility. Every worship service begins and ends with a hymn. For Amish persons, singing evokes the deepest emotions of the human spirit and is thus a source of social unification and group catharsis. No other ritual has such a sustained emotional appeal as does the blending of the individual voice with that of the spiritual community.

Text and tunes take one deep into the roots of Amish culture. An outsider, whether trained in music or not, finds it impossible to participate in the singing, which may sound to him like mournful droning or chanting. The Amish have adhered faithfully to the singing of sixteenth-century hymns long abandoned by other Anabaptist groups. The hymnbook of the Amish is called *Ausbund*, a term probably meaning "selection" or "anthology."[4] The texts appear as poetry

4. Translated into English, the title of a recent edition reads: "Selection (anthology): that is, some beautiful Christian songs as they were now and then composed in the prison in Passau in the castle by the Swiss Brethren and by other orthodox Christians. To each and every Christian, of whatever religion they may be, impartially very useful. Besides an appendix of six songs, 13th edition. Published by the Amish congregations in Lancaster County, Pa., 1970" (translation courtesy of William I. Schreiber, "The Hymns of the Amish Ausbund in Philological and Literary Perspective," *Mennonite Quarterly Review* 36 [January 1962]: 37).

Prison tower in Passau, Germany, where in the
sixteenth century persecuted Anabaptists composed many of the
hymns that form today's Amish hymnbook

without musical notations. These hymns were written by Anabaptists
who were confined to prison from the year 1535 in the great castle of
Passau, Bavaria, situated at the mouths of three rivers, the Rhine, Inn,
and Ibbs. In ballad fashion they recount the unusual occurrences and
the tragic fate of the believers who fell victim to intolerant religious
rulers.[5] The verses narrate in dialogue form the conversations between
victims and interrogators, accusers, authorities, and executioners.[6] A

5. For the history of this event and the hymnal, see *Mennonite Encyclopedia*,
s.v. "Ausbund" and "Phillipites." See also Harold S. Bender, "The First Edition
of the Ausbund," *Mennonite Quarterly Review* 3 (April 1929): 147–50; A. J.
Ramaker, "Hymns and Hymn Writers among the Anabaptists of the Sixteenth
Century," *Mennonite Quarterly Review* 3 (April 1929): 101–31; Paul M. Yoder,
Elizabeth Bender, Harvey Graber, and Nelson P. Springer, *Four Hundred Years with
the Ausbund* (Scottdale, Pa.: Herald Press, 1964); and David Luthy, "Four Centuries with the *Ausbund*," *Family Life*, June 1971, pp. 21–22.
6. Schreiber, "The Hymns of the Amish Ausbund," p. 49.

dominant theme running through the texts is that of protest against wicked tyrants; there is an undertone of loneliness and sorrow, but not of despair. A firm conviction that God will not forsake His people, but will lead them through sorrow to everlasting joy and eternal life, also is expressed. Composed in prison, the verses were meant to be sung and committed to memory, and it is likely that the prisoners shouted them to each other in secluded dungeons.

The first known edition of the *Ausbund* in Europe was printed in 1564. The book was first printed in America at Germantown in 1742. The present edition contains 140 hymns, or 812 pages of verse. In Europe the hymnbook went through fourteen printings, and in America there have been over twenty editions. The American editions contain an additional section describing forty Swiss martyrs who suffered hardships between 1635 and 1645.[7] The authors, texts, and tunes have received the attention of scholars, especially musicologists.

Since there are no musical notations in the *Ausbund*, all melodies are learned by ear. The *Vorsinger* ("song leader") sets the pitch and sings the first syllable of each line as a solo before the congregation joins in by singing in unison. The singing moves along at an extremely slow pace, and some appear to know, while others feel, where each succeeding note begins.[8] Those who sing out of tune are younger persons who have not yet mastered the tunes, or persons who do not have an ear for music. The *Vorsinger* is never formally chosen to lead the singing. The person with greatest natural ability simply becomes the song leader by common consent, and he in turn recognizes the ability of younger ones, whom he sometimes asks to lead. The Amish seldom sing more than four or five verses of a hymn, for some of the hymns have as many as thirty-seven verses. Although the tunes are indicated by name at the beginning of the text, it is only the person who has learned them aurally who can hold the melody.

The most familiar Amish hymn, the *Loblied* or *'S Lobg-sang*, is reproduced here as it is sung by the Iowa Amish (Figure 13). This

7. The biographies of Swiss martyrs appear in English translation in John E. Kauffman, *Anabaptist Letters from 1635 to 1645: Translated from the Ausbund* (Atglen, Pa.: By the author, 1975).

8. The singing has been described in greater depth by John S. Umble, "The Old Order Amish: Their Hymns and Hymn Tunes," *Journal of American Folklore* 52 (1939): 82–95; J. William Frey, "The Amish Hymns as Folk Music," in *Pennsylvania Songs and Legends*, ed. George Korson (Baltimore: The Johns Hopkins Press, 1960), p. 129–62; Charles Burkhart, "The Music of the Old Order Amish and the Old Colony Mennonites: A Contemporary Monodic Practice," *Mennonite Quarterly Review* 27 (January 1953): 34–54; and Robert K. Hohmann, "The Church Music of the Old Order Amish of the United States" (Ph.D. diss., Northwestern University, 1959).

'S Lobg'sang
(The Hymn of Praise)

Library of Congress 1

Ausbund 131

Figure 13.
'S Lobg'sang, or "The Hymn of Praise"

hymn is always sung as the second hymn at every preaching service in every Amish district. Normally it takes about thirty seconds to sing one line of a verse. To sing all four verses of this song takes twenty minutes in some of the most orthodox Amish communities; in others it can be sung in eleven minutes. Amish music reflects culture, and the speed of singing can be positively correlated with the rate of the community's assimilation.

George Pullen Jackson, a musicologist, compared Amish tunes with European tunes and found that many have their origin in secular melodies that were common at the time the texts were written.[9] (Each hymn has a headline indicating the name of the tune to be used.) The *Lobelied*, for example, is sung to the tune *Aus tiefer Not schrei ich zu Dir*, which corresponds to the secular tune "There Went a Maiden with a Jug." The question arises, Were the Anabaptist composers ignorant of religious melodies and therefore sang the religious texts to secular tunes? A European scholar has suggested that the prisoners used current folk tunes in order to conceal the contents of the songs from their persecutors.[10] He explained that as soon as the persecution abated, the Anabaptists began using the sacred melodies from the body of Lutheran and Reformed chorales. When the Swiss and southern German groups adopted newer hymns and hymn tunes in the eighteenth century, the Amish alone kept the ancient musical tradition.

Since the tunes were transmitted orally, the Amish melodies vary slightly from one settlement to another. Some began to embellish the phrases and sing them slower than others. Noting this tendency, Joseph W. Yoder, an Amish Mennonite of Mifflin County, Pennsylvania, who attended Elkhart Institute in Indiana and became an accomplished song leader at teachers' institutes, reduced the tunes to musical scores.[11] His purpose was to produce a song book that the Amish would adopt as their own to aid them in singing the tunes uniformly. Although he carefully prepared instructions for reading the music, the Amish did not accept his book or his progressive methods. Nevertheless, musicians and folklorists have had much praise for Yoder's efforts to preserve a knowledge of Amish music.

9. George P. Jackson, "The American Amish Sing Medieval Folk Tunes Today," *Southern Folklore Quarterly* 10 (June 1945): 151–57; and idem, "The Strange Music of the Old Order Amish," *Musical Quarterly* 31 (July 1945): 275–88.

10. Christian Hege (1869–1943); see *Mennonitisches Lexikon*, s.v. "Melodien."

11. Yoder, *Amische Lieder*. Several Amish hymns have been recorded on magnetic tape and have been deposited in the Library of Congress. Hymns sung by Indiana Amishmen Eli J. Bontreger and Joni Easch were recorded by Alan Lomax in 1938. Marcus Bach of the University of Iowa made recordings of the "Hay" John Miller family in Iowa in 1943.

The slow and doleful singing prompted Yoder to suggest that the tunes derive from the Gregorian chant. It would appear from the studies of others, however, that the tunes have simply been embellished, that in uncontrolled group singing each tune is dragged out, which leads to all kinds of strange ornamentation foreign to the original tune.[12]

Amish young people, who are often frustrated by the slow singing, find much more enjoyment in singing the "fast tunes" used at Sunday evening singings. These tunes are used with the *Unpartheyisches Gesang-Buch* ("nondenominational song book") and in the *dinn Bichli* ("the thin book"), called *Liedersammlung*. These German hymns are sung to the tunes of popular nineteenth-century gospel songs, though the Amish sing them *a cappella* and in unison and much more slowly than they are sung in English. Examples are *Wo ist Jesus, mein Verlangen* ("What a Friend We Have in Jesus"), *Du unbegreiflich hochstes Gut* ("Sweet Hour of Prayer"), and *Herr Jesu Christ, dich zu uns wend* ("He Leadeth Me"). In many places the young people will switch to the English language for the last half of their evening "singing." These faster tunes are also sung at the wedding table.

The slow tunes, or *langsam Weis*, as the Amish call them, are characteristic of all singing in worship. It is assumed that the congregation will learn the melodies by heart. In singing these hymns an Amish person is reminded of all that is worldly and sinful. There is little subjectivism in either text or spirit; rather, there is a mustering of the will to identify with Christ in cross-bearing, suffering, and sharing. The hymns symbolize much of the drama of the Amish life style and world view.

12. See Mary Oyer's review of Yoder's *Amische Lieder* in *Mennonite Quarterly Review* 24 (January 1950): 97–98; and also the interpretations of George P. Jackson cited in note 9 above.

CHAPTER 11

The Symbolism of Community and Exclusiveness

THE AMISH ARE a multibonded group. Families and individuals within the group are dedicated to a common welfare and bound by a network of historical, social, economic, ceremonial, kinship, and symbolic ties. Aside from these sociological patterns, the Amish maintain a spiritual charter that requires unity within the community and separation from the worldly or disobedient who live without. The social rules for living constitute a way of life that is delineated by explicit social boundaries. These boundaries are clearly marked by signs and symbols distinguishing Amish culture from worldly culture. The Amish individual acquires maturity and competency by learning the thought patterns that make up his culture and his individual identity. The individual is a member of the ingroup or *unser Satt Leit* "our sort of people"), as distinguished from "English people" or *anner Satt Leit* ("other sorts of people").[1] When sharply drawn, this line of distinction tends to

1. The Amish practice of calling outsiders "English" (and in some places "Yankee" or "American") can be traced to language and ethnic-group differences in colonial times. Compact settlements of Germans were distinguished from the English, French, and Spanish colonies in the New World. The Germans did not have a colony, so when the English spoke of Amish and Mennonite groups, they simply called them "Germans." Today, when an Amish person calls someone an *Englischer*, it does not imply any disloyalty to America; it simply indicates that the person is non-Amish.

231

Homogeneous culture patterns provide a sense of community
that sets Amish social realities apart
from worldly standards.

produce stereotypes in both worlds. The Amishman will have grossly
exaggerated information about the world, and worldly people will
have unreasonable perceptions of the Amish people.

The symbol system itself, the grooming and garment language in
particular, is indeed complex when viewed from without. Common
traditions and ideals that have been revered by the Amish people
from generation to generation embody the expectations of all. A separate language is used for communication among members, and competence in the speech of the outside world provides an orientation to
the ways of the world around them. Physical property, including
family farms passed down through the generations, acquire symbolic
associations. All relatives are Amish or of Amish descent. Smallness of
scale is cherished. The size of each district is kept to a minimum so
that it can function as an intimate and informally controlled community. The social structure of the community remains relatively
unchanged as long as the basic needs of the individual are met from
cradle to grave.

SIGN, SYMBOL, AND CONVENTION

In the world around them, the Amish constantly see the signs of
worldly civilization and progress: the skyscraper, the high-powered
automobile, mass-produced suburban housing, television, and modern

fashions. These reminders of the danger of "worldliness" and secular progress signify to the Amish person what is to be avoided.

The Amish have their own symbolism, which provides a basis for common consciousness and a common course of action. The horse and buggy, proper grooming and styles of dress—all take on symbolic meaning. Every Amish person knows the accepted way of doing things. Symbolism is an effective means of social control; the nonconformist can quickly be distinguished from the conformist. Universal traits in all Amish communities include hook and eyes on the Sunday coat and vest of all men; trousers that have no fly-closing but a flap that buttons along the waist; wide-brimmed, black felt hats for men; suspenders instead of a belt; white organdy caps and uncut hair for women; and long hair (to the middle of the ear) with bangs for men. These symbols constitute a social reality that teaches people how to live and what to imitate.

Actions rather than words are typically used to express courtesy. In a small society where convention is understood, few words are needed to make meanings precise. Words of courtesy, as expressed by the English-speaking world, are conspicuously absent among members of the Amish family and community. In Amish speech one can scarcely observe any terms of endearment between husband and wife. If young people of courting age use such terms, they are frequently English words. This does not mean that acts of courtesy are absent. Nonverbal behavior patterns are supportive and considered more appropriate. When Amish parents hear "English" couples exchange words like "honey" and "sweetheart," they regard such labels as superficial or suspect. The dialect words equivalent to "pardon me" or "excuse me" are seldom heard. Children might use such English terms in their play, but persistence in using them in family relationships would not be approved. They would be accused of trying to be "society" persons. "Oops" is sometimes used to indicate that a certain act was not intentional. The dialect words for "please" and "thank you" are not a part of the table manners or a part of everyday conversation. On the other hand, children are taught to use *Denki* ("thank you") and *Willkomm* ("You are welcome") when giving or receiving gifts on special occasions. The wife may brush the husband's hat on Sunday morning before he gets around to it. The act requires no "thank you." If the husband is thoughtful, he will carry the toddler, help his wife into the carriage, and tuck the blankets around her. Belching is normal at the dinner table, a sign of good appetite, and is not considered rude. However, in the presence of "English" people the Amish will adopt the polite language of the outsider. Once, when an Amish woman encountered a woman washing her sidewalk, she said "pardon me" as she stepped over the washed part. Polite language in medieval Europe was far more characteristic of the nobility and not of the rural people, and this practice is still viable in Amish life. The relative absence of words of courtesy in Amish speech heightens the power of symbols and gestures in the community.

DRESS AS A LANGUAGE OF PROTEST

The religious symbolism of the Amish is conveyed in dress and physical appearance. The styles of grooming and of dressing are an expression of obedience to God and of "protest" to the proud and disobedient world. As explained in Chapter 1 (in the section entitled "The View from the Inside"), godly knowledge derives from obedience to God and pride derives from "knowing better than God." Men must wear a full beard; black, simple clothing with no outside or hip pockets; suspenders; and black hats with a three-inch brim. For women there must be no silk, showy, form-fitting garments; dresses must be within eight inches of the floor; and hair must remain uncut, with no adornment or curling. Aprons, shawls, and bonnets of proper size and color must be worn at the appropriate time. Young children must not be adorned in worldly styles.

In Amish society styles of dress are important as symbols of unity and community.[2] The garb not only admits the individual to full fellowship but also clarifies his age, sex, and position within his society. The hat, for example, distinguishes the Amish man from the outsider and also symbolizes his role within his social structure. When the two-year-old boy discards his dress and begins wearing trousers for the first time, he also receives a stiff, jet-black hat with three or more inches of brim. Hat manufacturers produce at least twenty-eight different sizes and a dozen different styles of Amish hats. The bridegroom in Pennsylvania gets a telescopic hat that is worn during the early married years. The hat is distinguished by a permanent crease around the top of the crown, which is slightly rounded, and a wide seam around the brim. A flat crown is worn by the rank and file of Amish fathers. The outsiders may never notice these differences, or if he does he may regard them as accidental. But to the Amish these subtle differences indicate whether people are fulfilling the expecta-

2. Details of the relationship of dress to cultural boundaries are given in John A. Hostetler, "The Amish Use of Symbols and Their Function in Bounding the Community," *Journal of the Royal Anthropological Institute* 94, pt. 1 (1963): 11–22. For a structural analysis of folk costume, see Petr Bogatyrev, *The Function of Folk Costume in Moravian Slovakia*, trans. Richard Grimm (The Hague: Mouton, 1971).

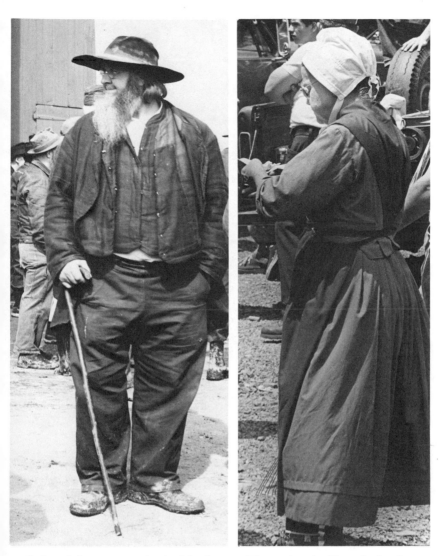

Styles of dress among the Amish of central Pennsylvania. Note the hooks
and eyes on the man's coat and the bustle on the woman's dress.

tions of the group. A young man who wears a hat with a brim that is
too narrow is liable to be sanctioned.

Very strict Amish congregations can be distinguished from the more
progressive ones by the width of the brim and the band around the
crown. Thus, when my family moved from Pennsylvania to Iowa, one
of our first adaptations involved taking out the scissors and cutting

A man's attire for ceremonial occasions
requires the *Mutze*, or "frock coat,"
with the split tail.

off some of the brim. This act made my brother and me more acceptable to the new community of Amish. At the same time, the act symbolized other adaptations that had to be made to adjust to a more
"westernized" group of Old Order Amish.

The Amishman has two kinds of coats. Their function is not only
one of warmth; there is also a proper time and place to wear these
coats. A vest is worn under the Sunday dress coat. An ordinary coat
can be a Sunday dress coat or a work coat, and after baptism the
Mutze is always worn to preaching service. An Amish man may appear
in full dress with a coat (*wamus*) when he goes to town or to visit
relatives on Sunday, but for the preaching service he will wear the
Mutze. This garment is longer than the ordinary coat and has a split
tail. All vests and coats worn for dress fasten with hooks and eyes. On
work coats, buttons, and in recent times, zippers and snaps are permitted in some communities and not in others. All Amish men wear
shirts and trousers that button. All these garments, as with Amish

costume in general, were common in Europe among the rural people.[3] The Amish merely retained them as a result of convention. Traits of culture once ordinary in Europe have been retained by the Amish community, where they have become symbolic of a way of life.

The dress of women is more colorful than that of men, as variation in color is permitted so long as it is a solid color and without pattern. One-piece dresses are made from traditional patterns. Over the bodice an Amish woman wears what she calls a *Halsduch*, which is similar to what plain-dressing Mennonite groups call a "cape." The name for this in the Palatinate was *Bruschttuch* ("breast cloth"). The *Halsduch* consists of a triangular piece of cloth about thirty inches long. The apex is fastened in the back, the two long ends go over the shoulders, and after crossing in the front, are pinned around the waist. Girls wear white organdy capes and white aprons to preaching service, but married women wear aprons and capes that match the color of the dress. These garments are fastened to the dress with numerous straight pins, for buttons are allowed only on a child's dress.

One of the most symbolic of all garments among the women is the *Kapp*, or "head cap," worn by every woman and even by infants. Girls from about the age of twelve until marriage wear a black cap for Sunday dress and a white cap at home. After marriage a white cap is always worn. The size, style, and color of caps vary slightly among regions and with degrees of orthodoxy in a single community (Figure 14). The ironing of fine pleats into some of these caps requires hours of tedious work. The specific way in which the caps are made, including the width of the *fedderdale* ("front part") and the *hinnerdale* ("back part"), and the width of the pleats and seams, is a sacred symbol of the community. Though this headpiece has undergone some changes in detail, the present Amish cap is essentially the same as that worn by the Palatine women of earlier centuries. Among partially assimilated Amish or Mennonites of Swiss-German origin the cap has become a "covering," "prayer cap," or "veiling" required of women "when praying or prophesying" (I Cor. 11:5). The most traditional Old Order Amish typically do not make this association.

Whether as a language of "protest" or as custom, Amish patterns of dress form a strong basis of identity and exclusion. Like all boundary mechanisms, dress serves to keep the insider separate from the world and to identify the outsider. These shared conventions are given

3. Palatine costume is documented by Karl A. Becker, *Die Volkstrachten der Pfalz* (Kaiserslautern, 1952). In his treatment of Mennonite attire, Melvin Gingerich discusses several aspects of Amish dress; see his *Mennonite Attire through Four Centuries* (Breiningsville, Pa.: Pennsylvania German Society, 1970).

sacred sanction and biblical justification: *unser Satt Leit* ("our sort of people") are distinguishable from *englische Leit* ("English people") or *anner Satt Leit* ("other people"). The attempts by theatricals to reproduce the dress of the Amish never quite measure up to the authentic. They appear ludicrous, if not hilarious, to the Amish.

LANGUAGE AND SPEECH

Although the Amish came from Switzerland, from Alsace and Lorraine in France, and from the Rhineland of Germany, their household conversational speech is remarkably uniform. The reason for this is that their diverse points of origin were all within the same (Alemannic) dialect-speaking area. Some of the Alsatian Amish could speak French when they arrived in America, and a few French words have been incorporated into their dialect, called Pennsylvania German or Pennsylvania Dutch. Here "Dutch" does not refer to the language of the Netherlands. Rather it is a folk-rendering of the dialect term *Deitsch* ("German"). In Adams and Allen counties, Indiana, descendants of nineteenth-century Amish immigrants speak a Swiss dialect, but it poses no real barrier to interaction with other Amish. An Amish person traveling from Pennsylvania through the Midwestern states on a kinship visit can speak his own familiar dialect and be understood.

The Amish speak three distinctive tongues, with some elements of each occurring in all.[4] They can read, write, and speak English without any interference from either of their other languages, although on informal occasions such interference may obtain. Their native Pennsylvania German dialect is primarily an oral language. A passive knowledge of High German is demonstrated in reading the Bible aloud or quoting it with their own distinctive pronunciation. Roles and functions tend to organize around each language. When speaking English the Amishman adapts to the English-speaking person.

Pennsylvania German is the familiar tongue of children at home and in informal conversation. It is the mother tongue of children born to Amish parents. Professor Albert Buffington has made it clear that this speech is not a "garbled English" or "corrupted German in the mouths of ignorant people who speak with a heavy accent," but a distinct dialect of the German language.[5] The dialect resembles the Palatine German folk speech. It is, of course, spoken by people of other religious

---

4. J. W. Frey, "Amish Triple-Talk," *American Speech* (April 1945): 84–98; and idem, "Amish Hymns as Folk Music," in *Pennsylvania Songs and Legends*, ed. George Korson (Baltimore: The Johns Hopkins Press, 1960), pp. 129–62.

5. Albert F. Buffington, "Pennsylvania German: Its Relation to Other German Dialects," *American Speech* (December 1939): 276–86.

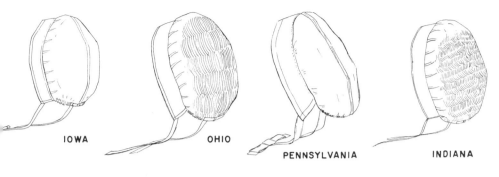

IOWA   OHIO   PENNSYLVANIA   INDIANA

Figure 14.
The white organdy caps worn by these young girls
are one of several regional styles
of the Amish *Kapp.*

denominations, including Lutheran, Reformed, and Church of the Brethren, who also originated in German-speaking areas.

The second language of the growing Amish child is English. A child first hears English extensively when he attends school. Prior to this time he has been exposed to the English loan words in his native dialect and perhaps to some use of English by older siblings. Amish children learn to speak the two languages without difficulty and without noticeable accent. Upon entering school the child frequently has only a very limited grasp of English, but readily learns English as a second language.

English is used when speaking with non-Amish persons in town, at school, or when talking to an "English" visitor or salesman. Thus Amishmen employ the English language on "forced" occasions. An Amish person may shift his conversation from the dialect to English, or from English to the dialect, whichever he finds most appropriate for the situation. When an outsider dines with an Amish family, he may hear dialect chatter at the other end of the table, but out of courtesy, the general conversation will probably be in English. The Amish use of English is influenced to some degree by their native Pennsylvania German language patterns, but in general, they experience little difficulty in speaking English correctly.[6]

High German, or more precisely "Amish High German," is used exclusively for the preaching service and on formal ceremonial occasions. An Amish person does not converse in High German, and most Amish adults know High German only passively, and then only as it is quoted from the Bible. The ordained officials must be able to preach from and quote their High German Bible, a version of the original Lutheran translation. The prayers read from the prayer book, and the hymns sung from several hymnals, are in German. High German is taught today in Amish schools.

Amish religious exercises require the use of High German, but even so the sermons are mixed with dialect and some English words. For example, this phrase was heard from the lips of an Amish preacher: "Heit sin viel Leit voll religion, avver sie hen kenn salvation" ("Today many people are full of religion, but they have no salvation"). Passages are memorized from s'Teschdement ("the New Testament") and from the whole of the Biewel ("the Bible"). English loan words frequently occur in the dialect with the German prefix and suffix, which is also the case with High German. The endings that have been weakened or dropped altogether in the dialect are frequently retained in the High German. The letters written with an umlaut, such as ö or ü, are not pronounced with lip-rounding as in modern Standard German, and were never pronounced in such fashion in the Palatine vernacular. Thus frölich ("joyous") is pronounced fray-lich. A passing knowledge of High German is preserved through its use and association with ceremonial functions.

The general term for a non-Amish person is Englisher or Auswendiger, meaning someone from the "outside." Little distinction is made between persons of other religious affiliations such as Methodists, Baptists, or Lutherans. There is some affinity to other "plain people" who practice separation from the world: Old Order Mennonites, River Brethren, Hutterites, Old Colony Mennonites, and the plain Quakers. The Mennonites are not classed as Englisher. Since the Mennonites

---

6. I am grateful to Steven M. Benjamin of Michigan State University for advice on language patterns and for placing two unpublished papers at my disposal: "The Old Order Amish: Their History, Culture, and Language" (18 pp.); and "The Amish: A Working Bibliography, 1951–1977" (36 pp.).

are only a step removed from the Amish, they are *Mennischte* and are
not considered as "English" as other people. On the other hand, a person of Catholic affiliation is called a *Gedolischer* (from the German
word *Katholischer*) and is clearly an outsider. Outsiders who are neighbors of the Amish people often refer to the Amish as "the Dutch."

Conversation in the dialect becomes an especially important function of community life, for the Amish are very sociable and hos-
pitable people. Visits to homes, preaching services, funerals, weddings,
sales, quiltings, barn-raisings, frolics of various kinds, sewings, singings,
and Sunday visiting are all occasions for conversing at length.

NAMES

In the little homogeneous community, conversational speech must
differentiate between people with the same last name (and in many
cases with the same first name also). The post office at Kalona, Iowa,
must distinguish between 450 Miller and 85 Swartzendruber families
on the rural mail routes. Under such conditions a middle initial or
even a nickname becomes crucial. To keep the mail straight the carrier
must "read between the lines" on the addresses, develop a knowledge
of relatives and family histories, and keep a fair check on the location
of the friends of a family.

Among the 85,000 or so Amish today, there are 126 family names.
Forty-three names (33 percent) are American in origin and represent
converts to the Amish faith, but they constitute a small proportion of
the population. At the present time, 18 of the 43 names represent only
single households. The family names in each of the three largest settlements vary (see Table 6). In all three of these settlements over half the
population is accounted for in 5 family names. Of 34 names in the
Lancaster County settlement, 25 percent of the households are Stolz-
fuses. Incidentally, the name Stoltzfus originated with Nicholas Stoltzfus, of Lutheran background, who joined the Amish prior to his emigration to America in 1766.[7] Following Stoltzfus, the most frequent
names are King, Fisher, Beiler, and Lapp. In the Ohio settlement
(Holmes County and vicinity), Miller, Yoder, Troyer, Raber, and
Hershberger are the most frequent family names; in Indiana (Elkhart
County and vicinity) the five highest in rank are Miller, Yoder, Bon-
trager, Hochstetler, and Mast. By comparing the three settlements it
will be noted that Pennsylvania has the least variation in naming
patterns. There are fewer family names and fewer first names for both

7. Paul Schowalter, "Pioneer Nicholas Stoltzfus," *Mennonite Research Journal*
4 (April 1963): 13.

Table 6
Amish names: Number and frequency in the three largest
Old Order settlements

	Pennsylvania[a]		Ohio[b]		Indiana[c]	
Number of households	2,051		2,561		1,204	
Number of family names	34		47		64	
Number of male first names	77		157		154	
Number of female first names	68		137		121	
Most common family name (%)	Stoltzfus	25	Miller	27	Miller	25
	King	13	Yoder	17	Yoder	14
	Fisher	11	Troyer	10	Bontrager	11
	Beiler	10	Raber	6	Hochstetler	5
	Lapp	7	Hershberger	9	Mast	4
Most common male first name (%)	John	10	Eli	8	John	5
	Amos	8	John	6	Levi	5
	Samuel	7	Levi	2	Joseph	5
	Daniel	6	Dan	5	Daniel	4
	David	6	Jacob	3	Perry	3
Most common female first name (%)	Mary	9	Mary	10	Mary	10
	Rebecca	7	Katie	7	Katie	7
	Sarah	7	Anna	6	Anna	7
	Katie	7	Fannie	5	Edna	6
	Annie	6	Sarah	5	Susie	5

[a] *Pennsylvania Amish Directory* (1973); includes Lancaster and Chester counties.

[b] *Ohio Amish Directory* (1973); includes Holmes County and vicinity.

[c] *Indiana Amish Directory* (1970); includes Elkhart and Lagrange counties.

males and females than in either the Ohio or the Indiana settlement. These naming practices support the view that the Midwestern communities have been more open to outside influences and perhaps not as vigorous in maintaining closed communities.

With so many similar names, whether last name or first name, some means of differentiation is a necessity. The use of a middle name or initial is not enough. It is an established principle that for any subject which becomes important in a given society, many words will be used to differentiate meanings. The Eskimos have not one word for snow, but over thirty, which distinguish what kind of snow. The Trobriand Islanders, who depend upon yams for their livelihood, have many words for yam, indicating precisely what kind of yam. In the Amish community, persons are in need of differentiation. Nicknaming is common to all Amish settlements, and through their speech patterns the Amish develop means of differentiating between very similar names. Maurice Mook observed that "nicknaming runs rife, almost as an onomastic necessity, and it is easily obvious to all observers that the Amish employ more nicknames than their non-Amish neighbors."[8]

Name differentiation is achieved by adopting an abbreviation, describing the physical traits of the person, noting individual preferences or habits, relating a humorous happening, practicing the matronymic and patronymic naming of children, enunciating the first name and initial uniquely, or by referring to the person's occupation or place of residence. Genealogists today are grateful that progenitor "Strong Jacob" Yoder (reputed to be very strong physically) can be distinguished from many other Jacob Yoders in the eighteenth century. "Huddle Jake" was another early American nickname, but the origin of this nickname remains unknown. "Seven Thick" (from *Sivve Dick*) identifies a Jacob Yoder whose overcoat was so large that seven young men got into it one Sunday after church.

In nicknaming, Solomon becomes Sol, and Benjamin becomes Ben. Chubby Jonas, Curly John, and Shorty Abner are indicative of physical traits. Applebutter John, Butter Abe, and Toothpick John derive from personal habits. Gravy Dan stuck with one Amishman when he poured gravy instead of cream into his coffee at a threshing dinner table. When first name and middle initial fail to identify, the paternal line is employed to single out a person. Thus John Yoder becomes Ruben Joe's John. Nancy John and Nancy Jake are identified by their mother's first name. Jockey Joe is a horse trader, Chicken Elam operates a chicken farm, and Chickie Dan works for Chicken Elam. Gap Dave, Gap Elam, and Gap Joe live near a village named Gap. When my own family moved from Pennsylvania to Iowa, my father was nicknamed "Pennsylvania Joe" to distinguish him from other family heads with the same name. "Peach Orchard Mike" distinguished one Mike from others in Mifflin County, Pennsylvania.

In the proliferating "interest" groups of young people, and among young people themselves, there is a great deal of nicknaming. The profuse use of nicknames, especially among boys—some of them named

8. Maurice A. Mook, "Nicknames among the Amish," *Names* 15 (June 1967): 111–18. See also Lester O. Troyer, "Amish Nicknames from Holmes County, Ohio," *Pennsylvania Folklife* 17 (Summer 1968): 24; and Eleanor Yoder, "Nicknaming in an Amish-Mennnonite Community," *Pennsylvania Folklife* 23 (Spring 1974): 30–37. The Yoder article deals with Somerset County, Pennsylvania, and Garrett County, Maryland.

after famed cartoon characters or baseball players, or given a name in purely arbitrary circumstances—helps to ensure ingroup solidarity, seclusion from outsiders and from the "straight" world of adults. Examples of nicknames among boys are Ashpile, Beanbag, Blip, Bull, Dog, Fatz, Fegs, Fuddy, Gomer, Pinky, and Yo-Yo. Nicknames are used exclusively in speech and seldom appear in writing.

UNPRETENTIOUS KNOWLEDGE

Amish people quote the Bible in warning of the dangers of high-mindedness: "Do not be haughty, but associate with the lowly; never be conceited" (*Trachtet nicht nach hohen Dingen, sondern haltet euch herunter zu den geringen. Haltet euch nicht selbst für klug*) (Rom. 12:16). Higher education—indeed the very phrase "high school"—is symbolic of self-advancement, of knowledge that comes from pride and disobedience to God. It typifies forsaking the lowly path of humility and faithful service to the community.

Like other societies, the Amish perpetuate a core of practical knowledge that has been adapted to ensure their survival. Knowledge is limited on the one hand by restrictions on what may be imported from the outside, and on the other, by taboos within the society. Two sources of knowledge are pertinent to the Amish: practical agrarian skills and a knowledge of the Bible as interpreted by the Amish. Their preference for useful or practical knowledge, a feature the Amish have in common with many folk societies, contrasts sharply with the worldly emphasis on speculative, abstract, or modern scientific knowledge. Book learning (also called chair-mindedness) is held in suspicion. How to plow a straight furrow is more important to the Amish boy than knowledge of the spatial relationships of geometry. Practical knowledge is acquired in the most effective way known to man, by means of an apprentice-like system that permits learning by participation in the rewards of work and in the goals of the society. The attitudes that are of utmost importance in Amish society—cooperation with other human beings and learning to like work—are acquired informally by working with others in the family and community, not by attending school. There is an evident disinterest in theoretical questions among the Amish.

The Bible is an important source of knowledge. It is the basis of the ethic that compels the Amish to live as they do. This ethic is transmitted by the family and the church and is reinforced in the ritual of community life. No successfully socialized Amish person seeks individuality or prominence through intellectual activity; rather, he seeks the shared wisdom that comes from spiritual communion and identification with his brothers. Individuality tends toward high-mindedness, self-praise, and pride. "Self-praise stinks" is a common Amish saying.

"The Amish," wrote one Amishman, "are very much interested in teaching their children the three basic parts of learning: reading, writing, and arithmetic. We feel that they can develop their minds better by working with their parents and by experience, than from books and the influence that surroundings of a college education would give them."[9] The Amish do not despise outsiders who are capable of going through college, for they understand that the world has need of such people. The same spokesman said: "We feel that anyone who is capable of making a decent living, helping his neighbors in need, raising a family that will be an asset to the community, and living at peace with God and his fellow men has attained about the most practical and best education there is to get."[10]

After the elementary grades, the children are put to work on the family farm. The emphasis on work as a form of discipline and as a means of preparation for adult life underlies all Amish thought: "Our people are engaged in some form of agriculture and we feel positive that as farmers we are better off with only a common school education. Education does not build muscle like tilling the soil in the open field and sunshine with lots of hard work. If a boy does little hard work before he is twenty-one, he probably never gets to like it afterward. In other words, he will not amount to much as a farmer."[11]

The Amish opposition to consolidation of schools and to high-school attendance has become widely known in America. The Amish do not want their children exposed to the "wisdom of the world," for they are repeatedly taught in their preaching services that "the wisdom of the world is foolishness with God" (I Cor. 3:19). The "world" is educated, and to the Amishman, "worldly education" leads to sinfulness, manipulative powers, and moral corruption. To the Amishman, the grossest distortions of education are perpetuated by the scientists, who have invented the theory of evolution and who have made bombs to destroy the world. Such ends are held to be contradictory to the teachings of the Bible.

The practice of limiting formal schooling and of not permitting the young to enter public high schools or colleges limits the amount of exposure to scientific knowledge and reduces knowledge of other life

9. Letter from Ezra Kanagy, Mifflin County, Pa., to the author, 1964.
10. Ibid.
11. A spokesman who wishes to remain anonymous.

styles. The practice of disciplining members who do not abide by this rule, coupled with positive rewards for practical knowledge, are effective means of maintaining the boundaries of the society.

MUTUAL AID AND GENEROSITY

Intense interaction in the little homogeneous community makes members feel responsible for each other's welfare. Although community aid is often a form of economic sharing, the feelings are the result of intense social concern. While the Amish do not practice complete "community of goods," as do their Anabaptist cousins the Hutterites, they find many ways to help each other. Perhaps the most dramatic form of mutual aid is the barn-raising. But there are many additional neighborly associations that result in an exchange of services. They include sawing and cutting wood, erecting milk houses or remodeling buildings, painting, fencing, and butchering. Among the women there are quiltings, sewings, and housecleaning activities. Baking, cleaning, and preparing both house and barn for the preaching service often involve the help of neighbors or relatives. In the case of an unexpected death, illness, or accident, the community comes to the rescue by taking care of the farm chores, harvesting the crops, or caring for the children. The young farmer just getting started may acquire a loan with modest interest. When there is a fire, the Amish have their own system of insurance. Each family contributes to the cost of restoring the building or raising a new one. Commercial insurance is avoided wherever possible.

The whole community supports all its members. If a member is sick, in distress, or is incapacitated, the community knows about it and takes action. While the Scriptures admonish the believer to do good to all men, the Amish are especially serious about the advice with respect to their own "household of faith" (Gal. 6:10). The care of the aged has never become a problem with the Amish. Old people retire on the farm. Many Amish farms have two household units, one for the grandparents and another for the younger farming couple and their children. The older people are often supplied with products from the farm and their needs remain simple.

These are some of the techniques by which the Amish community remains a multibonded social unit. The charter, which is rooted in the Bible and in Anabaptism, outlines the ideology of the society and sets limits within which persons may express themselves. The ecological community, the limited need for outside consumer goods, and the integration of rituals are in keeping with symbolic expectations. Tradition and experience tend to become highly symbolic in struc-

The traditional barn-raising, a form of economic sharing
in times of need, symbolizes the concern Amish members have
for one another's welfare.

tural elements such as the shared style of dress, language, limited
education, and mutual-aid practices. The Amish have been successful
in repelling the trends that characterize the modern American rural
community—migration to the cities, consolidation of schools, greater
dependence on government, urban recreation, general secularization,
and urban associations. They have diverted these trends not only by
means of the substitutionary forms of intense sharing but also by
meeting the social needs of the individual. The society provides for
the needs of the people in a cradle-to-grave arrangement.

The meaning inherent in Amish symbols keeps the group from
deteriorating into a sentimental community with a precarious existence. The traditions and social structure of the Amish community
contrast sharply with those of modern intentional communes. Of
course, the Amish have no flag, motto, or totem pole, but they live by

Noontime at a barn frolic. These hats symbolize
the strength of the Amish community.

many emblems[12] that are rooted in religious concepts and expressed
in specific ways of dressing and grooming. An emblem expresses social
unity in a material form. It clarifies the view a society has of itself.
It is only as the individual reacts to the community emblem that he
informs himself of his own appearance or position. The signs expressing the community's common sentiments are themselves fused into a
bond of identification. This bond informs individuals that they are
in harmony and makes them conscious of their moral unity. Thus
symbols are indispensable for ensuring the continuation of the social
structure.

12. For a discussion of emblems, see Emile Durkheim, *The Elementary Forms
of Religious Life,* trans. Joseph W. Swain (Glencoe, Ill.: The Free Press, 1954),
pp. 230–31.

Part III

Patterns of Change

CHAPTER 12

Government and the Amish

THUS FAR Amish society has been presented as a functioning whole. But distinctive, small subcultures such as the Amish are in a constant state of being and becoming, suspended between competing value systems, subjected to enticements from the external world, and confronted by the forces of lethargy and dissension from within. The Amish in particular are confronted with special problems of coping with regulations and bureaucracies in ways that most people are not aware of. In Part III some of the external and internal threats to Amish society will be discussed.

Several threats to Amish community and family organization stem from laws made to serve the industrial-military complex. They are: (1) consolidation of small elementary schools, (2) lengthening of the period of compulsory school attendance and the subsequent requirement of high-school attendance, (3) compulsory welfare systems, and (4) conscription. In addition there are many informal threats, such as the easy access to automobiles, television, and radios. Fundamentalist religious influences, with their stress on individualistic and charismatic experiences, pose a threat to the nonverbal solidarity of the Amish. It is impossible to describe here all the potentially disruptive forces in detail. This chapter emphasizes one of the most pervasive threats to the Amish way of life, compulsory education, and touches upon compulsory social security and conscription as well.

The *attitude of the Amish toward government* is essentially un-

changed from that of their Anabaptist forefathers. They acknowledge
the necessity of government and its prerogative to rule over its
citizens. In the words of Menno Simons, government functions "to
punish the evil, to protect the good, to administer a righteous justice
. . . to provide a police force that is not against God and his word."[1]
Rebellion against the state is considered un-Christian and unthink-
able. The function of government is to maintain order in the natural
or carnal world.

But like the Anabaptists, the Amish place a major limitation on the
authority of the state. As far as they are concerned the state has no
jurisdiction over the spiritual realm, no right to promote religious
and ecclesiastical uniformity or to suppress dissent. (In this respect
the Anabaptists' concept of church and state differed from the
Catholic and Protestant concepts of state and church during the
Reformation.)[2] The state may not assume the function of conscience
or assume the individual's responsibility to God. Amish persons do
not run for public office and they avoid any kind of political activity
that would require the use of force, for this would violate the higher
law of Christian love as they understand it.

The Amish do not resort to courts of law to settle disputes among
themselves or with outsiders. They are admonished to suffer injustices
rather than instigate legal suits or defend themselves in the courts.
They are forbidden to take an oath, serve on juries, or collect debts
by using the courts. The Amish have an outstanding reputation as
law-abiding citizens and they are rarely prosecuted criminally. However, in matters that violate their conscience and religion they
resolutely stand their ground, and as a consequence have advanced
the cause of religious liberty for everyone.

In reality, some Amish have made use of the law in the past,
depending on the circumstances and their conscience. Family heads
do have some choice in the matter. When fined for refusing to send
their children to high school, Amish parents refused to pay. To pay
the fines was to admit guilt. In such cases attorneys have represented
them in courts. Their ambivalence about going to court was expressed
to me by an Amishman who said: "The trouble with a lawsuit is that
if you lose you lose, and if you win, you lose too (in good will)." Some
Amish have an almost superstitious fright of going to court, fearing

---

1. *Mennonite Encyclopedia*, s.v. "State, Anabaptist-Mennonite Attitude Toward."
2. For an excellent discussion of these differences, see Thomas G. Sanders,
Protestant Concepts of Church and State (New York: Holt, Rinehart & Winston,
1964). For present-day practices, see Paul C. Kline, "Relations between the Plain
People and Government in the United States" (Ph.D. diss., American University,
1968).

that if the powers of evil are coerced, greater evil will result. This fear is an outgrowth of their experience with totalitarian governments in Europe and their limited knowledge of how American legal processes function to improve human rights.

Although holding public office or any position of worldly power is forbidden, voting in local or national elections is not. Voter turnout is heaviest in local township elections. The Amish will vote for persons they know and for persons they have learned by experience to trust. In the past some Amish people have served as school directors and supervisors of roads. Few of the Amish voluntarily register to vote, but they will often respond to local committee persons who offer transportation for registration and voting. Once registered, they are inclined to vote. In some Pennsylvania townships up to 40 percent of the Amish have voted. They are generally conservative and are opposed to taxation, school consolidation, rezoning of farmland, and liberalization of liquor laws. Most register as Republicans. Some of the Amish who live near villages serve as local fire company volunteers.

THE SCHOOL CONTROVERSY

It was not until well into the twentieth century that most Amish communities developed widespread objections to the public schools and founded their own. When public schools and compulsory education were first established in the various states, Amishmen frequently served as school board members. When attendance was required beyond the fourth grade a few Amish parents were summoned to court for refusal to comply. Reluctantly and gradually the Amish acquiesced to required attendance through the eighth grade. The conflict was brought into the open with the enforcement of school consolidation and the extension of compulsory attendance beyond the elementary grades.

The one-room rural elementary school served the Amish community well in a number of ways. As long as it was a public school, it stood midway between the Amish community and the "world." Its influence was tolerable, depending upon the kind of resources the Amish were able to bring to the situation. As long as it was small, rural, and near the community, a reasonable influence could be maintained over its worldly character.[3] Many Amish parents attended

3. In 1886 a former superintendent of public instruction, James P. Wickersham, wrote that the Amish "freely assisted their neighbors to establish schools, and their children were everywhere quite as well educated as the children of the other early settlers." See his book *A History of Education in Pennsylvania* (Lancaster, Pa.: Inquirer Publishing Co., 1886), p. 168.

Families build, maintain, and operate their own elementary schools.
Parents and children identify closely with their school.

parents' meetings, raised money for school equipment, donated labor
to the school, and attended cleanup frolics and school picnics. They
helped elect school board officers and influenced the choice of teachers.
The school building and its facilities were generally acceptable to
the Amish, even though they included some things forbidden in
Amish homes. The interior had electricity, central heating, and frequently a phonograph or piano, which was tolerated. The country
school often had no indoor plumbing and only modest play equipment. The school was the Amish child's first experience with the
world, and through it he discovered by personal experience the contrast between his world and the other world. The teacher dressed
differently and spoke a different language. With the help of an older
brother or sister, the Amish child acquired competence in both
cultures.

Amish parents often say that their children need some contact with
"English" children. It was in attending the traditional country school
with other children that the Amish child experienced "a little contact," which it was believed would make being Amish more desirable

and more secure. In the country school the Amish child was treated as a member of a group rather than as a unique personality. The songs learned were largely religious; they were copied into notebooks and sung in unison, as is the custom in the Amish community. The state curriculum was carefully followed and there was little room for individual variation. Amish children achieved basic skills in reading, writing, and arithmetic, and the public schooling was accepted, even though a considerable portion of the program was neither meaningful nor related to the Amish way of life.

With large-scale consolidation and the collectivization of school facilities, all this changed. The Amish feared what was being taught to their children by teachers they did not know in a large school away from the farm community. They resented the school's taking too much time away from the family and from the discipline of farm work. Although the Amish founded a private school in Delaware as early as 1925, it was not until 1938 that they founded their own schools in Pennsylvania. The Amish prevailed upon the school boards to keep the one-room schools open, but most were gradually closed. In the process of consolidation, the public school officials often regarded the heavily populated Amish areas as a "problem" in attaining their goals of reorganization. Never did they view consolidation as a disruption of the Amish family and community.

OBJECTIONS TO HIGHER EDUCATION

None of the arguments in favor of school consolidation are acceptable to the Amish.[4] The long struggle to retain the small school in their community and to allow it to function on a human scale rather than on an organizational scale has centered on four major issues: (1) the location of the school, (2) the training and qualification of the teacher, (3) the number of years of schooling provided, and (4) the content of the curriculum. The controversy in the various states has differed, but the major issues have remained the same.

High school comes at a time in the life of the Amish young person when cultural isolation is most important for the development of personality and social maturity. During this period the young person is learning to understand his own individuality within the boundaries of his society. As an adolescent he is learning for the first time to

4. The arguments for school consolidation and a recent refutation of those arguments are contained in Jonathan P. Scher, ed., *Education in Rural America: A Reassessment of Conventional Wisdom* (Boulder, Colo.: Westview Press, 1977).

relate to a group of peers beyond his family. As with most adolescents, he is testing his powers against his parents and the rules of the community. In the eyes of the community, it is important that his group of peers include only other Amish persons. If he acquires competence in the "English" culture at this stage, he will very likely be lost to the Amish fellowship. The period during which the parents loosen their direct control, but in which the community has not yet assumed much control, is too critical a time to expose the young person to outside influences.

High-school attendance would break down this needed period of isolation by taking the youth away from the family farm and by teaching him to identify with non-Amish acquaintances. This is what the Amish mean when they say that the high school is "a detriment to both farm and religious life." The public high school also teaches ideas that are foreign to the Amish culture. The "way of life" of the high school is feared perhaps even more than the curriculum itself. If the child is removed from the community for most of the working hours of the day, there is virtually no chance that he will learn to enjoy the Amish way of life.

Like most parents in American society, the Amish recognize the teen period as critical. The Amish family needs the help of its teen-age child more than the typical American family, and the child feels the family's need of him. Knowledge that the family needs his physical powers and that he is an economic asset to the welfare of the family is important to the individual. Quitting school after the elementary grades for greater identification with family and for the rewards of participation in adult society is normative. The typical Amish young person who learns to enjoy his family and his way of life has little regret when leaving school. Rather than rely on authority as a means of control, the parents now exercise control by showing the adolescent clearly how much the family needs him. The young person who works on the farm can understand and feel the contribution he is making to his family.

These are some of the informal and "real" reasons for objection to higher education. The formal or "ideal" objections are based on religious precepts for maintaining social boundaries. The biblical passage "The wisdom of the world is foolishness with God" (I Cor. 3:19) is frequently quoted. The world is educated, the Amishman would point out, but is plainly corrupt. The Amish do not attempt to prevent outsiders from educating their own children, but they themselves do not want to be contaminated by the harmful effects of higher education.

THE PENNSYLVANIA COMPROMISE

In 1937 a large consolidated school supported by federal funds was planned for East Lampeter Township in Lancaster County, Pennsylvania. The Amish leaders were concerned about its meaning and were initially divided over what action to take. One element wanted to withdraw their children from the public schools. Others feared disobeying the law. An "Old Order Amish School Committee" of sixteen members was formed, and representatives of the Old Order Mennonites also were invited.[5] An attorney advised the Amish to use legal processes to stop construction of the school. A petition was then sent to the state officials. Signed by 3,000 persons, it asked for eight months of schooling per year, exemption from schooling after completion of the elementary grades, and the privilege of attending one-room schools. The petition was of no avail, however, and the consolidated school was soon built.

Pennsylvania law required children to attend school until their seventeenth birthday, but children engaged in farm work were permitted to apply for a permit that would excuse them when they reached the age of fifteen. However, many had repeated the eighth grade (in order to stay out of high school) and were still not old enough to apply for a farm permit. A conflict erupted when the schools stated they were no longer willing to tolerate the practice of allowing the Amish children to repeat the eighth grade. School officials tried withholding the farm permits. The state threatened to withhold funds from districts that did not comply with the law. When the parents did not send their children to the consolidated high school, they were summoned to court and fined. They refused to pay the fines on the grounds that this would constitute an admission of guilt. The parents were then sent to the county jail. Anony-

5. Bishop Stephen F. Stoltzfus presided as chairman. After he moved to Maryland in 1941 as a consequence of the school controversy, he was succeeded by Aaron E. Beiler. Beiler was an Amish layman of persistent ability who over a period of thirty years appealed for Amish religious freedom through his personal correspondence with citizens, lawmakers, and newspapers, a life's work that earned him the nickname "Lawyer Aaron." With no one to turn to for help, he wrote pleading letters to President Franklin D. Roosevelt (January 31 and February 16, 1938) and to Supreme Court Justice Hugo L. Black (March 16, 1938). After his death in 1968, Beiler was succeeded by his son-in-law Elam H. Beiler and by Andrew S. Kinsinger. Meanwhile Kinsinger was instrumental in organizing the Old Order Amish Steering Committee—National, whose stated purpose is "to try and find a reasonable solution to any major problem that would concern or hinder our Amish way of life."

mous friends and businessmen frequently paid the fines to release the parents from prison. Some parents were arrested as many as ten times.

The Amish fathers and mothers took the position that compulsory attendance beyond the elementary grades interfered with the exercise of their religious liberty and that the values taught in the public school were contrary to their religion. Attorneys and friends of the Amish who took the case to the courts found no legal solution.[6] After many confrontations and much embarrassment, Governor George Leader in 1955 arranged for a reinterpretation of the school code which legitimized a compromise plan, the Amish vocational school. Under this plan the pupils would perform farm and house-hold duties under parental guidance, keep a daily journal of their activities, and meet in classes three hours per week. The vocational schools were required to teach certain subjects, and to file attendance reports, but teachers were not required to be certified.

Other states began to follow the Pennsylvania plan. In Ohio there were many legal attempts to force the Amish to attend public schools.[7] In Indiana the state superintendent of schools encouraged the Amish to organize their own schools and develop standards in keeping with their prerogative as a religious body.[8] In all three states the Amish began to form their own country schools and to hire experienced teachers who had retired from the public school system. When this was no longer possible they staffed the schools with their own Amish teachers.

THE IOWA CONFRONTATION

While the conflict in the various states has taken different forms, the controversy in Iowa during the mid-1960s illustrates the intensity of feelings involved. In the Amish settlement centered in Buchanan County, Iowa, school authorities forced their way into a private Amish school in order to compel the children to board a bus to take them to the consolidated town school. The press got wind of impending events and recorded the scene as frightened youngsters ran for

6. See Albert N. Keim, ed., *Compulsory Education and the Amish: The Right Not to Be Modern* (Boston: Beacon Press, 1975), especially chap. 5, "A Chronology of Amish Court Cases."

7. Ohio has not modified any of its laws to meet Amish objections. The state issued a report entitled *Amish Sectarian Education* (Columbus: Ohio Legislative Service Commission, Research Report no. 44, 1960). For a subsequent treatment, see Frederick S. Buchanan, "The Old Paths: A Study of the Amish Response to Public Schooling in Ohio" (Ph.D. diss., Ohio State University, 1967).

8. See Richard D. Wells, *Articles of Agreement regarding the Indiana Amish Parochial Schools and the Department of Public Instruction* (Bloomington: Indiana Department of Public Instruction, 1967).

cover in nearby cornfields and sobbing mothers and fathers were arrested for noncompliance with an Iowa school law.[9]

The little Iowa community became the subject of world-wide publicity. School officials were deluged with adverse reactions from people who sympathized with the Amish. The eruption was the culmination of long-standing intercommunity tensions broader than the "Amish problem." Tensions had been building up between two school districts for some years prior to the widely publicized crisis. Unwittingly, the Amish had served as pawns in a local school election involving old feelings of hostility.

Two Amish schools were established in Buchanan County. As time passed they tried to comply with the state's growing requirements for certified teachers, but the Amish said that when they sought and found qualified teachers, the school authorities refused to certify them, or the teachers were offered more pay in town. In the two Amish schools the children ended up being taught, as in Pennsylvania and Ohio, by Amish girls who were selected for their teaching aptitude.

The two local school districts, Hazelton and Olwein, were in the process of merging. Many people in the Hazelton district opposed the merger, and remembering the years of rivalry between the two towns, opposed the takeover by the Olwein district. The people in Hazelton fought the merger and town officials refused to put the matter before the voters. Finally, a few residents who desired the alliance pushed the legal petitions needed to require a referendum. The Hazelton-Olwein reorganization was particularly bitter. Old friends stopped talking, vicious rumors spread, and secret meetings were held. The Amish wanted to be attached to the adjoining Fairbank Township area, where one-room schools were still maintained, and in keeping with the required procedures, they petitioned a meeting of the various county officials who were responsible for drawing the boundaries of the new districts. The Olwein officials helped to arrange the rejection of the Amish petition, for they hoped to gain the extra tax income from farm children in the district who attended nonpublic schools. The superintendent of the Olwein district, who was described as brilliant and an expert in virtually every aspect of school affairs, was worried about getting the required votes

9. The controversy is described in detail by Donald A. Erickson in *Public Controls for Non-Public Schools* (Chicago: University of Chicago Press, 1969), chap. 5, "Showdown at an Amish Schoolhouse." I am grateful to the author and publisher for permission to use excerpts. See also Erickson's "The Plain People vs. the Common Schools," *Saturday Review*, November 19, 1966.

in both districts. The Amish might sabotage his efforts by casting their ballots against the referendum. In consultation with state officials, the Olwein superintendent arranged a "deal" with the Amish: if they would vote in favor of reorganization, they could keep their one-room schools. The task of persuading the Amish was not easy, for their schools were in the opposing Hazelton district. But on the promise of the superintendent—"I expect to be superintendent for many years to come, and I will always recommend that the board honor our agreement"—they consented.

The vote in Olwein was overwhelmingly in favor of merging, and in Hazelton the measure passed by a narrow margin. The people of Hazelton were furious when they discovered that the Amish had voted favorably but could easily have defeated the referendum by voting against it. Residents to this day insist that the Amish swung the election and forced Hazeltonians to come under the Olwein school board. Those who wanted the referendum to pass had transported many of the Amish to town to cast their ballots, and numerous local people saw what was happening. Old grievances were revived and the bitter prejudices that were activated formed the groundwork for intense pressures against the Amish. Local residents were prepared to see that the Amish obeyed every "inch" of the new school code.

The Amish, who had cited religious principle as the basis of their action, now were accused by Hazeltonians of "using religion as an excuse for everything they want to do." Locally the Amish were branded as hypocrites, as people motivated by economic greed, as wanting only to keep their school costs down and to exploit child labor in the fields.

Meanwhile the Olwein school officials arranged for help from the state level. Two state inspectors visited the Amish schools, and "shocked" by the outdoor privies and the austerity of the facilities, found them "impossible." This action allowed the Olwein school board to "get off the hook," and from this point on, the Olwein school board took the position that it was helpless to aid the Amish unless they agreed to the state's requirements. Meanwhile the Amish returned to running their schools with their own staff of teachers. The time was right for the local officials to take revenge.

The Amish were summoned before the justice of the peace. The parents were found guilty of violating the law by staffing their schools with uncertified teachers. Nightly for several weeks fourteen Amishmen showed up Monday to Friday to be fined twenty dollars plus four dollars in "costs" each day. On religious grounds, each parent refused to pay. They were warned that their farms would be sold to pay the levies if they did not pay. The amounts levied soon reached into the thousands of dollars, and at this rate it would not have taken long to ruin the Amish financially. It was at this point—on November 19, 1965—that the Olwein school bus came to take some forty Amish pupils from their private school, against the wishes of their parents, to the consolidated school. The plan, according to the school officials, was to load the children into the buses in spite of Amish resistance. After a few days, it was thought, compliance would be achieved and the trouble would be over. Against the advice of the Iowa attorney general, the showdown proceeded and was greeted with widespread national repercussions.

Governor Harold E. Hughes ordered a truce of three weeks to permit exploration of alternate solutions. There were to be no more attempts to take the Amish children to town, and prosecution of parents was to cease. County officials seized Amish corn and real estate to collect the unpaid fines, but most sales were forestalled because the fines were paid by anonymous donors. The governor visited one of the Amish schools, then talked to the students at the local junior high school, and met with the school board for two hours. A cooling-off period of two years was made possible when a private foundation offered to pay the salaries of certified teachers for two years.

The Iowa case called attention to a number of educational and legal problems in running nonpublic schools. This prompted Donald A. Erickson of the University of Chicago to organize a two-day National Invitational Conference on State Regulation of Nonpublic Schools for the purpose of discussing "Freedom and Control in Education."[10] Attending were members of state departments of education, members of the law profession, representatives of religious denominations operating private schools, and a few university professors. A group of concerned citizens organized the National Committee for Amish Religious Freedom, with the Reverend William C. Lindholm, a Lutheran pastor, as chairman. The immediate task was to appeal to the U.S. Supreme Court a Kansas Supreme Court decision against Amishman Leroy Garber.[11]

Meanwhile a number of religious leaders, politicians, and educators wrote articles in national magazines advising moderation. Governor Hughes of Iowa said: "I am more willing to bend laws and logic than

10. The papers were subsequently published in Erickson, *Public Controls for Non-Public Schools*.

11. In a 4 to 3 decision the high court declined to hear the case. See Donald A. Erickson, "The Persecution of Leroy Garber," *School Review* 78 (November 1969): 81–90.

human beings. I will always believe that Iowa and America are big enough in space and spirit to provide a kindly place for all good people, regardless of race, or creed."[12]

Franklin H. Littell, Reformation historian and president of Iowa Wesleyan College, said: "These people are exemplary American citizens of long duration. This is a test case to see whether we believe in religious liberty when it is for others and not ourselves. Certainly we are sick of soul if we cannot put up with 23,339 frugal, law-abiding 'peculiar people.' "[13]

"The Amish people's approach to education," said Donald Erickson, "is one of the most effective yet devised, with little unemployment, crime, and juvenile delinquency. In time, given some liberty, the unequivalent schools may even teach us something. The public school approach has worked well for many, but it has been an obvious failure outside the cultural main."[14]

In 1967, after a great deal of effort, the Iowa legislature amended its school code to permit a religious group to apply for exemption from compliance with the educational standards law. Application must be made annually. Proof of achievement in certain basic skills was made conditional. In the same year, Maryland amended its school law; the Amish were classified as a bona fide church organization and therefore not required to obtain approval of the superintendent of schools to continue to operate schools in that state. Many people began to take the position that unless it could be shown that the Amish were endangering the state or becoming welfare charges, the arrests were unjustified. If it was not illegal to be Amish, how could it be illegal for a parent to send his children to a school where Amish traditions were taught?

THE SUPREME COURT RULING

The U.S. Supreme Court settled the long-standing controversy on May 15, 1972. In *Wisconsin* v. *Yoder*, the court ruled that the states may not constitutionally force the Amish to send their children to public high school. The context of the suit arose at New Glarus, in Green County, Wisconsin, where a new Amish settlement was being formed. Three Amish fathers were arrested in the fall of 1968 on complaint of the local school administrator that they had failed to

12. Quoted from William Lindholm, *Do We Believe in Religious Liberty—for the Amish?* (East Tawas, Mich.: National Committee for Amish Religious Freedom, 1967).

13. Ibid.

14. Ibid.

enroll their three children, Frieda Yoder and Barbara Miller, both fifteen years old, and Vernon Yutzy, aged fourteen, in high school. All had completed the eighth grade in the public schools. Wisconsin law required attendance until the child's sixteenth birthday.

Since the Amish will not defend themselves in court, the National Committee for Amish Religious Freedom, a citizens group organized in the previous year, came to their assistance. The committee hired an attorney, Mr. William B. Ball, an expert in constitutional law and religion, and raised the needed funds. In laying the groundwork for a First Amendment religious issue, Mr. Ball attempted to show that a true religious liberty claim was involved, that the state was violating the Amish religion, and that the state's willingness to waive compulsory high-school attendance would not present any significant threat to society.[15] As in many previous court cases, the county court and the circuit court ruled that even though the Amish were sincere and their religion was being violated, the compelling interest of the state was greater. The Wisconsin Supreme Court held that the state had failed to prove its case and ruled in favor of the Amish. The Department of Education in Wisconsin was not satisfied to let the matter rest. It appealed to the U.S. Supreme Court and was granted a review of the case. Wisconsin argued that compulsory education is necesary to maintain the political system, that the state has a right to free children from ignorance, and that only state legislatures can determine educational policy.

In a 7 to o vote delivered by Chief Justice Warren Burger, the high court held that the First and Fourteenth amendments prevented the states from compelling the Amish to attend formal high school to the age of sixteen. The court said: "States undoubtedly have the responsibility of improving the education of their citizens, but this interest must be measured against the legitimate claims of the free exercise of religion."[16] The Amish victory was a significant one. In the words of Leo Pfeffer, a recognized authority on church and state, it was "a landmark case in American Constitutional history."[17] Never before in U.S. history had laws dealing with compulsory education been successfully challenged on the basis of religious freedom.

The threat of the large school and its associated values has been stopped, at least temporarily. It is clear that the Amish will not tolerate the removal of their children to a distant school where they

15. William B. Ball, "Building a Landmark Case: Wisconsin v. Yoder," in *Compulsory Education and the Amish*, ed. Keim, pp. 114–23.

16. *Wisconsin v. Yoder*, 406 U.S. 205 (1972).

17. Leo Pfeffer, "The Many Meanings of the Yoder Case," in *Compulsory Education and the Amish*, ed. Keim, p. 136.

are placed in large groups with narrow age limits, taught skills useless to their way of life, and exposed to values contradictory to their culture. They have won legal protection in some respects. But they still have little guarantee, other than public sentiment, that they will be permitted to maintain their schools. The certification of teachers remains a thorny problem in a few states. Meanwhile the Amish willingly comply with state requirements of attendance, length of the school year, length of the school day, health and safety standards, and the teaching of basic skills.

COMPULSORY WELFARE

The Amish people maintain positive religious teachings and attitudes toward helping all their needy members. They are deeply sensitive to any forces that would erode the principle of self-sufficiency in caring for their old people, widows, and orphans. Self-sufficiency is the Amish answer to government aid programs such as farm subsidies and social security payments. They comply with crop reduction programs but refuse payments for raising fewer crops. Amish leaders have repeatedly gone to Washington to seek freedom from federal aid. It is not that they are opposed to paying taxes, but they are opposed to any form of dependency on government.

The Amish opposition to compulsory insurance was widely publicized when social security benefits were extended (Public Law 761, January 1, 1955) to cover self-employed persons, including farmers. A delegation of Amish bishops made numerous trips to Washington seeking exemption from the tax and its benefits. Before congressional committees they contended that "Old-Age Survivors Insurance is abridging and infringing to our religious freedom."[18] In support of their stand they quoted the Bible: "if any provide not . . . for those of his own house, he hath denied the faith, and is worse than an infidel" (I Tim. 5:8). To pay social security tax, the Amish say, is to admit that the government has a responsibility for aged Amish members, and to admit this is to deny the faith. They know that this alliance with government would make future generations dependent on the government. Federal means of providing for these needs are viewed as purely secular, if not sinful.

Some Amish paid the self-employment tax and others maintained bank accounts against which levy action could be taken. IRS agents met with the Amish to try to persuade them to comply with the law.

18. Leaflet entitled "Our Religious Convictions against Social Security" (April 1960).

Amish spokesmen in Washington, D.C., seeking exemption
from federal welfare programs and benefits

When this failed, the Internal Revenue Service took legal action to
seize horses from as many as thirty delinquent Amish farmers. Valen-
tine Byler of New Wilmington, Pennsylvania, for example, was approached in his field on May 1, 1961, by law enforcement officers.
Three horses were unhitched, taken to market, and sold. His tax and
the expenses of transporting and feeding the horses were deducted
from the proceeds, and the balance was returned to him. The incident
received such widespread publicity that the chief of the Internal
Revenue Service placed a moratorium on any further collections,
pending a test of their constitutionality.[19] Finally, on July 30, 1965,

19. Clarence W. Hall, "The Revolt of the Plain People," *Reader's Digest*,
November 1962.

President Lyndon Johnson signed Public Law 89-97 to provide medical care for the aged under the Medicare section of the Social Security Act. Section 319 of the bill contains a subsection (sec. 1402h, I.R.S.) that permits an individual to apply for exemption from the self-employment tax (Form 4029). Such a person must be a member of a religious body that is conscientiously opposed to social security benefits but that makes reasonable provision for its own dependent members. The waiver applies only to self-employed persons and not to individuals who are employed and work for wages. In Canada the Amish were granted total exemption from the Canadian Pension Plan, not only from the self-employment taxes. The Amish are deeply grateful for these provisions, but they are still faced with other compulsory entanglements such as unemployment insurance, accident compensation, and workman's compensation taxes.

In all communities the Amish have formulated agreements covering the sharing of losses by fire, lightning, and storm. The Amish Aid Society of Lancaster, Pennsylvania, also serves the smaller nearby communities of Mifflin, Juniata, Lebanon, Saint Mary's (Maryland), and the newer settlements spawned from Lancaster County. Likewise in Indiana, the Lagrange-Elkhart area encompasses many smaller settlements, including some in Michigan. Each region elects its own officers. Finance companies generally honor Amish Aid Plans. When there is a loss an impartial committee is chosen to estimate the dollar amount. All members are assessed annually. The Aid Plan covers the dollar loss. In addition, the community donates free labor, especially on cleanup days and on the day of the barn-raising. Amish Aid Plans must incorporate the rules of the church. For example, automobiles or tractors that are stored in Amish barns or sheds are not covered by Amish insurance. Likewise, church districts that are not "in fellowship" with the main body of Old Order Amish cannot come under the provisions of the Aid Plan. By having their own fire insurance the Amish avoid "the unequal yoke" (II Cor. 6:14) and avoid paying losses on property they themselves are not permitted to own.

Two other types of insurance, liability and hospitalization, have been formed in recent years by the Amish people themselves. Liability insurance was necessitated by legal claims filed against Amish persons involved in highway accidents. The Amish Liability Plan is voluntary. Buying liability insurance from commercial insurance companies is not forbidden, but members stop short of buying insurance to protect their own property or life.

Among the Lancaster Amish a Hospitalization Plan was adopted in 1966 by families who felt the need for a means of meeting high hospital costs. Since not all Amish members and not all Amish bishops agreed to the plan, it is voluntary. The plan began with a $200 deductible policy, then gradually rose to a higher amount. Through a local district representative the treasurer collects a fee of $30 per person frequently enough to maintain a minimum balance. There are still many Amish who are opposed to hospitalization insurance. Some districts forbid it. When a family is faced with a large hospital bill, members are urged to give donations. Officers who direct the Hospitalization Plan are elected and volunteer their services.

The Amish people understand natural disaster and human need. When a flood, fire, or tornado strikes, the Amish often come in large numbers to aid the stricken family or community. They volunteer their services to Mennonite Disaster Service, Inc. When Indiana and southern Michigan were struck by serious tornadoes in 1965, Amish from other states came by train and bus to provide help in rebuilding homes and farm buildings.[20] They have also gone to Alabama and other areas, where there are no Amish settlements, to contribute their labor to the rebuilding of homes.

When the Occupational Safety and Health Administration (U.S. Department of Labor) ruled that employees in construction and carpentry work must wear hard hats, the Amish refused to give up their traditional broad-brimmed felt hats. Hard hats would in effect obliterate their identity as Amish persons. They had no dispute with the safety standard, but since the regulation affected their own safety, and not the safety of others, they considered the requirement a violation of their religion. After 400 Amish were furloughed from their construction jobs in Allen and DeKalb counties in Indiana, they sought and won an exemption from the regulation. They did not file a legal suit, but asked for an exemption, which was granted in June 1972. When the safety of others is directly involved, as in the laws requiring lights on horse-drawn vehicles and SMV (slow moving vehicles) emblems on the rear of such vehicles, the Amish generally comply. Only in a few regions have the Amish objected to SMV emblems, on the grounds that they are too ostentatious for their way of life.[21]

20. Two publications by Amishmen describing tornadoes and cleanup operations are David Wagler, *The Mighty Whirlwind* (Aylmer, Ont.: Pathway Publishing Corp., 1966); and Gideon L. Fisher, *Alabama Tornado* (Ronks, Pa.: By the author, 1975).

21. Objections to SMV signs are discussed by David Wagler in "Not Afraid of Persecution," *Family Life*, July 1970, p. 10.

CONSCRIPTION

The Amish have had a consistent record of conscientious objection to war since their arrival in America. During World Wars I and II they were permitted to serve out their military obligations in some type of civilian public service. Ninety-four percent of their young men who were drafted in World War II served time as conscientious objectors.[22] In most cases, those who chose military service were young men who wanted either to see the world or to run away from home.

The conscription of young men is especially disruptive to the Amish community. Not only during World War II, but from 1946 to 1976, the Amish were subjected to conscription, making them liable for two years of alternative service as conscientious objectors. Selective Service regulations specified that the service should "constitute a disruption" in the life of the conscientious objector.[23] In addition to being a disruption it was required that the work (1) contribute to the national health, safety, or interest; (2) be performed outside the community in which the person resides and (3); be a position that cannot be readily filled from the competitive job market. Those who were drafted had to live outside the Amish community, often alone, in a city, perhaps wearing non-Amish uniforms or clothing while at work. These measures separated the young men from community control. To a limited extent this period of service made them non-Amish.

By living in the city and giving up the distinctive Amish garb, the individual soon lost his symbols of identity. Young men began to acquire forbidden possessions such as automobiles and television sets. If the young man had taken the vow of baptism before entering alternative service, he could no longer live physically separated from the world as pledged in his vow. If he entered alternative service before baptism, he was not morally committed to the rules of the community, and was more vulnerable to outside influences.

Conscription also disrupted Amish marriage traditions. If the young man went into service without a wife, he was prone to form friendships with non-Amish girls.[24] Because marriage must be "in the Lord" (with an Amish member), such friendships are dangerous. If he had

22. Guy F. Hershberger, *The Mennonite Church in the Second World War* (Scottdale, Pa.: Herald Press, 1951), p. 39.

23. Local Selective Service Board Memorandum no. 64, September 1968.

24. The temptations of marriage to a non-Amish girl and the problems associated with work in the city are frequently fictionalized in Pathway publications. See, for example, "Al Can Take Care of Himself," *Family Life*, October 1971.

a wife, she helped to protect him from worldly influences. Nevertheless, by starting their married life with modern conveniences (electricity and telephones), the couple formed patterns that were difficult to relinquish when they returned to the Amish community.

In some cases the Amish were able to have their young men assigned to places where other Amish were working, in agriculture rather than in hospital care. But having their young men exposed to other objectors, liberal Amish and Mennonites, who were highly articulate and persuasive, also was disruptive. The Amish boys maintained their Amish life style, but were frequently unable to articulate it. The problem was somewhat alleviated when local draft boards honored farm deferment requests from the Amish. The Selective Service also honored a plan whereby a conscripted young man could go to another Amish community and serve for two years doing farm work where help was essential.

Several of the most traditional Amish took a hard line against alternative service and found even civilian service unacceptable. They reasoned that it was better for their young men to go to prison, for "God is with them there."[25] The few who went to prison generally returned to the Amish community stronger in their faith and more secure in their convictions. They did not go through a period of uncertainty when they returned. The time they spent outside the community served to strengthen their baptismal vow and clarify the boundaries between community and world. It enabled them to identify with the martyrs among their forefathers.

25. For a description of the problems encountered by the Amish in prison, such as length of hair and grooming styles, riots, and religious persecution, see "Behind Prison Walls," *Family Life*, August/September 1968.

CHAPTER 13

Change and Fragmentation

ALL SOCIETIES risk the hazard of change and ultimately of disintegration. Human beings in the same society do not think precisely alike. All do not have the same tendencies toward conformity. Some are tradition-directed, while others are creative and inner-directed. Traditional societies are particularly vulnerable to economic and social stagnation. New groups are formed when the traditions are perceived to be dysfunctional. We turn here to an examination of groups, as distinguished from individuals, that break from Amish tradition.

DIVERSITY AMONG THE OLD ORDER AMISH

Amish society appears remarkably uniform to the outsider. The person who does not participate in it cannot know how much the customs and rules of one community differ from those of another. There are differences not only from one settlement to another but also between Amish affiliations in the same settlement. The carriages or buggies of the Amish, for example, have many subtle variations. In Lancaster County most two-seated carriages have gray tops, and in Ohio and farther west the carriages have black tops. But there are also groups living in the same region in Pennsylvania who drive "yellow tops" and others who drive "white tops." In Lancaster County the single-seated buggy has been interpreted by the outsider

The symbols that differentiate Amish groups from one another are reflected in the styles of their carriages. Variations may indicate regional differences, functional differences, or differences in church rules.

as a "bachelor" or courting carriage. But single-seated carriages are also driven by the married Amish for other than churchgoing activities. In Midwestern communities, black tops appear on single-seated carriages. There are groups, however, that do not allow tops on their buggies. The presence or absence of dashboards, whipsockets, battery-operated lights, roll-up side and rear curtains, and brakes varies from one group to another. Even the harness used on the horses and the amount and type of ornamentation is subject to the *Ordnung*.

One accurate indication of social change is the style of singing at the Amish preaching service. While all Old Order Amish groups sing in German from a common song book, the embellishments of the orally transmitted tunes differ, as does the time it takes to sing a

Left: An Amishman whose church does not allow suspenders.
Right: Member of a one-suspender group.

particular hymn. In all Amish districts the *Loblied*, with four stanzas of seven lines each, is sung as the second hymn of the service. But one traditional group takes thirty minutes to sing this song, while another takes twenty minutes, and still another sings it in only eleven minutes. The slow-singing groups are invariably more traditional in their total culture than the faster-singing groups. Where tunes are sung more slowly, the dresses of the women are longer, the hair of the men is longer, and the men's hat brims wider. Where the tunes are sung faster, more modern conveniences have been accepted. The diversity of singing comes into focus when Amish people from different states and settlements are suddenly thrown together. This has occurred, for example, when Amish from various states lived temporarily in Florida. Difficulty in singing together is frequently experienced, particularly if the song leader is not from the same settlement as the majority of the congregation.

Singing styles and carriage technology are only two of many illustrations of the wide range of Amish cultural traits and patterns. The style of clothing, the shape of women's head coverings, the use of labor-saving technologies, and travel patterns are other differentiating features. How did these differences develop? What is their function?

Some differences can be attributed to cultural fusion, others to unequal acceptance of change. In the evolution of travel, for example, the first Amish communities assembled for worship by foot and by horseback. The first carriages had no tops, and they were followed by carriages with white tops, since the unpainted oilcloth was made from flax. Later the tops were dyed yellow, gray, and black. A similar development can be illustrated in styles of dress—e.g., the suspender. The Old School Amish in Pennsylvania do not wear suspenders, another group wears a single suspender over one shoulder, and other groups wear suspenders on both shoulders. These variations in Amish culture today can be attributed to unequal adoption of innovations. Some Amish groups were more opposed to changes than others. What is permitted or not permitted has been the source of fragmentation and splitting into various factions, some of which will shun other groups for their progressive stances.

MAJOR TENSIONS AND SPLITS

The main cleavages among the Amish are listed in Table 7. Before 1850, settlements were small, scattered, and isolated. As American industry, commerce, and agriculture grew, and communication and travel increased, differences in culture and in ceremony began to be perceived by the Amish leaders. In order to reconcile differences in religious practices and to provide opportunity for regular consultation, an annual General Ministers' Conference was begun in 1862.[1] The conferences, open to all members, were often held in a large barn and were attended by ministers from various states. Preachers brought their concerns and questions for clarification. Difficult questions were assigned to a committee that studied the problems thoroughly and brought recommendations to the assembly. Unanimity was reached on some of the major doctrines, but it soon became apparent that disagreements on practices would be difficult to resolve. During the Civil War it was agreed that participation in war was contrary to Scripture, that members could not engage in teamster service under the military control, and that former members who had joined the army but had been reinstated into the church could not receive government pensions. Occupations closely allied with business were forbidden, such as managing a store, post office, or express office.

---

1. C. Henry Smith, *The Mennonites in America* (Goshen, Ind.: By the author, 1909), p. 239. Proceedings of these conferences are located in the Mennonite Historical Library, Goshen, Ind. For a discussion of their content, see John A. Hostetler, "Amish Problems at the Diener-Versammlungen," *Mennonite Life* 4 (October 1949): 34–39.

Lightning rods, lotteries, photographs, and insurance were considered worldly. Several major issues, however, were not resolved in the Amish Ministers' Conferences. Some of the congregations had established meeting houses. Several communities were divided on the practice of shunning, and whether a member who refused to shun an expelled member also should be excommunicated. The failure to reach common consensus on many issues, and the inability to reconcile differences, brought the sessions to an end in 1878.

After this attempt at national organization the course of Amish history took three general directions. First, the congregations that favored retaining the old traditions unchanged as much as possible became known as "Alt Amisch" or Old Order Amish. Before this the word "Amish" or "Amish Mennonite" had been sufficient to describe any group. A second cluster of churches affiliated with the more progressive factions such as the Egli and Stuckey groups, both of Alsatian origin, which had already lost their ties with the traditional groups. A third group comprised the middle-of-the-road churches that favored moderate changes. These, under the name "Amish Mennonite," organized into three regional conferences and eventually merged with the Mennonite Church (see Table 7). "House Amish," who met in their homes for preaching, were now distinguished from "Church Amish," who met for worship in meeting houses.

Table 7
Amish cleavages, 1862–1966

Year	Name of division or movement
1862	General Ministers' Conference (Verhandlungen der Diener-Versammlungen)
1866	"Egli Amish" or Defenseless Mennonite Church, (later Evangelical Mennonite Church)
1872	"The Stuckey Mennonites" or Central Conference Mennonites (merged with the General Conference Mennonite Church)
1888	Indiana-Michigan Amish Mennonite Conference (merged with the Mennonite Church in 1917)
1890	Western Amish Mennonite Conference (merged with the Mennonite Church in 1920)
1893	Eastern Amish Mennonite Conference (merged with the Mennonite Church in 1927)
1910	Conservative Amish Mennonite Conference (affiliated with the Mennonite Church)
1927	Beachy Amish Mennonite Church (unaffiliated).
1956	Nonconference Conservative Mennonites (later Conservative Mennonite Fellowship)
1966	"New Amish"

A major cleavage among the Alsatian Amish immigrants occurred with the emergence of the "Egli Amish" in 1866. Henry Egli, a bishop of the Amish group near Berne, Indiana, claimed to have experienced regeneration of heart and restoration from a prolonged illness. In his home church he preached the necessity of a vital religious conversion. He charged his church with formalism, lack of spiritual vitality, and looseness in maintaining the old customs, and began rebaptizing persons who had not experienced regeneration at the time of their first baptism. The Amish conference was unable to heal the breach in Egli's local church. The small congregation divided over the issue. The followers of Egli organized a separate church, but the same issues sprang up in other Amish groups in Illinois, Missouri, Kansas, Nebraska, and Ohio. Egli visited these places and gained many supporters. Those who emphasized individual religious experience and broke with tradition soon lost the outward symbols of the Old Order Amish such as plain dress, strict group discipline, and the German language. After Egli's death in 1890, the group developed interest in missionary work after the manner of Protestantism. In 1898, another division occurred within the Egli Amish, over the question of immersion. As a result the Missionary Church Association was formed. The remaining Egli Amish adopted the name "Defenseless Mennonite," which they later changed to Evangelical Mennonite Church.[2]

In 1872, another cleavage resulted in the development of the "Stuckey Mennonites."[3] Joseph Stuckey, bishop of a congregation in Illinois, and a leading figure in the Amish Ministers' Conference, was more open-minded on some questions than other Amish bishops. Stuckey was well liked by his district but suddenly found himself under censure by the Amish Ministers' Conference. A schoolteacher in his congregation had published a poem in which the thought was expressed that all men would eventually be saved.[4] The idea was viewed by some as rank heresy. Several of the verses were read at the next Amish conference, and the decision was reached to expel members who did not believe in eternal punishment. But Stuckey refused to excommunicate the man who had written the poem. His refusal was regarded as insubordination, and after committee deliberations on the subject, Stuckey was requested to make a public confession.

2. *Mennonite Encyclopedia*, s.v. "Evangelical Mennonite Church."

3. Known as the Central Conference of Mennonites, the Stuckey group is discussed by C. Henry Smith in *The Story of the Mennonites* (Newton, Kans.: Mennonite Publication Office, 1950), 612.

4. For a biography of this poet, see Olynthus Clark, "Joseph Joder, Schoolmaster-Farmer and Poet, 1797–1887," *Transactions of the Illinois State Historical Society*, 1929, pp. 135–65.

This he also failed to do, and in 1872 he severed ties with the Amish Ministers' Conference. Stuckey's congregation stood behind his decision, so there was no split in his group. The churches under his pastorate prospered and in 1899 his group was organized as the Central Illinois Conference of Mennonites. The word "Amish" dropped into disuse. Stuckey died in 1902 and his group merged with the General Conference Mennonite Church, a progressive denomination.

Generally, the members of the Old Order Amish congregations who chose a more forward-looking course tended to affiliate with Amish Mennonite congregations. Among the three regional conferences of Amish Mennonites organized after 1878 there were no sharp cleavages, and affiliation with the larger Mennonite bodies occurred peacefully. But several small groups of Old Order Amish have occasionally formed new separatist groups independently from an existing Mennonite body. In 1910 a group of congregations formed an association called the Conservative Amish Mennonite Conference. This conference attracted congregations from Iowa to Pennsylvania. The name "conservative" was used to chart a course between progressive Amish Mennonite congregations and the Old Order congregations. Members began to hold Sunday Schools, promote evangelism, and support charitable institutions. The name "Amish" was dropped from the conference title in 1954.

Another group, called Beachy Amish, emerged from the Old Order in 1927. The movement began in Somerset County, Pennsylvania, and was named after Bishop Moses M. Beachy.[5] As bishop in the Casselman River district, Beachy experienced mild disagreement with other leaders of his district over the practice of conducting Sunday School and the use of electricity and the automobile. When Beachy refused to excommunicate and shun members of his congregation for joining the Conservative Amish Mennonite churches in the area, a segment of his congregation allied with the traditional Old Order Amish congregations. Not many years passed before other Amish districts were following Beachy's example. Those Amish families (or congregations) that wanted automobiles, electricity, meeting houses, and field tractors generally turned "Beachy." Other names arose for localized groups of this movement. In Lancaster County the "John A. Stoltzfus Church" or the "Weavertown Amish" began to affiliate with the Beachy Amish group. In Indiana the group was called the

5. Alvin J. Beachy, "The Amish of Somerset County, Pennsylvania: A Study in the Rise and Development of the Beachy Amish Mennonite Churches" (M.A. thesis, Hartford Seminary Foundation, 1952), published in *Mennonite Quarterly Review* 28 (October 1954) and 29 (April 1955).

"Burkholder Amish." Although the present ninety or more congregations of this affiliation are not organized into a formal conference, they function as a separately organized denomination. The use of the German language has given way to English in worship services, singing is increasingly four-part, and in dress and other customs the gap between the Old Order Amish and the Beachys is widening.

A movement describing itself as "Nonconference Conservative Mennonites" began to appear about the year 1956. Its members consist of former Beachy Amish persons and some who withdrew from Mennonite congregations to find a more conservative climate. They have occasionally published a periodical, and presently issue *The Harvest Call*. Representatives of this group meet at unspecified times to survey the "drift toward worldliness" and to support one another against more organized forms of Mennonitism.

Finally, a group called the "New Amish" began to emerge in 1966 in Pennsylvania and Ohio. The movement for a "new order" occurred among families that favored telephones, tractor-driven farm machinery, and power-driven generators for cooling bulk milk. Their members also speak out against the use of tobacco and emphasize a "cleaner" life style and conduct. The New Amish continue to meet for worship in their homes. They differ from the Beachy Amish in that they do not permit automobiles or meeting houses.

ISSUES AND CONFRONTATIONS

The Amish, who work so hard to maintain unity and uniformity, nevertheless suffer the consequences of a fragmented social order. The symbols over which they dispute appear to be diverse. Some have polarized over the shape or color of a garment; the style of a house, carriage, or harness; the use of labor-saving farm machinery or the pace of singing. The list is mind-boggling. Beneath the surface are extended families, frequently fraught with envy or jealousy, that take opposing sides. At the root of many divisions are members who suffer from stagnation and others who suffer from too much change. The Amish tend to suppress their feelings since no one wishes to become the cause of disunity and division. Typically, dissatisfied members migrate to a more compatible Old Order community or start a new settlement. When moving away does not solve the problem, an open split and shunning assures continued social distance between the factions. A few examples will illustrate the nature and intensity of these confrontations. There is the notorious case of Moses Hartz, which has been called a *Huttlerei*, "a tangle of confusion." The incident occurred several generations ago but is still vivid in the minds of some.

Moses Hartz was a prosperous Amish farmer, a preacher regarded by many in his district as an unusually intelligent man and an able speaker. He often expressed affection for the Amish churches. Moses had a son, also named Moses, who took up the occupation of mill-wright. The son became an expert in selling and installing machinery in mills for a manufacturing company. To make a success of this occupation, the son felt that he could not keep all the rules of the Amish church; for one thing, he wanted outside pockets on his coat, which the rules forbade. As a millwright and maintenance man, he felt he needed outside pockets in which to keep his wrenches. Eventually he "quietly went to the Mennonites."

The young Moses Hartz was excommunicated from the Amish church, as is customary for transgressors, but without the full consent of the members. Although the decision to excommunicate him was not unanimous, the bishop pronounced him "out." Preacher Moses Hartz felt he could not shun his son just for joining the Mennonites. For his refusal he was "silenced" as a preacher. Contention followed, and no reconciliation seemed possible.

Finally, Preacher Moses Hartz and his wife Lena made application to join the Conestoga Amish Mennonite Church. This was a meeting-house church made up of Amish who were progressive in their ways. The Amish Mennonites were hesitant about taking into their membership a silenced preacher from the Old Order church, but consented to take Moses and his wife as lay members. This resulted in shunning by the Old Order group, and provoked contention in both churches. Some of the Amish Mennonites said it was wrong to receive members who were not in good standing in the Old Order church. The decision of the Old Order church to shun the Hartzes had the effect of dividing the members of the Amish Mennonite church. Of course, many of the people in the Old Order group were close relatives of those in the Mennonite group.

An out-of-state committee was asked to investigate the entire affair and to make recommendations. After hearing the story from all sides, the committee recommended that Moses and Lena be given the choice of going back to the Old Order Amish group or making a confession upon their knees in the Amish Mennonite church. The Amish Mennonite group agreed to stand by the recommendation of the committee. The couple chose to make the confession. After their full reconciliation with the Amish Mennonite group, the trouble finally appeared to be settled. A delegation carried the news back to the Old Order Amish bishop. The bishop expressed pleasure with the decision. Moses and Lena had acknowledged their faults, and a way had been cleared for discontinuing the shunning. It was decided to drop the *Meidung*.

It appears, according to the meeting-house group's explanation, that one influential minister had been absent when the reconciliation was reported to a meeting of the ministers. At the next meeting of the Old Order ministers, this minister used his influence to upset the decision and to renew the *Meidung* against Moses and Lena Hartz. They were then shunned for the rest of their lives. The incident culminated in a cleavage when one hundred members withdrew from the Old Order. Years of bitter feelings prevailed, bringing stress between families and relatives. As one survivor of the Hartz incident said: "The old people rehearsed the doings until the people of my age grew sour on the avoidance principle."[6] There are always two sides to a dispute, as the Old Order Amish are prone to point out. But all the factors from the viewpoint of the Old Order may never be known, for the account in the record comes from the meeting-house side of the dispute.

Several circumstances may have contributed to the Hartz affair. Moses Hartz, of Lutheran background, had lost his parents at the age of four. At eighteen he took to the road in search of employment and found it on the farm of Amishman David Mast. During his years of employment he served as teamster with a Conestoga wagon line, hauling supplies between Philadelphia and Pittsburgh. He joined the Amish church, married Magdalena Nafziger, became a prosperous farmer, and was ordained as an Amish minister in 1855. Moses was an able speaker who emphasized Scriptural teachings rather than tradition. During the Millwood meeting-house division of 1877 he was the only minister who remained with the Amish district. He owned the largest farm in Conestoga Valley and was one of its most noted farmers. After he introduced the first combined reaper-binder in 1880, considerable alarm was expressed about the consequences of the new implement.

Whether there was envy on the part of other Amish farmers is not clear from the record, but such appears to have been the case. Furthermore, Moses's son Moses was employed as an agent of a machine company in Chambersburg, Pennsylvania, and traveled much of the time. In California he became part-owner of a gold mine. He installed

6. C. Z. Mast, in a letter to the author (July 3, 1960). Biographical material on Moses Hartz (1819–1916) and his son Moses (1846–1946) appears in Amos Hartz and Susan Hartz, *Moses Hartz Family History, 1819–1965* (Elverson, Pa.: By the author, 1965).

a mill in New Mexico and established a business in Philadelphia, all before he was married at the age of thirty-four. No wonder he sensed the need for outside pockets on his garments and left the Amish church! The Old Order leaders must have seen clearly that his excommunication and that of his father and mother, despite their respected character, were necessary for maintaining separation from the world. Although there are descendants of Moses and Magdalena Hartz who are Amish, there is today no Hartz family name among the Amish.

The heavy-handed manner of bishops, without the support of fellow ministers and members, is frequently associated with fragmentation. Occasionally an excommunicated member who moves from one state to another "to get away from it all" becomes the key figure in a division. Such a member in Ohio moved to an Amish settlement in Indiana. In Indiana he was received into the Amish church upon confession in good faith. After several years the Indiana church sought fellowship status with the Ohio group. The Ohio bishop replied that this could be achieved only if so-and-so, the former erring Ohio member, were excommunicated. The Indiana bishop excommunicated the member and announced that all who did not favor affiliating with the Ohio group could not take communion. The Indiana church was split when over half of its members decided to withstand the decision of the presiding bishop. Five of the bishop's brothers and two of his sisters were among the dissenters.

Another example is a preacher in Indiana, Christian Wary, who in 1884 moved to the state of Iowa. "He intended to join the Old Order church and attended their services on his first Sunday in the community, but he was not asked to preach because he had a folding top buggy and a raincoat, two conveniences that were not tolerated by the Iowa group. When he was approached on the question, he replied that he was unwilling to give up anything that protected his health."[7] A group of seceding members then asked him to be their minister. This group developed into the East Union Mennonite Church near Kalona, Iowa.

When outsiders join, or attempt to join, the Amish church, issues may arise that polarize the group. This occurred when a Detroit workingman was overjoyed in his discovery of the Amish people. While in a state of uncertainty about the adequacy of his religion, he read a newspaper account of Amish in Kansas who had sold their farms and moved away because oil was discovered on them. Maniaci

7. Melvin Gingerich, *The Mennonites in Iowa* (Iowa City: State Historical Society of Iowa, 1939), p. 137.

concluded that "either these people were fools or their religion was real," and in hopes that it was "real," he wrote to one of the Amish farmers asking how he could join their group. He was referred to an Amish family in his own state of Michigan. But the Amish had no precedent for taking in outsiders and referred Maniaci and his family to a small Mennonite mission in Detroit, which they joined. Still aware that it was the Amish who had won him to Christ, Maniaci began to arouse the Amish to do missionary work. The Amish expression of the Christian life, he felt with deep sincerity, should be proclaimed far and wide. He began publishing an evangelistic news sheet, *Amish Mission Endeavor,* and to all Amish ordained persons sent specially prepared letters in which he said: "My only interest is to see the Amish Church on fire for the Gospel. What about the debt that you as a leader owe to the unsaved? There are many young people in your church who are willing to launch out. . . . Will you lead them or will you cause them to join other churches?" Maniaci's efforts brought some results, and he succeeded in forming a "mission-minded" group in several states. The first of several Amish mission conferences was held in Kalona, Iowa, in 1950. Amish persons attended against the advice of their bishops. In some of these conferences a Mennonite missionary speaker was engaged. A Mission Interests Committee was organized and began publishing the periodical *Witnessing* in 1953.

Maniaci was considered a dangerous innovator by the Amish leaders. After all, he could not speak the language of the Amish and was regarded by them as an intruder. To offset this criticism from the leaders, his Amish sympathizers conducted the annual missionary conferences in German. Maniaci concluded that "they did not like an outsider running their affairs." Nevertheless, with his pointed, mimeographed messages, he had helped to form a special interest group within Amish society and had put like-minded persons into communication with one another.

Meanwhile an Old Order Amish minister, David Miller of Oklahoma, who was active in the missionary movement, traveled through several states preaching the Gospel in an evangelistic manner. He not only preached and prayed at the traditional Amish services in an unorthodox way but also spoke to large crowds gathered on the lawns of Amish homes in the evening. He won the admiration of hundreds of Amish people with his new "biblical" messages, stripped as they were of the usual Amish singsong delivery and terminology. Miller was promptly denied fellowship with the Old Order churches, and his own congregation eventually affiliated with the Beachy group.

The missionary movement, as articulated by Maniaci and Miller, attracted a considerable body of sympathizers from among the Amish, some of them young people who had been holding secret prayer and Bible study meetings. Parents who no longer took the trouble to teach their children the German language also were among its supporters, as were young people who were troubled by the rowdy behavior among Amish youth. But no overt division occurred as a result of the missionary movement. The Amish leaders strictly forbade attendance at missionary conferences, and sympathizers either yielded or joined congregations (Beachy and other churches) with similar sympathies.

DIVISIONS WITHIN A SINGLE COMMUNITY

What has just been sketched is a picture of the Amish movement showing its many branches. When such diverse groups live in a single community there is an even greater complexity. A prime example is Mifflin County in central Pennsylvania. This region encompasses Kishacoquillas Valley or "Big Valley," which has in it twelve Amish-related groups. All originated in whole or in part among the Amish who came to this region from southeastern Pennsylvania as early as 1791. These groups rank themselves by the degree of their assimilation into the prevailing American culture with the terms "low" and "high" church. A low church is one that has retained the old traditions, while a high church is one that is more like "the world" (see Figure 15). They are described below in the order of most-to-least traditional.[8]

The "Old School" Amish (Figure 15, divisions 1 and 2), also known locally as the "Nebraska Amish,"[9] date from 1881. The name Nebraska derives from an Amish settlement in the state of Nebraska, and specifically from its bishop Yost H. Yoder, who assisted a small fraction among the Mifflin County Amish in ordaining its leaders. Later a few families in Nebraska moved to Mifflin County to join

8. The early divisions of this community are discussed in part in John A. Hostetler, "The Life and Times of Samuel Yoder, 1824–1884," *Mennonite Quarterly Review* 22 (October 1948): 226–41. The nearby Union County division is described by John Umble in "The Amish Mennonites of Union County, Pennsylvania, Part I, Social and Religious Life," *Mennonite Quarterly Review* 7 (April 1933): 71–96; and idem, "The Amish Mennonites of Union County, Pennsylvania, Part II, A History of the Settlement," ibid. 7 (July 1933): 162–90.

9. See "The Amish in Gosper County, Nebraska," *Mennonite Historical Bulletin* 10 (October 1949); and Maurice A. Mook, "The Nebraska Amish in Pennsylvania," *Mennonite Life* 17 (July 1962): 27–30. For illustrations of this group, see ibid. 16 (July 1961).

Big Valley, central Pennsylvania, an area noted
for its many affiliations of Amish,
traditional and modern

them. The seceding group was nicknamed the "Nebraska Amish" or
"Old Schoolers." The men wear their hair about shoulder length in
the style of William Penn. They wear white shirts, brown denim
trousers and gray coats, wide-brimmed hats, no suspenders, and no
belts. Their trousers are laced up in back. The women wear a black
kerchief tied on the head over a white covering, as bonnets are prohibited. When working in the fields the women wear the "scoop" or
flat hat, made of straw, which resembles the Swiss and Alsatian peasant
hats worn two centuries ago. The wide brim is folded down at the
sides by means of a string that is tied beneath the chin. Of all Amishwomen, these wear the longest dresses, in dark, plain colors. In winter,
women wear the *Mandel*, a long outer garment like an overcoat, and
no shawls. Modern farm equipment is taboo. Until about 1940 these
Amish people were grinding their grain by means of horse power.
Traction engines are taboo, but one- or two-cylinder engines are

used for belt power. Lawn mowers, screens at the windows or doors, curtains, and carpets are taboo. All buggies are two-seated with a white top. There are no single-seated or open buggies, though spring wagons, or "market wagons" as they are called, some with brown tops, are used. Dashboards and whipsockets are not allowed. Barns remain unpainted, as do most houses. A projecting roof at the gable ends of buildings is forbidden.

As the most traditional of all Amish in the New World, they have retained the oldest customs. When most Amish accepted the bonnet in the nineteenth century, this group retained the head scarf. Their carriage tops and men's shirts are white, presumably because the material was made of flax and was unbleached and undyed. At funerals they observe the old custom of serving to all who attend a slice of sweet bread, cheese, and wine after the viewing and prior to going to the cemetery to lay the body to rest.

The Zook faction of Old Schoolers broke from the Yoders in 1933, but to the outsider these groups appear identical. Each group has its own worship service on the same Sunday, and each has two bishops to insure its independence from the other. According to tradition, a difference of opinion arose between two Old School ministers when a member bought a farm formerly owned by "English" people. The question was whether the new owner would need to saw off the projecting roof on the gable ends of his buildings. The group took sides on the question. All of the present eight Nebraska districts have tended to segregate themselves in the northeastern regions of Mifflin County, with small offshoots extending into Center and Union counties. Living between Philadelphia and Pittsburgh and away from large urban centers as they do, they are less accessible than most Amish to tourists, but photographers have seized upon them to compete for national and international awards in photography.

The "Byler Church" is sometimes called *die Alt Gemee* ("the Old Church") (Figure 15, division 3) and by a more descriptive phrase, the "Bean-soupers." The name comes from the practice of serving bean soup at lunch after the preaching service, although the same practice holds for the Old Schoolers. Generically this group traces its connection to the Samuel B. King division in 1849 and in its oral tradition regards itself as the stump from which other groups originated. One of its most distinguishing traits of culture is the use of yellow tops on.two-seated buggies. The color of men's shirts may be other than white, and blue is very predominant. In 1948 the group affiliated and began to exchange ministers with the Rennos (see Figure 15). The Byler Amishmen wear their hair shorter than do the Old Schoolers, but it still covers the ears. The women wear brown

Figure 15.
Cognitive orientation from "low" to "high" church
in Mifflin County, Pennsylvania

The concentric circles are labeled, from the center outward:

1 Old School (Yoder)
2 Old School (Zook)
3 Byler Church
4 Peachey Amish (Renno)
5 "New" Amish
6 Beachy Amish (Valley View)
7 Beth-El Mennonite
8 Holdeman Mennonite
9 Allensville Mennonite
10 Locust Grove Mennonite
11 Brethren in Christ
12 Maple Grove Mennonite
13 Protestant

bonnets and a *Mandel* (overcoat with a cape). Tractors are used for belt power but not for field work. Single-seated buggies are used by the unmarried men of this group. Spring wagons—one-horse buggies with one seat in the front and a long compartment in the rear—are used to haul bags of feed or other light loads. Buildings are generally painted and in good condition. Half-length curtains (lower half), window blinds, and screens are used, but the woven carpets so typical of other Amish groups are absent.

The "Renno Amish" (Figure 15, division 4); named after John Renno and his son Joshua, maintain "full fellowship" with their Lancaster brethren in practicing the *Meidung* and conform culturally to the same general standards, but with some exceptions.[10] The men wear a single suspender and their hair covers the ears. The women wear dark, plain-colored dresses; black bonnets; white, starched head coverings; and black shawls. The Sunday dress of unmarried girls past the age of puberty includes a white *Halsduch*, a white apron, and a black head covering. Families drive two-seated, black-top buggies to the preaching service. Single boys drive a one-seated, open buggy with dashboard, whipsocket, and battery lights. Spring wagons are used for hauling materials from nearby villages. Barns are typically red and houses white, though there is no colored trimming on the buildings. Carpets, window blinds, and half-length curtains are common. Indoor plumbing is allowed.

The "New Amish" (Figure 15, division 5) or Old Order Valley District (the official name) emerged in 1972 when members began to study and articulate the meaning of salvation, especially assurance of salvation. With Christian Peachey and Ezra Kanagy as ministers, approximately seventeen families from both the Renno and Byler groups formed the initial body. From the viewpoint of the traditional groups, these members were affiliated with "a strange belief" that created disunity in the congregations. The "New Amish" insisted that an individual could have the "assurance of salvation" instead of a mere, vague "hope" of salvation. According to the old bishop, it was permissible to have such thoughts, but to advocate such beliefs was to display a dangerous kind of pride.[11] Two ministers sympathetic to a knowledge of salvation tried to avoid an open split by containing their views, but circumstances led them otherwise.

One circumstance was the accident and final words of Aquilla, son of the minister Ezra Kanagy. The young married man was kicked by a horse, lay suffering in the hospital for thirty-eight days, and died of a staph infection. In his last hours the young man revealed to his father: "Jesus talked to me and comforted me and said I was on the right path." To his young wife he revealed a dream: "Satan

10. This main-line Old Order group descends from the faction of Abraham Peachey, who in 1863 opposed Solomon Beiler, who allowed baptism in streams and under whose leadership meeting houses were established at Allenville and at Belleville (Maple Grove).

11. John R. Renno, Jr., writes of his personal encounter with assurance of salvation and of his excommunication from the Amish by his own father. John R. Renno, *A Brief History of the Amish Church in Belleville* (Danville, Pa.: By the author, 1976).

came to get me, but Jesus came and took me away and showed me some wonderful beautiful things." While Aquilla was receiving his thirty-eighth pint of blood he quietly passed away. Those close to the young man attest that he lived and died with the assurance of salvation.

In charting the course of the new group, one of the ministers explained that "New Order" would be a fitting name for their group, "for afterall we do have the 'New Birth', as the district is not interested in members without the new birth, and especially not those (regardless of how plain they dress) who teach we cannot know we are born again but can only hope so. This is unscriptural and against the Old Order doctrine and faith which goes back to our forefathers, the Anabaptists, and the apostles."[12] The group meets for preaching each Sunday in the homes of members. It permits telephones, but unlike some New Amish, does not use high-line electricity or tractor machinery for farming. The New Amish group was greatly diminished when its bishop Christian Peachey with many members joined the Holdeman group (Figure 15, division 8) in 1979.

The Beachy Church (Valley View) or "Speicher'" group (Figure 15, division 6), named after Bishop Jesse Speicher, but traditionally known as the "Zook" church, was formed in 1911 as a progressive offshoot of the Peachey Amish. When a seceding group in Lancaster County, Pennsylvania, requested ministerial help from Mifflin County and John B. Zook came to their assistance, the division was initiated. Thus a division spread from one settlement to another in this instance.

A small faction in Lancaster County known as the "King Amish" was without leadership. Not being in sympathy with some of the strict Amish rules, it appealed for ministerial help to Big Valley, where there were three districts, each with a bishop: John B. Zook, Sam Peachey, and David Peachey. Bishop Zook thought the small Lancaster group should be helped and the three bishops decided to take the *Rat* ("council") of the congregations on this question. Zook reported a favorable vote from his district, but the Peachey bishops reported: "Mir hen kenn einger Rote katt." ("We had no unanimous decision"). Zook responded: "If you would have taken the vote the right way you would have gotten a favorable decision." (Instead of asking their members for consent to aid the Lancaster group, the Peachey bishops asked their congregations to approve refusal of the ministerial aid.) The outcome was a division in the Big Valley group,

12. *The Budget,* July 12, 1973; the accident is discussed in the issues of June 30 and July 6, 1972.

for the Zook district came to the aid of the King group in Lancaster County and the Peachey districts did not. The King faction was the forerunner of what was to become the John A. Stoltzfus or Weavertown Amish group.

Until 1954, when the Zook group adopted the use of automobiles, it conformed generally to the typical Amish pattern of culture, although the men wore two suspenders instead of one, wore their hair shorter than the Renno group allowed, and were permitted to use sweaters and zippered jackets. Men's hat brims were narrower, the dresses of the women shorter. Electricity was adopted by the group in about 1948. The use of rubber-tired tractors preceded the adoption of the automobile in 1954. Gradually carpets, linoleum, modern kitchen appliances, and wall mottoes have become commonplace. The adoption of the automobile resulted in considerable social distance from neighboring Amish groups, as well as in changes in occupation and in travel. The group built the "Valley View" meeting house in 1962, and exchanges ministers with "Beachy" Amish churches in other states.

The Beth-El Mennonite Church (Figure 15, division 7), organized in 1973 with J. Ellrose Hartzler as its leader, consists of several families that withdrew from the long-established Allensville Mennonite congregation. These families were not pleased with the modernizing trends they saw in the congregation and built a separate meeting house. They seldom vocalized their views but quietly withdrew. They emphasize the wearing of plain clothing—black stockings and cape dresses among women; plain, collarless coats and no neckties among men—and are not affiliated with any conference body.

The Holdeman group (Figure 15, division 8), first formed a small congregation in 1958, although the denomination (known as Church of God in Christ Mennonite) was founded over one hundred years ago. They emphasize, in their own terms, "repentance, forgiveness, the new birth, self-denial, nonconformity, nonresistance, excommunication of transgressors and the shunning of apostates."[13] Their dress is plain but in style is distinctive from that of other plain sects. The men wear beards. The group conducts evangelistic (often tent) revivals and practices a high degree of exclusiveness. The local congregation was organized in an abandoned schoolhouse after several individuals from the Renno group, including Bishop John R. Renno's

---

13. *Histories of the Congregation of the Church of God in Christ, Mennonite* (Moundridge, Kans., and Sainte Anne, Man.: Gospel Publishers, 1975), p. 10. For a comprehensive history, see Clarence Hiebert, *The Holdeman People* (South Pasadena, Calif.: William Carey Library, 1973).

son Eli, came in contact with itinerant evangelists of the group. The congregation has grown with the influx of members from several Amish groups that "were expelled from the old order Amish due to an experimental knowledge of having received the New Birth and its subsequences."[14] Traditional Amish members who join this group appear to exchange one strict discipline for another, but gain greater personal freedom, for the group permits automobiles and modern farm machinery.

The Allensville Mennonite Church (Figure 15, division 9) traces its origin to the Amish group organized in 1861 by Solomon Byler, the group that established meeting houses in 1869. The congregation is affiliated with the Allegheny Conference of the Mennonite Church, the largest body of Mennonites in North America. Its meeting house is located on Route 655, a short distance from the village of Allensville. A distinct style of dress is still discernible, for women wear white prayer coverings and print dresses, and a few still wear plain Mennonite bonnets.

The Locust Grove or Conservative Mennonite Church (Figure 15, division 10) was organized in 1898 under the leadership of Bishop Abraham D. Zook by members of the Allensville and Belleville meeting-house churches who felt that change in their community was taking place too rapidly. The congregation is affiliated with the Conservative Mennonite Conference, but the styles of dress that once distinguished it from the Allensville or Maple Grove Mennonite churches no longer prevail. The earlier plain style of dress among women, including black stockings, cape dresses, and white coverings with strings and small black bonnets, has disappeared. Support for Mennonite schools and colleges, foreign missions, relief, and benevolent giving are part of the church's effort. Many of the group's young people, like those of other Mennonite congregations in the area, attend college.

The Brethren in Christ Church (Figure 15, division 11), a revivalist group, built a meeting house in Belleville in 1959. It gained adherents when members of the Beachy group, who by this time were allowed to have automobiles, began to attend Brethren in Christ revival meetings outside Big Valley. Like the Holdeman group, this group stresses repentance and conversion and conducts revival meetings, but does not require beards, a distinctive way of dressing, or avoidance of apostate members. The group has remained active but small in numbers.

The Maple Grove Mennonite Church (Figure 15, division 12) was

14. *Histories of the Congregations of the Church of God in Christ,* p. 177.

organized at Belleville by the meeting-house Amish under the leadership of Solomon Byler in 1868. The congregation first affiliated with the Eastern Amish Mennonite Conference, but when that conference was disbanded, it affiliated with the Allegheny Conference of the Mennonite Church. The congregation has had the reputation of being the most progressive Mennonite group in Big Valley. Its members were among the first to attend college, and its recent pastors have received seminary training. Maple Grove was also the first to support nearby small mission congregations, organize radio broadcasts, and conduct choral programs. Professional men and businessmen of the group belong to civic and community organizations. The discipline is the most relaxed of any of the above groups. Nevertheless, the congregation remains distinct from the general Protestant churches in the area, which are regarded as "higher" or more worldly.

These twelve groups, coexisting in a single community, represent one of the most diverse expressions of Anabaptist-Mennonite culture anywhere in North America. Various degrees of social distance are maintained between orthodox groups. In secular activities, at auctions and farm sales, and in mutual-aid practices there is limited interaction. The "lowest" church has very little to do with Amish who are "higher" and has tended to segregate its members in the least congested region of Big Valley.

This stratified system of religious groups performs a number of functions associated with the maintenance of community boundaries. Except for the two proselyting groups (Figure 15, divisions 8 and 11), each respects the customs and rights of the others. No effort is made to gain members from another group. Each Amish sect is highly endogenous and is so maintained by the threat of *Meidung*. This system of stratification permits the person to move gradually from a "lower" group to a more progressive one in a natural and voluntary manner. The greater the social distance between the groups, the less likely it is that members will drop out and affiliate with the group most like it in *Ordnung*. Among the "lowest" two groups, there is very little tendency to join the "higher" groups. Though very few in number, defecting young Amish in the "lowest" ranks tend to make abrupt changes like joining the army. This tendency to reject religious affiliation rather than accept a Mennonite-related congregation has been observed in other contexts.[15]

15. Gingerich, *The Mennonites in Iowa*, p. 173; see also ibid., chap. 11, "Differences of Opinion." Hutterite defectors also have shown a disinclination to join other denominations; see John A. Hostetler, *Hutterite Society* (Baltimore: The Johns Hopkins University Press, 1974), p. 275.

The problem of land availability is alleviated when persons leave the stricter Amish groups (to whom land is most vital) and join a Mennonite congregation. Often the move to a "higher" church precipitates a change from farming to another occupation. The boundaries of each religious community are preserved by expelling the deviant person; the expelled person simply moves up the ladder to a "higher" church and in this way establishes a new identity without "contaminating" other members. Each ceremonial group thus remains small and retains its character.

In Ohio, as in Big Valley (Mifflin County, Pennsylvania), there are many different gradations or groups of Old Order Amish concentrated in the same community which do not exchange ministers or join in fellowship.[16] These are usually named after the bishop of each group. The gradations in Indiana and Iowa are less pronounced. In Lancaster County, Pennsylvania, there has been little splitting into divergent groups except for the Weavertown Amish-Mennonite group, the New Amish, and groups that have split off from the New Amish. Daughter settlements originating in Lancaster County since 1966 have been in full fellowship with their parental community. The bishops and ministers here have met more consistently over the years to assess their differences, as they still do twice annually. Others, both ordained and lay members, who have been inclined to disagree with the rules, have by common consent moved to new settlements. Migration in such instances prevents open cleavages.

In summary, the loss of Old Order Amish group identity typically begins with increased verbalization of religious beliefs, interest in evangelism, and Bible study, which in turn lead to Sunday Schools, automobiles, and nonfarming occupations. These periodic schisms are sparked by vocal innovators, by both lay members and leaders. The schisms are supported by persons who seek greater freedom from the strict discipline of Amish life, from social stagnation, on the one hand, and on the other hand, by those who suffer from the prospect of too much change.

16. For the chronology of the Ohio cleavages, see *Ohio Amish Directory*, comp. Ervin Gingerich (Star Route, Millersburg, Ohio, 1973), p. 14.

CHAPTER 14

Deviation and Vulnerability

ALTHOUGH THE AMISH stress the unity of the corporate church-community living in a state of obedience and readiness, "unspotted" and "without blemish," we have seen in the previous chapter how tensions arise and subgroups are formed. We shall now turn to the subject of individual conformity and deviation. As in any society, conformity to community rules and expectations varies among Amish members. Rules are not understood by all individuals in the same way, nor are they emphasized with equal intensity in the various districts. Certain kinds of actions are tolerated more than others. Amish leaders recognize the various tensions within their congregation, as is evident in the following comment made by an Amish minister: "We have a minority who resist the rules. They are of two classes. One group is prone to look for 'greener grass' and they will usually find their abode on the outside. The other element is unconcerned. They disregard the lessons of the past and just want to live for today."[1]

MODES OF INDIVIDUAL ADAPTATION

Of the major modes of individual adaptation to culture, all types are found among the Amish, but in different proportions. A useful scheme for comprehending individual adaptations is presented in

1. Interview with Joseph Beiler.

Figure 16, where four major ways of adaptation are differentiated: *conformity, ritualism, innovation,* and *retreatism.*[2] No individual fits any one mode of adaptation perfectly, for a person might be a conformist in some ways and an innovator in others. Let us then illustrate some of these modes in Amish society.

Conformity. Conformity to the goals of Amish life and to the approved means of achieving them is the most common form of adaptation. Individuals conform to the goals through institutional and approved means. This assures the maintenance of the status quo. In a society where most people conform to these expectations there is great stability and strong resistance to change. To the extent that the conforming members have their basic needs met, the pattern of life is orderly and predictable. By conforming to Amish norms, Amish society as a whole resists conformity to the dominant society. "In Amish society," said a former Amish girl after graduation from college, "one is always conscious of keeping as many rules as one can, and each person tends to feel an obligation to see that other members of the family also keep these rules." From data presented earlier (Table 4), it may be recalled that of children born to Old Order parents (from 1880 to 1939 in Lancaster County), about 22 percent did not remain Amish. Since persons voluntarily join the church at baptism, the percentage who defect from membership is much smaller, possibly 6 percent. Of all Amish young men who were drafted during World War II, only 4 percent went into military service. In light of the high birth rate (see Chapter 5), this is a remarkable record of conformity.

As used here, conformity implies that persons are committed to the goals and means of their culture, voluntarily accept them, and live in a state of commitment to the appropriate rewards. If, however, goals are unattained for any reason, individuals may emphasize rules and adapt to their culture ritualistically.

Ritualism. Ritualism is a mode of adjustment in which an individual makes a virtue of overconformity to the rules, usually at the cost of stagnation. Typically these are the "bureaucrats" who slavishly follow the rules without regard for the ends for which they were designed. In Amish society they might also include individuals who for any number of reasons cannot achieve the highest goals (large families, farm ownership, and children who stay Amish), and who alleviate their anxieties

2. Based on Robert Merton, *Social Theory and Social Structure* (Glencoe, Ill.: The Free Press, 1957), p. 140. Merton's "rebellious" type is excluded from the diagram because it assumes a complete rejection of the culture.

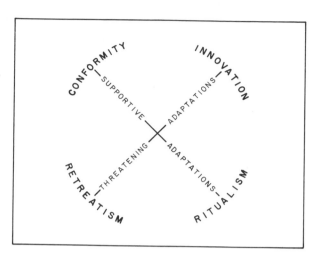

Figure 16.
Modes of individual adaptation
to the Amish community

over not measuring up by emphasizing the rules. Aside from practicing ardent conformity themselves, they gain status by seeing that others also conform. The most ritualistic status role in Amish society, that of the deacon, is a position that is held for life. The deacon is typically an older (rarely a younger) man who is above reproach in keeping the rules. In his official duties he must ascertain the facts and attitudes with respect to offenders and seek the help of others in maintaining conformity. Because Amish society has strong sanctions against most changes, ritualistic behavior is acceptable, and is much less threatening than the innovative type.

Innovation. Innovation is a type of adaptation in which the goals of the society are accepted, but other than approved means are used to achieve them. Working and saving money to buy a farm, for example, is an approved Amish goal, but the means of achieving that goal (where one works and what one does) is an area in which innovation is apt to occur. Changes generally are not encouraged, vocalized, or rewarded in Amish society as they are in the dominant American culture. For example, the Amish style is " 'Tis better to remain quiet and let people think you are dumb, than to speak and remove all doubt."[3] Changes may occur in subtle ways, or as an afterthought. Amish inno-

3. A motto posted in the repair shop of Gideon L. Fisher.

vators may be divided into two broad categories: those who are toler-ated and those who are expelled. Those who try to be Amish without conforming in language, dress, or attitude are of the latter category.

Deviant tendencies are quickly detected. The slightest deviation is apparent not only to the ordained on Sunday but to members of the family or neighbors on any day of the week. As one young man who was under instruction for baptism said, "I had some chrome rings on my harness and I did not have enough brim on my hat soon enough, so they excluded me." Deviation varies with status roles in Amish society. Deviant behavior of certain types is normally expected of the single rather than the married. Youth is the normal time for deviation in the otherwise stable group. Before marriage, deviation tends to take a "wild" or "worldly" character. Grooming the hair in worldly fash-ion, wearing clothes with extra frills, and driving an automobile are all ways of expressing deviation. Smoking may or may not be a sign of deviation, depending on the local *Ordnung*. Where smoking is nor-mally practiced, quitting may be taken as a sign of "changing one's thinking" by identifying with the Mennonites. Since many young people who leave the Amish group become Amish Mennonites or Mennonites, signs of identifying with the Mennonites are avoided as much as possible.

Mature Amish males who become successful entrepreneurs are inno-vator types. If their enterprises serve the needs of the community, as for instance a manufacturing or servicing operation for horse-drawn farm equipment would, their attitudes and innovative skills are not perceived as a threat. In fact, these enterprises may be widely accepted or later proven indispensable. However, one Amishman who invented a farm implement—who produced and marketed it for the American farm population in partnership with a non-Amish relative, in a shop utilizing high-line electricity—was expelled from membership.

Jonathan B. Fisher achieved what many a young man might have dreamed of. Traveling alone, he went to Europe and later around the world, and published two books containing his observations.[4] In many respects he was an atypical Amishman—an unwilling farmer, possessed of an insatiable appetite to read and travel, willing to subsist on a poverty standard of living—but he never flaunted the Amish beliefs or rules of dress. Working on freighters, finding accommodations in benevolent institutions and in Mennonite communities around the

4. Both books were published from serialized accounts in *The Budget*. They are Jonathan B. Fisher, *A Trip to Europe and Facts Gleaned on the Way* (Bareville, Pa.: By the author, 1911); and idem, *Around the World by Water and Facts Gleaned on the Way* (Bareville, Pa.: By the author, 1937).

world, he achieved his objective: "to peep into foreign lands, to note the customs of the natives, the beauty of their sceneries, and to glean facts one may learn on the way."[5] His accomplishments were achieved in spite of an unsympathetic wife and children, none of whom remained Amish.

Retreatism. Innovators who do not succeed typically tend to become retreatists. Retreatism is a mode of adjustment in which the person rejects both the cultural goals and the institutional means. Retreatists are indifferent to the values of the society, and while they conform to the society, they make an apathetic adjustment. They are mentally capable of achieving the goals, but the perceived contradiction between approved goals and disapproved means becomes so great that they give up the competitive struggle. "Defeatism, quietism, and resignation are manifest in escape mechanisms which ultimately lead him (the retreatist) to 'escape' from the requirements of the society."[6] Though retreatists may hold to the supreme goals of the society, they are unwilling to use the legitimate means because of internalized blocks. They become a nonproductive liability among peers and in their society. It is unlikely that Amish society could tolerate many individuals of this type, but they do absorb some. As long as retreatists do not violate the norms, they are usually included in group activities and tolerated in the society. To retreat from the goals because they are not worth striving for, yet to keep the rules because there are no alternatives, presents the Amish person with a peculiar type of adaptation. Amish society has no socially approved place for tramps or vagrants, but on close examination it is possible to identify individuals who are nonproductive and a liability to their society. Persons who are mentally handicapped, or those who may be considered "queer," and who accept such a role, are nevertheless included in the community's activities.

Several years ago two adventurous, independent families, the David Bylers of Ohio and the Eli Garbers of Pennsylvania, estranged from their native communities, traveled eight hundred miles in horse-drawn caravans to Hartland, Maine. As followers of a presumed convert to the Amish church, they set out to escape their "backslidden" home communities. Their canvas-covered wagons, on which were printed several Bible verses (not an Amish practice), were barred by law from entering expressways, including the bridge over the Hudson River, and attracted national news coverage. By overconforming in dress they

5. Jonathan B. Fisher, *Around the World*, p. 7.
6. Merton, *Social Theory and Social Structure*, p. 156.

were ritualistic, but in their rejection of the usual Amish goals and means they were retreatist.

Rebellion. Rebellion lies outside the scope of adaptation, for through it the individual rejects his own culture, alienating himself from the parent social structure. Rebellious behavior is manifested in "diffuse feelings of hate, envy, and hostility; or in a sense of being powerless to express these feelings actively against the person or social stratum evoking them."[7] The rebellious type regards the institutional system as a barrier to satisfactory achievement of the goals. Organized movements of rebellion must advance new myths that define the large-scale frustrations and at the same time provide an alternative social structure. The new myth provides the justification for separatism, as was originally the case with the Amish rebellion against the Swiss Brethren.

The rebellious Amish person today typically rejects the rules of grooming or dress and affiliates with another religious group, usually an Anabaptist-related group. When this occurs the individual does not need to seek a new myth, but simply adapts to an existing group outside the Amish society. The rebellious type will use all available rationalizations for his or her actions, and may express (1) explicit disagreement with Amish doctrine, (2) interpersonal friction with members in the society, and (3) personal frustration and dissatisfaction. The rate of deviation from Amish norms is higher among children of families that are marginal to the culture than among conforming families. If either the mother or the father shows nonconformist tendencies, or if one of the parents has had difficulties with the church rules, there will be a greater tendency among the children to reject the Amish way of life.

The children of parents who are marginal, or who for any one reason may feel insecure in the Old Order discipline, are especially vulnerable to alien influences. If the parents flaunt the church rules, the children will flaunt still other rules. The children may respond with rebellion, bringing sorrow and pain to their parents. When the parents are estranged from the great stability of the Old Order culture, gentleness may turn into rigidity, as indicated by an informant who explained: "Who wouldn't run away? All the teaching they get is rules and the command they get from their parents, 'You must stay Dutch.' My brother ran away from home last year and I can tell you why. Dad was awful rough with him. He gave us boys one licking after another. Even when I was eighteen he tried to lick me, but that's when I said 'It's enough.' I didn't let him." The incident illustrates the inability

7. Ibid.

of parents to cope with rebellious attitudes they may have inadvertently implanted in their children.

Although these categories of individual adaptation are helpful for gaining a knowledge of the general characteristics of deviation, they fall short of explaining the process of Amish deviation. The theory is a static, structural model, which misses the subtle signs and important indicators of deviation. We now turn to a description of the vulnerability of individuals who come under the influence of alien movements.

THE INFLUENCE OF PIETISM AND REVIVALISM

Like other Christian churches, the Amish church teaches "the new birth" or "regeneration," but its understanding of the language of religious commitment is totally different from that of revivalistic groups. Though the biblical texts are the same, the interpretations are different. The Amish understanding of regeneration, in the words of Dirk Philips, is "submissiveness, obedience, and righteousness," without "flowery and embellished rhetoric" or "lofty and arrogant language."[8] The Amish emphasize "partaking of the divine nature" (II Pet. 1:4), being "made heirs of the hope of salvation" (Tit. 3:5–7), and taking on the attributes and sufferings of Christ.

Most fundamentalist churches and independent revivalistic movements stress individual liberation from sin more than submission to the corporate community of believers. They stress enjoyment rather than suffering, assurance of salvation rather than hope, a subjective rather than a submissive experience, a vocal rather than a nonverbal (silent) experience. As can be demonstrated from historical sources, the Amish stress the Anabaptist theme of *Gelassenheit* with its many meanings: resignation, calmness of mind, composure, staidness, conquest of selfishness, long-suffering, collectedness, silence of the soul, tranquility, inner surrender, yieldedness, equanimity, and detachment. "We must reside quietly in Christ" ("Wir müssen in Christus still halten") is an oft-repeated phrase in Anabaptist writings.[9]

8. Dietrich Philip, *Enchiridion or Hand Book* (Aylmer, Ont.: Pathway Publishers, 1966), p. 295.

9. See Robert Friedmann, "Anabaptism and Protestantism," *Mennonite Quarterly Review* 24 (January 1950): 22. For Anabaptist implications of regeneration, see John C. Wenger, "Two Kinds of Obedience: An Anabaptist Tract on Christian Freedom," ibid. 21 (January 1947): 18–22. For the characteristics of pietism, see Robert Friedmann, *Mennonite Piety through the Centuries* (Goshen, Ind.: Mennonite Historical Society, 1949), pp. 28–54, 72–77. For a discussion of fundamentalism, see James Barr, *Fundamentalism* (Philadelphia: Westminster Press, 1977).

When members take on revivalistic tendencies, they are likely to erect
meeting houses, drive automobiles, modernize their farms,
and lose their sense of community solidarity.

The Amish person today who has been taught to live by example
rather than through the development of a specific, rational vocabulary
with respect to his religious experience, and who comes under the
sway of articulate fundamentalist individuals, may fall prey to prose-
lytizing groups. This is especially true if such Amish persons entertain
doubts about the goals of the Amish way of life, or if they are of the
ritualistic or retreatist types. Among the signs of taking on an alien
belief is that of seeking "assurance of salvation." When an Amish person embraces this teaching, it is disruptive to the community and
considered a manifestation of pride rather than humility. By asserting
his own knowledge, experience, or views over those of the community,
the individual becomes a threat to the unity of the church.

These differences in religious experience between the Amish and
other Christian groups, which often lead to misunderstandings, are
rooted in historical traditions. During the first hundred years in America, many Amish individuals were absorbed into pietistic and revivalistic movements. Abraham Draksel (Troxel), an Amish preacher in
Lebanon County, Pennsylvania, in the eighteenth century, was notified that he must stop preaching and was thus nicknamed "the silent
preacher." His error was that he "made too much of the doctrines of
regeneration" and "the enjoyment in the Holy Ghost."[10]

In the nineteenth century an Amish boy who was converted in a
revival meeting became a Methodist preacher. He wrote an account

10. C. Brane, "Landmark History of United Brethrenism in Pennsylvania,"
The Pennsylvania German 4 (1903): 326.

of his own conversion against the background of "the stricter sect of the Mennonites." "He was led from darkness to light, and from ignorance, error, and superstition, to the knowledge of the truth; and [was] afterward made instrumental in the conversion of his father's family." The book of sixteen chapters, which was used as part of the Sunday School and revivalistic literature of the mid-nineteenth century, is a revealing picture of how revivalist groups viewed the Amish.[11] The autobiographical account is without author, but from genealogical sources we can be certain that it was written by Adam Hostetler Miller (1810–1901).

The trance or "sleeping preacher" phenomenon that was so widespread in eighteenth-century Europe and nineteenth-century America also emerged in Amish communities.[12] At least two Amish persons delivered scintillating sermons to large audiences while in an apparently unconscious state in the late nineteenth century. They were both lay members: Noah Troyer of Iowa and John D. Kauffman of Indiana. Following an illness, Troyer developed convulsions that left him unconsciousness, and it was during these periods that he delivered long sermons. The spells would come in late afternoon, and with the assistance of several persons, he could stand and speak for several hours. Troyer's and Kauffman's sermons were not specifically threatening to Amish traditions, but Kauffman's followers insisted that he be regarded as a prophet introducing a new dispensation. Although not Old Order Amish, several congregations still exist (in Illinois, Oregon, and South Carolina) that have their roots in the Kauffman element of the movement. Once when some members asked whether they should go to hear a sleeping preacher, one bishop remarked: "The Bible has something to say about watching and praying but nothing about sleeping and praying."

The following account of the influence of revivalistic thinking on an Amish boy is typical of modern times:

Mike was a young man who grew up in a strict Old Order Amish community. He was personally conscientious and practiced his religion zealously, but when he was drafted as a conscientious objector and assigned to a Civilian Public Service camp with other objectors, he

11. [Adam Hostetler Miller], *Hostetler; or The Mennonite Boy Converted: A True Narrative by a Methodist Preacher* (New York: Carlton & Foster, 1848), p. 18. For genealogic information, see Harvey Hostetler, *Descendants of Barbara Hochstedler and Christian Stutzman* (Scottdale, Pa.: Mennonite Publishing House, 1938), entry 3331.

12. Harry H. Hiller, "The Sleeping Preacher: An Historical Study of the Role of Charisma in Amish Society," *Pennsylvania Folklife* 18 (Winter 1968/69): 19–31.

came in contact with non-Amish religion for the first time. As he relates the experience: "Church trouble was going on at the time. My wife and I would visit on her side, the more liberal one, and then in my district. We would listen to them seesawing all the time.

"Then I got my notice to go to camp. My mother was very much concerned and when I left she cried her eyes out. She was afraid I would slip and not stay with the Old Order. So I made up my mind to be a good example of the Old Order. But when I marched up to get on the train, two Pentecostal boys played 'God Be with You till We Meet Again.' Inside the train the other boys started to sing. This was something I was not accustomed to, and it gave me a spurt. I felt strange. I sat down beside a sober-looking boy and I thought, I'll cheer him up.

"Across from me were two Christian boys. One of them reached over and asked my name. He asked my background, church, locality, and said we might as well get acquainted. I noticed that these two boys were friendly, and they always had cheerful friends and talked spiritually. This impressed me and I was attracted to them. Then I met a Negro boy who was a Christian. He began talking to me, telling me how surprised he was that so many C.O. boys smoke. This was a surprise to me because that is what I had always done. Then he said he doubted whether many of the boys had had a conversion experience. This struck me, and I expect he noticed it on me.

"That night the Mennonite preacher who accompanied us began to conduct a devotional period right on the train. He went right ahead even though there were soldiers walking through the coaches. I thought, that's just the way it should be. Then I thought to myself, would our Amish preachers have done this? I thought, no. Would my preachers have held a service, or would they have kept quiet and kind of hid their religion? When we arrived the minister said we were going to have a prayer meeting to thank the Lord for taking care of us. This was a new experience for me. Everybody knelt down and nobody had a prayer book. It was just spontaneous, and when one was done the other would pour out his praises. I was there on my knees, all ears, and I could hear this colored boy pouring out his heart to God. After the meeting I thought, well, that's just the way it should be.

"On Sunday I sat in my first Sunday School class. They gave me a book but I could not discuss any spiritual depth. Here the boys were discussing the lesson and really enjoying it. Then on Sunday night the minister said we were going to have a testimony meeting. The boys got up, one after another, with faces aglow, giving Scripture verses and testimony. Each boy said how he was saved, but I thought, no, we do not know whether we are saved until we get over yonder. I got uneasy. Was I supposed to be on guard for false doctrine in this group? I pondered this after the service, yet these boys had a joy I did not have. After church one of the boys nudged me and asked me to go for a walk.

"We got to talking about the meeting that night. I told my friend that I enjoyed the enthusiasm of the boys but that what they said was far-fetched. They said they were saved, but they are still living here. My friend said we can know that, but I tried to change the subject. I sensed that the boys were on one side of the fence and I on the other. I did not want to lose them as friends. One night they asked me to take charge of prayer meeting for the next time. I agreed because I did not want to disgrace the Old Order church. That day I started memorizing a prayer, but when the time came it did not go very well, but I got through.

"One night a Pentecostal boy and I went for a walk downtown and we passed the poolroom. He asked if I played pool and I said yes. He said he wouldn't. 'It's just a game and lots of fun,' I said. Then we began discussing movies. He said he would not attend any. 'Why not?' I said. 'Once I saw how a submarine worked in a movie.' He said, 'Do you know who is putting on that show? . . . just a bunch of adulterers and fornicators who are living after the dictates of the flesh; then we pay to see it and expect to get some good out of it.' This made me think. Another thing I noticed was the difference in speech. In my home community we used to tell a lot of filthy stories, but these boys in camp just wouldn't tell stories like we did back home. I noticed that their standards in this regard were above mine, but I had the outward appearance. This bothered me.

"In my heart I felt the spirit starting to convict me. When I worked in the timber I had a few close calls. What if I would be killed, I thought. What was the value of my being in camp if I should die as a hypocrite? I could see that the other boys were saved and now they were giving their life back to God. I had long hair and plain clothes, and I had always been taught that their clothes were worldly. I was as confused as I could get. Then I came home for Christmas.

"I thought, maybe the Old Order preachers did preach salvation by faith, and that perhaps I was too indifferent that I never caught on. So when I went home I listened carefully to them. They used the same Scripture verses, but explained it differently and just seemed to explain away the meaning. I had decided not to drink when I got home. It worked all right for a few places, but then I got to my brother-in-law's place and he brought up a pitcher of cider and started laughing when I refused. 'So you want to be good, do you,' he said. That was too much for me so I took a little, but then there was no stopping. Then I felt miserable.

"I talked to my dad about how different the Christian boys were in camp. I told him that the victory of the boys lies in the point that they believe they are saved, that Christ died for them and now they have a desire to live better. I could see it. 'Well,' Dad said, 'I heard a story one time. A man told how sure he was that he was saved; he was as sure as taking the next forkful of meat. But at the point of putting it in his mouth, it fell from the fork and the dog swallowed it.' So dad gave me little help. I was uneasy, miserable, and wretched.

"I spoke to my youngest brother, telling him how the boys were so clean and pure, how it seemed to come from the fact that they have assurance, or they say they have. 'Well,' he said, 'when you read the stories in the Bible it seems to imply that.' Yet my brother didn't seem to have this experience, nor my parents.

"I dreaded to go back to the boys at camp. I knew that if I got to camp, conviction would get deeper within me. Then I returned to camp, and I never felt more wretched. I was caught between what the boys were in camp and what the preachers said at home. I kept my misery camouflaged as much as I could. I tried to be cheerful. It was the same at camp. These boys had something. They met every night for worship and always gave a testimony. What they talked about meant so much to them. Everybody at prayer meeting would give a testimony but me. Those who were not Christian would not attend the service. I attended because I did not want to let down the Old Order Amish church, to have it look as though we were not a spiritual people. But I was as miserable as I could get. I went to bed that night and turned to the wall, and I was just beat. The boys told me what they thought, but the preachers at home told me what they thought. The gap was as wide as you could make it.

"When a missionary preached about the foolish virgins, I just knew I was one of them. I knew I should raise my hand and ask for prayer but I was too proud. I couldn't face it. If I went home this way, I would be thrown out of church, I would have to part company with my wife. I felt I was going to be a nervous wreck."

It was not long until Mike reached a crisis that relieved his contradictory expectations. According to his own words, he became converted like the other boys. This opened the way for him to meet the expectations of the other boys in camp, but still left problems that had to be solved when he reached home, his wife, and family. In Mike's resolution to defend his Old Order faith and to be loyal to his mother, we can see the development of conflicting expectations. The camp experience was the first he had had with other Christian boys of his own age. His own religious training had given him no familiarity with audible praying, testimony, or with the taboos of fundamentalist religion. Later in life, after his return to his community, he faced the ridicule of his kin and then affiliated with a Protestant group.

It will be observed that deviation is associated with religious experience. Amish society is religiously oriented, and defection from it takes the form of religious rather than secular symbolism. An Amish person would not likely become an atheist; in finding reference groups outside his society, he would choose religious groups. In spite of the strong antipathy toward Mennonite teaching, this barrier is overcome, and a Mennonite (pacifist) group is usually more acceptable to the deviating Amish person than is a Protestant, Catholic, or fundamentalist group. In recent decades, however, those Amish who have been prone to travel, including some who have gone to Florida for vacations, have been strongly influenced by fundamentalism.[13] Even so, the ethnic, nonverbal character of Amish socialization, the strong moral training and sense of kinship, tends to influence the Amish for the rest of their lives. Guilt, conversion, revival, and cultural shock play important roles in transforming the insecure Amish person into a person who accepts a new set of aspirations.

THE TEMPTATION OF HIGHER EDUCATION

Before the Amish operated their own schools, more Amish youths were exposed to the possibilities of higher education and to teachers who inspired them to continue their education than is the case today. To become a committed Amish person, a boy or girl who likes school for its own sake must learn to be indifferent toward it. If formal schooling is extended beyond the expectations of parents and community, the adolescent may be headed for serious conflict.

The cultural gap between the Amish elementary school and the public high school is presently so great that virtually no Amish are tempted to attend the secular school. Those who entertain aspirations of continuing their education will defer the effort until they reach late adolescence or the age of twenty-one. With the development of Amish schools, however, it has become possible for Amish persons to exercise their intellectual interests within the Amish culture by teaching.

---

13. See, for example, "From Buggy to Rambler" and other Amish testimonials in *Spiritual Awakening among the Amish*, ed. Gerald Derstine (Sarasota, Fla.: Gospel Crusade, n.d.)

The following three case histories, based on interviews, illustrate ways in which motivation can lead to education beyond the limits of the Amish norm. All three young people had attended small public schools during the elementary period.

Sam recalls his early interest in schooling, which led to his decision to enter college: "I always loved school, from the day I started. My parents didn't start me until I was seven, so I wouldn't have to go to high school. They thought I couldn't learn very well and I wanted to show them I could. When my mother was young she taught school. She wanted to go on to school, but never had a chance. I sort of caught this desire from my mother." In school Sam could succeed, but at home he was less certain of success. He said: "It made me mad when my father kept me home for a day's work. Sometimes when I was to stay at home, I would switch into my school clothes at the last minute and get on the bus."

Sam was adept at making friends in school, and during his last grades in school, he said, "I hated that I came from such a backward family." The animosity for his backwardness grew as he learned to know his classmates and especially a certain non-Amish girl. "We were always the top two in the class. I could beat her in arithmetic, but she always beat me in reading. It was always tit for tat between us. We were always together in those early years. I always hated that I was an Amishman. My older brother was a 'good' boy and listened to Daddy but was always getting into trouble. Sunday after Sunday I would go to church, and all we would do after church was sit out on the buggies and tell stories. I was the cockiest guy, I guess, as I was more or less the leader of our group of boys. My, how I used to get whippings from my father. I heard other people brag how they thanked the Lord for their whippings, but mine just did not make sense."

With the completion of grade school Sam wanted to go on to high school but could not. "I felt there was nothing to do but stay home and work for Dad till I was twenty-one. My life was terribly lean during those years." Sam was baptized in the Amish church. After he reached legal age he was drafted into wartime conscientious-objector service. Here he was exposed to a wider association of friends, most of them Mennonites. Following his release from service he entered a Mennonite college. Although for some years he attempted to retain his Amish affiliation, eventually he became a member of the Mennonite church.

The second case is that of *Rebecca*, who at the age of eighteen turned from her Amish background without having been baptized. "I read a great many books and anything I could get my hands on. I tried to persuade my father to let me go to high school. But he would not.` After grade school I was Amish another six years and this was a very difficult time in my life. My dissatisfaction began to show in physical ways. I had no energy, I was anemic. Nothing interested me. I didn't fit in with the Amish young people and I sort of despised them for their lack of learning. I made attempts to be popular among the Amish and dated a few times, but I didn't like it very much. I was the oldest of eight, and mother kept on having children, and this tied me down and I was constantly resenting this. I was always running away to read, and I hid books. When mother was not watching I would read everything I could.

"When I was eighteen, I thought mother had reached the age when she could have no more children. Finally, I thought, I could begin to see daylight, have a little more time to myself, and to keep the house neat without working so hard. Then I learned that mother was pregnant again, and this was the last straw. I simply could not face this. I went to the basement and just cried. I told father I had had enough, I was leaving. While I packed my suitcase, mother became very upset. Father knew that mother needed my help. So we worked out a compromise. Father said if I would stay until the baby was born, the next year I could go to Bible school. Two of my father's brothers had gone away for a six-week term of school. This was enough for me; then I could get away and go where there was a library and read."

Rebecca went to college and left the Amish way of life. Later her brothers and sisters followed her example, and after several more years the whole family left the Old Order Amish faith and joined a Mennonite group. It is not uncommon for one or two children in a family to break with the tradition with the result that the parents do so later.

A third case, *Chris*, says: "I wanted to go to high school so badly that I remember crying about it, trying to persuade my parents. They gave us achievement tests after grade eight and I found out I was the highest in the county. I competed from grade one through grade eight very closely with a girl who went on and became valedictorian. In the cumulative tests, which included all eight grades, I had all A⁺'s except for one A, and she had all A⁺'s except two. My principal talked to my father several times and told him I had possibilities. I was only fourteen, so my father made me repeat the eighth grade the next year. After getting all A⁺'s in grade eight, I barely got A's the second time. I was very athletic, though, and even though I was not going on to high school the principal let me go all out for athletics. All the time the kids and neighbors (non-Amish) wanted me to go to high school.

In my second year in the eighth grade, I quit when April came because it was time to start plowing. I went home and remember how terrible I felt."

With all his chums now in high school, Chris returned to the principal and explained his painful experience. The school principal gave him ninth-grade books, and Chris promised that he would study them and appear for the semester tests. He said: "I hardly touched the books but I took the first semester test and got all A's and B's. But I finally gave up and returned the books. I knew I would never stay Amish because the principal convinced me the Amish should not keep their children home from school. He told me I had brains. He told me I could be more than a farmer.

"Most of the next two years I spent at home brooding. I was insecure within myself. I wouldn't work at home very much. When I had to work for another Amish farmer for no wages I felt that my leg was being pulled. I did a lot of local-diner-and-gas-station-hanging-out with my non-Amish friends, and though I dressed Amish I fitted in somehow."

A few years later Chris achieved financial independence by working as a hotel waiter in Florida, then entered and was graduated from college.

The traditional rationale against higher education was no longer convincing to the above defectors. In all cultures certain anxieties are inculcated in individuals as part of their socialization experience in order to motivate them in the direction of approved behavior.[14] They are taught that certain types of deviation bring painful or dangerous results. The traditional way of reducing these threats and of relieving the psychic pain experienced in Amish society is no longer meaningful to the defectors. Defectors organize their lives around goals outside the Amish system of values.

THE EFFECTS OF TOURISM

The development of tourism among the Amish communities in the past three decades has created a situation in which the Amish are potentially vulnerable. Tourists are a growing proportion of the urban population, and each year they schedule time and money for periods of deliberate change of scenery, pace, and experience. They have been described as a class of people who are seeking a "cooling" experience

14. See, for example, A. I. Hallowell, "Social Psychological Aspects of Acculturation," in *The Science of Man in the World Crisis*, ed. Ralph Linton (New York: Columbia University Press, 1945), p. 194.

An eating establishment owned and operated
by former Amish members

from the "hot" pursuit of progress.[15] The Lancaster County Amish,
who are within two hours of New York, Baltimore, and Washington,
are an attraction for city dwellers.

Tourism as an enterprise has invaded all major Amish communities,
but the most developed and promoted is Lancaster County, Pennsylvania. Staged "Amish farms" thrive not only here but also at places
like "Amishville" and "Amish Acres" in Indiana. Restaurants, tours,
pamphleteering, evangelizing, and merchandising have become part
of the Amish tourist scene from Kansas to Pennsylvania, and from
Florida to Ontario. The major attraction is the Old Order Amish
people themselves, their farms, their tradition of farming, and their
dress and customs. Directly or indirectly, Amish communities are
promoted as living museums, amusement parks, or in the words of a
tourist brochure, "a happy hunting ground for the visitor." In all of
this the Amish have not been a willing partner, and ironically, the
harder they have tried to remain loyal to their faith, the more attractive they have become to the tourist.

15. Roy C. Buck, "Bloodless Theatre: Images of the Old Order Amish in
Tourism Literature," *Pennsylvania Mennonite Heritage* 2 (July 1979): 2–11.

Between the tourists and the Amish there is a strong cultural wall that delineates two different realities. Tourism from the Amish viewpoint is "a nuisance and a bunch of foolishness."[16] In defense of his view, the orthodox Amishman cites Maccabees 1:14: "Whereupon they built a place of exercise at Jerusalem according to the customs of the Heathen." In German "a place of exercise" translates into *Spielhaus*, or "playhouse." Play or pleasure house is the Amish metaphor for the tourist world. Tourism is "empty pleasure-seeking," or "leisure lust" as one Amish minister put it.

How does the presence of tourism affect the Amish community itself? An initial reaction is that tourism will eventually engulf, swamp, and destroy the Amish community unless the members move elsewhere. Some have moved. But one recent study of tourist enterprises suggests that if the boundaries are maintained between the Amish and the tourist enterprises, both may survive and benefit from each other.[17] As in Jerusalem or Athens, tourism among the Amish is here to stay. It has, however, important influences upon the individuals and institutions in the community.

The most adverse affect of tourism on the Amish is the clogging of their small roads and the inconvenience caused by leisurely, gawking tourists, who peep into schoolhouses, farms, meadows, and fields. Many Amish families forgo their weekly shopping visits to the local village during the summer months when the tourists fill the towns. "No tourists" signs may be found at schools and Amish repair shops. Indifference to the many visitors is expressed in other ways. Amish persons working in the field typically greet one another and the passer-by, but tourism has turned a friendly people into a people of "cool" disposition. As one Amishman explained, "If we waved at every tourist, we would soon have a sore arm."

There is little the Amish can do to stop the intrusion by tourists. Although zoning ordinances could prohibit buses from traveling on the small township roads, the Amish are unwilling to use legal means to protect themselves. Humor, joking and laughter, making the tourist activity look like "a bunch of foolishness," is virtually the only informal means of self-defense.

The high praise enjoyed by the Amish people as a by-product of tourist promotion is another factor to which the Amish may prove vulnerable. Persecution has been experienced by the Amish people

16. I am indebted to a colleague, Roy C. Buck, for this quotation and for insights on tourism in this chapter. The quotation and the reference to Maccabees are cited in his article "Boundary Maintenance Revisited: Tourist Experience in an Old Order Amish Community," *Rural Sociology* 43 (Summer 1978): 226.

17. Ibid.

in the past, and they have been able to survive it. Worldly praise is quite another matter. The national attention given to Amish communities has accorded to Amish individuals something of a celebrity status. Tourists who respond to colorful promotional brochures expect to find the Amish a special kind of people. This high expectation was recently verified by an Amishman who observed: "They come in here and think we are angels or better than other people, and expect to find us floating several feet above the ground."[18]

Because visitors carry with them many stereotypes, there is a need for tourist bureaus or information centers to "assist" them. Ambiguous information leaves the tourists at the mercy of local informants. Not realizing that the Amish live in individual farm houses and have to work and earn their livelihood like rural farmers anywhere, tourists typically expect to see the Amish segregated in colonies or villages.

The tourist enterprise is structured in such a way as to minimize direct contact with the Amish. This is accomplished, according to Roy C. Buck, by reassuring tourists that they are "strangers in a strange land" and therefore in need of assistance.[19] The tourist enterprises and their guides appear to be performing a service for the Amish by routing tourists into staged attractions in the name of education, convenience, and sensitivity. Because the tourists spend their time at such places as the Wax Museum, Dutch Wonderland, Kitchen Kettle, Strasburg Railroad, and the Amish Homestead, the Amish themselves are somewhat protected from personal encounters with them, and the tourists find a place to spend their money. There are approximately 241 present-day tourist-related enterprises in Lancaster County.[20]

Although Amish rules forbid members from working in or conducting establishments specifically for the tourists, some Amish profit indirectly from the economic flow of tourist activity. A few Amish— single individuals and those who have not been able to secure a farm —are involved to some extent in supplying products for tourist shops. Some make quilts, rugs, or other needlework in their homes and sell the products to gift shops.

The Camera and the Amish. One of the major objections of the Amish people to tourism is the snapping of photographs. In the words of one young Amishman, "I just don't enjoy living in a museum or a

---

18. Gideon L. Fisher, *Farm Life and Its Changes* (Gordonville, Pa.: Pequea Publishers, 1978), chap. 31.
19. Buck, "Boundary Maintenance Revisited," p. 229.
20. Ibid.

The Amish have become a captive tourist attraction.
They lament the traffic that clogs their roads and the intrusion
of spectators with cameras.

zoo, whatever you would call it." According to another, "They invade your privacy. They are a nuisance when I go to town, for I can't go to any public place without being confronted by tourists who ask dumb questions and take pictures."

The camera is an object of intrusion and prevents normal reciprocity between the photographer and the Amish. Objections of the Amish to the camera are widely known. The reasons given are based on religious grounds, ranging from the prohibition of the graven image (Exod. 20:4–5) to a variety of other biblical teachings against a show of personal pride and vanity. To take photographs or pose for pictures is specifically forbidden in Amish law. The tourist who wishes to capture some of the scenery, people, and lore of the Amish community is confronted with a dilemma. If he asks Amish persons for permission to photograph, they are obliged to decline politely.

When photos are taken without asking, how do Amish people feel? "If they don't respect us enough when we tell them in a kind way that we don't approve, there is really not much we can do," said one Amishwoman. She added: "Most people don't even bother to ask. It would not fit with our nonresistant beliefs to use force. Getting upset and making a scene would hardly be a light to the world." Another offered this advice: "In my opinion the best thing to do is ignore them. By all means, don't go to great extremes to hide. You'll only draw more attention to yourself, plus giving the cameraman a good story to go with his picture."

Several photographic treatments of the Amish have been published, and many fine collections of photographs of the Amish are owned by individuals. The illustrations for this book were selected from many such collections. Some of the best photographs were made by local, professional photographers who formed neighborly relationships with Amish people over a period of many years. Some Amish do not object, but would not be seen having their pictures taken. The sanctions against having one's picture taken do not apply with equal force to children and those who have not been baptized.

Tourist Experience and Reciprocity. A few visitors establish meaningful contact with the Amish people, but generally not as tourists. Virtually every Amish family has friends in the outside (non-Amish) world, people who come periodically for farm produce, to exchange experiences or favors, or who enjoy talking in unstructured and nonthreatening circumstances. In these exchanges there are elusive moments of communication between the Amish and the outsider. Both know that they come together from different stances and have identities that are not "for sale." Both are in a sense "tourists" temporarily having an "experience." As tourists they occupy a liminal territory.

The Amish person enjoys temporary relaxation from the routine, and this may be momentarily experienced when he rides in an automobile with an outsider. The destination matters little. What matters is the excursion, the new scenery, the gratifying experience, and the exchange of words and gestures with another human being. The outsider is typically a person from the "urban" world who relishes temporary relief from the complex, competitive struggle in the industrial world. For the outsider, "an Amish experience" constitutes an ahistorical moment, a moment that denies the actuality of the present; it may approximate a religious experience. For the Amish person, who is "touring" the outside world, it is a moment of illusion; it is for him a reality without community and therefore without spirit.

CHAPTER 15

Health and Healing

WHAT EFFECT does Amish culture have on the health of the individual?
Are any illnesses peculiar to the Amish people? What culturally induced diseases, if any, occur because of the values and standards
demanded of the Amish person by his social system? The outsider
frequently assumes that the Amish must have extraordinary stress
patterns, for they are denied many of the conveniences and pleasures
that are taken for granted in mainstream society. In reality, the reverse
is often the case. Individuals in a highly integrated group who share
significant meanings may deny themselves personal gain and convenience and still achieve a high degree of personal fulfillment. Alien-
ation, listlessness, alcoholism, and suicide are typically found in societies where individuals have lost meaningful social discourse.

MEDICAL BELIEFS AND PRACTICES

The Amish are very health conscious and are quick to recognize
individuals who are sick or incapacitated. Concern for the sick is of
major importance in every Amish community. Elderly persons who
for reasons of health cannot attend religious services are visited by
relatives and friends. Illness and recovery are major topics in Amish
newspapers. The Amish emphasize hard work, and for them, a healthy
person is one who has a good appetite, looks physically well, and can
do rigorous physical labor. A poor appetite means poor health. Per-

313

sons who sit in offices, fail to get fresh air and sunshine, and do not engage in physical work are often considered by the Amish to be "unhealthy." When college students visited the Amish community in which I grew up, my mother commented, "They look so pale and sickly." This was her deft way of discouraging any thoughts I had of going to college.

The social environment in which people live, as well as the society's belief system, can be correlated with many symptoms of physical and mental illness. For the individual who cannot find fulfillment in life, the "sick role" has increasingly become one alternative to the problem of personal adjustment. Thus the person faced with a stressful situation may become sick and thereby find an advantageous or tolerable existence. In Amish society, sickness is a socially approved form of deviation. For a person with low self-esteem, going to "the doctor" is good therapy, and especially so if the physician, chiropractor, or reflexologist affirms the individual and makes him feel good.

Attitudes toward sickness, health care, and disease prevention are conditioned by the Amish world view (see Chapter 1, "The View from the Inside"). One important paradigm that influences the medical behavior of the Amish is the Genesis account of Creation. God created the human body. It should not be tampered with. Medicine may help, but it is God who heals. Another basic belief is the necessity of obedience to God and separation from the world. The Amish do not have trained physicians of their own, since attendance at institutions of higher learning conflicts with the doctrine of separation. By relying on worldly society for medical knowledge and medical services, the Amish live in a state of liminality when securing these services. They rely on their own tradition when diagnosing illnesses, but they also seek the technical and scientific knowledge of the trained physician. The Amish person must find ways of trusting persons who are not members of his community in order to secure the knowledge and services that do not exist within it. Thus far in their history the Amish have been unwilling to permit their members to attend medical or technical schools to acquire competence in medically related fields for fear the higher knowledge (and pride) gained in worldly society would overtake their own value system.

Physician-Patient Relationships. The Amish obtain medical care from physicians they know in nearby villages, clinics, and hospitals. Their inclination and readiness to seek health services varies greatly from family to family. Nothing in the Amish understanding of the Bible forbids them from using modern medical services, including surgery, hospitalization, dental work, anesthesia, blood transfusion, or immunization. Some are more reluctant than others to accept immunization, but it is rare that an Amish person will cite a biblical text to object to a demonstrated medical need.

The misunderstandings that exist between the Amish and local health authorities were well illustrated in the outbreak of polio that occurred in a small community of Amish in 1979. According to newspaper accounts, the health authorities reported that the Amish refused to take immunizations on religious grounds. The accounts also stated that the Amish bishops refused to permit the use of polio vaccine. Both of these assumptions were false.

If the Amish are slow to accept preventive measures, it does not mean they are religiously opposed to them. The Amish are cautious, and they are viscerally conservative about accepting government programs of any kind, including health plans. Their reluctance stems from not knowing what sources of knowledge to trust and from waiting for consensus and hints from among their own spokesmen. They dislike publicity, and whether a bishop or the head of a family is involved, no one likes to take action in a crisis without the knowledge, and preferably the approval, of others. In the case of the polio outbreak, after a series of visits by health officials, the Amish arranged for mass immunization sessions in their homes and schools.

With few exceptions, physicians rate the Amish as desirable patients. They are generally dependable, stable, and appreciative. The transportation problems of the Amish tend to make it difficult for them to observe the office hours of small-town physicians. The more affluent Amish frequently demand prompt attention. Some physicians hold that the Amish pay little attention to preventive medicine. They ascribe this to a lack of formal education. Others report a tendency to wait too long to consult a physician, especially in the case of children, with respect to cuts and bruises. By horse and carriage, going to the physician takes time, and the Amish tend not to visit a doctor's office for what they consider minor illnesses or colds. The high cost of medical services is another deterrent. Access to a physician in case of an emergency is frequently a problem, since most physicians do not make house calls. Physicians may fail to appreciate the urgency of a telephone call from an Amish family.

Certain complaints occur with higher frequency among the Amish than among other patients, according to an opinion survey made among physicians.[1] Among them are chronic bed-wetting, digestive

1. John A. Hostetler, "Folk Medicine and Sympathy Healing among the Amish," in *American Folk Medicine*, ed. Wayland W. Hand (Berkeley: University of California Press, 1976), p. 254.

disturbances, and mental disorders. The Amish are not reluctant to "change doctors" when the desired improvement is not obtained, or if the manner and explanations of the physician are not satisfactory. Patients whose illnesses are not understood and who do not respond to professional treatment may be treated with folk remedies or taken to folk practitioners. The following case illustrates the tension-field of the Amish in utilizing their traditional knowledge, on the one hand, and medical physicians and folk practitioners in the outside world, on the other.

A tumor was observed on the arm of a middle-aged woman; she was taken to the family physician, who found more tumors. The specialist wanted to remove one tumor, but the informant reported: "We didn't let them as we were afraid it might be cancer. We tried other things for a year, then we had one taken out." Following this, the woman was given the Koch cancer treatment, "which didn't do any good." She was then taken to special medical centers in two large cities, and finally to the Hoxsey cancer clinic. To relieve the suffering woman's pain, the doctors removed about two hundred tumors from under her right arm, but finding no relief, she went to the Mayo Clinic. "They could not help her either, so she went to different chiropractors, took foot treatments, tried iodine and all kinds of medicine, and is now taking strong pills which cost a lot." The length to which the Amish will go to find relief from sickness is exhaustive, and some visit devious folk practitioners. "Too many pills" and "strong medicine," according to some Amish people, "are not good for a person."

Because the Amish have a general distrust for worldly knowledge and university training, they have a problem in finding physicians whom they feel they can trust. For them, demonstrated scientific knowledge is not enough. They look for signs of integrity and sympathy. In their normal associations, they have little opportunity to become acquainted with doctors as human beings. Although the Amish must have access to physicians and surgeons, they are inclined to patronize chiropractors, possibly because chiropractors spend more time talking with their patients and also provide more body contact.

In choosing a physician, the Amish seek a cooperative and trustworthy person, and his technical skill and competency are taken for granted. They expect a physician to be trained, but they will respect him more for his ability to be "a common guy" than for his "high" learning. Their perception of the physician's attitude and manners plays a large part in the patient-physician relationship. In addition to "strong medicine," a cold, abrupt manner and "no satisfaction" (meaning poor communication), are signs that discourage Amish people from patronizing professional physicians.

The health-care practices of the Lancaster County Amish were reported in a survey made by The Johns Hopkins Hospital in the summer of 1978.[2] The survey was conducted among 100 married women between the ages of twenty and forty-five who had given birth during the previous year. The sources of their health care were reported as follows: 76 percent of the respondents had visited a medically trained doctor, while 20 percent had visited "alternative" practitioners. The latter category included chiropractors, homeopaths, pow-wow doctors, and reflexologists. (Reflexologists specialize in manipulation of the feet to relieve bodily ills.) The "alternative" practitioners, however, had been visited more frequently than the medically trained doctors. Only 26 percent of the children had been immunized against DPT (diphtheria, whooping cough, and tetanus); 23 percent had been immunized against polio; and 16 percent had been given immunization against measles and mumps. The survey was completed before the 1979 outbreak of polio.

Of the 472 pregnancies reported in the survey, there had been 55 miscarriages and 3 stillbirths, or a fetal loss rate of 12 percent (58/412). Ninety percent of the first births had occurred in a hospital, while 59 percent of the "last births" had been home deliveries. The average cost of a home delivery was $272, while hospital deliveries averaged $750. Clearly, cost and preference are principal reasons for the high rate of home deliveries. Although many children were born at home, 22 percent of the women did not seek prenatal care until the sixth month of pregnancy.

Preventive Health Care. Preventive health care in modern society requires a rather sophisticated knowledge and familiarity with disease theories. Some Amish do not see the importance of being immunized against diseases that are outside the scope of their knowledge or experience. They will do what "is necessary" when such outbreaks occur, but to take measures against all types of diseases that might occur in the future is, in their view, to rely too much on worldly knowledge.

Most states require proof of immunization of beginning school pupils whereby parents must provide the proper certification from a family physician. However, only a small proportion of Amish children receive the prescribed vaccines, for states also permit a waiver for those who object to vaccination on religious grounds. Although the Amish church

2. Unpublished data, The Johns Hopkins Hospital, Baltimore, Md. The survey was supervised by Victor A. McKusick and was conducted by Clair Francomano, Louis Weiss, Barbara Verde, and Chris Laspia.

has no *Ordnung*, or "rule," forbidding vaccination, a few parents object. To accommodate the few, the Amish print shop provides exemption forms for the Pennsylvania Amish who want them. Some Amish school teachers and parents believe that the forms are "much too handy" and are "used for the sake of convenience." Hence, most Amish children are not immunized against diphtheria, tetanus, polio, measles, or mumps. Chemical properties and their long-term consequences, including their dangers, tend not to be understood by some Amish. Knowing the difference between food additives and toxins, and appreciating the changes that take place during cooking and food preparation, are some examples.

When the Amish attended one-room public schools in the past, they were visited routinely by public health authorities who checked their hearing, sight, and health habits. They received some instruction in health and hygiene. Today many Amish schools are not visited by medical authorities, and the children suffer the consequences of inattention.

The Amish have officers for their religious life and ceremonies, designated leaders for fire insurance and hospitalization, and school board members and teachers, but neither a veterinarian nor a health officer is designated to assume leadership in matters of health and sanitation. Before there were licensed physicians in France, the government appointed health officers in various localities.[3] Several Amish individuals held these appointments, and a few who emigrated to America were recognized as doctors. In America, however, there have been no such designations.

Among the Amish, utilization of health care practices is the decision of the family head. Families vary greatly in their attitudes toward preventive care and health practices. During recent years the Amish have been disproportionately influenced by articulate "back to nature" movements, special health-food interests, and vitamin and food-supplement industries that seek to sell their literature, ideologies, and products. The Amish lack of familiarity with good medical practices has made them vulnerable to such influences. The defense of folk medical practices and the opposition to modern health care is transmitted in certain family lines. In a few isolated cases, dietary beliefs are associated with delusions of political conspiracy in which government and hospitals are viewed as food-poisoning enterprises serving Communist interests.

3. Jean Séguy, "Religion and Agricultural Success: The Vocational Life of the French Anabaptists," trans. Michael Shank, *Mennonite Quarterly Review* 47 (July 1973): 209. Hans Blanck, an immigrant of 1751, was recognized as a doctor.

HEREDITARY DISEASES

Several hereditary diseases have been discovered by geneticists who began studies of the Amish population in 1962.[4] The Amish are a natural find for geneticists, for the essential requirements of the study of human genetics are found here. The Amish, along with the Hutterites, are the best-defined inbred group in the United States. They are a closed population with extensive genealogical records; because they have large families that reside in one place (they do not travel to seek employment), medical observations can be made on many relatives in a restricted geographic area.

The Amish population is not, however, a single genetically closed population. Within it are separate inbreeding communities or demes. Deme refers to a local inbreeding community or consanguineal kin group. The Lancaster County, Pennsylvania, Amish represent one deme, the Holmes County, Ohio, Amish another, and so on, for relatively little intermarriage occurs between them. The separateness of these groups is supported by the history of the immigration into each area, by the uniqueness of the family names in each community, by the distribution of blood groups, and by the different hereditary diseases that occur in each of these groups. The Amish themselves recognize family lines that are especially "bright."

In each of the three largest settlements of Amish, five names account for over half of the total population. Different family names prevail in each area (see Table 6). The name Stoltzfus accounts for 25 percent of the Amish people in Lancaster County. Yet among the immigrant founders, there was only one male by the name of Stoltzfus. Clearly Nicholas Stoltzfus contributed disproportionately to the present Lancaster Amish gene pool. The number of family names, as well as the

4. The major findings, combining many separate studies, are contained in Victor A. McKusick, *Medical Genetic Studies of the Amish: Selected Papers, Assembled, with Commentary* (Baltimore: The Johns Hopkins University Press, 1978).

Several factors combined to make extensive genetic studies possible. The Amish keep extensive genealogical and family records, and nearly four hundred separate family genealogies have been published. (For lists of published genealogies, see Harold E. Cross and Beulah S. Hostetler, *Index to Selected Amish Genealogies* [Baltimore: The Johns Hopkins University School of Medicine, Division of Medical Genetics, 1970]. Subsequent titles appeared in *Family Life*, January and March 1977.) Collaboration between the Amish and The Johns Hopkins Hospital resulted in projects of mutual benefit. Geneticists compiled computerized genealogies for the study of genetic diseases. The Amish received printed community directories listing household heads with children by church districts; they also received maps of the settlement (directories are listed in McKusick, *Medical Genetic Studies of the Amish*, p. 523).

pattern of first names, varies in these three large settlements. The number of names and the patterns of naming lead one to believe that the Lancaster County Amish have a more homogeneous culture than the Amish in Ohio or Indiana. Previous observations on fertility patterns and agricultural practices tend to support this conclusion.

The hereditary diseases that occur in the different settlements (demes) are indicators of the distinctness of the groups. Of at least twelve "new" recessive diseases ascertained, four are especially pronounced. The occurrence of Ellis–van Creveld syndrome (EVC) or dwarfism is extremely high among the Lancaster County Amish. At least fifty-two cases were found there prior to 1964, or about the same number as had been reported in the entire world.[5] The overall frequency of its occurrence is about 2 per 1,000 living persons. The disease is a cause of stillbirths, and over a third of the cases die before the age of two weeks. However, among those examined who were over the age of nineteen, one was fifty-eight years old. One male had married and was the father of seven children, two of whom also were dwarfs. Their physical features include short limbs, disproportionate dwarfism, polydactyly (six-fingered hands), and dysplasia of the fingernails. Their teeth are poor, and the upper lip is short. Some malformation of the body cavity and respiratory problems also are present. In no other community of Amish has this type of syndrome occurred. All the affected sibships have been traced to Samuel King and his wife, immigrants of 1767.

A second type of dwarfism, discovered and named cartilage-hair hypoplasia (CHH) by Victor McKusick, has been found among the Amish throughout the country.[6] In affected individuals, the hair is abnormally fine, sparse, and short, and is lighter in color than that of normal sibs. Baldness is likely to occur. The hands are short and pudgy. Fingernails and toenails are short, and deformity of the ankles has been observed in some. The condition is evident at birth because of the abnormally short extremities. Height varies from 42 to 48 inches, but intelligence is not impaired. Over eighty cases of CHH have been found.

A rare blood-cell disease (pyruvate kinase deficiency anemia) is unusually frequent in central Pennsylvania and is not found among Amish families outside this state. Affected children are often jaundiced and anemic at birth and require blood transfusions. If they can be saved by transfusions in the first year or two of life, they can be cured

5. McKusick, *Medical Genetic Studies of the Amish*, pp. 93–117.
6. Ibid., pp. 231–72.

by removal of the spleen. The twelve sibships affected by this disease have been traced to "Strong" Jacob Yoder, an immigrant of 1742.

Hemophilia or bleeders disease is frequent among the Ohio Amish, but it has not been found among the Pennsylvania Amish. Limb-girdle muscular dystrophy is unusually frequent among the Swiss Amish of Adams and Allen counties in Indiana. Its frequency is about four times that found elsewhere. The disease has also been found in Switzerland in the areas from which the Amish came.

The frequency of blood types A, B, and O varies among the Amish communities. In the Holmes County, Ohio, community there is a relatively high frequency of blood group A (50 percent). Among the Lancaster County, Pennsylvania, Amish about three-fourths of the individuals have type A blood, but type O is unusually low. These unusual frequencies are attributed by geneticists to founder effect, a form of genetic drift.

Several chromosomal variants have been identified in Amish society. Males with the name Beiler have been found to have a very short Y chromosome.[7] More recent immigrants from Switzerland and persons still living in Switzerland also have the short Y chromosome. Hypertension is rare among the Lancaster County Amish, and on the average their blood pressure is lower than that of the white populations in other rural communities. The occurrence of cervical cancer is less frequent among Amish women than among women in other rural populations. Many heretofore unknown genetic disorders have been observed by the geneticists. The Amish have cooperated, and by allowing researchers to study their hereditary problems, they have aided in advancing medical knowledge.

Of 1,850 Amish couples in Lancaster County, it was found that all but 3 were related. The inbreeding coefficient was about the equivalent of each couple being more closely related than second cousins. Although there is a conscious effort to avoid close marriages, about 250 couples were found to be second cousins. Some were second cousins several times over. Two couples were first cousins once removed. Multiple distant relationships, such as quadruple second cousin marriages, also occur.

Inbreeding does not inevitably result in hereditary defects. Close marriages have occurred in many human societies in past centuries without giving rise to any known adverse affects. Among the Amish, however, inbreeding has this tendency. If the gene pool of a group of people contains certain recessive tendencies, the probability that a child will be born with a birth defect is greater when the members

7. Ibid., pp. 465–70.

intermarry and the gene is carried by both father and mother. This explains why the Amish have certain birth defects and why these defects occur in certain areas more than in others.

MENTAL ILLNESS

The Amish people are by no means free from mental illness. On the Eastern Seaboard there are two Mennonite-operated mental hospitals: Brook Lane Hospital in Maryland, founded in 1948; and Philhaven Hospital in Pennsylvania, founded in 1952. In Elkhart, Indiana, the Oaklawn Psychiatric Center serves the Amish and Mennonite populations. These centers operate on a self-sustaining basis, offering comprehensive inpatient and outpatient services to persons of all faiths. Not all Amish who become mentally ill are admitted to these hospitals, but some have preferred the services of these centers to state institutions. The diagnostic treatments in these centers are made by professionally trained psychiatrists.

The Amish themselves have developed little explicit therapeutic knowledge to deal with cases of extreme anxiety. Patients are admitted to the above centers for treatment on the advice of family physicians. Individuals who are physically or mentally handicapped are cared for in their homes following treatment in institutions. In Amish society the behavior patterns that indicate psychological problems are frequent visits to doctors, failure to find full satisfaction in a day's work, preoccupation with problems of religious orthodoxy, rigidity of attitude, and among males, the failure to marry. Mental illnesses among the Amish include those that are typical of the American rural population, including a variety of manic-depressive types.

The literature of the Amish people themselves—fictional narratives and letters from readers—suggests that some wives have crying spells and problems their husbands do not understand. Some are afraid. Women who believe that their husbands are at fault do not feel free to criticize them or to express themselves. Their role is one of submission. Depression is a common symptom. Since there is no legitimate way of expressing frustration through aggression, turning sorrow inward and becoming depressed is a common mechanism. Women, as well as men, infrequently seek out physicians who will prescribe tranquilizers.

Although there are strong social supports for the individual, some Amish people have difficulty coping with contradictory expectations Young or newly installed officers who must bear the responsibility for maintaining the Amish standards as interpreted by the older bishops are subjected to extrardinary stress. In one large settlement two informants could recall a total of fifteen suicides. The frequency of suicide is higher among Amishmen than among Amishwomen, and higher among the younger Amish than among those over fifty. The rate of suicide appears to vary in the different communities. In some counties it appears that the reported rate is about as high as that for the rural non-Amish. In others it appears that the rate is only about half that for the overall U.S. non-Amish population.[8]

Amish culture, however, provides some "common sense" approaches to persons who are mentally disturbed. Persons who are considered abnormal are urged to "work, rather than sit around and read too much." Their families and community try to provide a sense of belonging and of being needed. The mentally ill are normally cared for at home. Visiting and traveling provide occasions on which to renew connections with relatives and friends, and sick persons are given an opportunity to visit as well. A certain tolerance for deviants, especially "sick" persons, is permitted within the society. Although there is strong informal and familial support, there is little formal recognition or ceremony, such as an opportunity for confession, in dealing with the sick.

Mental Retardation. Mentally retarded individuals in Amish society are given favorable attention and care. Whether the Amish have a greater proportion of mentally retarded than other cultures has not been demonstrated. The Amish define a retarded person as one "who is not normal." This includes victims of birth defects, brain damage, or accidents—conditions that will not respond to treatment.

Retarded persons are not considered a social problem, for differences in ability and intellect are taken as gifts from God.[9] An individual's worth is not measured by his performance in school or the wages he can earn. The presence of abnormal children is accepted as part of God's will. An abnormally gifted child is also accepted as a "handicap."[10] A "problem child" is one who is dissatisfied or disobedient, not one with a disability.

The Amish believe that all children should go to school, including the "hard learners" or even those "who cannot learn," for they should not be excluded from group participation. In several regions the

8. Richard F. Hamman, "Mortality Patterns in the Old Order Amish" (Ph.D. diss., The Johns Hopkins University, 1979).

9. Corroborated by James A. Melton, "Old Order Amish Awareness and Understanding of Mental Retardation" (Ph.D. diss., Ohio State University, 1970).

10. In describing her gifted child, an Amish mother wrote an article: "Our Child Was Handicapped and We Didn't Know It," *Family Life*, July 1974.

mentally retarded attend local, public-supported schools. A few Amish schools have separate facilities and a separate teacher for the retarded. The retarded are part of the Amish family and community, are accepted and loved by all, and are not excluded from voluntary participation in community activities. Some perform useful tasks in the family. In general, the Amish are aware of and concerned about their mentally retarded members and are involved in seeking appropriate ways to assist them.

The Physically Handicapped. For the physically handicapped, as for the mentally retarded, the Amish community provides an atmosphere of consideration and affection. The handicapped include blind persons, polio victims, those disabled as a result of accidents, and those who suffer from genetic diseases such as dwarfism or muscular dystrophy. Periodically the Amish handicapped conduct a national meeting to share their interests and to become acquainted. A catalog of handicrafts made by the handicapped lists the name and address of each individual (with directions to his home), the nature of the handicap, and a description of the products offered for sale. These include, among other things, leather goods, needlework, beads, dolls, birdhouses, rocking chairs, coat hangers, and decorative dishes. Many manage their own retail shops, selling watches, books, and greeting cards, and offer a variety of repair services.

FOLK AND SYMPATHY CURES

The Amish have retained folk attitudes and cures common to the Germanic tradition and rural American culture. Family lines vary greatly in this respect, however. With each decade more of the European occult practices have been lost, but other folk cures from American culture have been syncretized into the Amish belief system.

Traditional home remedies judged to be effective in restoring good health are common to folk healing. The belief in folk healing is perpetuated by testimonies and the authority of respected members of the group. Oral tradition has preserved a knowledge of various teas, ointments, tonics, salves, liniments, and poultices. This knowledge is augmented by contemporary sources of folk knowledge found in farm almanacs, in the weekly Amish newspapers, and in the publications of "natural" health-food and vitamin dealers.

The patent names of medicines advertised in *The Budget* have changed over the years, but the ailments they claim to cure remain the same. Remedies for rheumatism and arthritis are most numerous, but there are also testimonials associated with vitamins, tonics, and bitters to cure constipation and to relieve itch. Testimonials from English persons are accepted as readily as those from Amish persons. An Amishwoman who found relief for severe croup offered her formula to other readers: "Boil vinegar, and if it is a severe case of croup, hold the child over full steam, enough that the child can breathe easily." For infections, she recommended a poultice of milk and linseed meal. Teas and homemade formulas constitute another source of treatment. "They use all kinds of teas for all kinds of ills," said one physician, "and I don't interfere with it unless I know it to be detrimental." Old-favorite home remedies are passed around from family to family.

In search of better health, some Amish will travel great distances—to places like Florida, Arizona, or South Dakota—to visit "hot springs" or chiropractic centers. At the present time some travel to Montana to sit in old uranium mines to obtain relief from arthritic pains. One state inspector who investigates quasi practitioners states that he invariably finds Amish patients at these places, which are often far from an Amish community.

Food supplements and vitamins, natural health foods, along with juicers and vibrators, are used by many of the Amish people. Some have established health-food stores and have become distributors for brand-name products. Knowledge of the use of herbs and their sale and distribution were greatly advanced by William McGrath in his weekly column in *The Budget*.[11] He has conducted lectures and seminars for a fee in most of the major Amish communities, offering herbal certificates to those who enroll in his seminars. These presentations are arranged by local Amish families who either are dealers in health products or are sympathetic to herbal foods. McGrath's own testimonials, first as a convert to the "plain Christian faith" from a military career and a worldly church background, and later upon his dramatic recovery from rheumatism after using natural plants, add credibility for his Amish audiences.

Sympathy Curing. Sympathy curing, also called powwowing, plays a minor role in Amish healing even though some Amish condemn the practice. Powwowing is defined as a native brand of faith healing—using words, charms, amulets, and physical manipulations in an attempt to heal man or beast.[12] Other terms used for powwowing are

11. William McGrath, *God-Given Herbs for the Healing of Mankind* (N.p.: By the author, 1970).
12. For further discussion of these concepts, see Don Yoder, "Folk Medicine," in *Folklore and Folklife*, ed. Richard M. Dorson (Chicago: University of Chicago Press, 1972), pp. 191–215.

"charming," "conjuring," "to try for," and "to use" (a direct translation from the German term *Brauche*). Powwowing apparently has no direct connection to Indian folk medicine, but was transplanted to America by immigrants from the Rhineland and Switzerland. The practice is not unique to the Amish, for at one time it was a common healing art among Pennsylvania Germans.[13]

Many of the charms and formulas used in powwowing can be traced to a book by John George Hohman, *Der Lang verborgene Schatz und Haus-Freund* (The Long Lost Friend), published in Reading, Pennsylvania, in 1820. Some of the spells in this collection have been traced back to Albertus Magnus, who died in Cologne in 1280, and some are apparently more ancient. The Amish, however, have no knowledge of these books, nor do they use them. The tendency to rely on oral testimony, so pervasive in Amish life, is especially manifest in the healing arts. The following are illustrations of charms used in powwowing.[14] To insure safety from an angry dog, repeat three times:

> Dog, hold thy nose to the ground;
> God has made me and thee, hound.

To cure a person from worms, repeat in silence the following verse while encircling the patient three times:

> You are a little worm, not entirely grown.
> You plague me in marrow and bone.
> You may be white, black, or red,
> In a quarter of an hour you will be dead.

One of the Amish healers in the early nineteenth century was Solomon Hochstetler (b. 1785) of Walnut Creek, Ohio.[15] By trade he was a mechanic skilled in making brace bits and augers. He combined the art of "magnetic healing" with powwowing, treating such disorders as cancer, ringworm, tetter, and other ailments. Using saliva, he rubbed the affected part with the forefinger of his right hand. Each time the finger was removed he blew on the affected part with great

13. Thomas Brendle and Claude Unger, *Folk Medicine of the Pennsylvania Germans, Proceedings of the Pennsylvania German Society*, vol. 45 (Norristown, Pa., 1935).

14. Both of these charms are published in *Der Reggeboge* (quarterly of the Pennsylvania German Society), vol. 13, 1979, and various versions have been handed down by the Amish.

15. Harvey Hostetler, *The Descendants of Jacob Hochstetler* (Elgin, Ill.: Brethren Publishing House, 1912), p. 272.

force and spoke magical words taken from a book of charms. Following the treatment, his right arm weakened and his muscles appeared emaciated. He maintained that the cures took power out of his body. Solomon had an ambiguous status in the community, for he had a drinking problem, and for over fifty years he was suspected of having murdered his brother's child. After the real murderer confessed, he was baptized into the Amish church at the age of seventy-three. It appears that most healers among the Amish today are marginal in some respects.

A present-day Amish healer, not necessarily typical of others, is Elam Lapp (fictitiously named), a retired farmer.[16] His son operates the family farm. His "grandfather house" is large enough to accommodate a treatment room and a waiting room for twenty people. He sees patients three days a week from nine to five o'clock. Some have appointments, especially those who come great distances, while others do not. Elam receives from thirty to fifty callers per day. Aside from the local people who come by horse and carriage, Elam has had clients from eleven states during the course of a single month.

Elam is reluctant to talk about powwowing, though his technique appears to have begun with powwowing, moved to chiropractic, then to "nerve" treatment, and now incorporates elements of all three. He explained: "If a nerve hurts, I can feel it. The electric in my hand can feel when a nerve hurts; when it does not hurt I do not feel it. I follow the nerve to the place where it is pinched, then I give treatment."

Persons who are crippled, those suffering from birth defects, from rheumatism, backaches, cold feet, paralysis, headaches, or swelling, and others who have no obvious complaints, come to his waiting room. His description of the ailment is one that his patients readily accept. His hand has "electric," which locates the pinched nerve, and the area is then relieved by chiropractic.

Elam claims to have gained his knowledge of healing from a wide range of people, including retired chiropractors. He himself takes treatments from chiropractors when he visits other towns. He learned much from a previous Amish healer who farmed during the day and treated patients in the evenings. Elam thinks he could pass an examination and get a chiropractor's license, but that would require him to charge a fee and manage a business, both of which he does not want to do. He says he only wants to help people. Elam does not "take" any

16. The writer is grateful to Levi Miller for sharing this case study with him (unpublished, 1975).

money, but those who wish to give something leave a few dollars on a table. As is typical of other folk healers, he does not return any change. Accepting contributions while not stipulating a fee is an apparent safeguard against the unlawful solicitation of fees for medical services.

Many people testify to the beneficial help they receive from Elam. Elam's intensity and self-confidence reflect a kind of enthusiasm and hope one finds among new believers. A visit with him inspires hope, and the ritual of going to see Elam is an exercise in building hope. Typically, the ill Amish person takes the day off from work, and some hire an automobile and chauffeur to make the trip—a treat for one who usually drives a buggy. One or two persons may accompany the ill person to keep him company. In the waiting room, relatives and others tell how they were relieved of their illnesses. Hearing the descriptions of other illnesses and testimonials of recovery inspires the confidence that one's ailments are manageable, if not curable.

There are two kinds of Amish sympathy healers: those who become practitioners, set up a treatment room, and accept the role of "doctor"; and, typically, sages and grandmothers who are pressed into pow-wowing when all else fails. The latter do not accept contributions for their services. The patient does not always need to be present when the actual incantations are performed, but the ailing person must have faith to obtain results. One who desires to acquire the skill can obtain it only from an older person of the opposite sex upon the promise that the formulas will be kept secret. The chief feature of *Brauche* is the silent incantation of the proper charms at appropriate times. Some of the incantations are forceful commands that direct the disease to leave the patient. Some common ailments taken to the *Brauch-Doktor* are bed-wetting, erysipelas (a skin condition also known as wild fire), homesickness, livergrown, and abnemme (wasting away). Incantations may also be done for parasites, bleeding, warts, burns, toothaches, and intestinal pains.

Livergrown is a mysterious ailment which in years past was common among Amish infants. In the dialect (*ah-gewachse*), it means "hidebound" or "grown together." The symptoms are crying and discomfort, which are not alleviated by food or physical care. It is often thought to be caused by sudden exposure to the outside atmosphere or being shaken up too vigorously by a carriage ride. The diagnosis is made by placing the child on his abdomen on a table, then bringing together, if possible, the child's left arm and right foot. If the two do not come together without ease, the child has livergrown. Livergrown seems to have no equivalent in modern medical literature, though it was once a common ailment among Pennsylvania Germans.

Many Amish young people today know nothing of *Brauche*, and most will deny that it still exists. However, in some of the cures involving spirit intrusion, a demonic personification is implied. *Brauche* became the subject of a debate among the Amish in 1961.[17] In some cures, the healer believes that the disease is transferred to the practitioner himself. Following a treatment, the healer feels the need to rest and recover from the "poisonous element" he has acquired from the patient. One Amish healer experiences profuse belching following treatments.

There are Amish persons who are embarrassed by those who patronize folk healers, and by those who travel great distances to find "special doctors." Several Amish communities in the past have been strife-ridden because of the controversy over powwowing, especially the use of black magic or hexing. The early Amish community in Chester County (near Malvern), Pennsylvania, faced deterioration when those who wanted to rid themselves of the influence of sorcery moved to other places.

Magic in Europe. Amish sympathy healing has its roots in Europe, especially Alsace. The productive research of the French scholar Jean Séguy in modern times has brought new knowledge to bear on the subject.[18] Among the Swiss and Austrian Anabaptists, medicine was a specialty. Listed in an eighteenth-century census are several Anabaptist doctors—Ulrich Neuhauser, Christ Ummel, Jacob and Nicolas Augsburger, and Pierre Graber. Neuhauser, who drew criticism from the authorities, was allowed by the prince "to practice surgery only among those belonging to his creed."[19] Several, including Jacob Augsburger of Celles and Peter Graber of Montbéliard, were health officers in their districts. Elder Nicolas Augsburger of Salm practiced both human and veterinary medicine.

Among the Anabaptist "virtues" noted in public records was the art of treating cattle and protecting them from epidemics. Among those listed as quacks was an Anabaptist at Moutiers-Grandval who "lives in a withdrawn area" and whose house "is always full of people who come to consult him from one dawn to the next."[20] He utilized medicinal plants of the region but also diagnosed sicknesses by in-

17. The various views were expressed in *The Budget* from September to November 1961.
18. Jean Séguy, *Les Assemblées anabaptistes-mennonites de France* (The Hague: Mouton, 1978), pp. 509–14. For the English narrative, see idem, "Religion and Agricultural Success."
19. Séguy, "Religion and Agricultural Success, p. 209.
20. Ibid., p. 210.

specting specimens of urine. Botanists of the area observed that the Anabaptists had medical books, especially books on herbs. A medical or healing tradition appears to have been passed down through certain family lines. Klopfenstein's almanac contained numerous hygienic, medical, and veterinary prescriptions, such as cures for sprained ankles, bloating in cows, and the removal of warts. In the eighteenth century it appears that the cures were largely herbal remedies and lore that were not unique to the Anabaptists, but in the nineteenth century the populace began to patronize Mennonite healers, and the Mennonite healers then began to practice magic.

An Anabaptist healer, it is recorded, cured sprained ankles in the following manner. "Between eleven and twelve o'clock at night he came to the patient's bed, opened a book of spells from which he read a few cabalistic formulas, while touching the injured foot from time to time with the tip of his outstretched hand, as to form a cross."[21] Following this the healer continued reading beside the fireplace in a grave, deep-set voice for half an hour. The healing was not to take place until a second set of operations was concluded. To cure a sick horse the same healer hung a small bag containing a preparation around the horse's neck. One curious owner who examined the contents afterward found a mixture of oats and sawdust.

An official in Belfort writing in 1850 called the Anabaptists "gypsy manias," saying: "Like all the sects that live outside the law, like all those that live among themselves without having invited society [to see] the mysteries that surround their life, the Anabaptists are very superstitious; almost all of them have family secrets; they practice medicine illegally in the country, especially on animals, and take advantage of herbs, powders and invocations in which they see many virtues."[22]

How and why did the Anabaptists acquire the practice of magical healing? One possible explanation for this transmutation is suggested by Séguy.[23] To those around them, the Anabaptists seemed a strange people ethnically, linguistically, and religiously (with distinctive dress). They lived on the margin of society, away from the population centers. Their open violation of religious laws and customs aroused suspicions, but their neighbors recognized their influence as good. Many of the native people began to regard them as a people endowed with special powers. After all, they grew crops and raised livestock where others

21. Ibid.
22. Ibid., p. 214.
23. Ibid., pp. 214-17.

could not make a living. Popular beliefs forced the Anabaptists to accept the image of themselves as a people possessing magical powers, though all their religious beliefs ran counter to these practices. They may have fought this reputation, since there is little evidence of practitioners of magic among them before about 1850. The magical element may simply have been similar to that of the peasants, and when outsiders began to view Anabaptists as bearers of special powers, of religious secrets, the Amish accepted this view of themselves. Their aloofness from society, their separation and marginality, was supportive of their own view of themselves as a special people. Had they been robust in their historic faith, they would never have accepted the role into which society was forcing them. It was during the nineteenth century, from about 1830 to 1850, when magical healing was at its peak, that the Amish migrated out of Alsace to America. These practices did not affect all Amish families or all congregations, but at least one Alsatian congregation early in the twentieth century experienced a division when the bishop was asked to desist from the practice of magical healing.

The apathetic and stagnant character of the Amish communities may have induced the Amish to be receptive to magical thinking, as did some of the literature they were reading. The French and Swiss groups read widely *The Wandering Soul*,[24] a book of miracles and allegorical material they probably came to view as history, as Séguy has suggested. The miracles associated with the last Bernese martyr, Hans Haslibacher (some of which are recounted in a thirty-two-stanza ballad in the *Martyrs Mirror*[25] and in the *Ausbund*), are familiar themes. According to tradition, after attempts by the Reformed preachers to force Haslibacher to recant, he prophesied on the basis of a dream that three signs would accompany his execution: his severed head would jump into his hat and laugh, the sun would turn crimson, and the spring water in his village would turn to blood. The poem claims that all three occurred. The Swiss and Alsatian Anabaptists frequented the Haslibacher village and drank its water on various occasions before coming to America. Spurious books that still have an attraction for the Amish in American are the *Apocrypha*, *The Gospel of Nicodemus*, and the *Testament of the Twelve Patriarchs*.

How the Amish came to practice magic is not easily explained.

24. For a description of this book, see Irvin B. Horst, "The Wandering Soul: A Remarkable Book of Devotion," *Mennonite Historical Bulletin* 18 (October 1957).
25. Thieleman J. van Braght, *The Bloody Theatre; or, Martyrs Mirror* (Scottdale, Pa.: Mennonite Publishing House, 1951), p. 1128. American editions of the *Ausbund* (no. 140) also contain the ballad.

There is a strong suggestion, however, that the transition from medicine to magic was associated with the perception outsiders had of the Anabaptist groups as bearers of special powers. The Anabaptists apparently accepted this view for themselves, for they too saw themselves as a separate people possessing a history with many miracles.

CHAPTER 16

Backstage Amish Life

THE BACK STAGE of a culture is everything that is concealed from public view—the mistakes, ills, or varieties of behavior that are deliberately or structurally shielded from the public. All cultures have some roads that lead to disastrous ends. In American culture as a whole it has been observed that insanity is as highly developed as technology and that psychosis is the final outcome of all that is wrong with a culture.[1] What are the wrongs and cultural ills in the Amish community? In this chapter we will consider the recurring afflictions of Amish life. Some are structured and unconscious. This is not to suggest that the Amish have more ills than other cultures in the United States but rather to note that they too experience tragedies.

Throughout this analysis we must distinguish between two levels of reality—that of the Amish and that of the larger society. We must therefore ask several questions: What do Amish people shield from other Amish? What is concealed from the larger society? Do the Amish conform to two standards of behavior, and if so, how are such apparent contradictions resolved?

RIGIDITY AND THE ILLUSION OF GENTLENESS

Many people have commented on the gentle and considerate nature of the Amish people. Indeed, the Amish are often called the "gentle

1. Jules Henry, *Culture against Man* (New York: Random House, 1963), p. 322.

333

people" by outsiders.[2] A religious seeker who approached large numbers of both Old Order Amish and Old Order Mennonite farms observed that the dogs on Amish farms were friendlier than those on the Mennonite farms. In view of the rigidity of Amish mores, how can one account for this gentle quality? Do the finer human qualities emanate from the Amish culture, or are such attributes ascribed to the Amish people by idealistic outsiders?

The Amish, who are secure in their traditions, appear to be less defensive in their actions and far less judgmental of outsiders than most other religious sect members, including their cousins the Mennonites. This style of living is supported by their formal teachings (namely, "Judge not that ye be not judged" [Matt. 7:1]) and by their emphasis on humility and cooperation in the home and community.

Nevertheless, this gentleness is contradicted by the history of the Amish. The reforms of Jacob Ammann were anything but gentle. Not only did he ban attractive apparel and insist on simple grooming, but he taught social avoidance and imposed this practice on his fellow ministers. He even maintained that outside sympathizers who favored his people with good deeds were, after all, intruders "trying to enter the sheep-fold some other way." "There is," he said, "but one people who are the bride of Christ."[3] He expelled from fellowship those who did not share his stern views, calling them liars and blasphemers. This uncompromising rigidity has been perpetuated in the social fabric of the society and confronts the Amish persons with dialectic tensions: insider vs. outsider, acceptance vs. exclusion, separation vs. acceptance, and friendliness vs. severity. The rational, spiritual striving is upward, out of the pit of "the fallen church," toward "a holy nation," "a chosen people," a church "without blemish," the "bride of Christ." These metaphors signify for the individual the appropriate attitudes: resignation, powerlessness, nonresistance, restraint, guarded participation in human affairs, and separation from non-Amish social life. Worshiping in a language that is incomprehensible to the outsider is part of the enigma.

In their work ideology, the Amish try to express the same modesty they show in their dress. Manual labor and farming with horses is the norm. Working in cities or factories is off limits, and sons or daughters are not to work for worldly people except in the case of an

2. James M. Warner and Donald M. Denlinger, *The Gentle People: A Portrait of the Amish* (New York: Grossman Publishers, 1969).
3. Jacob Ammann letter (1963); see John B. Mast, ed., *The Letters of the Amish Division* (Oregon City, Oreg.: C. J. Schlabach, 1950), p. 35.

emergency. Musical instruments, commercial insurance, life insurance, and buying or selling on Sunday are not permitted. Electricity may not be affixed to one's property. Radio and television also are off limits. In all relationships with worldly people, one must guard against being too friendly.

These distinctive practices are grounded in the basic Amish metaphors, specifically that of the "bride," which relates the "inside" community to Christ. The Amish have maintained such distinctions for centuries, and their will to transmit them to their children remains strong. Persecutions and insults have strengthened the group. What, then, is the relationship between these cultural restrictions and the apparent gentleness of the Amish?

The Amish experience brief periods of relief from the constraints of their own culture when they come in contact with non-Amish persons. Such periods occur when Amish people associate with outsiders, when the Amish engage in conversation with the visitor, the antique collector, the neighbor, the salesman, the storekeeper, or the auctioneer. Many Amish are good conversationalists, and visiting with people from faraway places is, for them, very special. Through such encounters the Amish person obtains insight into the human problems in the outside world, which frequently makes him more content with his own community. When temporarily relieved of his cultural constraints, the Amish person appears to the outsider to be happy, contented, tolerant, and at peace with himself.

Within the baptized group, rigidity may give rise to certain types of social ills—problems associated with exclusion, jealousies between families, church divisions, and their consequences. An extreme measure is exclusion from church membership. There is normally no problem when the transgression is clearly defined, as in the case of moral lapses, and the accused accepts the severity of the offense. Excommunication can, however, turn "sour" under certain circumstances. This tends to happen when accused persons feel that they were the victims of spite and unjust accusations and were dealt with in an arbitrary manner. A person in such circumstances has no recourse, no court of appeal, and no alternative, for only the church has the power "to bind or to loose" (Matt. 16:18). In keeping with Amish practice, an excommunicated person must show submission, even if no wrongs have been committed. Should such a person seek justice for himself or engage in arguments, he would certainly bring shunning on himself. The reason for this extreme action is that the church-community as the "bride of Christ" cannot tolerate arrogance or disunity.

In 1947, in a highly publicized case, Andrew Yoder of Wayne County, Ohio, retaliated by suing each of four Amish ordained officials for $10,000.[4] Yoder had been excommunicated and shunned after he joined an Amish group that permitted the use of automobiles. Claiming that he needed an automobile to transport his daughter to the doctor for frequent medical attention, Yoder had begun to attend the church that allowed automobiles. For this he was excommunicated. Yoder claimed economic hardship as a consequence of the shunning. In a trial by jury, Yoder was awarded $5,000 in damages, and when the defendants refused to pay, the farm of Bishop John Helmuth was put up for sheriff's sale. Such legal cases are rare, but several have occurred.[5] In some there appears to have been envy between individuals or families, where in Amish journalistic jargon, spite turned into "mite" (a shortened derogatory rendering of *meide* or *meidung*, meaning "to shun").

In less-dramatic shunning cases, the ensuing stresses and consequences for individuals and family members are nevertheless far-reaching. A father (I will call him Henry Stoltzfus for purposes of illustration) was excommunicated for his progressive tendencies at the age of forty-seven. As an enterprising farmer, he was also involved in construction, sawmilling, cattle-raising, maintaining a dairy herd, and horse-trading. He became the focus of community criticism, possibly also of envy among other Amish members. In other respects, such as dress and grooming, he and his family more than conformed to Amish rules. After a sequence of accusations, each followed by visits from the ordained officials, he was excommunicated for reasons he could not accept. His passive and compliant wife requested that she be excommunicated with him. The accusations against him ranged from embezzlement to pride manifested in various farm enterprises.

After three years, the parties to the case still could not be reconciled. The couple had no inclination to liberalize by joining another Amish affiliation. When it became apparent that no reconciliation was possible, the couple sold their Pennsylvania farm and moved to

4. John H. Yoder, "Caesar and the Meidung," *Mennonite Quarterly Review* 23 (January 1949): 76–98.

5. Ibid., p. 78. Not to be confused as Amish is the widely publicized suit of Robert Bear, a former member of the Reformed Mennonite church, who asked that the court order the church to desist from the practice of shunning. See his book *Delivered unto Satan* (Carlisle, Pa.: By the author, 1974).

Joseph W. Yoder, an otherwise sympathetic writer and the author of *Rosanna of the Amish*, wrote a fiery denunciation of Amish shunning practices and other traditions. See *Amish Traditions* (Huntington, Pa.: Yoder Publishing Co., 1950).

Iowa "to get away from church trouble." On their arrival in Iowa they applied for membership in the local Amish church. Since they did not have a church letter, they were received as members on the basis of their confession of faith. When the Pennsylvania bishop learned that the couple had been granted membership, he wrote to the Iowa bishop explaining that if he did not promptly exclude the couple and honor the Pennsylvania shunning policy, the whole Iowa church would be excluded from fellowship. Not prepared for a confrontation, the Iowa bishop promptly complied with the Pennsylvania bishop's ultimatum, excluded the couple, and advised them to return to Pennsylvania to make the necessary reconciliation. But four separate journeys to Pennsylvania to "make peace" did not bring a satisfactory reconciliation. After seven years of living without membership in any church, the couple joined a Mennonite congregation, but only after their children had done so, and at the urging of the Mennonite bishop.

The consequences for the growing children in the family were far-reaching. Three of the seven children were baptized into the Amish faith. Only one remained with the Old Order. All the others affiliated with Mennonite groups, and later some joined Protestant churches. The children and grandchildren became scattered throughout the United States. Relatives and friends who remained faithful to the Amish church were obliged to shun the couple for as long as they lived, a span of over forty years.

What had Henry Stoltzfus done to merit exclusion? No single offense stands out, but one obtrusive fact remains: he "talked back" to his accusers and to the ordained Amish officials—something which no excommunicated person must ever do if he wishes to be reinstated. As indicated, no amount of argument, justification, or logic will aid in reconciliation. A submissive attitude is absolutely necessary.

Marital avoidance, which is required when a spouse is excommunicated, also may threaten the unity of the family. In most cases the innocent spouse of an accused party will request excommunication so that shunning need not be practiced between them, for in shunning not only must there be avoidance at the table but abstention from sexual relations is required. One wife who lived with her excommunicated husband for thirteen years gave birth to four children. After each birth she was asked to confess a transgression. After the fourth child she said, "I can't confess to a sin," and she joined the church of her husband.

In the large Amish settlements there is the problem of not knowing who is to be shunned. A member who knowingly eats with an excommunicated person is liable to be shunned. However, if in in-nocence a person eats at the same table with an excommunicant, the offense is overlooked. Visits with excommunicated relatives become awkward in extended families. The presence of such persons at family gatherings is unavoidable and the problem is resolved by eating at separate tables. The problem is less acute at outdoor gatherings or picnics, where the shunned ones can be inconspicuously seated at a separate table with the children and nonmembers. Those who flinch at shunning their friends at the table, but nevertheless feel they must practice the formalities, may make symbolic gestures to mitigate the harshness of the practice. One mother prepared two separate tables, placed them within several inches of each other, and covered both with one large tablecloth. Each table had separate benches. The children and the excommunicated ate at one table and the members at the other. Only the adults knew what had transpired.

The rule of not accepting services or favors directly from excom-municated persons has complications in the modern world. Awkward, embarrassing, or annoying situations will transpire. While driving his automobile to town, an excommunicated person stopped along the highway to give a ride to an Amish pedestrian, a young relative. After the two were driving down the road, the young passenger asked:

"Are you Henry Zook?"
The driver replied: "Yes, I am."
"Well," said the passenger, "I don't believe I want to ride with you."
"I didn't think you did," was the reply.

Nevertheless, the driver of the automobile took his unwilling pas-senger to his desired destination.

Some excomunicated persons will accommodate their Amish rela-tives by not forcing them into difficult social situations. A waitress in a restaurant (a former Amish member) does not serve Amish members, so as not to offend them. A clerk (also formerly Amish) calls the Amishman's attention to a new product or book, but instead of handing it to him, lays it on the counter so that the Amish person may examine it on his own accord.

Other evidence of social ills includes disunity, fragmentation, and church divisions, as discussed earlier. Although the Amish family in-stitution is not threatened by divorce, Amish society itself suffers from a fragmented social order. Here, as in other aspects of the dialectic, the Amish are suspended between the search for social harmony and the forces that would destroy it.

CULTURAL CONTRADICTIONS

Maintaining Amish standards, but accepting some modernization to solve the human problems of living, requires compromises that must not disrupt the social structure. By rejecting certain types of modernity and accepting others, some Amish appear to the outside to be contradicting themselves. From the viewpoint of Amish culture there is no contradiction. But the outsider who sees no logic to Amish selectivity may be inclined to point out apparent hypocrisy. The more pronounced inconsistencies concern the use of modern conveniences, which the Amish person is not allowed to own.

Although he may not own an automobile, a member will accept rides and willingly hire an automobile with a driver to transport him from place to place. Telephones are forbidden in Amish homes, but in an "emergency" most Amish will use their neighbor's telephone or nearby coin-operated telephones. Electricity from the public-utility or highline is not to be hooked up to Amish homes, but the use of generators powered by diesel or gasoline motors is permissible for operating welding and shop equipment, milking machines, and refrigeration units. When an Amishman rents a farm home furnished with electricity, he may use the power to operate electrical appliances. As a renter in a new community he may even borrow a tractor from a neighbor to do his field work. Some Amish groups permit tractors for crop production but forbid the use of pneumatic tires. Others allow tractors for belt power but not field work. The rule that all field implements must be pulled by horses does not prevent the Amish from using a mounted motor to operate the unit.

Adult patterns of adaptation have their counterparts among the young. The practice of secretly acquiring a driver's license or secretly owning an automobile has become common among the young men in densely populated Amish settlements. Many boys, and some girls, have a driver's license. The unbaptized youth cannot be punished by the church for this; parents must deal with such offenders. Some of the boys leave their vehicles in a nearby town, parked in a used-car lot, a service station, or on a quiet street. They typically do not flaunt or openly display their deviation. Sympathetic parents raise little objection, and in some instances they too violate an Amish rule by giving their son financial assistance. In this way the parents gain access to convenient and probably less costly transportation. Some boys who seriously intend to join the church delay baptism until their approaching marriage and gradually relinquish their forbidden practices.

In obtaining a driver's license, auto registration, insurance, or other types of assistance disapproved by their parents, the young are frequently shielded by neighbors, by relatives who have left the Amish church, or by their employers.

The ease of access to automobiles and the threat this deviation poses to the Amish community has given rise to special rules made by the Amish for both members and their children. On Sunday one may ride with an outsider in his auto, but not with a driver who is a relative. For example, a parent may not accompany an unbaptized child who has access to an automobile. This effectively prevents members from going to or returning from the Sunday service in automobiles.

When arrested for speeding or charged with a felony, Amish youths have frequently been released on their own recognizance and their names have been withheld from newspapers. Young Amishmen are frequently not aware of the dangers of an automobile, for today they no longer drive inconspicuous "old plugs" but choose high-powered sports cars. When pursued by patrolmen, Amish boys are prone to drive recklessly, crossing a major highway at excessive speed, for example. They have been known to perform daring and foolish feats. More youths are working off the farm than was true twenty years ago, and consequently, there is more conflict with the law according to local (Lancaster County) authorities. Although they are not involved in "hard" crime (where force is employed), shoplifting and passing bad checks occur occasionally.

Parents do not report the offenses of their children to the police unless, of course, they feel they have already lost control of their young. (The Amish typically do not report anyone to the police.) However, Amish leaders have recently told Lancaster County law enforcement officers that they should no longer withhold the names of Amish offenders from the news media.

Former Amish persons who now serve in educational, legal, and law enforcement institutions in the Amish community know how to deal effectively with Amish youths who transgress the law. A police officer stopped an automobile packed full of Amish boys. He checked the license of the driver and was about to leave. Not knowing that the officer was a former Amishman who understood "Dutch," one boy in the back seat snickered in the dialect, "If only he knew what we had in the trunk!" The officer, who understood all, returned and ordered the trunk opened. Inside were several cases of beer. The boys, who were minors, argued: "If you take it away from us, you will drink it yourself, so why not dump it right here?" To the dismay of the Amish boys, the officer agreed: "All I need is one can for proof of evidence." The officer then forced the boys to open each can of beer and pour the contents into the ditch.

Not only the single youth but even some church members walk a tight rope with respect to Amish rules or local laws. Those who are engaged in plumbing, painting, and building trades often rent or own trucks, although the vehicles are operated by their non-Amish employees. Zoning laws have been enacted in some places to protect the agricultural character of Amish farmland. When the Amish farmer builds a repair or service center on his own acreage, he may ignore the zoning ordinance, assuming that the law was intended for "English" people.

The tension between the inside and outside communities requires that the individual Amish person acquire a high degree of discretionary knowledge. The individual must discern what is a transgression and what is approved by Amish standards. Acquiring this discretionary knowledge is part of the process of learning to be a responsible Amish adult. In speaking of her teenage son, an observant mother noted: "If he smokes and hides it, he knows he shouldn't be doing it."

The Scriptural passage that admonishes the Amish person to perform his good deeds in secret appears also to work well for concealing contradictory behavior: "Do not let your left hand know what your right hand is doing" (Matt. 6:3). Those Amish who oppose smoking, for example, are more concerned about members who smoke openly, in front of English people, than about those who smoke habitually, but do it with discretion. Such indulgences enjoyed in private are more tolerable than overt behavior that reflects on the whole group. Some of the young derive great satisfaction from the seemingly insignificant deviations they conceal from the group.

SOCIAL STAGNATION AND APATHY

Apathy affects some individuals in all societies, and when large numbers are affected in a single society, extinction of the culture becomes a real possibility. It is claimed that some migrant populations have died of nostalgia, and that whole societies in Melanesia have withered away from weariness. Hermits in the fourth century who withdrew from society to live in isolation suffered from an affliction known as *acedia*, a Greek term meaning "a state of not caring."[6] The symptoms, loneliness and fatigue, were attributable to the conditions of withdrawal. The affliction was particularly evident among monks who in the midst of their monastic lives fell into lassitude, laxness, and apathy. *Acedia* implies religious hopelessness and the failure to find the world and its activities meaningful.

6. Bert Kaplan, "Acedia: The Decline and Restoration of Desire" (unpublished manuscript).

A condition of progressive wasting away known as marasmus has been observed especially among babies and children when human support and affection are insufficient or are withheld. Among adults, various types of depression occur when there is insufficient human contact and support.

Amish communities, like any traditional society or institution, tend to suffer from social stagnation. Stagnation can result when the designated leaders exercise an unusual measure of autonomy. Whether leaders wrest this authority from the group or the group passively conforms to the wishes of its leaders, the results are the same. Personal growth diminishes, and discourse on ethical issues tends to disappear. When all members acquiesce there are no tensions, no more goals to strive for, and there is little meaning in existence. When, like victims of bureaucracy in modern society, large numbers of Amish members slavishly follow the rules without regard for the ends for which they were designed, motivation declines.

There are two periods in the life of an Amish person in which he is particularly vulnerable to apathy. One occurs during childhood, often at the onset of school attendance, when the child (typically from a large family) fails to find adequate feelings of acceptance. The other occurs during the sensitive period of adolescence, when the person is confronted with moral imponderables. Though most children do not lack role models, they appear to suffer the effects of heavy informal indoctrination. One symptom is bed-wetting, a recognized and recurring problem among the Amish. Some recognize it as a symptom of an emotional problem and believe that "the child needs extra love and encouragement."[7]

Since rebellion and flagrant disobedience are not acceptable outlets, Amish boys (but rarely girls) run away from home as a last resort. A boy of sixteen in a very orthodox family suddenly disappeared one Saturday afternoon. His Amish hat was found a mile from home. The alarmed father could do nothing but wait and hope. Two days later a neighbor received a telephone message from a large city stating the time and place where the boy could be picked up. The boy had discarded his Amish clothing, had had his hair cut in a barber shop, and had traveled to the city, but shortly thereafter had become despondent and had notified the police. The boy had secretly entertained the notion of running away for many months. An unhappy encounter with his father at work had been the occasion for the actual break.

Sensitive Amish youths who cannot identify with rowdy gangs

7. David Wagler, "How to Stay Dry," *Family Life*, June 1971, p. 9.

Individuals from two subcultures retain their identity
while using the same modern facility.

frequently experience ridicule and loneliness. Individuals of courting
age must associate with their peer group or "gang," for to do otherwise
is to invite ostracism. A typical victim of this predicament was a
young man who described his childhood days as happy ones and his
home as devout, but said: "I was not happy with the few social
activities of the young people, so I went to fairs and farm shows to
satisfy my longings. Without my parents knowing it, I attended
movies, and I began drinking. This led to card playing and gambling.
I pretended to be a Christian when I was home, then I would go
away and seek the pleasure of the world to satisfy my own desires. In
this way I was deceiving both my parents and the church." This
young man respected his parents but could not accept the standards
of Amish youth. His deviation was not deliberately rebellious, but after
two years of living a "double-faced life," as he put it, he abruptly ran
away from home. He recognized the contradictions but found no
solution except "to break the heart of my parents." Although he
could not accept the mildly coercive aspects of his rowdy peer group,
his passive individualism was probably taken as a form of rebellion.

Individualism is extremely difficult to accommodate in the Amish
subculture during adolescence and the period of courtship, for it is
during this time that the person must demonstrate his loyalty to the
peer group. When an individual refuses to comply with the demands

of his peers, whether in smoking, drinking, attending movies, or bundling, he tends to be viewed as disloyal to his group. This "gang" or group he associates with will set the standards of conduct. Individuals who are sick or incapable of performing the normal work load of a young person have difficulty feeling accepted by their group. A boy of fourteen, for example, who found that because of his physical condition he could not load a wagon with barnyard manure by himself, became so depressed that he walked from the scene and cried for hours.

One Amish couple recognized the unwillingness of their children to associate with the Amish young people at their "singing" and began holding regular Bible study and discussion sessions each evening in the home. This activity solved the problem in the short run, but the children did not remain Amish. A group of youths who began to meet secretly for "Bible study and prayer" were ordered to stop their meetings. A mother told her seventeen-year-old son: "We know it can't be the Lord's will for the young folks to come together like that to study the Bible."

There is, of course, no rule that individuals may not read or study the Bible in private. What is feared by Amish adults is a form of evangelical piety which leads to the rejection of the Amish way of life. That fear is well grounded, for Amish persons influenced by fundamentalism typically leave the faith. Amish parents and leaders frequently are inarticulate when confronting these alien influences in their children.

The heavy emphasis on humility in Amish culture gives rise to eccentric expressions of stagnation when, for instance, there are restricted means of social recognition. The temptation to become proud of one's humility may have a negative or repressive effect on the young, but among adults it may be a form of passive aggression. This occurs when members overconform to avoid any possible criticism of being worldly. By wearing Sunday clothes that are a little dirty, one cannot be accused of being too proud. When giving up tobacco would raise suspicions about one's orthodoxy, one continues to use it so as not to raise suspicions. Mistakes in spelling, whether in letters or in printed matter, are tolerated on the grounds that "it will keep us humble." This "humility game" among seekers of humble status not only limits intellectual interests and technical competency but renders the pursuit of such goals unattractive. The effect of social stagnation on personality is to starve personal growth and to make the individual the prey of apathy and self-complacency.

Of the many uses made of silence among the Amish, some bring pain and misery to human relationships. Silence following excommunication is a punishment wrought with finality, as is the silence of shunning at the table. Silence is turned into aggression when an offended father does not speak to his family at the table. He expects his wife to know from the context and the series of past events what the trouble is. The silenced preacher, bereft of his audience, suffers the punishment of his calling, for there is much he would say but he is "benched." No one will ever know how many crimes are smothered in silence. When a bishop's house burned to the ground well after midnight, two persons lost their lives. Although the police found evidence of arson, the investigation was met with silence. For three years the bishop had been harassed for his unpopular policy by the young people in his dwindling congregation.

POPULATION DENSITY AND ROWDYISM

When Amish settlements become large, so large that the Amish people scarcely know each other's families, the quality of interpersonal relationships changes and social controls weaken. Although ceremonial activities discipline the former adult world of the Amish, this is not the case with adolescent activities. Courtship extends far beyond the church district, and informal networks proliferate without formal control.

The accepted occasion for association among the young people is the "singing" held on Sunday evening. Here young people sit at a long table, with the boys on one side and the girls on the other. In small settlements there is one singing or place of meeting. As settlements become larger, two or more singings may be held, and the young opt to go to the singing of their choice. In Lancaster County, Pennsylvania, where the area occupied by the Amish has greatly expanded, there are many singings, and no formal organization regulates the singing institution. As a consequence, there are not only "singings" (in the traditional sense) but special-interest groups that organize their own peer-group activities.

Evidence of the differences among Amish young people is manifest in the proliferation of nicknaming for the various groups or "gangs." Two decades ago (in Lancaster County) there were, according to older informants, three main groups: the Groffies, the Ammies, and the Trailers. The Groffies were the most liberal; the Ammies and their subgroups, Lemons and Keffers ("bugs") were moderate; and the Trailers were conservative. Each of the three groups had a number of subgroups, and their names and interests changed over time. "Under the Groffies were the Hillbillies, Jamborees, and the Goodie-Goodies." The Groffies were named after the village of Groffdale. The

Hillbillies occupied the hilly region of southern Lancaster County. The Jamborees "were called that because they acted unruly and were not exactly liked by the larger groups." The Goodie-Goodies, who called themselves Christian, were sympathetic to the use of automobiles, but their apparent self-righteous stance made them objectionable to most other Amish gangs.

In the last twenty years, the Lancaster County young people have regrouped themselves into about ten gangs ranging from orthodox to most worldly. The Kirkwooders (named after a village) are one of the largest conservative groups that conduct the singings according to Amish tradition. Slightly less orthodox are the Lemons and Pioneers, followed by the Sparkies, Luckies, Quakers, and Antiques. The most deviant are reputed to be the Shotguns, Happy Jacks, and Ammies, who have automobiles and conduct "hops." The Groffies, Hillbillies, and the Keffers have become extinct, as have the Goodie-Goodies, who were lost to the Old Order when the New Amish division was formed. Some individuals have become "Sod" (a Lancaster County young person's term for "English" or "worldly") in their dress and behavior.

The large Amish settlements in Ohio and Indiana have experienced the same sort of differentiation among the young, with, of course, their own set of nicknames. In Indiana, young people's groups have generally followed the assimilation patterns of the three main adult groups: Clearspring, Barrens, and Clinton. Typically, the "good" young people, especially the girls, start the Sunday evening singing and sing for an hour or longer, while the "cut-ups" have no intention of sitting around the singing table. They mill around in small groups in other parts of the house or barn. In Ohio, an individual who is borderline, neither a "goodie" nor a "cut-up," is called a *Schwaddy* (literally, "a piece of gristle"). In Ohio and parts of Pennsylvania, a derogatory name used by some to describe the group of Amish boys with the longest hair is *Gnoddelwoller* ("hairy-waddles"). Some of the young men have distorted the name into "Noodle-roller." Early in this century in Iowa, a progressive group was labeled *die hochmüdiche Deer Grieker* ("the proud Deer Creek people"), while a strict group earned the name *die schlappiche Laplander* ("the sloppy Lapps" or "patches").[8] Such descriptive labeling may be indicative of repressed feelings.

The consumption of alcohol has reached intemperate proportions among some of the gangs. "Hoedowns [or "hops"] are not hoedowns

8. Sanford C. Yoder, *The Days of My Years* (Scottdale, Pa.: Herald Press, 1959), p. 33.

unless you have music and beer, and a dance every Sunday night after the singing," said one participant. "On Sunday afternoons the Amish young people, boys and girls, who are close to large cities will go to horse races, parks, attend movies, or attend big league ball games too." The traditional harmonica and guitars have been displaced by electric guitars and transistor-operated tape recorders. At the urging of parents who have lost control over their teenagers, the police have occasionally conducted raids on Sunday night singings. In one instance several juveniles were arrested for drunkenness, and hundreds of empty beer cans were found on the premises. An Amish father explained: "What can I do? I know it's wrong for minors to drink beer, but the boys would get down on me if I didn't allow it." In an earlier era, when saloons were built too close to the Amish community, Amish fathers would band together to buy out the saloon in order to stop the excessive drinking. That technique is no longer a solution.

Most "hops" are arranged without the consent of the parents. The young wait on their farm until their parents go away for the evening. If the parents are unable or unwilling to leave, they remain in the house and "look the other way" while the festivities proceed in the barn. After a barn floor holding 150 persons collapsed, injuring several people, the church enjoined parents from allowing parties on their farms. Although the frequency of the "hops" has declined, they have not stopped.

Many of the small or moderate-sized Amish settlements do not experience such rowdyism or gang behavior, and it would be unfair to attribute such problems to all Amish. Social harmony in Amish society is best maintained when the institutions are on a face-to-face, human scale rather than a large, bureaucratic scale. In the larger settlements the young constitute a subculture within Amish society, a peer pressure group so strong that parents have little or no control over the activities of their young people. Nevertheless, many of these young people later change radically and become steadfast church members.

Amish adults are careful not to deliberately intrude into the activities of their children and their friends. They respect their right to privacy. Adults do not participate in the gatherings of the young, and they ignore much of the behavior of adolescents. The Amish resemble the Chinese and other high-context cultures in dealing with rebellion in their children.[9] When confronted with difficult situations,

9. For the meaning of "high context," the reader may wish to turn to Chapter 1, the section entitled "A High-Context Culture." See also Edward T. Hall, *Beyond Culture* (New York: Doubleday, 1976), p. 142.

one acts as though nothing had happened. The great stability of the culture and the tremendous latitude within the system make this possible. Clashes of personality, dissent, and mild rebellion "are handled by pretending that they do not exist."[10] If a father acknowledges the things that happen, then he must choose a course of action, and to act is disruptive. An Amish father, like a Chinese father, "will put up with a lot from his son without ever saying anything."[11] The boy is allowed to express himself, and in both cultures there is confidence that the strong family system, rooted as it is in the ancestors, will ultimately bring the son around.

Florida Activities. One of the most powerful networks among deviant Amish youth emerged with the development of an institution known as the "Florida Reunion." As early as 1927 some elderly Amish people, in search of a better climate for their health, began vacationing in Florida for several weeks or months during the wintertime. A few miles east of Sarasota, a suburban settlement known as Pinecraft became a "resort" center for a wide variety of Amish and Mennonite people. Persons who suffer from heart trouble, asthma, sinus trouble, and other ailments attest to the area's excellent climate. They travel south with a Mennonite neighbor, or go by train and bus. The men like to fish and the women conduct quiltings.[12] While away from home, some of the Amish adults do things they would not do at home, like playing shuffleboard or working as carpenters in the Barnum Circus barns.

The older folks were soon followed by single young men who were normally employed in seasonal occupations but who had came south looking for winter work. In Florida they found ready employment as builders, painters, and masons. Single girls began working as domestic servants in Sarasota homes for high wages. The youths who go to Florida for extended periods are the foot-loose or marginal Amish. Here they experiment with worldly dress and behavior. They no longer live within the Amish community in the village of Pinecraft, but both girls and boys rent rooms or apartments in all parts of Sarasota. While in Florida the young people maintain close contact with one another and hold regular gatherings. During the Christmas season large parties attract virtually all the Amish youths

10. Ibid.
11. Ibid.
12. "Amish Families Winter in South," *New York Times*, April 1, 1952. See also John S. Umble, "The Mennonites in Florida," *Mennonite Life*, June 1957.

in the area, and many young people come to Florida from the northern states especially for these occasions.

The Sarasota activities have provided the setting and the rationale for an annual gathering, in the northern states, of friends who have been to Florida. Each year the "Florida Reunion" is held during a weekend in late summer in either Indiana, Ohio, or Pennsylvania. The purpose of the reunion is to mingle with friends, share food and beer, and dance to "wild" music. In each of the three states there is a reunion committee consisting of marginal Amish persons—those who have not yet been baptized or those who may have been excommunicated. The reunions are generally held at a large country club or campground, and the financing, logistics, and security are carefully arranged in advance.

These reunions of several hundred people are carefully executed without the consent of parents, and if possible, without the knowledge of the local police. The several thousand dollars required for expenses are raised through donations and the selling of admission tickets. The funds cover the cost of renting the premises, food, alcoholic beverages, one or two outside bands that play for two nights, and the cost of hiring a security guard. To make certain that unwanted persons do not come to the reunion, tickets are issued to those who are personally known by members of the reunion committee, or who are invited by an approved acquaintance. They arrive sleek and sporty in automobiles and brightly painted vans. A security guard and a member of the reunion committee carefully check all persons at the gate. Having their own security guard not only helps to ensure order within the group but prevents local police from raiding the grounds by surprise.

The Old Order Amish are apologetic about the "Florida Reunion" and the "hops" conducted by the young. Those young people who are most loyal to the Amish faith strongly disapprove of the reunion, saying, "they do terrible things there." The constant growth rate of the Amish population appears to be related to the growth of rowdyism and its networks in Amish communities. The differentiated gangs, however, perform a number of functions. They permit a period of limited self-determination by the individual, they provide personal satisfaction in small groups that are not totally unrelated to the Amish community, and they regulate dating patterns. The young people express some of the hostilities that marginal adults feel but suppress. The exclusiveness maintained by the gangs and their factions, and the different degrees of conformity to Amish norms they manifest, all in some measure prepare the young for adult life in the highly differentiated Amish church.

Amish parents and the church are limited in any direct action they may wish to take to squash the rowdy activity of the young. Their teaching on nonresistance prevents them from taking coercive measures; offenses are reported to the police only as a last resort. Furthermore, parents often feel that "the young folks must sow their wild oats and get it out of their system."[13] Amish young people sin sufficiently to remind themselves and others that human nature is flawed, that a time is coming when the "Old Adam" must be put away.

13. Editorial comment in *Young Companion*, January 1979, p. 18.

Part IV

Survival

CHAPTER 17

Responses to Change

SOME MINORITIES have managed to achieve stability and integration after periods of change and stress while others have not. Some, according to sociologist Everett Hughes, are "swept out by the broom of our industrialized civilization." Hughes carefully avoids making any predictions, however: "How long it will take to mop them up, no one knows. The process seems to be going on rapidly now, but it will probably last longer than any of us would predict."[1]

Small societies respond to perceived environmental stress in different ways. Some respond to a challenge and others do not. The Fox Indian tribe, for example, made "a good adjustment" to the American culture, "while the Sauk sank into apathy on a reservation, and the Kickapoo fled the country."[2] One tribe succumbed rapidly to acculturation, one tribe fled to Mexico, and one purchased land as a way out of its difficulty. As transplanted Europeans who have maintained a minority status over a long period, the Amish have acted in

1. Everett C. Hughes, *Where People Meet* (Glencoe, Ill.: The Free Press, 1952), p. 25.

2. William Caudill, *Effects of Social and Cultural Systems in Reactions to Stress*, Pamphlet no. 14 (New York: Social Science Research Council, 1958), p. 12. For a discussion of defensive adaptation, see Bernard J. Siegel, "Defensive Structuring and Environmental Stress," *American Journal of Sociology* 76 (July 1970): 11–32.

an integrated manner so as to preserve their identity. What are the major ways in which the Amish have responded to perceived threats and to environmental stress of long duration? In this chapter we will discuss some of their major responses to change. Although Amish attitudes toward change remain fairly stable, the number and kinds of changes vary from those of a generation ago. First, we will describe some of the mechanisms of social control.

SOCIAL CONTROL AND CHANGE

In a small society where virtually everyone is related by blood and where life is governed by informal rather than formal organizations, change occurs slowly. It took an Amish church fifty years from the time it adopted a moderate policy of *Meidung* (that of not shunning members who join other churches) until it adopted the automobile. Change is slow where members give common adherence to the core elements of the culture. In folk cultures "new items do not appear with any great frequency," says Ralph Linton, and the "society has plenty of time to test them and to assimilate them to its pre-existing patterns. In such cultures the core constitutes almost the whole."[3]

Deviation from established rules is prevented by a series of mild-to-severe constraints, including the following: (1) Conscience or personal inhibitions keep the individual from transgressing the rules of the church. The person who says "I dress Amish but I sure think different on the inside" is not restrained by these means. (2) Informal talk or gossip is an effective way of controlling behavior. Even though gossip is generally frowned upon within families, it remains one of the most effective moderating devices in the small, face-to-face Amish community. Those not controlled by consience or by informal talk are (3) admonished by the deacon or a preacher if guilty of an offense. The official determines the attitude of the offender, and if that person manifests disobedience and remains unchanged in intent, (4) the offender is admonished by two persons, usually ordained men. For minor offenses (5) the offender may voluntarily refrain from taking communion or confess the wrongdoings to the church by standing, or for major offenses, by kneeling. As additional warning and punishment (6) the offender may be asked not to take part in the upcoming communion. Major offenses recognized by the church, such as adultery, drunkenness, or buying an automobile or tractor (where forbidden), subject the transgressor to (7) immediate excommunication

3. Ralph Linton, *Acculturation in Seven American Indian Tribes* (New York: D. Appleton Century, 1940), p. 283.

and shunning until such time as a change of attitude is manifest. Most severe of all is (8) excommunication and shunning for life.

Social change may initially come about in an Amish community in one or all of the following ways. First, the rules are not enforced uniformly; enforcement is differential even for members within a single church district. Second, the attitudes of the bishop and the ordained men in a given district may differ from those in other districts. Third, an aspect of behavior which is most affected by change is economic productivity. (An example of economic change is the adoption from general to specialized farming.) In the fourth place, leaders and parents tend to be tolerant of youthful activity (often rowdy in character) because they know that the risk of having children "go English" is great.

Sanctions are not always uniformly enforced between old and young members and between persons of different occupations. An old man who was under the strain of having a chronically ill wife and who was generally thought to be slightly senile was the first to obtain battery-powered electricity in his house. His argument with the church officials was that in order to keep medications and dietary preparations for his sick wife, he must have a refrigerator. The incident forced a change in the community's *Ordnung*. Old people are frequently the first to be allowed privileges others do not have, such as indoor plumbing. The making of such exceptions may lead to community-wide acceptance of the innovation. An old, feeble man who needed to use the toilet several times a night built a small light fixture and switch into his toilet. The source of energy was flashlight batteries. Today in that community, battery lights are used on nightstands, and plumbing has been installed in many dwellings.

Persons who travel from their home community are expected to conform to the rules of their own district, but those who travel far from home, as for example the many older Amish persons who spend the winter months in Florida, sometimes deviate from the rules of their home church until they return. This temporary relief from the rules has made travel a popular and accepted alternative for many retired Amish couples.

Innovations that are accompanied by economic rewards have a greater chance of being accepted than do changes that are noneconomic in character. Innovations in styles of hair or clothing, or the taking of photographs, are examples of the latter type. On the other hand, persons engaged in nonfarming occupations such as carpentry, masonry, contracting, building, and sawmilling must make a living. These occupations require equipment and institutionalized means of communication and travel that are not allowed by the whole Amish community. The pay telephone just across the road from the Amish mill or cabinet shop is mainly used by the Amish proprietor. Utility and farm-machine companies that service the general farm population are knowledgeable about Amish rules, and adaptations are made so that benefits may be realized without bringing the sanctions of the church against any specific family. Amish persons who work in local factories or processing plants travel to and from work with the non-Amish. Such accepted patterns of behavior, which are directly related to economic rewards, tend to become institutionalized. Persons who are saving money to make a down payment on a farm are usually the ones who engage in this form of activity, which is accepted as temporary until they become established on a farm. But these diverse, "temporary" occupations are potential sources of change, especially where there is differential enforcement of the *Ordnung*.

Agricultural ideas and practices that are not visually perceivable are more likely to be accepted than are objects that have visual symbolic value. A new fertilizer or a new hybrid chicken will be more acceptable than a tractor or a farm truck. All these objects have economic values, and no one can object to a crop of hybrid corn as appearing "worldly." When hybrid seed first came on the market, it did not take the Amish long to adopt it. Contour farming was jokingly put aside as "book farming" three decades ago, but today it has been widely accepted.

The rules of a church district apply to all members, but change occurs when discipline is not uniformly enforced. The punishment that applies to the baptized member cannot apply to the unbaptized young man who wants an automobile. Renters, rather than owners of farms, are frequently the innovators and the agitators for the tractor. The well-established, traditional Amish farmer with a large family has less need for a tractor than the young couple faced with problems of labor, capital, and the necessity of financial success. Renters were often the first to engage in specialized farming, such as raising cash crops and poultry. In this way, prevailing farm practices and ideas were slowly but quietly accepted as normal.

MODERNIZATION

The term *modernization* here refers to the acceptance of technology and material culture, as distinguished from assimilation, meaning the absorption of the group into the dominant society. As an acculturation process, modernization implies the acceptance of electricity, telephones, automobiles, and artifacts but stops short of participation in the social functions of worldly society (religious, political, or status-enhancing clubs) or intermarriage with outsiders. Modernization has affected all Amish settlements in one way or another. In some, modernization fragmented the Amish into many affiliations (see Chapter 13), and in others the Amish preserved their way of life by moving away.

To the Old Order Amish, the automobile, as an object and as a symbol, represents "a way of thinking" that is forbidden by their charter. How is the *Ordnung* changed to legitimize the automobile? To illustrate the process, we will describe the case of a Pennsylvania Amish district which, to the surprise of outsiders, suddenly allowed its members to have automobiles. The news that automobiles "were allowed" soon spread through the entire region, and the secular community became accustomed to seeing bearded fathers driving their automobiles on the highways. Automobile dealers in nearby towns experienced a sudden boom in sales. This Amish church had voted almost unanimously in 1954 to allow automobiles.

Upon reconstructing the sequence of events that led to this decision, it becomes apparent that the decision was not reached as easily as taking a vote among the members. A number of events reaching back half a century combined with contemporary problems to produce this extraordinary development. Seceding from the "strict" *Meidung* church in 1911, this church had already relaxed its rules by making changes from the strictest Amish in the community. Although it retained the dress and the *Ordnung* generally, slight modifications were made over the years. Men began wearing buttons on work jackets and cut their hair shorter, single women were permitted to work as cleaning maids for non-Amish people, and tractors were adopted for farming. With the development of pneumatic tires and improved tractors with higher speeds, the Amish began using them on the road to pull wagons to town, run errands to neighbors, and for the daily delivery of milk to market. Children and boys became completely familiar with the mechanics and skills of driving a tractor.

It was common for Amish parents to engage licensed cab drivers, often Mennonite neighbors who spoke and understood the Amish dialect, to transport them to other states and communities. The Amish drove their carriages to the homes of the drivers to make the appointments. Cab drivers were booked in advance for trips to Ohio, Indiana, Iowa, or even as far west as California and Oregon. Short trips, often emergency in nature, such as trips to the doctor and hospital or to the county courthouse, were arranged by using a non-Amish neighbor's telephone. Use of the telephone became institutionalized among members of this church. Amish parents with a son (not yet old enough for baptism) who owned an automobile did not have need of the services of a cab driver. In some instances the young sons who owned automobiles and had no intention of becoming Amish joined nearby Mennonite churches. They could not be punished by *Meidung*, for no one can come under this sanction unless he has been baptized. Amish fathers who were not inclined to uphold the old rules of behavior helped their sons to finance the purchase of an automobile. The desire for the automobile became very apparent among the young men and the married nonfarming men who were employed in such occupations as milling, carpentry, masonry, and butchering. Farm hands ribbed their employers about the inconsistency of hitching up horses for road work when transportation was easier and more efficient with the tractor. Sons complained about the slowness of the horses, saying that they were too much trouble and that it was dangerous to drive a carriage on the open highway. This informal conversation and "egging" by younger members to Amish landowners, some of them ministers, over a period of several years appears to have set the stage for a favorable nod in the church. The verbalization of a forbidden norm was important in creating an atmosphere conducive to change.

But no amount of discussion on informal occasions could bring up the subject of automobiles for a vote in church. Formally there was nothing to discuss. The only way to own an automobile was to leave the Amish church and transfer to a Mennonite group. But these Amish did not want a different religion, just automobiles.

Early one spring a young man, a baptized member of a respected family, purchased an automobile. The youngster had secured a driving permit and drove his new possession to the farm of his parents. The whole family was shocked. The father objected to having the automobile on his property. After much persuasion the son returned the automobile to the dealer with the hopes of regaining it later.

A few days later a married man, employed in a nearby village, purchased an automobile. He kept it at his place of employment and commuted to and from the village on his farm tractor. The church officials deliberated as to a course of action. The man was advised to "put it away," meaning to sell the car, until the church could come to a unanimous decision. He refused the advice of the assembly and was excommunicated. Meanwhile a third member, a young married farmer, purchased an automobile, but he too was excommunicated. Many members were in favor of automobiles but were waiting for a change in the *Ordnung*. With the commission of these offenses, the officials had reason to bring the question of ownership of automobiles before the church. Though the offenders had to be punished for their disobedience, the question of whether or not to allow automobiles could now be formally discussed.

In the meantime, informal discussions continued among the members. Amish fathers conversed with each other informally, sometimes far into the night. In desperation, two of the excommunicated men shared their predicament with the bishop of a nearby Mennonite church. They applied for membership in the Mennonite church. The bishop advised caution in changing churches and suggested that the two men call an informal meeting of all the Amish members who wanted to have an automobile. The meeting was arranged and about thirty Amish persons came to hear what the Mennonite bishop had to say. The bishop read the Bible and prayed with the group. He then explained that people who join a new church because they want an automobile "usually do not help the church they jump into." He advised the group of Amish people to take the question to their own ministers to see if they could not come to some solution. The bishop's church was already a large one and he was weary of accepting former Amish members who wanted membership for no other reason than to have the liberty to own an automobile. The members went home and talked to their ministers. The attitude of the Mennonite bishop undoubtedly caused the Amish officials to come to a firm decision. He had helped to crystallize opinions among the Amish members and this brought pressure to bear on the Amish church.

The ordained men of the Amish church were forced to decide on a proper course of action, and it was up to the bishop to obtain unanimity among his fellow ordained men. By custom, recommendations brought to the assembled body must have the unanimous backing of all the ordained persons. The bishop in this church was a middle-aged man with considerable experience. When single, he had worked as a farm hand in the Midwestern states, had been drafted into conscientious-objector service, and had participated in the camp worship and Sunday School services there. This exposure to the wider society before his ordination to the office of bishop provided him with reasoned viewpoints. The views of his fellow ministers were compatible with his. The six ordained men did not oppose the oncoming automobile issue, and they made their recommendation to the assembly. The result of the automobile vote was practically unanimous, with only four old persons not giving their assent. (These four soon joined the Old Order Amish group in the community.) Members were instructed to buy only black automobiles or to have them painted black. Within a few weeks most of the members were coming to church in automobiles, and only a few of the older members continued to come in carriages. The acceptance of the automobile forced still other changes in this community of Amish. The young people, who had formerly courted with horse and carriage and in traditional ways, now had many new freedoms. Overnight, a people who had been limited to travel in horse-drawn vehicles were thrust into a territory that included much of the eastern United States. One woman who opposed the automobile vote said: "Where will this lead to, if our young people are given the privilege of going wherever they want?" The forces of adjustment that were necessary in this small community within a few weeks, an adjustment that in the secular society required half a century, gave rise to other intense pressures for accelerated change.

Today this church, the Valley View Amish Mennonite Church, in Mifflin County, Pennsylvania, belongs to the Beachy Amish group (see Figure 15, division 6). The group erected a meeting house and now also conducts Sunday School. The church has modernized but has not been assimilated.

The automobile was the object that forced a change in the *Ordnung* of the church just described. Such a major change was preceded by a relaxing of discipline in a number of other areas of life, even before the present generation. The idea of farm efficiency that prevailed in the general American society found acceptance among the middle-aged Amish farm couples who were in need of "tractor farming." The widespread practice of hiring automobiles (with drivers) and the use of tractors on the road were institutionalized before the change came about. Patterns of travel and communication had developed to the point that they could no longer be maintained under the old norms. Stress resulted, the rules were violated, and eventually the rules were changed. Change among the Amish is often less dramatic than was the case in this Pennsylvania community, and it is rather rare that so nearly unanimous a decision was possible.

OVERCONFORMITY

Those opposed to modernization may respond in negative or opposing ways. They suffer from the prospect of too much change, and consequently seek to delay the influence of change on their lives by calling for stricter rules. Such persons find it difficult to adjust to change, even though they believe it may be logical or unavoidable. Imminent decisions concerning issues not emotionally acceptable to them may create emotional blocks. This is well illustrated by what happened in the Amish church that accepted the automobile. As one of the participants explained: "The automobile seemed progressive to our Old Order thinking. Our older people went along with the decision. . . . Theoretically they could see it, but to be part of it was quite a different thing. It caused quite a stir. Ten years before, they had resolved within themselves never to be anything but Old Order. They had changed in the meantime; they had to accept the decision, but they didn't want to. They began to stress customs they had never thought of emphasizing before, like parting the hair, which had not been mentioned for years."

An Amish adult man who overconforms to the rules will let his hair grow longer than the *Ordnung* requires just "to play it safe." Older members and ministers frequently adhere to stricter practices than is required, just for the sake of avoiding any possible criticism. Some of the aged Amish persons of very conservative groups have observed that the hair is worn longer today than it was fifty years ago. The most conservative Old Order Amish groups today may in fact be groups that have become more conservative by overconforming through the years, just as other groups have become more progressive. There is a kind of aggressive humility in seeing who can conform the most. However, sons may not have longer hair than their father. All such actions tend toward overconformity and greater withdrawal.

When there is a crisis in the church, young people have noted how parents tend to become more rigid. A young man who had been excommunicated from the church for advocating assurance of salvation remembered that when he was a boy his mother normally sang gospel songs in English while working at home. After "all this church trouble got stirred up," he said, "she stopped all English singing at home. I was the only boy that had left the Amish church for a long time, and my parents could not stand to think that it was their boy." In this instance, the parents avoided all signs of being "English" that might be interpreted as lending support to his views. The boy also observed that his parents became stricter in their relationships with other members who had been put under the ban.

After returning home from the preaching service, one boy checked his Bible to see if the preacher had quoted it properly. He said: "I told my mother I did not agree with one point. She said I should not find fault with the sermon. She did not think it right to look it up in the Bible to see if it was true. If the preachers said it, she believed it was true. From that time on, I felt my mother was extreme." Overconformity requires an uncritical attitude toward the preachers as well as toward the traditional practices. In the opinion of one informant, "The preachers who do not have very much depth or insight into the Bible make up for it by teaching tradition."

Some Amish who suffer from the prospect of too much change
are prone to overconform to tradition. A boy and a girl
in a traditional Ohio group.

MOVEMENT TO NEW SETTLEMENTS

Unfavorable reactions to change are manifested by schisms or migration over what appear to the outsider to be trivial questions. Amish history is a history of divisions and migration. The many divisions are possible because of the sacredness with which the Amish consider their mode of life, and because of the abundance of land and the freedom of movement in America. Divisions prevent change in that they exclude those who would be innovators. The question of shunning, the degree of strictness with which it should be practiced, has formed the basis of many Amish divisions (see Chapter 4, under "Exclusion and Social Avoidance"). Where strict shunning has not been the policy, it is generally acknowledged that modernization and outside influences have been the greatest.

Bishops who have a broad perspective and who know the devastating results of division use their influence to avoid issues that might develop into splits. The question of whether to allow meeting houses caused considerable tension among the Amish from 1860 to 1890. One region where the Amish built meeting houses but kept the Old Order way of life in other respects was Somerset County, Pennsylvania. In 1880 and 1881 two districts voted favorably on having one meeting house. After the meeting house was built, the question remained as to what kind of seats to install. There was a difference of opinion: some thought backless benches were sufficient; others felt that the benches should have backs. During the week a few of the carpenters quickly but quietly built seats with backs and put them in the church. When the people arrived on Sunday an opponent said: "We have to do something." With a sense of humor the bishop replied: "Ich denk sie hen uns gebodde" ("I think they have beat us to it"). A division was avoided.

Seldom are the unanimous suggestions of the ordained men overruled by the lay members in council, but it can happen. A member who had been steaming tobacco beds with equipment mounted on a truck had been seen driving the truck when he was supposed to have hired a driver for it. When the driver was temporarily absent the owner would sometimes drive it short distances himself. A member complained to the preachers, who in turn recommended excommunication. Other members, many of whom had hired the services of the accused member, were opposed to excommunication. The bishop was "very understanding" and the decision was modified from excommunication to confession of a fault. What might have developed into a serious cleavage of the group was thereby forestalled.

When unanimity on an issue cannot be achieved in a local church, migration is another form of adjustment. The opportunity for family heads to move from a district that is "too strict" to one that has fewer restrictions, and/or from one that is "too worldly" to one that is "keeping the old faith," prevents many potential conflicts from arising. If a member has difficulty keeping one aspect of the *Ordnung*, he may find conditions easier elsewhere. Ordained leaders have less freedom to move from one community to another, but some movement cannot be prevented and is often peacefully achieved through consultation with the officials in the recipient community. A stricter-than-ordinary bishop in one settlement was allowed by common consent of the ordained to expand his community geographically in the direction of a non-Amish settlement. Thus the "stricter" family heads moved to his territory, creating a very odd-shaped community.

When Amish migration occurs the outsider is inclined to interpret it as a search for new land where prices are more reasonable. While this may be true, the underlying motivation is often the resolution of a religious problem. The migrations to Oxford County, Ontario, from Pennsylvania, Maryland, and Ohio were precipitated by disagreements in the large, well-established settlements. In commenting about this movement, a father in Lancaster County said: "Those people want to go back fifty years, but I don't think it can be done." The major settlements in Missouri and Wisconsin were instigated by conservative-minded elements that did not wish to tolerate milking machines or to allow their members to work in factories.

Many fathers who realize that the *Ordnung* is "not being kept the way it should" bring pressure to bear on the bishop to excommunicate the offenders. In the case of boys who own automobiles secretly, one bishop has taken the position that "we must be patient." The only alternative for those who cannot "be patient" is to move to other communities.

The expansion of the Amish into the southern part of Lancaster County was predominantly a conservative movement. The Amish group in Elgin County, Ontario, is made up of families from different states who have similar attitudes and are interested in re-creating a "clean" Christian community. They have made it clear to other Amish that they wish to get away from smoking, drinking, party games, and bed courtship, and that they want to have a private school, as well as a Sunday School, for their children. Yet they are opposed to tractor farming and the automobile. Their leaders are aggressive in writing and defending their practices. The Amish in Grey County, Ontario, are an offshoot of the Swartzendruber group in Ohio, which took a firm stand against bundling. The leaders of this group had objected to this old custom in their home community in Ohio. Over a century ago some of the Somerset County, Pennsylvania, Amish moved to Iowa for similar reasons.

Without freedom of movement the Amish would encounter serious difficulties in trying to resolve and maintain the essential elements of their community life. Still, the decision to sell a farm and relocate is not an easy one, particularly when the farm is a very productive one and the family is large.

CONTROL OF THE SOCIALIZATION EXPERIENCE

Early Training. The Amish know that early childhood training and community control of education are absolutely essential for the maintenance of a distinctive way of life. Worldly success and worldly standards are a threat to Amish society when their children are placed in schools that promote these values. For over one hundred years the Amish remained with the public school system. They did not establish their own schools until they were threatened by the monocultural public school, which in essence would not grant them an identity of their own and would not permit them to be raised as both Amishmen and Americans. The most uncertain period began with the onset of the school consolidation movement (1937) and continued until the U.S. Supreme Court decision in *Wisconsin* v. *Yoder* upheld the Amish school system in 1972. This period of defensive structuring, in which the Amish had to cope with an uncertain future, challenged their institutions and resulted in greater cultural vigor.

When the Amish began to withdraw from the public school system to set up their own private schools, their neighbors and state officials alike believed that it would be impossible for them to give their children an adequate education. The schools had very little equipment, and neither their teachers nor their board members were high-school graduates. The schools were financed entirely by the Amish. The Amish schools are not intended to train scientists, businessmen, or musicians, nor do they prepare people for upward mobility in the modern industrial complex. They have, however, proved successful when judged by public school standards (standardized tests), independent school certification standards (goal attainment), and the traditional Amish community.[4] Amish schools prepare the children for life as Amish persons in the twentieth century. The children aspire to the occupational roles available to them, they succeed in them, and they enjoy their chosen vocations. Amish schools are successful in that the teacher and the pupils understand and identify with one another.

The Amish are committed to the assumption that learning should be practical, related to life, and should lead to social responsibility. They hold that schooling that is committed primarily to abstract and analytical learning is useless to them. Social cohesiveness, rather than intellectual creativity or critical analysis, is the goal of Amish schooling. Amish education emphasizes cooperation, responsibility, and humility. Facts that are learned, are learned thoroughly. The basic conditions for education are created with very limited educational equipment when trust, respect, and honest needs and wishes are shared by teacher and pupil.

---

4. For achievement-test scores, see John A. Hostetler and Gertrude E. Huntington, *Children in Amish Society: Socialization and Community Education* (New York: Holt, Rinehart & Winston, 1971), pp. 80–96.

Adult Socialization. The need for literature appropriate to the Amish way of thinking became obvious with the founding of Amish schools. The small number of older Amish periodicals are still read, but new ones have been introduced to support new institutions, new situations, and a larger, more varied readership. The main means of printed communication remains *The Budget*, founded in 1890, and to a very limited extent the *Herold der Wahrheit*, a German-English publication first printed in 1910. According to its masthead, *The Budget* is "A Weekly Newspaper Serving the Sugarcreek Area and Amish-Mennonite Communities Throughout the Americas." It is printed in Sugarcreek, Ohio, by a non-Amish publisher.[5] The paper has been an important institution, serving as the major means of communication among all Amish settlements, informing them of agricultural activities, visits and travels, sicknesses, accidents, and weddings. With the appearance of *Die Botschaft* (The Message) in 1974 (published by Berkshire Publishers, Lancaster, Pennsylvania), Amish readers gained a periodical that is written by "approved" Old Order persons (Amish or Mennonite) and that is relatively free of objectionable advertising. Some *Budget* writers are former Amish members, and since some of them are under the ban and use their writings to "liberate" the more orthodox Amish, the Amish readers wanted an alternative. A committee of deacons is responsible for "keeping out [of *Die Batschaft*] the writings of unsound writers, especially those who have left the faith of our fathers."[6]

With the formation of Pathway Publishers in 1964, new periodicals and books written and produced by the Amish themselves began to appear. The planning for this enterprise began in a wheatfield, as sheaves were being loaded for threshing, when two Amish farmers, David Wagler and Joseph Stoll, discussed the possibility of starting an Amish publishing company. Both men knew of old books that they believed should be reprinted. At the same time, an Amish minister had written a manuscript, "Worth Dying For," and was seeking a publisher. Wagler decided to open a bookstore and mail-order service in his farm home. The following year a third Amish farmer, Jacob Eicher, an experienced operator of threshing machines and sawmills, volunteered to operate a printing press. Near Aylmer, Ontario, the nonprofit organization was formed in 1964, and Levi J. Lambright

5. For an analysis of this weekly, see William I. Schreiber, *Our Amish Neighbors* (Chicago: University of Chicago Press, 1962), pp. 145–72. For articles by Harvey ...:: David Luthy, see Selected References.

6. *Family Life,* December 1977, p. 22.

of Lagrange, Indiana, offered to become the distributor for its publications in the United States.

The offices of Pathway Publishers are housed in a single building on Rural Route 4, Aylmer, Ontario. There are no electric wires running from the community's power line to the building, for the presses and "electric" typewriters are operated with hydraulic fluid from a diesel motor. Printed in an edition of 5,500 copies, the first book published, *Worth Dying For* (an imaginative narrative based on Waldensian persecution), was sold out before a year had elapsed. *The Mighty Whirlwind*, an account of the 1965 Palm Sunday tornadoes in Indiana and Michigan by David Wagler, reached a distribution of 12,000 copies within a few months. Since the founding of Pathway, over one hundred books and pamphlets have been published, including a steady seller, *Amish Cooking*.

In addition to publishing books by Amish authors, classical Anabaptist literature, and a catalog, Pathway publishes a school curriculum, including Pathway Readers—a complete set of readers for grades 1 to 8 that combines workbooks and teachers' guides. The management has hired additional staff members (all of them Amish), including editors, writers, and illustrators (some of them single girls), which brings the total number of employees to eight. The principal staff consists of farmers and laborers whose work in publishing is part-time. In conjunction with its writing and historical research, Pathway has developed a comprehensive Amish Historical Library under the direction of David Luthy. Although not owned by the Old Order Amish church, Pathway is careful to operate within the pattern of its constituency, serving "plain" or Old Order Amish and Old Order Mennonite groups.

Three monthly periodicals are published by Pathway, each of which has a circulation of over 13,000. The *Blackboard Bulletin* is directed to those involved with Amish schools—teachers, parents, and board members. The journal carries letters, stories, and articles that are relevant to the maintenance of Amish and Mennonite schools. *Young Companion* (formerly *Ambassador of Peace*), a paper for young people, was initiated for young men of draft age who served in various places during peacetime conscription. Today it contains short stories, serials, discussions, and editorials. *Family Life* is "dedicated to the promotion of Christian living among the plain people." Most of its stories and articles are written by the Amish themselves and include articles on new settlements and migrations, human-interest and historical articles, recipes, interpretations of world events, housekeeping, a page for shut-ins, poems, puzzles, and the reactions of readers to various ethical problems.

The founding of a publishing house by and for the Old Order Amish people was a significant accomplishment. The organizers were mature men, heads of households who themselves had moved to Elgin County, Ontario, from various places in the United States to form a "clean" community. As spiritually concerned individuals, they combined their skills and formulated their plans with the same sympathetic attitude that had guided the editor of *Herold der Wahrheit*. Their community lacked the older ethnic element that characteristically regards new ventures with suspicion. Most, but not all, of the Amish are pleased with their publication work.

In Pennsylvania, the Gordonville Print Shop has served the Amish by reprinting their family genealogies, tracts, and broadsides. The firm also reprints old public school texts and curricula for the Amish schools. As a member of the Amish School Committee and the Old Order Amish Steering Committee, the proprietor, Andrew S. Kinsinger, publishes the rules for Amish schools and the minutes of committees on which he serves.

Renewed interest in Amish history is reflected in the publication of a monthly periodical, *The Diary*, which was begun in 1969 "by a group of Amish brethren in Lancaster County, Pennsylvania, dedicated to the preservation of fundamental movements of our church in America as well as Old Order religious literature and its virtues."[7] The periodical is produced and printed in an Amish print shop known as Pequea Publishers and is operated by Joseph F. Beiler and his family near Gordonville. It carries community news, crop and weather reports, births, marriages, baptisms, ordinations, obituaries, and migrations. It prints primary source material such as old letters and documents of the early Amish settlements and genealogical accounts of various Amish families. *The Diary* also communicates the major findings of Joseph Beiler and his network of researchers, who have set out to find the early Amish homesteads, deeds, land records, wills, letters, and lore connected with the first settlements in America. The interest of geneticists in family records has further stimulated the Amish effort to record vital statistics and issue directories of the Amish communities.

What is the net effect of this new literature on Amish society? The Amish person of yesteryear is not the Amish person of today. The contemporary Amish person, a product of the Amish school rather than the public school, reads Amish periodicals. A new self-consciousness is being created. Clearly the farm and family magazines produced in the outside world, with their exposure of the human

7. Masthead, *The Diary* (Gordonville, Pa.).

body, consumer appeal, and symbols of violence, are out of character for the Amish people. Faced with these challenges, they have produced a literature which is appropriate to their circumstances.

The new thrust in Amish publishing is to articulate many of the assumptions of Amish culture that have never been written down. Older basic beliefs are being reexamined and new interpretations for changing circumstances are presented. Fiction, true stories by anonymous authors, and question-and-answer columns are techniques used in all Pathway periodicals. Reader response is of great interest. A column entitled "What Do You Think?" has covered in-law troubles, zodiac signs and superstitions, the use of nicknames, unwanted baby gifts, new settlements, what to do with offensive salesmen, women working in the fields, vitamin addiction, tourists, borrowing, working in factories, hired girls, hunting, bed-wetting, use of tobacco, conveniences, and other sensitive topics. Some of the Amish object to having too much of their way of life in print. Readers are sensitized to customs they never before considered "bad." Pathway expressed its view in this manner: "We at Aylmer feel very strongly that our church is not becoming a 'dead' culture; therefore, we try to instruct our young people in the whys and wherefores of all practices." The thrust toward greater literacy and articulation may meet the needs of the present, but in the long run, like previous movements of enlightenment, articulation may tend to undermine the nonverbal character of the Amish religion.

APPROPRIATE TECHNOLOGY

In modern industrial society there is an irresistible trend, dictated by technological thinking, for units of production to become larger and larger. The Amish have responded by adapting to a technology that is appropriate to their scale.[8] When tractor power overtook horse power in American agriculture, the Amish remained with horse power. For their farm equipment they relied on used horse-drawn machinery. When old farm implements could no longer be secured at farm sales or in junk yards, the Amish began to produce them themselves. When gasoline and kerosene lanterns could no longer be bought, they began to manufacture them. When the making of harnesses and carriages became obsolete, and when blacksmithing

---

8. The Amish practice the ideals so ably presented by E. F. Schumacher in *Small is Beautiful* (New York: Harper Colophon Books, 1973), though neither seems to have found the other.

An Amish service center that also houses a harness,
saddle, and shoe store

shops were rendered extinct in the American economy, the Amish
took over these enterprises for themselves.

Today there is a thriving enterprise of small shops and industry
in the Amish community. Products that can no longer be bought in
the mass market are made in Amish shops, most of them located on
Amish farms and operated by Amish families. An estimated four
hundred Amish establishments provide for the nonfarming Amishman "a job at home with or near his family, self-dependent, self-
supporting, making, repairing or selling a product that he knows is
useful."[9] Listed in the *Old Order Shop and Service Directory* are accountants, bake shops, battery service centers, bee supplies, blacksmiths, bookbinderies, buggy shops, butcher shops, cabinet shops,
carpentry shops, casting and foundry works, cheese houses, clock and
watch repair shops, country stores, dry goods stores, engine shops,
farm equipment suppliers and repair, and many others. One
appliance firm in the large Ohio Amish community issues a mail-order
catalog entitled *The Good Neighbor Heritage Catalog: Merchandise*

9. Preface to *Old Order Shop and Service Directory of the Old Order Society
in the United States and Canada*, 1st ed. (Gordonville, Pa.: Joseph F. Beiler, Compiler, November 1977).

That Reflects an Undying Culture, a Reverence for Tradition, and Meets Today's Needs.[10] Like *The Whole Earth Catalog* of the back-to-earth movement, it provides access to many tools, rendered obsolete in the larger American society, that are still functional in the Amish community.

The development of a technology that is suited to the scale and thinking of the Amish has enriched their culture and their social arrangements. Labor-intensive activities are performed best by small groups on or near the Amish farm homes. These decentralized industries have rendered the Amish more self-sufficient and less dependent on the outside world for services and manufactured goods. Their own enterprises accommodate diverse skills, and for those who cannot obtain a farm or who do not wish to farm, these provide a means of livelihood within the Amish community.

The machine metaphor, stressing bigger and more efficient operations in worldly society, stands in sharp contrast to Amish thinking about the use of tools. The logic of expanded technology points toward infinite industrial growth and infinite energy consumption. The energy crisis is for the Amish a crisis not of supply but of use, not of technology but of morality. By carefully restricting the use of machine-developed energy, the Amish "have become the only true masters of technology."[11] The Amish have problems, but with respect to energy and the balancing of human life with machines, they have mastered one of the contradictions so puzzling to modern society. By holding technology at a distance, by exercising restraint and moderation, and by accepting limitations and living within them, the Amish have maintained the integrity of their family and community life. They have escaped many of the noxious side effects of ambitious technology—haste, aimlessness, distraction, violence, waste, and disintegration.

10. Lehman Hardware and Appliances, Kidron, Ohio.
11. The quote and the ideas suggested here are from Wendell Berry, *The Unsettling of America: Culture and Agriculture* (New York: Avon Books, 1977), p. 95.

CHAPTER 18

The Discourse with Survival

MANY OUTSIDERS perceive the Amish as an anachronism, a people misplaced in time, or an ethnic community that will eventually be assimilated into the mainstream of American life. Social theorists have assumed that it is only a matter of time before the Amish will become absorbed into the dominant society. Amish survival has been explained largely on the basis of a static sociological model. Amish continuity has been attributed to social and geographic isolation, agrarianism, distinctive dress and language, and religious devotion. But contrary to expectations, the Amish not only have survived but have more than doubled in number in the past twenty-five years. The Amish population is larger now than it has ever been in its history.

Will the Amish be able to continue their distinct way of life much as they have in the past? The future of Amish society will be discussed here in the context of social discourse, i.e., from the viewpoint of the Amish themselves. Amish survival is a dialectic process. There is a constant dialogue among the Amish themselves on points they consider important for survival. Each community is constantly striving to resolve its problems by weighing its heritage against its needs. Bound by a common tradition, each local community attempts to resolve the problem of achieving community self-realization within the limitations of its charter. The dialogue of what is good for the community and what is a threat runs through all of Amish history and is reflected in *Ordnung* and practice.

THE AMISH VIEW OF THE FUTURE

The Amish are oriented to the past, though they live in the present. Their past is alive in their present. They do not ignore what may happen in their earthly future and they anticipate heaven after death. They accept the biblical teaching of the end of the world and the great judgment, but they are not preoccupied with waiting for the return of Christ or with speculating about the nature of life after death. The best preparation for the end of the world is faithfulness to the believing community, which they express by going about their daily work and duties. The Amish stress "not knowing the time of his [Christ's] coming," yet acknowledge that one must be ready, for "one will be taken and the other will be left" (Matt. 24:40). When the nuclear reactor accident occurred near Harrisburg, Pennsylvania, in 1979, most Amish were unaware of the event or the danger until they were approached by reporters. Similarly, when the end of the world comes, the Amish hope to be found doing their normal duties faithfully.

Theological, denominational, and revivalistic terms are conspicuously absent from the Amish vocabulary. The Amish have escaped the influence of many religious movements in American life—the revivals of the nineteenth and twentieth centuries, premillennialism, fundamentalism, and dispensationalism—by living behind boundaries of separation from the world. Their central beliefs oppose those movements whose military style thrives on conquest, converts, and worldly progress.[1]

As in the early Anabaptist-Mennonite view, the kingdom of Christ is for the Amish a reality within the disciplined and gathered community. The best preparation for the future is obedience to the community of personal believers who have been awakened and called by God and who accept the gift of God as their spiritual possession. Like other brotherhood-type communities, including the Quakers, the Amish conduct themselves in a quiet, moderate, and eminently conscientious way.[2]

---

1. Amish attitudes toward Protestant movements are similar to those of the Mennonites in eastern Pennsylvania described by Beulah S. Hostetler in "Franconia Mennonite Conference and American Protestant Movements, 1840–1940" (Ph.D. diss., University of Pennsylvania, 1977).

2. For the structure of conduct, see Max Weber, *The Protestant Ethic and the Spirit of Capitalism* (New York: Charles Scribner's Sons, 1958), p. 149.

Since both rejection of the world and blameless conduct are important to salvation, the conditions for maintaining the redemptive community are subject to perpetual discourse. The maintenance of the church-community is a delicate function, for its priorities are unity, sacrificial suffering, brotherly love, humility, and peaceableness. The future of the church-community is never ensured by making a more stringent *Ordnung* or by allowing each member to disregard the views of others. As corporate offering to God, the believers constantly strive to be worthy as "a bride for the groom." Constant communication and the search for consensus attune the members to the group idea of what constitutes humility as distinguished from pride, and brotherly love as distinguished from love of the world. Thus the language of consensus is crucial to the maintenance of group harmony, identity, and solidarity. Each community or region has its own discourse, which may vary slightly from the others. Here we will deal with observations that apply generally to the Old Order Amish in North America rather than to one particular community.

THE SILENT DISCOURSE

The Amish dialectic is suspended between the impulse of community self-realization and the desire for individual fulfillment. The Amish themselves recognize these tendencies as "old order" vs. "new order." On a deeper level this dialectic can be described as *silent discourse* versus *verbal discourse*.[3] Social relationships are greatly affected by these two ways of thinking and perceiving, as we will demonstrate. Silent and verbal forces usually meet head-on among the Old Order Amish just before a division takes place. The two tendencies are manifested in the Amish orientation to the future and what they do about it.

Silent discourse prevails where people are deeply involved with one another. The collective awareness is developed to such an extent that it becomes a religious experience, and it can be neither uttered in sound nor communicated in words. People committed to the *silent way* are highly integrated, for whole, unstated realms of culture act as extremely effective conveyors of information. Loyalties are concrete and people work together to settle their problems. By screening the flow of information that comes into the community, and by developing a sensitivity to signs and symbols, the society expresses its traditions in life rather than in words or written records. Since this kind of re-

3. Silent vs. verbal discourse may be compared to Edward T. Hall's concept of "high-" vs. "low-" context cultures; see pages 18–21 above.

ligious experience cannot be communicated verbally, other forms of expression are sought. Those forms are human conduct. The sparseness of words implies neither ineptness nor lack of intelligence.

In Amish life, silence has many functions. Amish conversions tend to be silent rather than vocal. The Amish worship service begins with silence. Between hymns there are long periods of silence. The whole assembly kneels for silent prayer; the praying ends with a scuffling, or a clearing of the throat by the minister. Prayers before and after meals are periods of uninterrupted silence. Sundays at home are spent in relative silence—hammering, building, and other workday sounds are prohibited. Relaxed conversation, resting, and walking are silences that blend with attitudes of worship.

Silence is a defense against sudden change, an appropriate response to fright or supernatural intervention. Silence is appropriate during severe thunderstorms or in moments of disaster, accident, or death. Early-morning or late-night scenes on the farm, in spring or in winter, in sunshine, rain, or snow, with animals and hay under cover of roof, lend the environment varied shades of silence.

Silence is a way of living and forgiving, a way of embracing the community with charity and the offender with affection. The member who confesses all before the church is forgiven, and the sin is never spoken of again. Silence can aid in the restoration of good human relationships. By remaining silent when others would ask questions, one avoids the ugly subjects that would introduce disharmony. Silence in the face of hooligan behavior by the young allows adults to absorb the faults of the immature. When cheated by another Amish person in a shady financial deal, an Amish farmer may prefer to remain silent for fear of creating a scene.

In Amish life, silence is an active force, not a sign of introspection. Silence is used not in opposition to others, but with others, for the individual at work or worship faces the world objectively. The person who is possessed of silence (as distinguished from solitude) lives above verbal contradictions. The Amish are spared many of the arguments about words of Scripture or theology over which others haggle. For them, absolutes do not exist in words, whether in creeds or in position papers, for all such arguments are silenced by the character and example of Christ himself.

The Amish person who is possessed of silence does not need consciously to order everything.[4] Much is ordered without conscious knowledge, and in silence there is room to work out contradictions. Silence is a resource that is always at one's disposal. Many noises,

4. Max Picard, *The World of Silence* (Chicago: Henry Regnery Co., 1952), p. 66.

including "needless words," are a displeasure to God, for once they are spoken, words can never be taken back, never stricken from the record. They will surface again on the day of judgment. Swearing cannot make one hair black or white; a simple "yes" or "no" is sufficient, and "anything beyond this comes from the evil one" (Matt. 5:36, 37).

There is the silence of pacifism, of turning the other cheek, which reaches back to the martyrs and to Christ himself, who refused to answer the question of Pilate and who suffered silently on the cross. When confused by a bureaucrat, outwitted by a regulation, or cursed by an outsider, the Amish person answers with silence.

Verbal discourse, or preoccupation with words, whether spoken or written, prevails among those who emphasize literacy, rationality, and individuality. Study, reasoning, exegesis, and record-keeping lead to a way of thinking that is primarily linear in emphasis. Instead of collective unity there is a multiplicity of thought, which leads to individualistic revelations and knowledge. This way of thinking has been termed "low-context" because information is restricted primarily to verbal communication.[5]

We will compare the impact of silent discourse in three areas of concern: the meaning of separation, the scale of the community, and attitudes toward seekers.

ON THE MEANING OF SEPARATION

The Old Order Amish face the problems of reconciling the doctrine of separation with the practical problem of existence. Every human community must either resolve the question of community self-realization within its environment, perish, or move on to another locale. On the one hand, the Amish perceive as their highest goal eternal life, which they seek to achieve by conforming to the ways of the early Christians as described in the New Testament, including separation from the unbelieving world. On the other hand, the Amish are faced with the existential problem of a natural existence in time and space, in an environment where temperature, soils, and climatic conditions vary, and in a modern society where economic competition and profit are necessary conditions for survival.

Those Amish who are committed to *silent discourse* emphasize making a living from the soil and keeping the traditions of the past insofar as these are possible. The practice of separation is supported by other aspects of the Amish charter—the vow of obedience, the

Ordnung, and the practice of exclusion and avoidance. The consensus is supported by rules that keep out those technologies and disruptive influences that are perceived to be a threat to social solidarity. The rules of separation forbid ownership of field tractors, automobiles, electricity, or telephones in the home. In circumstances where these conveniences cannot be avoided, limited use may be permitted, as in an emergency, but habitual use is forbidden or discouraged.

Persons of the silent persuasion are emotionally committed to the doctrine and practice of separation. Not only do they think of themselves as "a peculiar people," but they practice separation in the mundane affairs of making a living. There is little ambiguity between church and world. The world is progressing, and since such progress is based on the knowledge of the unbelieving world, it can only mean that the world has forsaken God. When individuals fall prey to the temptations of the world, or turn to more worldly churches, the people of the silent persuasion firm their boundaries and withdraw even more from perceived worldly influences.

Those Amish who tend toward *verbal discourse* do not emphasize traditional ways of living, though they live by Amish customs. For them, separation from the world means spiritual rather than physical separation. Where making a living from the soil is considered impossible, the charter is no longer interpreted in this manner. The symbols of separation, distinctive dress, and grooming change markedly as the boundary between church and world becomes more ambiguous. The use of tractors instead of horses in the field symbolizes a more loosely drawn boundary. Midwestern communities, where farms are larger, have tended to permit the tractor for field work, but in some, only steel wheels are permitted. Such changes require greater capital investment. High-speed tractors with trailers soon compete favorably with horses on the hard-surfaced roads. In many Eastern communities there is a trend toward greater use of mechanized dairy equipment, including diesel-operated milkers and coolers.

Changes in clothing styles are verbalized on grounds of function. Among the young, change is evident in the wearing of store-bought suspenders, sweaters with zippers and buttons, and (among the young boys in winter) warm caps rather than rimmed hats. Secularization in apparel is greater among men than among women, and is more advanced among the young than among the older people. The outer garments of women are homemade. Changes in women's apparel have been confined largely to what is worn under the outer garment; underclothes were the first garments bought commercially. While the young men turn away from farm work, many single women turn to domestic housework in the town or in nearby cities. Given the attractive wages offered in "English" homes and the availability of buses, many young women are attracted to employment in villages and towns. Living-in with "English" people during the week may not be approved, but it is tolerated by parents who themselves are not farmers.

Amish of the verbal persuasion are influenced by greater contact with outgroups, by an awareness and concern for people outside the Amish boundaries. The charter of separation is modified to permit renewed study and informal discussion of the Bible. With such a slight change in world view comes greater personal freedom, an opportunity for intellectual activity, and physical mobility. According to this view, the Amish are not "a chosen people" any more than are other people who try to live by the teachings of the Bible. With the emphasis on an open mind to study and learn from others there emerges a readiness to think, evaluate, and critically examine propositions. Bible-study groups or secret prayer groups may emerge. Verbal discourse tends to produce two types of subgroups. One, a renewal effort, aims to maintain its identity within the tradition. The problem is how to keep new wine in old bottles. The other, a self-hate group, seeks to demoralize and abolish the traditional system.

Greater verbal orientation is reflected in sermon and preaching styles. There is a reaction to the traditional chanted sermon. Breaking with the tradition of secluded eyes and a rhythmic pattern, the verbally oriented preacher faces individuals in his audience eye to eye. His delivery is forceful. He may wander from his standing position as much as from four to eight feet for the sake of emphasis. He may step forward or backward or place his hands on the shoulders of a brother seated nearby. He is more inclined to use illustrations from contemporary life than from the Bible. Bible verses are quoted in full. He appears confident of himself, and many more English and mixed words creep into his delivery.

The tendency to use the English language develops with greater verbal facility. English words and phrases are adopted in sermons and on ceremonial occasions. The problem is twofold: It is hard for the minister to express new ideas in the old forms, and a decreasing familiarity with the German language makes it hard for the member to grasp the meaning. Dialect words are at first substituted in sermons for such English terms as *surely, accident, condition, peaceful, absolutely, flood, judgment, chance,* and *disappointment.* English words and idioms are also used with a German prefix, as in "Er hat unser sins aus [ge] blot" ("He hath blotted out our sins"), "Noah hat Gott nicht [aus] figur [a] kenna aber war gehorsum" ("Noah could not figure out God but was obedient"), or "Viel Leit heiligs daag hen religion awwer ken salvation" (Many people today have religion but no salvation"). The inability to use either standard German or English in its entirety introduces linguistic stress and ambiguity. When the language of the world is used to express sacred concepts, separation is rendered ambiguous.

The formal breaking point between those who practice silent discourse and those who favor verbal discourse comes when there is concern for "lost souls," open interest in "assurance of salvation," and missionary activity. The Old Order Amish are sometimes regarded as "a prospective mission field to whom the Gospel should be preached" by former Amish members with a verbal orientation. One Mennonite pastor cautioned his fellow pastors not to receive Amish applicants into their congregation too hastily, advising that "pastors should thoroughly indoctrinate them in the plan of salvation, of the grace of God, of faith and the Christian life, and root out the legalistic and negative thinking that has resulted from being under Amish discipline."

The Amish, it should be noted, have simply perpetuated the quiet forms of Anabaptism by defining salvation as obedience to community as it is rooted in the Gospel accounts. Many Mennonites who are descendants of the Anabaptists have shifted from Anabaptism toward Protestantism, with its emphasis on individual salvation as epitomized in the writings of the Apostle Paul. Thus a Mennonite pastor may feel that Mennonites have more in common with evangelical Protestants than with Amish. The question is well stated by Friedmann: "Is the Gospel to be understood through Paul, or is Paul to be understood through the Gospel?"[6] The Amish person simply understands *Nachfolge* ("discipleship") as commitment to love the community, while the view of Paul and much of Protestantism starts with sin, emphasizing experience and verbalization. The latter stresses personal enjoyment, while the former teaches submission and quiet suffering. Both emphases "should meet each other frequently," says Friedmann,[7] but this antipathy explains the diversity between community and individualistic tendencies.

THE SCALE OF THE COMMUNITY

Each Amish community faces the problem of fulfillment as a human group within the range of its limited potentialities and possibilities, including size and scale. The constant striving to resolve problematic

6. Robert Friedmann, *Mennonite Piety through the Centuries* (Goshen, Ind.: Mennonite Historical Society, 1949), p. 85.
7. Ibid.

Technology and convenience are held in check to maximize
the strength of family and community. This motorized hay baler
is pulled by horses.

situations by means of available natural and human resources, and
by means of the community's own unique local heritage, accounts for
differing perception patterns, and thus for variation in the practice
of silent and verbal discourse. In the Amish community, as in others,
the capacity to build a community is limited by man's own capacity
to integrate his experiences.

In terms of population, the Amish were a small society half a
century ago, when no settlement numbered more than a few hundred
people. Today, many Amish settlements are still small in scale, but
their most densely populated regions can no longer be classed as
small in terms of maximizing primary relationships. The three largest
settlements number from ten to twelve thousand persons. While the
lines along which their patterns of anonymity develop are different
from those of the larger society, they are similar in kind. The small
Amish settlements show less evidence of disorder than do the larger
settlements.

When a church district becomes too large, it is divided into two
meetings to prevent the ceremonial unit from becoming unmanage-
able. But even so, remoteness and anonymity develop as each group
expands geographically. Just from the standpoint of sheer numbers,
adults, to say nothing of the young, cannot know all other Amish
persons in primary, face-to-face relationships. Intimacy gives way to
cosmopolitanism and to indifferences toward those one does not know.
A knowledge of others cannot be maintained except through the kin-

ship system. Those who are not in the *Freundschaft* are least well known, and in some cases are altogether unknown.

Those who practice silent discourse resolve the problem of maintaining a community of scale, where intimacy and sharing can be maximized, in ways that are distinct from those who stress verbal discourse. Both ways are related to what the two groups consider to be important for the future good of the community.

Those who practice *silent discourse* know intuitively that if they lose their agricultural base, they will lose to a large extent the qualities that go into the making of an Amish community. Farm work binds people of all ages together. Each member of the family performs a task that contributes to the whole. Husbands and wives share goals, concerns, and responsibility. To them, the small farming community is the most promising setting within which to carry out the ultimate goals of life. To those who have experienced good will, mutual respect, and the sharing of risks and experiences, the community is an expression of supreme worth. The loss of an agrarian base is reason for grave concern to them.

The formation of new settlements is not simply a solution to the scarcity of available farmland, but usually occurs in conjunction with other group needs, such as the maintenance of the *silent* orientation. Those who migrate in order not to perish are of the silent type. Migration permits renewed attempts at isolation as families move from densely populated settlements to small settlements and to rural areas where no Amish have previously lived. A reformulation of leadership patterns and of community consensus usually precedes such a move. Two basic requirements for forming a new settlement are sufficient consensus as to the rules and a large enough group to permit marriages within the same settlement. Many attempts at resettlement have been unsuccessful due to the absence of one or both of these requirements. The occurrence of extinct communities does not mean that they have disintegrated, failed, or been assimilated. The Amish take their social patterns with them wherever they go. In most cases it means that the space dimension of community has not been resolved in relation to its needs.

The Amish are intuitively aware of the danger of large-scale enterprises. Bigger machines will involve large investments and concentrations of economic power. They will do violence to the environment and hence conflict with the Amish feeling of closeness to the soil. Limitless technology is, for them, greed and a denial of wisdom. Amish economic thinking is subjected to a traditional wisdom requiring the restraint of selfishness, greed, leisure, and expansionist thinking. The ideal of work is not to be done with it, but to utilize it in giving every member an opportunity to develop his faculties. The future of the Amish will be determined not solely by technology, or the means to life, but by the definition they themselves give to life.

Those who tend toward *verbal discourse* appear less inclined to move to new locations to preserve their social solidarity. Closer contact with more Amish persons and with outsiders is not perceived as a threat. The young married couple faced with the problems of farm ownership and of acquiring sufficient capital uses the short cuts of middle-class American farm families. The advantages of electricity and of tractor farming are more clearly comprehended and accepted. Amish people who rent farms from non-Amish owners in some areas use these conveniences, particularly if they reside on the fringes of the large settlements. The owner may not want to remove the electricity from his farm or to replace the power-operated machines. These Amish renters become accustomed to otherwise forbidden uses and find it inconvenient to "put away" lights and electricity.

With the development of larger settlements, the Amish are realizing more individual freedom and greater differentiation. Those who have turned to verbal discourse are striving to solve their community expansion problems by means of adaptation within redefined limits. Instead of staying with the hazardous buggy on the highway, the Amish are seeking substitute modes of travel. On a prosperous Old Order Amish farm, one finds neither electric lights, rubber-tired farm implements, nor a telephone. By avoiding them, the Amishman abides by the rules of his church. But there is a propane gas installation on his farm. His wife uses the latest-style gas range, a kerosene-burning refrigerator, and an automatic, gas water-heater with a gasoline engine to keep up the water pressure. Upstairs there is a fully equipped bathroom with toilet, sink, bathtub, and shower. The lighting in the house is by gasoline mantel lanterns. This Amish farmer has no automobile, but his neighbor lives nearby and may be summoned any time, day or night, as necessary.

Although this Amish farmer (typical of many) is abiding by the rules of his church, he has departed far from Amish behavior patterns of a generation ago. His farm operations have been revolutionized, and he depends upon the great industrialized society for his markets and his developing standard of living. In order to sell grade A milk, he has had to alter his barn, milk house, water supply, and habits of working with farm animals. To meet sanitation requirements, he has had to understand how the outsider thinks. The milk is collected by a company truck; eggs, produce, and livestock are transported to market by the city people. Butter, bread, and groceries are delivered to his farm on a weekly schedule.

ATTITUDES TOWARD SEEKERS

Amish survival cannot be accounted for by the revitalization theory[8] or by an influx of seekers who would be converts. Revivalistic movements have been conspicuously absent throughout the history of the Amish. In fact, when revivalistic and enlightenment movements have occurred, they have gradually broken up the social fabric of the Old Order by offering false prophets and by leading to the formation of factions tending toward modernization and individuation.

As the world becomes more complex, insecure, and stressful, many more seekers will be attracted to the Amish way of life. An increasing number of inquiries are coming to the Amish people themselves from outsiders who wish to join the Amish church. In the past there were relatively few, undramatic instances of outsiders who joined. The chance factors that accounted for some of these conversions brought into the Amish fellowship such present-day family names as Anderson, Cross, DeLagrange, Flaud, Girod, Headings, Helmuth, Huyard, Jones, Lambright, Lee, Luthy, Whetstone, Wickey, and others. Most, if not all, of the converts had lived and worked in Amish homes, or they entered through adoption. They were exposed to the Amish life pattern and attracted by *silent* rather than *verbal* discourse. Today, many of the counterculture-type seekers who expect to find among the Amish a reasoned discourse soon turn away in disappointment. The greatest difficulties for those who try to join the Amish are: the hard manual labor, learning to accept responsibility willingly, and developing the ability to understand directions communicated in a nonverbal way. For a young man who is a prospective convert, Amishness begins with the stable and a pitchfork. For the young girl, it begins with the work at hand—scalding tomatoes, preserving apples and fruit in glass jars, and preparing the family meals. The Amish may show great hospitality to the outsider who would join, but only those Amish who are disposed to verbal discourse would attempt to reason or persuade one to become a member.

The new Amishness that is emerging on the modern scene is a sense of worth as measured by outside standards. The traditional virtues of restraint and moderation have been combined with a new sense of diversity and community self-realization. Status is based on what the individual can produce, on how well he accepts responsibility, and

---

8. For this well-established theory in anthropology, see Anthony F. C. Wallace, "Revitalization Movements," *American Anthropologist* 58 (1956): 264–81. For a study of the Jews' return to ancestral patterns, see Egon Mayer, *From Suburb to Shtetl: The Jews of Boro Park* (Philadelphia: Temple University Press, 1979).

on the sense of being needed. The dialogue with the self is essentially "I'm really needed around here." Belief is integrated with social and economic life, and with status enrichment, in a family and generation system that manifests attainable goals.

The Amish of the silent persuasion have not separated redemption from community, the soul from the body, or labor from the soil. All of these are the works of God. The world is, of course, a place of spiritual trial, but it is also a place where body, flesh, and spirit interact to achieve some kind of ultimate reality. As understood by the Amish man, the Bible does not teach that the soul must be freed from all else in creation. Life is not meant to be fragmented into many separate parts, nor is the soul to be alienated from the whole travail of creation while awaiting its deliverance from earth to heaven. Reconciliation is achieved not in division but in works of virtue that help to restore unity and harmony.

Amish society is faced with the problem of community self-realization and personal fulfillment for its members in each new generation. The constant striving to achieve these ends has given rise to two general types of social discourse, silent and verbal. Each is characterized by a unique set of attitudes and practices as reflected in the possibilities and potentialities of each community's ongoing problem-solving process and perception patterns. We have observed directions of development in both types of discourse with respect to the charter of separation, the changing community, and attitudes toward seekers. Problems of stress are apparent in both types, and they differ in kind and intensity within each community. We have observed the manner in which communities resolve or fail to resolve their living problems. Amish society will thrive or perish to the degree that it can provide community and personal fulfillment for the children raised in Amish homes.

Selected References

Almanac, The New American
1930   Published annually by J. A. Raber, Baltic, Ohio. Also issued in German.

Amish Cooking
1977   Aylmer, Ont.: Pathway Publishers.

Ammann, Paul, and Ammann, Hans
1975   *Aus der Sippe Ammann von Madiswil, Stammregister, 1612–1955.* Zurich.

Ausbund, Das ist: Etliche schone christliche Lieder
1564   1st ed.

Bachman, Calvin G.
1942   *The Old Order Amish of Lancaster County, Pennsylvania.* Norristown, Pa.: German Society. Reprinted in 1961.

Ball, William B.
1975   "Building a Landmark Case: Wisconsin vs. Yoder." In *Compulsory Education and the Amish: The Right Not to Be Modern,* edited by Albert N. Keim, pp. 114–23. Boston: Beacon Press.

Barclay, Harold B.
1967   "The Plain People of Oregon." *Review of Religious Research* 8: 1–26.

Beachy, Alvin J.
1954   "The Amish Settlement in Somerset County, Pennsylvania." *Mennonite Quarterly Review* 28 (October): 263–93.
1955   "The Rise and Development of the Beachy Amish Mennonite Churches." *Mennonite Quarterly Review* 29 (April): 118–40.

Becker, Karl A.
1952   *Die Volkstrachten der Pfalz.* Kaiserslautern.

Beiler, Aaron E.
1937   *Backgrounds and Standards of the Old Order Amish Church School Committee.* Route 1, Gap, Pa. Reaffirmed in 1961.

Beiler, Joseph F.
1971   "Revolutionary War Record." *The Diary*, March.
1976   "Eighteenth Century Amish in Lancaster County." *Mennonite Research Journal* 17 (October).
1977   Comp. *Old Order Shop and Service Directory of the Old Order Society in the United States and Canada.* Gordonville, Pa.: Pequea Publishers.

Bender, Harold S.
1929   "The First Edition of the Ausbund." *Mennonite Quarterly Review* 3 (April): 147–50.
1930   "An Amish Church Discipline of 1781." *Mennonite Quarterly Review* 4 (April): 140–48. Article on Bishop Hanns Nafziger.
1934   "Some Early American Amish Mennonite Disciplines." *Mennonite Quarterly Review* 8 (April): 90–98
1937   "An Amish Church Discipline of 1779." *Mennonite Quarterly Review* 11 (April): 163–68. Article on Bishop Hanns Nafziger.
1944   "The Anabaptist Vision." *Church History* 13 (March): 3–24. Reprinted in *Mennonite Quarterly Review* 18 (April): 67–88.
1946   Ed. and trans. "An Amish Bishop's Conference Epistle of 1865." *Mennonite Quarterly Review* 20 (July): 222–29.
1946   Ed. and trans. "The Minutes of the Amish Conference of 1809 Probably Held in Lancaster County, Pennsylvania." *Mennonite Quarterly Review* 20 (July): two plates following p. 239.
1950   *Conrad Grebel, c. 1498–1526: The Founder of the Brethren Sometimes Called Anabaptists.* Goshen, Ind.: Mennonite Historical Society.
1953   "The Zwickau Prophets, Thomas Muntzer, and the Anabaptists." *Mennonite Quarterly Review* 27 (January): 3–16.

Bender, Wilbur J.
1927   "Pacifism among the Mennonites, Amish Mennonites, and Schwenkfelders of Pennsylvania to 1783." *Mennonite Quarterly Review* 1 (July): 23–40; (October): 21–48.

Berry, Wendell
1977   *The Unsettling of America: Culture and Agriculture.* New York: Avon Books.

Bishop, Robert, and Safanda, Elizabeth
1976   *A Gallery of Amish Quilts.* New York: E. P. Dutton Co.

Blackboard Bulletin
1957   Monthly periodical published in the interest of Old Order Amish schools by Pathway Publishers, Aylmer, Ont.

Blanke, Fritz
1961   *Brothers in Christ: The History of the Oldest Anabaptist Congregation.* Scottdale, Pa.: Herald Press.

Botschaft, Die
1975–   Lancaster, Pa. A weekly newspaper serving the Old Order Amish communities.

Braght, Thieleman J. van
1951   Comp. *The Bloody Theatre; or, Martyrs Mirror.* Scottdale, Pa.: Mennonite Publishing House. Originally published in Dutch (Dordrecht, 1660).

Brendle, Thomas, and Unger, Claude
1935   Folk Medicine of the Pennsylvania Germans, Proceedings of the Pennsylvania German Society, vol. 45. Norristown, Pa.
Bryer, Kathleen B.
1979   "The Amish Way of Death: A Study of Family Support Systems." American Psychologist 34 (March): 255–61.
Buchanan, Frederick S.
1967   "The Old Paths: A Study of the Amish Response to Public Schooling in Ohio." Ph.D. dissertation, Ohio State University.
Buck, Roy C.
1978   "Boundary Maintenance Revisited: Tourist Experience in an Old Order Amish Community." Rural Sociology 43 (Summer): 221–34.
1979   "Bloodless Theatre: Images of the Old Order Amish in Tourism Literature." Pennsylvania Mennonite Heritage 2 (July): 2–11.
Budget, The
1890   Sugarcreek, Ohio. A weekly newspaper serving the Amish and Mennonite communities.
Buffington, Albert F.
1939   "Pennsylvania German: Its Relation to Other German Dialects." American Speech, December, pp. 276–86.
Burkhart, Charles
1953   "The Music of the Old Order Amish and the Old Colony Mennonites: A Contemporary Monodic Practice." Mennonite Quarterly Review 27 (January) 34–54.
Byler, Uria R.
1963   Our Better Country. Gordonville, Pa.: Old Order Book Society.
1969   School Bells Ringing: A Manual for Amish Teachers and Parents. Aylmer, Ont.: Pathway Publishers.
Cavan, Ruth
1977   "From Social Movement to Organized Society: The Case of the Anabaptists." Journal of Voluntary Action Research 6 (July–October): 105–11.
Christlicher Ordnung or Christian Discipline
1966   Aylmer, Ont.: Pathway Publishers.
Clark, Olynthus
1929   "Joseph Joder, Schoolmaster-Farmer and Poet, 1797–1887." In Transactions of the Illinois State Historical Society, pp. 135–65.
Cline, Paul C.
1968   "Relations between the Plain People and Government in the United States." Ph.D. dissertation, American University.
Cohn, Norman
1970   The Pursuit of the Millennium. Rev. ed. New York: Oxford University Press.
Correll, Ernst
1925   Das schweizerische Täufermennonitentum. Tübingen: Mohr.
1951   "Master Farmers in France." Mennonite Life 6 (July): 61–62.
Cowley, W. K.
1978   "Old Order Amish Settlements: Diffusion and Growth." Annuals of the Association of American Geographers 68 (June): 249–64.

Cragg, Perry
1971   *The Amish: A Photographic Album.* Cleveland, Ohio: By Mrs. Perry Cragg.
Cronk, Sandra L.
1977   "Gelassenheit: The Rites of the Redemptive Process in Old Order Amish and Old Order Mennonite Communities." Ph.D. dissertation, University of Chicago.
Cross, Harold E.
1967   "Genetic Studies in an Amish Isolate." Ph.D. dissertation, The Johns Hopkins University.
Cross, Harold E., and Hostetler, Beulah S.
1970   *Index to Selected Amish Genealogies.* Baltimore: The Johns Hopkins School of Medicine, Division of Medical Genetics.
Cross, Harold E., and McKusick, Victor A.
1970   "Amish Demography." *Social Biology* 17 (June): 83–101.
DeWind, Henry A.
1955   "A Sixteenth Century Description of Religious Sects in Austerlitz, Moravia." *Mennonite Quarterly Review* 29 (January): 44–53.
Diary, The
1969   A monthly periodical devoted to Amish history and genealogy published by Pequea Publishers, Route 1, Gordonville, Pa.
Dukeman, John A.
1972   "Way of Life of Illinois Amish-Mennonite Community and Its Effects on Agriculture and Banking in Central Illinois." The Stonier Graduate School of Banking, Rutgers—the State University, New Brunswick, N.J.
Dyck, Cornelius J.
1967   *An Introduction to Mennonite History.* Scottdale, Pa.: Herald Press.
Eaton, Joseph W., and Mayer, Albert J.
1954   *Man's Capacity to Reproduce: The Demography of a Unique Population.* Glencoe, Ill.: The Free Press.
el-Zein, Abdul Hamid M.
1974   *The Sacred Meadows: A Structural Analysis of Religious Symbolism in an East African Town.* Evanston, Ill.: Northwestern University Press.
Ericksen, Eugene P.; Ericksen, Julia A.; and Hostetler, John A.
1980   "The Cultivation of the Soil as a Moral Directive: Population Growth, Family Ties, and the Maintenance of Community among the Old Order Amish." *Rural Sociology,* in press.
Ericksen, Julia A.; Ericksen, Eugene P.; Hostetler, John A.; and Huntington, Gertrude E.
1979   "Fertility Patterns and Trends among the Old Order Amish." *Population Studies* 33 (July): 255–76.
Erickson, Donald A.
1966   "The Plain People vs. the Common Schools." *Saturday Review,* November 19.
1969   "The Persecution of Leroy Garber." *School Review* 78 (November): 81–90.
1969   *Public Controls for Non-Public Schools.* Chicago: University of Chicago Press.

Everet, Glenn D.
1961   "One Man's Family." *Population Bulletin*, December.
Family Life
1969   Monthly publication of Pathway Publishers, Aylmer, Ont.
Faust, A. B., and Brumbaugh, G. A.
1920   *Lists of Swiss Emigrants in the Eighteenth Century to the American Colonies.* Reprint (2 vols. in 1) Baltimore: Genealogical Publishing Co., 1968.
Fisher, Amos L.
1957   *Descendants and History of Christian Fisher Family.* Compiled by the John M. Fisher Family, Route 1, Ronks, Pa.
Fisher, Gideon L.
1975   *Alabama Tornado.* Ronks, Pa.: By the author.
1978   *Farm Life and Its Changes.* Gordonville, Pa.: Pequea Publishers.
Fisher, Jonathan B.
1937   *Around the World by Water and Facts Gleaned on the Way.* Bareville, Pa.: By the author.
Fletcher, S. W.
1950   *Pennsylvania Agriculture and Country Life, 1640–1840.* Harrisburg: Pennsylvania Historical and Museum Commission.
Freed, S. A.
1957   "Suggested Type Societies in Acculturation Studies . . . the Jews of Eastern Europe and the Old Order Amish." *American Anthropologist* 59 (February): 55–68.
Fretz, J. Winfield
1977   "The Plain and Not-So-Plain Mennonites in Waterloo County, Ontario." *Mennonite Quarterly Review* 51 (October): 377–85.
Frey, J. William
1945   "Amish Triple-Talk." *American Speech*, April, pp. 84–98.
1960   "The Amish Hymns as Folk Music." In *Pennsylvania Songs and Legends*, edited by George Korson, pp. 129–62. Baltimore: The Johns Hopkins Press.
Friedmann, Robert
1949   *Mennonite Piety through the Centuries.* Goshen, Ind.: Mennonite Historical Society.
1973   *The Theology of Anabaptism.* Scottdale, Pa.: Herald Press.
Gangel, George O.
1971   "The Amish of Jamesport, Missouri." *Practical Anthropology* 18 (July/August): 156–66.
Gascho, Milton
1937   "The Amish Division 1693–1697 in Switzerland and Alsace." *Mennonite Quarterly Review* 11 (October): 235–66.
Gehman, Richard
1965   "Amish Folks." *National Geographic* 128 (August): 226–53.
Gerlach, Russel L.
1976   *Immigrants in the Ozarks: A Study in Ethnic Geography.* Columbia: University of Missouri Press.
Getz, Jane C.
1946   "The Economic Organization and Practices of the Old Order Amish of Lancaster County, Pennsylvania." *Mennonite Quarterly Review* 10 (January): 53–80; (April): 98–127.

Gilberg, Laura S., and Buchholz, Barbara B.
1977   *Needlepoint: Designs for Amish Quilts.* New York: Charles Scribner's Sons.

Gingerich, Melvin
1939   *The Mennonites in Iowa.* Iowa City: State Historical Society of Iowa.
1943   "Custom Built Coffins." *The Palimpsest* 24 (December): 384–88.
1970   *Mennonite Attire through the Centuries.* Breiningsville: Pennsylvania German Society.

Gingerich, Orlando
1972   *The Amish of Canada.* Waterloo, Ont.: Conrad Press.

Gratz, Delbert
1951   "The Home of Jacob Amman in Switzerland." *Mennonite Quarterly Review* 25 (April): 137–39.
1953   *Bernese Anabaptists.* Goshen, Ind.: Mennonite Historical Society.

Greenleaf, Barbara K.
1974   *American Fever: The Story of American Immigration.* New York: The New American Library.

Gross, Neal
1948   "Sociological Variation in Contemporary Rural Life." *Rural Sociology,* September, pp. 256–59.

Gutkind, Peter C. W.
1952   "Secularization versus the Christian Community: Problems of an Old Order House Amish Family in Northern Indiana." M.A. thesis, University of Chicago.

Haders, Phyllis
1976   *Sunshine and Shadow: The Amish and Their Quilts.* Clinton, N.J.: Main Street Press.

Hall, Clarence W.
1962   "The Revolt of the Plain People." *Reader's Digest,* November, pp. 74–78.

Hall, Edward T.
1976   *Beyond Culture.* New York: Doubleday.

Hamman, Richard F.
1979   "Patterns of Mortality in the Old Order Amish." Ph.D. dissertation, The Johns Hopkins University.

Hartz, Amos, and Hartz, Susan
1965   *Moses Hartz Family History, 1819–1965.* Elverson, Pa.: By the authors.

Henry, Jules
1963   *Culture against Man.* New York: Random House.

Heritage Productions
1976   *The Amish: A People of Preservation.* Documentary 16mm educational film. Available in two versions: no. 3499, 53 minutes; and no. 3399, 28 minutes. Distributed by Encyclopaedia Britannica Educational Corp., 1822 Pickwick Ave., Glenview, Ill. 60025.

Hershberger, Guy F.
1951   *The Mennonite Church in the Second World War.* Scottdale, Pa.: Herald Press.

Hershberger, Henry J.
n.d.   *Minimum Standards for the Amish Parochial or Private Elemen-*

tary Schools of the State of Ohio. Route 2, Apple Creek, Ohio. By the author for the Ohio Amish School Committee.

Hertzler, Silas

1952 *The Hertzler-Hartzler Family History.* Goshen, Ind.: By the author.

Hiebert, Clarence.

1973 *The Holdeman People.* South Pasadena, Calif.: William Carey Library.

Hiller, Harry H.

1968/69 "The Sleeping Preachers: An Historical Study of the Role of Charisma in Amish Society." *Pennsylvania Folklife* 17 (Winter): 19–31.

Hochstetler, John D.

1916 Ed. *Ein alter Brief.* Elkhart, Ind.: Letter of Hanns Nafziger in German to the Amish Church in Holland. For an English account, see Harold S. Bender, "An Amish Church Discipline of 1781," *Mennonite Quarterly Review* 4 (April): 140–48.

Hohmann, Robert K.

1959 "The Church Music of Old Order Amish of the United States." Ph.D. dissertation, Northwestern University.

Horsch, John

1950 *Mennonites in Europe.* Scottdale, Pa.: Mennonite Publishing House.

Horst, Irvin B.

1957 "The Wandering Soul: A Remarkable Book of Devotion." *Mennonite Historical Bulletin* 18 (October).

Hostetler, Harvey

1912 *The Descendants of Jacob Hochstetler.* Elgin, Ill.: Brethren Publishing House.

1938 *Descendants of Barbara Hochstedler and Christian Stutzman.* Scottdale, Pa.: Mennonite Publishing House.

Hostetler, John A.

1948 "The Life and Times of Samuel Yoder, 1824–1884." *Mennonite Quarterly Review* 22 (October): 226–41.

1949 "The Amish in Gosper County, Nebraska." *Mennonite Historical Bulletin* 10 (October).

1951 "The Amish Family in Mifflin County, Pennsylvania." M.S. thesis, Pennsylvania State University. Excerpts published in *Pennsylvania Folklife* 12 (Fall 1961): 28–39.

1951 *Annotated Bibliography on the Old Order Amish.* Scottdale, Pa.: Mennonite Publishing House.

1954 *The Sociology of Mennonite Evangelism.* Scottdale, Pa.: Herald Press.

1955 "Old World Extinction and New World Survival of the Amish." *Rural Sociology* 20 (September/October): 212–19.

1956 "Amish Costume: Its European Origins." *American-German Review* 22 (August/September): 11–14.

1963 "The Amish Use of Symbols and Their Function in Bounding the Community." *Journal of the Royal Anthropological Institute* 94, pt. 1: 11–22.

1969   Ed. *Conference on Child Socialization.* Philadelphia: Temple University, Department of Sociology.

1974   *Hutterite Society.* Baltimore: The Johns Hopkins University Press.

1976   "Folk Medicine and Sympathy Healing among the Amish." In *American Folk Medicine,* edited by Wayland W. Hand, pp. 249–58. Berkeley: University of California Press.

1977   "Old Order Amish Survival." *Mennonite Quarterly Review* 51 (October): 352–61.

1979   "The Old Order Amish on the Great Plains: A Study in Cultural Vulnerability." In *Ethnicity on the Great Plains,* edited by Fred Leubke. Lincoln: University of Nebraska Press, forthcoming.

Hostetler, John A., and Huntington, Gertrude E.

1967   *The Hutterites in North America.* New York: Holt, Rinehart & Winston.

1971   *Children in Amish Society: Socialization and Community Education.* New York: Holt, Rinehart & Winston.

Hostetler, John A., and Redekop, Calvin W.

1962   "Education and Assimilation in Three Ethnic Groups." *Alberta Journal of Education and Research* 8 (December).

Huntington, Gertrude E.

1956   "Dove at the Window: A Study of an Old Order Amish Community in Ohio." Ph.D. dissertation, Yale University.

1976   "The Amish Family." In *Ethnic Families in America,* edited by Charles H. Mindel and Robert W. Habenstein. New York: Elsevier Scientific Publishing Co.

Jackson, George P.

1945   "The American Amish Sing Medieval Folk Tunes Today." *Southern Folklore Quarterly* 10 (June): 151–57.

1945   "The Strange Music of the Old Order Amish." *The Musical Quarterly* 31 (July): 275–88.

Jantzen, Carl R.

1959   "Boundary Maintenance and Personality Test Score Differences between Old Order Amish and Non-Amish Children." M.A. thesis, Michigan State University.

Johnson, W. A.; Stoltzfus, Victor; and Craumer, Peter

1977   "Energy Conservation in Amish Agriculture." *Science,* October 28, pp. 373–78.

Kauffman, John E.

1975   *Anabaptist Letters from 1635 to 1645: Translated from the Ausbund.* Atglen, Pa.: By the author.

Kauffman, S. Duane

1978   "Early Amish Translations Support Amish History." *The Budget,* February 22, p. 11; March 1, p. 3.

Keim, Albert N.

1975   Ed. *Compulsory Education and the Amish: The Right Not to Be Modern.* Boston: Beacon Press.

Kepler, Luther F., Jr., and Fisher, Anne Kepler

1961   "The Nebraska Old Order Amish." *Mennonite Life* 16 (July): 122–27. Illustrations.

King, C. Wendell
1956   *Social Movements in the United States.* New York: Random House.
[Kingsinger, Andrew S.]
1978   *Guidelines: In Regards to the Old Order Amish or Mennonite Parochial Schools.* Gordonville, Pa.: Gordonville Print Shop.
Klaassen, Walter
1973   *Anabaptism: Neither Catholic nor Protestant.* Waterloo, Ont.: Conrad Press.
Kollmorgen, Walter M.
1942   *Culture of a Contemporary Community: The Old Order Amish of Lancaster County, Pennsylvania.* Rural Life Studies no. 4. Washington, D.C.: U.S. Department of Agriculture.
1943   "The Agricultural Stability of the Old Order Amish Mennonites of Lancaster County, Pennsylvania." *American Journal of Sociology,* November.
Kuhn, Manford H.
1954   "Factors in Personality: Socio-Cultural Determinants as Seen through the Amish." In *Aspects of Culture and Personality,* edited by F. Hsu. Scranton, Pa.: Abelard-Schuman.
Landing, James E.
1963   "An Analysis of the Decline of the Commercial Mint Industry in Indiana." M.A. thesis, Pennsylvania State University.
1967   "The Spatial Development and Organization of an Old Order Amish–Beachy Amish Settlement: Nappanee, Indiana." Ph.D. dissertation, Pennsylvania State University.
1970   "Amish Settlement in North America: A Geographic Brief." *Bulletin of the Illinois Geographical Society* 12 (December): 65–69.
1972   "Amish, the Automobile, and Social Interaction." *Journal of Geography* 71 (January): 52–7.
Lapp, Henry
1975   *A Craftsman's Handbook.* Introduction and Notes by Beatrice B. Garvan. Philadelphia: Philadelphia Museum of Art.
Lembright, M. L., and Yamamoto, K.
1965   "Subcultures and Creative Thinking: An Exploratory Comparison between Amish and Urban American School Children." *Merrill-Palmer Quarterly of Behavior and Development* 11 (January): 49–64.
Lemon, James T.
1972   *The Best Poor Man's Country: A Geographical Study of Early Southeastern Pennsylvania.* Baltimore: The Johns Hopkins Press.
Lenski, Lois
1963   *Shoo-Fly Girl.* Philadelphia: J. B. Lippincott.
Lindholm, William C.
1967   *Do We Believe in Religious Liberty—for the Amish?* East Tawas, Mich.: National Committee for Amish Religious Freedom.
1974   "The Amish Case: A Struggle for Control of Values." In *Controversies in Education,* edited by Dwight W. Allen and Jeffrey C. Hecht, pp. 488–95. Philadelphia: W. B. Saunders Co.

Littell, Franklin H.

1961   *A Tribute to Menno Simons*. Scottdale, Pa.: Herald Press.

1964   *The Origins of Sectarian Protestantism*. New York: Macmillan.

1969   "Sectarian Protestantism and the Pursuit of Wisdom: Must Technological Objectives Prevail?" In *Public Controls for Non-Public Schools*, edited by Donald A. Erickson, pp. 61–82. Chicago: University of Chicago Press.

Loomis, Charles P., and Beegle, J. Allan

1951   *Rural Social Systems*. Englewood Cliffs, N.J.: Prentice-Hall.

Loomis, Charles P., and Dyer, Everett D.

1976   "The Old Order Amish as a Social System." In *Social Systems: The Study of Sociology*, edited by Charles P. Loomis and Everett D. Dyer, pp. 7–38. Cambridge, Mass.: Schenkman.

Luthy, David

1971   "The Amish Division of 1693." *Family Life*, October, pp. 18–20.

1971   "Four Centuries with the Ausbund." *Family Life*, June, pp. 21–22.

1972   "New Names Among the Amish." *Family Life*, August/September, pp. 31–35; October, pp. 20–23; November, pp. 21–23. See also the following 1973 issues: February, pp. 13–15; and June, pp. 13–15.

1974   "Old Order Amish Settlements in 1974." *Family Life*, December, pp. 13–16.

1975   "A Survey of Amish Ordination Customs." *Family Life*, March, pp. 13–17.

1977   "Amish Family Record Books." *Family Life*, January, pp. 19–23; March, pp. 17–18.

1978   "A History of the Budget." *Family Life*, June, pp. 19–22; July, pp. 15–18.

McGrath, William

1970   *God-Given Herbs for the Healing of Mankind*. N.p.: By the author.

McKusick, Victor A.

1978   *Medical Genetic Studies of the Amish: Selected Papers, Assembled, with Commentary*. Baltimore: The Johns Hopkins University Press.

MacLeish, Archibald

1972   "Rediscovering the Simple Life." *McCall's*, April, pp. 79–89. Photographs by Lord Snowdon.

MacMaster, Richard K.; Horst, Samuel L.; and Ulle, Robert F.

1979   *Conscience in Crisis: Mennonites and Other Peace Churches in America, 1739–1789*. Scottdale, Pa.: Herald Press.

Madden, Robert W.

1977   "The Amish: A Simple, Ordered Life." In *Life in Rural America*, pp. 174–91. Washington, D.C.: National Geographic Society. A photographic essay.

Malinowski, Bronislaw

1944   *A Scientific Theory of Culture*. Chapel Hill: University of North Carolina Press.

Martin, William L.
1975   Photog. *The Peaceful People: A Photographic Profile of the Amish.* Edited by David E. Sill. N.p.: By the author.
Marty, Martin
1960   "Sects and Cults." *Annuals of the American Academy of Political and Social Science* 332: 125–34.
Mast, C. Z., and Simpson, Robert E.
1942   *Annals of the Conestoga Valley.* Elverson, Pa.: By the authors.
Mast, John B.
1950   Ed. *The Letters of the Amish Division.* Oregon City, Oreg.: C. J. Schlabach.
Melton, James A.
1970   "Old Order Amish Awareness and Understanding of Mental Retardation." Ph.D. dissertation, Ohio State University.
Mennonite Encyclopedia, The
1956   4 vols. Published by the Mennonite Publishing House, Scottdale, Pa.; the Mennonite Brethren Publishing House, Hillsboro, Kans.; and the Mennonite Publication Office, Newton, Kans.
Meyer, Carolyn
1976   *Amish People.* New York: Atheneum.
Meynen, Emil
1937   *Bibliography on German Settlements in North America, Especially on the Pennsylvania Germans and Their Descendants, 1683–1933.* Leipzig: Otto Harrassowitz.
Miller, D. Paul
1949   "Amish Acculturation." M.A. thesis, University of Nebraska.
Miller, Harvey J.
1959   "Proceedings of the Amish Ministers Conference, 1826–1831." *Mennonite Quarterly Review* 33 (April): 132–42.
Miller, Levi
1972   "The Amish Word for Today." *Christian Century* 90 (January): 70–73.
Miller, Mary
1976   "An Amish Farm." *Michigan Farmer,* July, pp. 8–11.
Miller, Wayne
1969   "A Study of Amish Academic Achievement." Ph.D. dissertation, University of Michigan.
Mittelberger, Gottlieb
1960   *Journey to Pennsylvania.* Cambridge: Harvard University Press, Belknap Press.
Mook, Maurice A.
1955   "The Amishman Who Founded a City." *Christian Living,* July.
1955   "An Early Amish Colony in Chester County." *Mennonite Historical Bulletin* 16 (July). (Photographs of the tombstones appear in *Christian Living,* October 1956.)
1960   "Nicknames among the Amish." *Keystone Folklore Quarterly* 5 (Winter): 3–12.
1962   "The Nebraska Amish in Pennsylvania." *Mennonite Life* 17 (July): 27–30. (Illustrations appear in the July 1961 issue.)
1967   "Nicknames among the Amish." *Names* 15 (June): 111–18.

396 SELECTED REFERENCES

Müller, Ernst
1895 *Geschichte der Bernischen Täufer.* Frauenfeld, Switz.
Myers, Isabell Briggs
1962 *Myers-Briggs Type Indicator.* Princeton, N.J.: Educational Testing Service.
Nagata, Judith
1968 "Continuity and Change among the Old Order Amish of Illinois." Ph.D. dissertation, University of Illinois.
National Geographic Society
1974 *Rural Life in America.* Photographs on pp. 20–21, 173–91.
Ohio Amish Directory
1973 Compiled by Ervin Gingerich, Star Route, Millersburg, Ohio. Also issued in 1959 and 1960.
Pennsylvania Amish Directory
1973 Compiled by the Old Order Map Committee, Gordonville, Pa., in cooperation with The Johns Hopkins Hospital.
Pennsylvania, Commonwealth of
1955 "Policy for Operation of Home and Farm Projects in Church-Organized Schools." Department of Public Instruction. October 5.
Philip, Dietrich
1910 *Enchiridion or Hand Book.* Reprint. Aylmer, Ont.: Pathway Publishers, 1966.
Picard, Max
1952 *The World of Silence.* Chicago: Henry Regnery Co.
Populations Reference Bureau
1968 "Pockets of High Fertility in the United States." *Population Bulletin* 24 (November): 25–55.
Ramaker, A. J.
1929 "Hymns and Hymn Writers among the Anabaptists of the Sixteenth Century." *Mennonite Quarterly Review* 3 (April): 101–31.
Randle, Bill
1974 *Plain Cooking.* New York: New York Times Book Co.
Redekop, Calvin W.
1969 *The Old Colony Mennonites.* Baltimore: The Johns Hopkins Press.
Redekop, Calvin W., and Hostetler, John A.
1977 "The Plain People: An Interpretation." *Mennonite Quarterly Review* 5 (October): 266–77.
Redfield, Robert
1947 "The Folk Society." *American Journal of Sociology* 52 (January): 293–308.
1955 *The Little Community.* Chicago: University of Chicago Press.
Reed, Thomas J.
1968 "The Amish—A Case Study in Accommodation and Suppression." *Notre Dame Lawyer* 43 (June): 764–76.
Renno, John R.
1976 *A Brief History of the Amish Church in Belleville.* Danville, Pa.: By the author. 26 pp.
Rice, Charles S., and Shenk, John B.
1947 *Meet the Amish: A Pictorial Study of the Amish People.* New Brunswick, N.J.: Rutgers University Press.

Rice, Charles S., and Steinmetz, Rollin C.
1956   *The Amish Year.* New Brunswick, N.J.: Rutgers University Press.

Richelin, Alice
1970   "Spatial Behavior of the Old Order Amish of Nappanee, Indiana." Ph.D. dissertation, University of Michigan. Published by the Department of Geography, University of Michigan, in 1976.

Richter, Conrad
1955   "Pennsylvania." *Holiday,* October, pp. 98–112.

Roberts, Ron E., and Kloss, Robert M.
1974   *Social Movements.* St. Louis: C. V. Mosby Co.

Rodgers, Harrel R., Jr.
1969   *Community Conflict, Public Opinion, and the Law: The Amish Dispute in Iowa.* Columbia, Ohio: Charles E. Merrill Publishing Co.

Rosen, Lawrence
1977   "The Anthropologist as Expert Witness." *American Anthropologist* 79 (September): 555–78.

Rosenberg, Bruce A.
1970   *The Art of the American Folk Preacher.* New York: Oxford University Press.

Rosenberg, Homer T.
1966   *The Pennsylvania Germans 1891–1965.* Breiningsville: Pennsylvania German Society.

Royce, Josiah
1908   *Race Questions, Provincialisms, and Other American Problems.* N.p.

Ruxin, Paul T.
1967   "The Right Not to Be Modern Men: The Amish and Compulsory Education." *Virginia Law Review* 53 (May): 925–52.

Sanders, Thomas G.
1964   *Protestant Concepts of Church and State.* New York: Holt, Rinehart & Winston.

Scherer, Karl
1974   "The Fatherland of the Pennsylvania Dutch." *Mennonite Research Journal* 15 (July): 25–29.

Schowalter, Paul
1963   "Pioneer Nicholas Stoltzfus." *Mennonite Research Journal* 4 (April): 13, 22.

Schrag, Martin H.
1974   *European History of the Swiss Mennonites from Volhynia.* North Newton, Kans.: Mennonite Press.

Schreiber, William I.
1962   "The Hymns of the Amish Ausbund in Philological and Literary Perspective." *Mennonite Quarterly Review* 36 (January): 37–60.
1962   *Our Amish Neighbors.* Chicago: University of Chicago Press.

Schrock, Alta
1943   "Amish Americans: Frontiersmen." *Western Pennsylvania Historical Magazine* 26 (March–June): 47–58.

Schwieder, Elmer, and Schwieder, Dorothy
1975   *A Peculiar People: Iowa's Old Order Amish.* Ames: Iowa State University Press.

Scott, Taylor C.
1949   "The Mennonites of Sarasota, Florida." M.A. thesis, University of Florida, Gainesville.
Séguy, Jean
1973   "Religion and Agricultural Success: The Vocational Life of the French Mennonites from the Seventeenth to the Nineteenth Centuries," translated by Michael Shank. *Mennonite Quarterly Review* 47 (July): 182–224.
1977   *Les Assemblées anabaptistes-mennonites de France.* The Hague: Mouton.
Shaner, Richard H.
1962/63 "The Amish Barn Dance." *Pennsylvania Folklife* 13 (Winter): 24–26.
Shetler, Sanford G.
1963   *Two Centuries of Struggle and Growth.* Scottdale, Pa.: Herald Press.
Showalter, Mary Emma
1950   *Mennonite Community Cookbook.* Scottdale, Pa.: Mennonite Community Association.
Shryock, Richard H.
1939   "British versus German Traditions in Colonial Agriculture." *Mississippi Valley Historical Review* 26 (June): 39–54.
Simons, Menno
1956   *The Complete Writings of Menno Simons.* Translated by Leonard Verduin. Edited by John C. Wenger. Scottdale, Pa.: Herald Press.
Smith, C. Henry
1909   *The Mennonites in America.* Goshen, Ind.: By the author.
1929   *The Mennonite Immigration to Pennsylvania.* Vol. 28. Norristown, Pa.: Pennsylvania German Society.
1950   *The Story of the Mennonites.* Newton, Kans.: Mennonite Publication Office.
1962   *Mennonite Country Boy.* Newton, Kans.: Faith and Life Press.
Smith, Elmer L.
1961   *The Amish Today: An Analysis of Their Beliefs, Behavior, and Contemporary Problems, Proceedings of the Pennsylvania German Folklore Society,* vol. 24. Allentown, Pa.: Schlechters.
Smucker, Donovan E.
1977   Ed. *The Sociology of Canadian Mennonites, Hutterites, and Amish: A Bibliography with Annotations.* Waterloo, Ont.: Wilfrid Laurier University Press.
Smucker, Mervin
1978   "Growing Up Amish: A Comparison of the Socialization Process between Amish and Non-Amish Rural School Children." M.S. thesis, Millersville State College, Pa.
Stoll, Joseph
1965   *Who Shall Educate Our Children?* Aylmer, Ont.: Pathway Publishing Corp.
1967   *The Challenge of the Child.* Aylmer, Ont.: Pathway Publishers.

Stoll, Joseph; Luthy, David; and Stoll, Elmo

1968   Pathway Reading Series: *Thinking of Others* (5th grade); *Step by Step* (6th grade); *Seeking True Values* (7th grade); *Our Heritage* (8th grade). Aylmer, Ont.: Pathway Publishers.

Stoltzfus, Grant M.

1954   "History of the First Amish Mennonite Communities in America." M.A. thesis, University of Pittsburgh. Published in *Mennonite Quarterly Review* 28 (October) 28: 235–62.

Stoltzfus, Victor

1973   "Amish Agriculture: Adaptive Strategies for Economic Survival of Community Life." *Rural Sociology* 38 (Summer): 196–206.

1977   "Reward and Sanction: The Adaptive Continuity of Amish Life." *Mennonite Quarterly Review* 51 (October): 308–18.

Strassburger, Ralph B., and Hinke, William J.

1934   *Pennsylvania German Pioneers.* 3 vols. Norristown, Pa.: Pennsylvania German Society.

Stroup, J. Martin

1965   *The Amish of Kishacoquillas Valley.* Mifflin County Historical Society.

Swartzendruber, Jacob

1937   *An Account of the Voyage from Germany to America.* N.p.: By the author.

Swope, Wilmer D.

1972   *The Genealogical History of the Stoltzfus Family in America, 1717–1972.* Seymour, Mo.: Englewood Press.

Toennies, Ferdinand

1957   *Community and Society.* Edited and translated by C. P. Loomis. East Lansing: Michigan State University Press.

Troeltsch, Ernst

1931   *The Social Teachings of the Christian Churches.* 2 vols. New York: Macmillan.

Troyer, Lester O.

1968   "Amish Nicknames from Holmes County, Ohio." *Pennsylvania Folklife* 17 (Summer).

Umble, John S.

1933   "The Amish Mennonites of Union County, Pennsylvania. Part I: Social and Religious Life." *Mennonite Quarterly Review* 7 (April) 71–96.

1933   "The Amish Mennonites of Union County, Pennsylvania. Part II: A History of the Settlement." *Mennonite Quarterly Review* 7 (July): 162–90.

1939   "Amish Ordination Charges." *Mennonite Quarterly Review* 13 (October): 236–50.

1939   "The Old Order Amish: Their Hymns and Hymn Tunes." *Journal of American Folklore* 52: 82–95.

1946   "Catalog of an Amish Bishop's Library." *Mennonite Quarterly Review* 20 (July): 230–39.

1948   "Justice Fails Again." *Gospel Herald*, February 3.

Wagler, David

1966   *The Mighty Whirlwind.* Aylmer, Ont.: Pathway Publishing Corp.

Warner, James M., and Denlinger, Donald M.
1969   *The Gentle People: A Portrait of the Amish.* New York: Grossman Publishers.

Wells, Richard D.
1967   *Articles of Agreement Regarding the Indiana Amish Parochial Schools and the Department of Public Instruction.* Bloomington: Indiana Department of Public Instruction.

Wenger, John C.
1937   *History of the Mennonites of the Franconia Conference.* Telford, Pa.: Franconia Mennonite Historical Society.
1961   *The Mennonites in Indiana and Michigan.* Scottdale, Pa.: Herald Press.

Wickersham, James P.
1886   *A History of Education in Pennsylvania.* Lancaster, Pa.: Inquirer Publishing Co.

Williams, George H.
1962   *The Radical Reformation.* Philadelphia: Westminster Press.

Wilson, Bryan
1970   *Religious Sects.* New York: McGraw-Hill.

Wisconsin v. *Yoder et al.*
1972   U.S. Supreme Court. No. 70-110. Argued December 8, 1971; decided May 15, 1972.

Wittmer, Joe
1970   "Homogeneity of Personality Characteristics: A Comparison between Old Order Amish and Non-Amish." *American Anthropologist* 72 (October): 1063–68.
1971   "The Amish Schools Today." *School and Society* 99 (April): 227–30.
1971   "Cultural Violence and Twentieth Century Progress." *Practical Anthropology* 18 (July/August): 146–55.

Yoder, Don
1969   "Sectarian Costume Research in the United States." In *Forms upon the Frontier,* pp. 41–75. Monograph Series, no. 16 (April). Logan: Utah State University Press.

Yoder, Eleanor
1974   "Nicknaming in an Amish-Mennonite Community." *Pennsylvania Folklife* 23 (Spring): 30–37.

Yoder, Harvey
1966   "The Budget of Sugarcreek, Ohio, 1890–1920." *Mennonite Quarterly Review* 40 (January 1966): 27–47.

Yoder, John H.
1952   "Mennonites in a French Almanac." *Mennonite Life* 7 (July): 104–6.
1973   *The Legacy of Michael Sattler.* Scottdale, Pa.: Herald Press.

Yoder, Joseph W.
1940   *Rosanna of the Amish.* Huntington, Pa. Yoder Publishing Co.
1942   *Amische Lieder.* Huntington, Pa.: Yoder Publishing Co.
1948   *Rosanna's Boys.* Huntington, Pa.: Yoder Publishing Co.
1950   *Amish Traditions.* Huntington, Pa.: Yoder Publishing Co.

Yoder, Paul M.; Bender, Elizabeth; Graber, Harvey; and Springer, Nelson P.
1964   *Four Hundred Years with the Ausbund.* Scottdale, Pa.: Herald Press.

Yoder, Sanford C.
1959   *The Days of My Years.* Scottdale, Pa.: Herald Press.

Zielinski, John M.
1975   *The Amish: A Pioneer Heritage.* Des Moines, Iowa: Wallace-Homestead Book Co.

Photo Credits

The photographs in this volume are reproduced by permission of the individuals and organizations listed below.

R. S. Beese: 283. Dick Brown: 271 (upper right). Bert Buller: 176, 239, 271 (lower right). Bill Coleman: ii-iii. James M. Cutrell: 247. John A. Hostetler: 38, 70, 226. Joan Liffring-Zug: 219. Pat Little: 160, 235 (right), 272 (left). National Geographic Society: 187. Richard Reinhold: 6, 80, 90, 122, 126 (right), 131, 132, 139, 143, 149, 151, 164, 169 (upper), 170, 178, 181, 188, 201, 204, 232, 254, 299, 311, 343, 380. Rowan P. Smolcha: 11, 209. Fred J. Wilson: 13, 89, 126 (left), 128, 145, 153, 158, 169 (lower), 174, 175, 184, 235 (left), 248, 271 (upper and lower left), 272 (right), 362, 370. World Wide Photos: 236, 265. Sam Yoder: 140, 308.

Index

❦

405

John A. Hostetler is professor of anthropology and sociology at Temple University and is director of the university's Center for the Study of Communal Societies. He is widely known for his publications and research on minority groups in the United States and Canada and is the author of *Hutterite Society*, also published by Johns Hopkins.

THE JOHNS HOPKINS UNIVERSITY PRESS

This book was composed in Linotype Baskerville text and Photo-typositor Lydian display type by Maryland Linotype Composition Company, from a design by Susan Bishop. It was printed on 60-lb. Glatfelter Offset paper and bound by The Maple Press Company.

Library of Congress Cataloging in Publication Data

Hostetler, John Andrew
 Amish society.

 Bibliography: pp. 385–401
 Includes index.
 1. Amish in the United States—Social life and customs.
2. Amish—Social life and customs. I. Title.
E184.M45H63 1980   301.45′28′87   79–23823

ISBN 0–8018–2333–1
ISBN 0–8018–2334–x pbk.